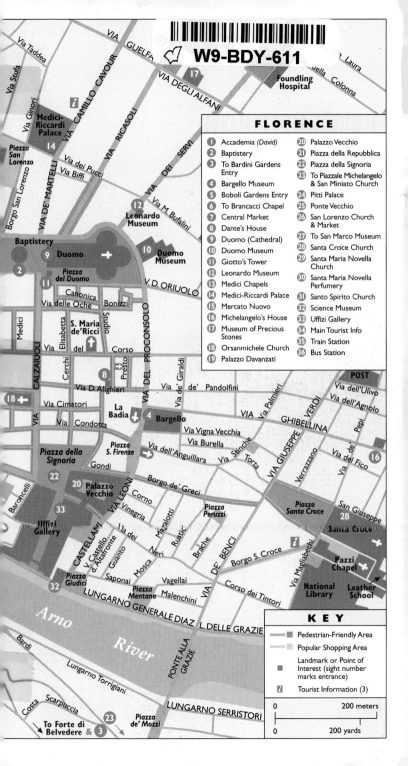

FLORENCE

1. Accademia (David)
2. Baptistery
3. To Bardini Gardens Entry
4. Bargello Museum
5. Boboli Gardens Entry
6. To Brancacci Chapel
7. Central Market
8. Dante's House
9. Duomo (Cathedral)
10. Duomo Museum
11. Giotto's Tower
12. Leonardo Museum
13. Medici Chapels
14. Medici-Riccardi Palace
15. Mercato Nuovo
16. Michelangelo's House
17. Museum of Precious Stones
18. Orsanmichele Church
19. Palazzo Davanzati
20. Palazzo Vecchio
21. Piazza della Repubblica
22. Piazza della Signoria
23. To Piazzale Michelangelo & San Miniato Church
24. Pitti Palace
25. Ponte Vecchio
26. San Lorenzo Church & Market
27. To San Marco Museum
28. Santa Croce Church
29. Santa Maria Novella Church
30. Santa Maria Novella Perfumery
31. Santo Spirito Church
32. Science Museum
33. Uffizi Gallery
34. Main Tourist Info
35. Train Station
36. Bus Station

KEY

- Pedestrian-Friendly Area
- Popular Shopping Area
- Landmark or Point of Interest (sight number marks entrance)
- Tourist Information (3)

0 — 200 meters
0 — 200 yards

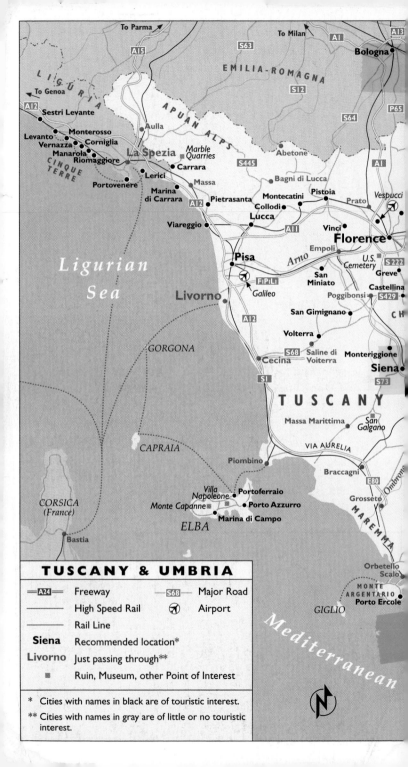

TUSCANY & UMBRIA

═A24═ Freeway		**─S68─** Major Road	
──── High Speed Rail		✈ Airport	
Siena Recommended location*			
Livorno Just passing through**			
■ Ruin, Museum, other Point of Interest			

* Cities with names in black are of touristic interest.

** Cities with names in gray are of little or no touristic interest.

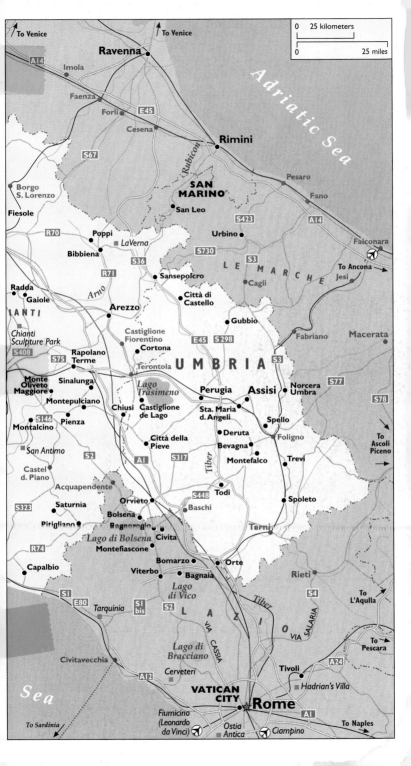

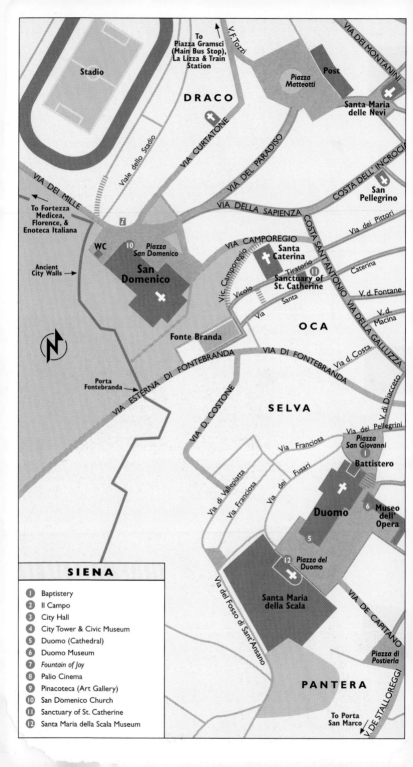

Stadio

DRACO

To
Piazza Gramsci
(Main Bus Stop),
La Lizza & Train
Station

V. F. Tozzi

VIA DEI MONTANINI

Piazza
Matteotti

Post

Santa Maria
delle Nevi

VIALE DELLO STADIO

VIA CURTATONE

VIA DEL PARADISO

VIA DEI MILLE

To Fortezza
Medicea,
Florence, &
Enoteca Italiana

VIA DELLA SAPIENZA

COSTA DELL'INCROCI

San
Pellegrino

Via dei Pittori

ℹ️

WC

10 Piazza
San Domenico

VIA CAMPOREGIO

Santa
Caterina

Caterina

11 Sanctuary of
St. Catherine

Tiratorio

COSTA SANT'ANTONIO VIA DELLA GALLUZZA

V. d. Fontane

Ancient
City Walls

**San
Domenico**

Vic. Camporegio

Vicolo

Via

Santa

V. d.
Macina

Fonte Branda

OCA

N

VIA DI FONTEBRANDA

Via d. Costa

Porta
Fontebranda

VIA ESTERNA DI FONTEBRANDA

SELVA

V. di Diacceto

VIA D. COSTONE

Via dei Pellegrini

Via Franciosa

Piazza
San Giovanni

Via dei Fusari

Battistero 1

Via di Vallepiatta

Via Franciosa

Via dei Fusari

Duomo

6 Museo
dell'
Opera

5

12 Piazza del
Duomo

Via del Fosso di Sant'Ansano

**Santa Maria
della Scala**

VIA DE CAPITANO

Piazza di
Postierla

PANTERA

To Porta
San Marco

V. DE STALLOREGGI

SIENA

1 Baptistery
2 Il Campo
3 City Hall
4 City Tower & Civic Museum
5 Duomo (Cathedral)
6 Duomo Museum
7 *Fountain of Joy*
8 Palio Cinema
9 Pinacoteca (Art Gallery)
10 San Domenico Church
11 Sanctuary of St. Catherine
12 Santa Maria della Scala Museum

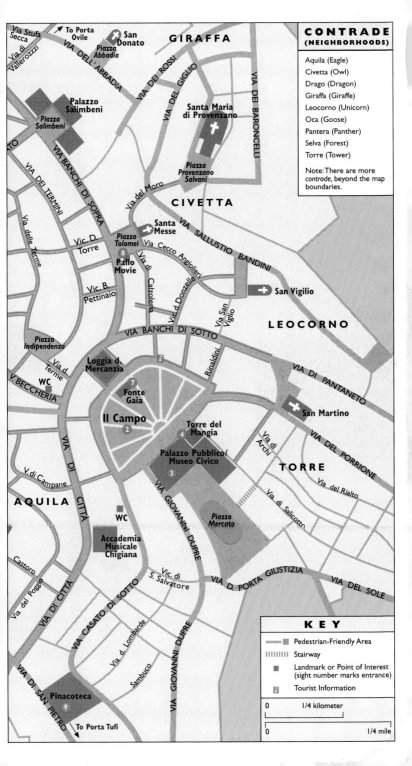

Rick Steves'
FLORENCE
& TUSCANY
2007

Santa Maria Novella

San Marco

David

Medici Chapels

Baptistery

Giotto's Tower

Duomo

Palazzo Vecchio

Ponte Vecchio

Uffizi

Bargello

Brancacci Chapel

Boboli Gardens & Pitti Palace

ARNO

DCH

AVALON TRAVEL

CONTENTS

INTRODUCTION

Florence is Europe's cultural capital. As the home of the Renaissance and the birthplace of the modern world, Florence practiced the art of civilized living back when the rest of Europe was rural and crude. Democracy, science, and literature, as well as painting, sculpture, and architecture were all championed by the proud and energetic Florentines of the 1400s.

When the Florentine poet Dante first saw the teenaged Beatrice, her beauty so inspired him that he spent the rest of his life writing poems to her. The Renaissance opened people's eyes to the physical beauty of the world around them, inspiring them to write, paint, sculpt, and build.

Today, Florence is geographically small but culturally rich, with more artistic masterpieces per square mile than anyplace else. In a single day, you could look Michelangelo's *David* in the eyes, fall under the seductive sway of Botticelli's *Birth of Venus,* and climb the modern world's first dome, which still dominates the skyline.

Florence can be a Botticelli wonderland, tinseled with Renaissance graffiti. But there's a reality, too: The surge of tourism is changing the city. Restaurants may be packed with local workers for lunch, but at dinner it's just tourists—locals don't want to deal with downtown driving restrictions. The willingness of tourists to pay high prices for a room is driving up the price of apartments. The result: Locals are moving to the suburbs, and their apartments are becoming fancy little hotels. And stores are going chic. Old shoemaker shops are morphing into upscale shoe boutiques. For eateries, rustic is the rage—everything is becoming a *trattoria* or an *osteria*. Nobody in particular is to blame. Tourists have the money...and locals want it. Florence is touristy, but where else can you stroll the same pedestrian streets walked by Michelangelo,

Leonardo, and Botticelli, while savoring the world's best gelato?

To round out your visit, see Florence and then escape to the Tuscan countryside. With its manicured fields, rustic farms, and towns clinging to nearly every hill, Tuscany is our image of village Italy. Venture beyond the fringes of Florence and you'll find a series of sun- and wine-soaked villages, each with its own appeal. Stretching from the Umbrian border to the Ligurian Sea, the landscape changes from idyllic (Crete Senese) to mountainous (the Montagnola) to flat and brushed with sea breezes (Pisa).

During your visit, you'll discover that peaceful Tuscan villages and bustling Florence—with its rough-stone beauty, art-packed museums, children chasing pigeons, students riding Vespas, artisans sipping Chianti, and supermodels wearing Gucci fashions—offer many of the very things you came to Italy to see.

This Information Is Accurate and Up-to-Date

This book is updated every year. Most publishers of guidebooks can afford an update only every two or three years (and even then, it's often by e-mail or fax). Since this book is selective, we can update it in person each summer. The telephone numbers and hours of sights listed in this book are accurate as of mid-2006—but once you pin Italy down, it wiggles. Still, if you're traveling with the current edition of this book, we guarantee you're using the most up-to-date information available in print. For any updates, see www.ricksteves .com/update. Also at our Web site, you'll find a valuable list of reports and experiences—good and bad—from fellow travelers who have used this book (www.ricksteves.com/feedback).

Use this year's edition. People who try to save a few bucks by traveling with an old book learn the seriousness of their mistake... in Tuscany. Your trip costs about $10 per waking hour. Your time is valuable. This guidebook saves lots of time.

About This Book

Rick Steves' Florence & Tuscany is a personal tour guide in your pocket. Better yet, it's actually two tour guides in your pocket: The co-author of this book is Gene Openshaw. Since our first "Europe through the gutter" trip together as high school buddies 30 years ago, Gene and I have been exploring the wonders of the Old World. An inquisitive historian and lover of European culture, Gene wrote most of this book's self-guided museum tours and neighborhood walks. Together, Gene and I keep this book up-to-date and accurate (though for simplicity, from this point "we" will shed our respective egos and become "I").

The book is organized this way:

Each **Orientation** includes tourist information and public transportation. The "Planning Your Time" section offers a suggested schedule with thoughts on how to best use your limited time.

Sights provide a succinct overview of the most important attractions, arranged by neighborhood, with ratings per sight:

▲▲▲—Don't miss.

▲▲—Try hard to see.

▲—Worthwhile if you can make it.

No rating—Worth knowing about.

The self-guided **Renaissance Walk** takes you through the core of Renaissance Florence, starting with Michelangelo's *David* and cutting through the heart of the city to the Ponte Vecchio on the Arno River.

The **Self-Guided Tours** lead you through Tuscany's most important sights, with tours of Florence's Uffizi Gallery, Bargello, Museum of San Marco, Duomo Museum, Medici Chapels, Medici-Riccardi Palace, Church of Santa Maria Novella, Brancacci Chapel, and the Science Museum, as well as Siena's Duomo, Duomo Museum, and Civic Museum, and Pisa's Duomo and Field of Miracles.

Sleeping is a guide to my favorite budget hotels, conveniently located near the sights.

Eating offers restaurants ranging from inexpensive eateries to splurges, with an emphasis on good value and quality.

Florence with Children, Shopping, and **Nightlife** contain my best suggestions on these topics.

Transportation Connections covers connections by train, bus, and plane, laying the groundwork for your smooth arrival and departure.

Siena covers the highlights in this captivating Gothic city, from the stay-awhile central piazza to the 13th-century cathedral. **Pisa** takes you beyond the Leaning Tower. **Lucca** introduces you to the charms of this little-touristed, well-preserved city. And **Tuscan Hill Towns** brings you the best of village Italy, featuring Montalcino, Montepulciano, Pienza, Cortona, San Gimignano, and Volterra.

History takes you on a whirlwind tour through the ages, covering eight centuries from ancient Tuscany to the present.

The **appendix** is a traveler's tool kit, with telephone tips, useful Italian phone numbers, a climate chart, a list of festivals, and a handy list of Italian survival phrases.

Throughout this book, when you see a ✪ in a listing, it means that the sight is covered in more detail in one of my self-guided tours. A page number will tell you where to look to find more information.

Browse through this book and choose your favorite sights. Then have a great trip! Traveling like a temporary local, you'll get the absolute most out of every mile, minute, and euro.

PLANNING

Trip Costs

Six components make up your trip costs: airfare, surface transportation, room and board, sightseeing/entertainment, shopping/
miscellany, and gelato.

Airfare: Don't try to sort through the mess. Find and use a
good travel agent. A basic, round-trip United States–to–Florence
(or even cheaper, Milan or Rome) flight should cost $700 to $1,000,
depending on where you fly from and when. Always consider saving time and money in Europe by flying "open jaw" (into one city
and out of another).

Surface Transportation: Most of Florence's sights, clustered
in the downtown core, are within easy walking distance of each
other. If you'd rather use taxis than walk, allow about $60–80
over the course of a one-week visit (taxis can be shared by up to 4
people). The cost of round-trip transportation to the recommended
nearby destinations is affordable (about $10 each for a second-class
train ticket to Pisa or Siena or for a bus ticket to San Gimignano).
For a one-way trip between Florence's airport and the city center,
allow $5 by bus or $25 by taxi (can be shared). The other cities and
villages covered in this book are made for walking.

Room and Board: You can easily manage in Tuscany in 2007
on $100 a day per person for room and board. This allows $10 for
lunch, $5 for snacks, $20 for dinner, and $65 for lodging (based
on 2 people splitting the cost of a $130 double room that includes
breakfast). If you have more money, I've suggested great ways to
spend it. Students and tightwads can enjoy Tuscany for as little as
$50 a day ($25 for a bed, $25 for meals and snacks).

Sightseeing and Entertainment: Figure about $10–15 per
major sight (Michelangelo's *David*, Uffizi Gallery), $6–8 for
smaller ones (museums, climbing church towers), and $30 for
splurge experiences (e.g., walking tours and concerts). An overall
average of $25 a day works for most. Don't skimp here. After all,
this category is the driving force behind your trip—you came to
sightsee, enjoy, and experience Florence.

Shopping and Miscellany: Figure $2 per postcard, coffee, soft
drink, and gelato. Shopping can vary in cost from nearly nothing
to a small fortune. Good budget travelers find that this category
has little to do with assembling a trip full of lifelong, wonderful
memories.

When to Go

Tuscany's best travel months (and busiest, most expensive months)
are May, June, September, and October. Between November and

April you can usually expect pleasant weather and none of the sweat and stress of the tourist season.

The most grueling thing about travel in Tuscany is the summer heat in July and August, when temperatures hit the high 80s and 90s. Most mid-range hotels come with air-conditioning—a worthwhile splurge in the summer—but usually available only from June through September. Florence is fine in the winter, when temperatures drop to the 40s and 50s. Spring and fall can be chilly, and many hotels do not turn on their heat until winter. For specific temperatures, see the climate chart in the appendix.

Travel Smart

Many people travel through Italy thinking it's a chaotic mess. They feel that any attempt at efficient travel is futile. This is dead wrong—and expensive. Italy, which seems as orderly as spilled spaghetti, actually functions well. Only those who understand this and travel smart can enjoy Italy on a budget.

Really, this book can save you lots of time and money. But to have an "A" trip, you need to be an "A" student. Read it all before your trip; note the days when museums are closed and whether reservations are mandatory. You can wait two hours in line to get into the Uffizi—or you can ask your hotel to book you a time, and you'll walk right in. Saving Michelangelo's *David* for your trip finale is risky, and on Monday, impossible. (Florence's major sights, along with some minor ones, are closed on Mondays.) If you cut your Siena day trip short, you'll miss the city's medieval magic at twilight. A smart trip is a puzzle—a fun, doable, and worthwhile challenge.

Reserve your hotel room well in advance if you'll be in Florence over a holiday. Hotels are often booked up on Easter (April 8 in 2007), April 25, May 1, June 24 (Florence's patron saint day), November 1, and on Fridays and Saturdays year-round. Religious holidays and train strikes can catch you by surprise anywhere in Italy.

Sundays have the same pros and cons as they do for travelers in the United States: Sightseeing attractions are generally open; banks and many shops are closed; and city traffic is light. Rowdy evenings are rare on Sundays. Saturdays are virtually weekdays with earlier closing hours.

Buy a phone card and use it for reservations and double-checking hours of sights. (I've included phone numbers for this purpose.) Enjoy the friendliness of the local people. Ask questions. Most locals are eager to point you in their idea of the right direction. Pack along a pocket-size notebook to organize your thoughts. Those who expect to travel smart, do.

RESOURCES

Tourist Offices in the US

Before you go, you can contact the nearest Italian tourist information office (abbreviated **TI** in this book) in the US to briefly describe your trip and request information. You'll get the general packet and, if you ask for specifics (city map, calendar of festivals, etc.), an impressive amount of help. If you have a specific problem, they're a good source of sympathy. Their Web site is www.italiantourism.com.

Their offices are...

In New York: Tel. 212/245-5618, brochure hotline tel. 212/245-4822, fax 212/586-9249, enitny@italiantourism.com; 630 Fifth Ave. #1565, New York, NY 10111.

In Illinois: Tel. 312/644-0996, fax 312/644-3019, enitch@italiantourism.com; 500 N. Michigan Ave. #2240, Chicago, IL 60611.

In California: Tel. 310/820-1898, fax 310/820-6357, enitla@italiantourism.com; 12400 Wilshire Blvd. #550, Los Angeles, CA 90025.

Web Sites: www.firenzeturismo.it (Florence tourist information), www.italiantourism.com (Italian Tourist Board in the US), www.museionline.it (museums in Italy), and www.trenitalia.com (train info and schedules).

Rick Steves' Guidebooks, Public Television, and Radio Shows

With the help of my staff, I produce materials to help you plan your trip and travel smoothly.

Guidebooks: This book is only one of a series of 30+ books on European travel that includes country guidebooks (including Italy), city guidebooks (like the one you're holding), and my budget-travel skills handbook, *Rick Steves' Europe Through the Back Door;* all are annually updated. My phrase books—for Italian, French, German, Spanish, and Portuguese—are practical and budget-oriented. My other books are *Europe 101* (a crash course on art and history, heavy on Italy), *European Christmas* (on traditional and modern-day celebrations, including Italy), and *Postcards from Europe* (a fun memoir of my travels over 25 years). For a complete list of my books, see the inside of the last page of this book.

Public Television and Radio Shows: My television series, *Rick Steves' Europe,* covers European destinations. My weekly public radio show, *Travels with Rick Steves,* features interviews with travel experts from around the world. All the TV scripts and radio shows are at www.ricksteves.com. You can listen to the shows at any time—or download them on your MP3 player to take along on your trip.

Other Guidebooks

For most travelers, this book is all you need. But when you consider the improvements it will make in your $3,000 vacation, $25 or $35 for extra maps and books is money well spent. The well-researched Access guide (which combines Florence and Venice) and the colorful Eyewitness guide (on Florence and Tuscany) are popular with travelers. Eyewitness is fun for its great, easy-to-grasp graphics and photos, and it's just right for people who want only factoids. But the Eyewitness books are relatively skimpy on content and they weigh a ton. You can buy them in Florence (no more expensive than in the US—see recommended bookstores on page 26) or simply borrow them for a minute from other travelers at certain sights to make sure you're aware of that place's highlights. If you'll be traveling elsewhere in Italy, consider the 2007 editions of *Rick Steves' Italy*, *Rick Steves' Venice*, and *Rick Steves' Rome*.

Recommended Reading and Movies

To get the feel of Tuscany past and present, consider reading some of these books or seeing these films:

Non-Fiction: *The City of Florence* (R. W. B. Lewis), *The Stones of Florence* (Mary McCarthy), *Brunelleschi's Dome* (Ross King), *Lives of the Artists* (Giorgio Vasari), *The Architecture of the Italian Renaissance* (Peter Murray), *Florence: A Portrait* (Michael Levey), *The House of Medici* (Christopher Hibbert), *The Prince* and *Florentine Histories* (Niccolò Machiavelli), *Italian Days* (Barbara Grizzuti Harrison), *Desiring Italy* (Susan N. Cahill), *The Italians* (Luigi Barzini), *That Fine Italian Hand* (Paul Hofmann), *Italian Neighbors* and *An Italian Education* (Tim Parks), *Travelers' Tales: Italy* (Anne Calcagno), *Under the Tuscan Sun* (Frances Mayes), *Fortune Is a River* (Roger D. Masters), and *The Hills of Tuscany* (Ferenc Máté).

Fiction: *The Agony and the Ecstasy* (Irving Stone), *A Room with a View* (E. M. Forster), *The Sixteen Pleasures* (Robert Hellenga), *The Light in the Piazza* (Elizabeth Spencer), *A Rich Full Death* (Michael Dibdin), *Death of an Englishman* (Magdalen Nabb), *Bella Donna* (Barbara Cherne), *Romola* (George Eliot), *The Passion of Artemisia* (Susan Vreeland), and *The Birth of Venus* (Sarah Dunant).

Flicks: *A Room with a View* (1986, Florence), *Under the Tuscan Sun* (2003, Tuscany), *Where Angels Fear to Tread* (1991, San Gimignano), *Life Is Beautiful* (1997, Tuscany), *Palio* (1932, Siena), *Prince of Foxes* (1949, San Gimignano), *The Light in the Piazza* (1962, Tuscany), *The Triumph of Love* (2001, Lucca), *The English Patient* (1996, partially shot in Montepulciano), *Stealing Beauty* (1996, near Siena), *Up at the Villa* (2000, Florence and Siena), *The Portrait of a Lady* (1996, Lucca), *A Midsummer Night's Dream* (1999, Montepulciano), *Much Ado About Nothing* (1993, set in Sicily, but

Begin Your Trip at www.ricksteves.com

At our travel Web site, you'll find a wealth of **free informa-tion** on European destinations, including fresh monthly news and helpful tips from thousands of fellow travelers.

Our **online Travel Store** offers travel bags and acces-sories specially designed by Rick Steves to help you travel smarter and lighter. These include Rick's popular carry-on bags (wheeled and rucksack versions), money belts, totes, toi-letries kits, adapters, other accessories, and a wide selection of guidebooks, planning maps, and DVDs.

Choosing the right railpass for your trip—amidst hun-dreds of options—can drive you nutty. We'll help you choose the best pass for your needs, plus give you a bunch of free extras.

Travel agents will tell you about mainstream tours of Europe, but they won't tell you about **Rick Steves' tours.** Rick Steves' Europe Through the Back Door travel company offers more than two dozen itineraries and 250+ departures reaching the best destinations in this book...and beyond. You'll enjoy great guides, a fun bunch of travel partners (with small groups of generally around 25), and plenty of room to spread out in a big, comfy bus. You'll find European adven-tures to fit every vacation length. To get our Tour Catalog and a free Rick Steves Tour Experience DVD (filmed on location during an actual tour), visit www.ricksteves.com.

filmed in Tuscany), and *Obsession* (1976, Florence). Two films by Franco Zeffirelli were also set in San Gimignano: *Brother Sun, Sister Moon* (1972) and *Tea with Mussolini* (1999). In 2005, PBS produced an excellent docudrama about Florence's first family, *Medici: Godfathers of the Renaissance* (with a fine Web site: www.pbs.org/empires/medici).

Maps

The black-and-white maps in this book, drawn by Dave Hoerlein, are concise and simple. Dave is well-traveled in Tuscany and Italy, and has designed the maps to help you orient quickly and get to where you want to go, painlessly. Any TI, and some hotels, will have free maps. Better maps that list all the roads are sold at news-stands for €3–4. Take a look before you buy to be sure the map has the level of detail you want.

PRACTICALITIES

Red Tape: You need a passport—but no visa or shots—to travel in Italy.

Time: In Italy—and in this book—you'll use the 24-hour clock. It's the same through 12:00 noon, then keep going: 13:00, 14:00, and so on. For anything over 12, subtract 12 and add "p.m." (14:00 is 2:00 p.m.) Italian time is generally six/nine hours ahead of the East/West Coast of the US.

Business Hours: Traditionally, Italy uses the siesta plan. People usually work from about 8:00 to 13:00 and from 15:30 to 19:00, Monday through Saturday. Nowadays, however, many businesses have adopted the government's recommended 8:00 to 14:00 workday. In tourist areas, shops are open longer.

Shopping: Shoppers interested in pursuing VAT refunds (the tax refunded on large purchases made by non-EU residents) can refer to page 217.

Discounts: Discounts for sights are not listed in this book because they are generally limited to European residents and countries that offer reciprocal deals (the US does not).

Watt's Up? If you're bringing electrical gear, you'll need a two-prong adapter plug (sold cheap at travel stores in the US) and a converter. Travel appliances often have convenient, built-in converters; look for a voltage switch marked 120V (US) and 240V (Europe). If yours doesn't have a built-in converter, you'll have to buy an external one.

News: Americans keep in touch with the *International Herald Tribune* (published almost daily via satellite). Every Tuesday, the European editions of *Time* and *Newsweek* hit the stands with articles of particular interest to European travelers. Sports addicts can get their fix from *USA Today*. Good Web sites include www.europeantimes.com and http://news.bbc.co.uk.

MONEY

Banking

Bring plastic—ATM, credit, or debit cards—along with several hundred dollars in hard cash as an emergency backup. Traveler's checks are a waste of time (waiting at banks) and a waste of money (paying to purchase and cash checks).

To withdraw cash from an ATM, you'll need a debit card that can withdraw money from your bank account, plus a PIN code (numbers only; there are no letters on European keypads). Before you go, verify with your bank that your card will work and alert them that you'll be making withdrawals in Europe; otherwise, the bank may not approve transactions if it perceives unusual spending patterns.

Exchange Rate

1 euro (€) = about $1.20

To convert prices in euros to dollars, add 20 percent: €20 = about $24, €45 = about $54. Just like the dollar, one euro is broken down into 100 cents. You'll find coins ranging from €0.01 to €2, and bills ranging from €5 to €500.

Look carefully at any €2 coin you get in change. Some unscrupulous merchants are giving out similar-looking, gold-rimmed old 500-lire coins (worth $0) instead of €2 coins (worth $2.40). You are now warned!

Many debit and credit card companies have been tacking on additional fees (up to $5) for international transactions. Before you leave, ask the company about these fees to avoid being surprised when you get your statement.

It's smart to bring two cards in case one gets demagnetized or eaten by a temperamental machine. If your card doesn't work, try again, and request a smaller amount; some cash machines won't let you take out more than about €150 (don't take it personally). Also be aware that some ATMs will tell you to take your cash within 30 seconds, and if you aren't fast enough, your cash may be sucked back into the machine...and you'll have a hassle trying to get it from the bank.

Visa and MasterCard are more commonly accepted than American Express. Just like at home, credit or debit cards work easily at larger hotels, restaurants, and shops, but smaller businesses prefer payment in local currency (in small bills—break large bills at a bank).

Regular banks have the best rates for changing cash and traveler's checks. For a large exchange, it pays to compare rates and fees. Banks—not exchange offices—have the best rates for cashing traveler's checks. Banking hours are generally 8:30 to 13:30 and 15:30 to 16:30 Monday through Friday, but they can vary wildly. Banks are slow; simple transactions can take 15 to 30 minutes. Post offices and train stations usually change money if you can't get to a bank.

You should use a money belt (a pouch with a strap that you buckle around your waist like a belt and wear under your clothes). Thieves target tourists. A money belt provides peace of mind, allowing you to carry lots of cash safely.

Don't waste time every few days tracking down a cash machine—change a week's worth of money, stuff it in your money belt, and travel!

Damage Control for Lost or Stolen Cards

If you lose your credit, debit, or ATM card, stop people from using your card by reporting the loss immediately to the respective customer-assistance centers. If you promptly report your card lost or stolen, you typically won't be responsible for any unauthorized transactions on your account, although many banks charge a liability fee. Call these 24-hour US numbers collect: Visa (tel. 410/581-9994), MasterCard (tel. 636/722-7111), and American Express (tel. 336/393-1111).

At a minimum, have the following information ready: the name of the financial institution that issued you the card, along with the type of card (classic, platinum). Ideally, plan ahead and pack photocopies of your cards—front and back—to expedite their replacement. Providing the following information allows a quicker cancellation of your card: full card number, whether you are the primary or secondary cardholder, the cardholder's name exactly as printed on the card, billing address, home phone number, circumstances of the loss or theft, and identification verification (such as your Social Security number—memorize this, don't carry a copy). If you are the secondary cardholder, you'll also need to provide the primary cardholder's identification-verification details. You can generally receive a temporary card within two to three business days in Europe.

Tipping

Tipping in Italy isn't as automatic and generous as it is in the US, but for special service, tips are appreciated, if not expected. As in the US, the proper amount depends on your resources, tipping philosophy, and the circumstances, but some general guidelines apply.

Restaurants: Check the menu to see whether the service is included (*servizio incluso*—generally 15 percent); if not, a tip of 5–10 percent is fine (for details, see page 197), though Italians rarely tip.

Taxis: To tip the cabbie, round up. For a typical ride, round up to the next euro on the fare (to pay a €4.50 fare, give €5). If the cabbie hauls your bags and zips you to the airport to help you catch your flight, you might want to toss in a little more. But if you feel like you're being driven in circles or otherwise ripped off, skip the tip. Note that you'll be charged a supplement for luggage.

Special Services: It's thoughtful to tip a couple of euros to someone who shows you a special sight and who is paid in no other way (such as the man who shows you an Etruscan tomb in his backyard). Tour guides at public sites sometimes hold out their hands for tips after they give their spiel; if I've already paid for the tour, I don't tip extra, though some tourists do give a euro or two, particularly for a job well done. I don't tip at hotels, but if you do, give the porter a euro for carrying bags and leave a couple of euros in your room at the end of your stay for the maid if the room was kept clean. In general, if someone in the service industry does a super job for you, a tip of a couple of euros is appropriate...but not required.

When in doubt, ask. If you're not sure whether (or how much) to tip for a service, ask your hotelier or the tourist information office; they'll fill you in on how it's done on their turf.

TRANSPORTATION

The downtown core of Florence is walkable. For information on taking buses and taxis, see "Getting Around Florence" in the Orientation chapter. If you have a car, park it. Drivers who don't follow the strict rules get fined (see page 227).

Getting around the Tuscan countryside is easiest by rental car and doable by bus and train; you'll find specifics on public transportation in each chapter. For information on transportation throughout Italy, see *Rick Steves' Italy 2007*. For information on travel agencies in Florence, see page 27.

COMMUNICATING

Telephones

Smart travelers learn the phone system and use it daily to reserve or reconfirm rooms, get tourist information, reserve restaurants, confirm tour times, or phone home.

If you have to spell out your name on the phone when making a reservation, you might have trouble with *a* (pronounced "ah" in Italian), *i* (pronounced "ee"), and *e* (pronounced "ay"). Say "*a*, Ancona," "*e*, Empoli," and "*i*, Italia" to clear up that problem. If you plan to access your voice mail from Italy, be advised that you can't always dial extensions or secret codes once you connect (you're on vacation—relax).

Types of Phones

You'll encounter various kinds of phones in your European travels.

Telecom **pay phones** are everywhere, and take cards only (no coins). About a quarter of the phones are broken. The rest work reluctantly. Dial slowly and deliberately, as if the phone doesn't understand numbers very well. Often a recorded message in Italian will break in, brusquely informing you that the phone number does not exist *(non-esistente)*, even if you're dialing your

own home phone number. Dial again with an increasing show of confidence, in an attempt to convince the phone of your number's existence. If you fail, try a different phone. Repeat as needed.

Hotel room phones are fairly cheap for local calls, but pricey for international calls, unless you use an international phone card (see below).

American mobile phones work in Europe if they're GSM-enabled, tri-band (or quad-band), and on a calling plan that includes international calls (T-Mobile and Cingular have the best deals). For example, with a T-Mobile phone, you can roam all over Europe using your home number, and pay $1 to $2 per minute for making or receiving calls.

Some travelers buy a **European mobile phone** in Europe, but if you're on a strict budget, skip mobile phones and use phone cards instead. The cheapest new phones cost around $75, plus $20–50 for the necessary "SIM card" to make it work (includes some prepaid calling time). A cheapie phone is often "locked" to work affordably only in the country where you buy it, but can also roam (for high rates) in other countries. For around $25 more, you can buy an "unlocked" phone that allows you to use different SIM cards in different countries—which saves money if you'll be making lots of calls. If you're interested, stop by any European shop that sells mobile phones; you'll see prominent store-window displays. You aren't required to (and shouldn't) buy a monthly contract—buy prepaid calling time instead. As you use it up, buy additional minutes at newsstands or mobile-phone shops.

Paying for Calls

You can spend a fortune making phone calls in Italy...but why? Here's the skinny on different ways to pay, including the best deals.

Get a phone card for your calls. Italian prepaid **phone cards** come in two types: phone cards that you insert into a pay phone (best for local calls or quick international calls), and phone cards that come with a code number and can be used from virtually any phone.

The **insertable phone cards** are used to make calls from pay phones. You can buy these Telecom cards (in denominations of €5, €10, etc.) at tobacco shops, post offices, and machines near phone booths (many phone booths indicate where the nearest phone-card sales outlet is located). Rip off the perforated corner to "activate" the card, then physically insert it into a slot in the pay phone. It displays how much money you have remaining on the card. Then just dial away to anywhere in the world. The price of the call is automatically deducted while you talk. These cards give you your best deal for calls within Italy, and are reasonable for international calls. Each European country has its own insertable phone card, which means your Italian card won't work in a Swiss phone.

International phone cards are an even better deal for overseas calls (as cheap as a nickel per minute to the US). Unlike the official phone cards, an international phone card is not inserted into the phone. Instead, you dial the toll-free number listed on the card, reaching an automated operator. When prompted, you dial in a scratch-to-reveal code number, also written on the card. Then dial your number. You can use the cards to make local and domestic long-distance calls as well. Since they're not insertable, you can use them from any phone—including the one in your hotel room (if your phone is set on pulse, switch it to tone). Generally you'll get more minutes out of a card if you use it from your hotel room, rather than from a pay phone. (For a €5 card, for example, you may get 180 minutes from your hotel room phone, compared to 40 minutes from a pay phone.) Buy cards at small newsstand kiosks and hole-in-the-wall long-distance phone shops. Because there are so many brand names, simply ask for an international phone card (*carta telefonica prepagata internazionale*, KAR-tah teh-leh-FOHN-ee-kah pray-pah-GAH-tah in-ter-naht-zee-oh-NAH-lay). Tell the vendor where you'll be making most calls (*per Stati Uniti*—to America), and he'll select the brand with the best deal. Buy a lower denomination in case the card is a dud. I've had good luck with the Europa card, offering 180 minutes from Italy to the US for €5. If you have time left on your card when you leave the country (as you likely will), simply give it to another traveler—anyone can use it.

Dialing direct from your hotel room without using an international phone card is usually quite expensive for international calls, but it's convenient. I always ask first how much I'll be charged. Keep in mind that you have to pay for local and occasionally even toll-free calls.

Receiving calls in your hotel room is often the cheapest way to keep in touch with the folks back home—especially if your family has an inexpensive way to call you (either a good deal on their long-distance plan, or a prepaid calling card with good rates to Europe). Give them a list of your hotels' phone numbers before you go. As you travel, send your family an e-mail or make a quick pay-phone call to set up a time for them to call you, and then wait for the ring.

Metered phones are sometimes available in bigger post offices. You can talk all you want, then pay the bill when you leave—but be sure you know the rates before you have a lengthy conversation.

VoIP (Voice over Internet Protocol) is the latest trend in European communications. Basically, two VoIP users can talk to each other for free (via their computers) over a fast Internet connection. The major providers are Skype (www.skype.com) and Google Talk (www.google.com/talk). Unless you'll be traveling with a laptop, you probably won't need to bother with VoIP. But it's worth knowing about—it's only a matter of time before a new European friend who wants to keep in touch asks you, "Do you use Skype?"

US calling cards (such as the ones offered by AT&T, MCI, or Sprint) are the worst option. You'll nearly always save a lot of money by paying with a phone card.

How to Dial

Calling from the US to Italy, or vice versa, is simple—once you break the code. The European calling chart on page 372 will walk you through it. Remember that European time is six/nine hours ahead of the East/West Coast of the US.

Dialing Within Italy: Italy has a direct-dial phone system (no area codes). To call anywhere within Italy, just dial the number. For example, the number of one of my recommended Florence hotels is 055-293-451. To call it from the Florence train station, dial 055-293-451. If you call it from Venice, it's the same: 055-293-451. Italian mobile phone numbers are dialed direct like fixed phone numbers.

Italian phone numbers vary in length; a hotel can have, say, an 8-digit phone number and a 9-digit fax number.

Italy's toll-free numbers start with 800 (like US 800 numbers, though in Italy you don't need to dial a "1" first). In Italy, these 800 numbers—called *freephone* or *numero verde* (green number)—can be dialed free from any phone without using a phone card or coins. Note that you can't call Italy's toll-free numbers from America, nor can you count on reaching America's toll-free numbers from Italy.

Dialing International Calls: When calling internationally, dial the international access code (00 if you're calling from Europe, 011 from the US or Canada), the country code of the country you're calling (39 for Italy; see appendix for list of other countries), and the local number. Note that in most European countries, you have to drop the zero at the beginning of the number—but in Italy, you dial it. So, to call the Florence hotel from the US, dial 011 (the US international access code), 39 (Italy's country code), then 055-293-451. To call my office in Edmonds, Washington, from Italy, you dial 00 (Europe's international access code), 1 (the US country code), 425 (Edmonds' area code), and 771-8303.

How Was Your Trip?

Were your travels fun, smooth, and meaningful? If you'd like to share your tips, concerns, and discoveries, please fill out the survey at www.ricksteves.com/feedback. I personally read and value your feedback. Thanks in advance—it helps a lot.

E-mail and Mail

E-mail: I've listed several cafés (see page 26), though your hotelier or TI can easily steer you to the nearest Internet access point. Some hotels offer Internet access in the lobby.

When you see a cluster of orange public phones in a room off a busy street, you might see several computers in the batch. With these, you can use your Italian phone card to access the Internet. You won't be comfortable (no seat), and you'll get cut off if your phone card runs out of time, but this can be a handy, quick way to check your e-mail.

Mail: Mail service in Italy has improved over the last few years, but even so, mail nothing precious from Italy. If you need to receive mail while traveling, consider a few pre-reserved hotels along your route. Allow 14 days for United States-to-Italy mail delivery, but don't count on it. Federal Express makes pricey two-day deliveries. E-mailing and phoning is so easy that I've completely dispensed with mail stops.

TRAVELING AS A TEMPORARY LOCAL

We travel all the way to Italy to enjoy differences—to become temporary locals. You'll experience frustrations. Certain truths that we find "God-given" or "self-evident," such as cold beer, ice in drinks, bottomless cups of coffee, hot showers, and bigger being better, are suddenly not so true. One of the benefits of travel is the eye-opening realization that there are logical, civil, and even better alternatives. A willingness to go local ensures that you'll enjoy a full dose of Italian hospitality.

If there is a negative aspect to Italians' image of Americans (apart from our foreign policy), it's that we are big, loud, aggressive, impolite, rich, and a bit naive. Europeans don't respond well to Americans complaining about being too hot or too cold. To encourage conservation, the Italian government limits when air-conditioning or central heating can be used. Bring a sweater in winter, and in summer, be prepared to sweat a little like everyone else. Also, Americans tend to be noisy in public places, such as restaurants and trains. Our raised voices can demolish Europe's reserved and elegant ambience. Talk softly.

While Italians, flabbergasted by our Yankee excesses, say in disbelief, *"Mi sono cadute le braccia!"* ("I throw my arms down!"), they nearly always afford us individual travelers all the warmth we deserve.

Judging from all the happy postcards we receive from travelers who have used this book, it's safe to assume you'll enjoy a great, affordable vacation—with the finesse of an independent, experienced traveler.

Thanks, and *buon viaggio!*

BACK DOOR TRAVEL PHILOSOPHY
From *Rick Steves' Europe Through the Back Door*

Travel is intensified living—maximum thrills per minute and one of the last great sources of legal adventure. Travel is freedom. It's recess, and we need it.

Experiencing the real Europe requires catching it by surprise, going casual..."Through the Back Door."

Affording travel is a matter of priorities. (Make do with the old car.) You can eat and sleep—simply, safely, and enjoyably—anywhere in Europe for $100 a day plus transportation costs. In many ways, spending more money only builds a thicker wall between you and what you traveled so far to see. Europe is a cultural carnival, and time after time, you'll find that its best acts are free and the best seats are the cheap ones.

A tight budget forces you to travel close to the ground, meeting and communicating with the people. Never sacrifice sleep, nutrition, safety, or cleanliness in the name of budget. Simply enjoy the local-style alternatives to expensive hotels and restaurants.

Extroverts have more fun. If your trip is low on magic moments, kick yourself and make things happen. If you don't enjoy a place, maybe you don't know enough about it. Seek the truth. Recognize tourist traps. Give a culture the benefit of your open mind. See things as different, but not better or worse. Any culture has much to share.

Of course, travel, like the world, is a series of hills and valleys. Be fanatically positive and militantly optimistic. If something's not to your liking, change your liking.

Travel is addicting. It can make you a happier American, as well as a citizen of the world. Our Earth is home to six and a half billion equally precious people. It's humbling to travel and find that people don't envy Americans. Europeans like us, but with all due respect, they wouldn't trade passports.

Globe-trotting destroys ethnocentricity. It helps you understand and appreciate different cultures. Regrettably, there are forces in our society that want you dumbed down for their convenience. Don't let it happen. Thoughtful travel engages you with the world—more important than ever these days. Travel changes people. It broadens perspectives and teaches new ways to measure quality of life. Rather than fear the diversity on this planet, travelers celebrate it. Many travelers toss aside their hometown blinders. Their prized souvenirs are the strands of different cultures they decide to knit into their own character. The world is a cultural yarn shop, and Back Door travelers are weaving the ultimate tapestry. Join in!

FLORENCE
(Firenze)

ORIENTATION

The best of Florence lies mostly on the north bank of the Arno River. The main historical sights cluster around the red-brick dome of the cathedral (Duomo). Everything is within a 20-minute walk of the train station, cathedral, or Ponte Vecchio (Old Bridge). The less impressive but more characteristic Oltrarno area (south bank) is just over the bridge. Though small, Florence is intense. Prepare for scorching summer heat, kamikaze motor scooters, slick pickpockets, few WCs, steep prices, and long lines.

Planning Your Time

Plan your sightseeing carefully. The major sights—the Uffizi Gallery and the Accademia (starring Michelangelo's *David*)—are closed on Monday. While many travelers spend several hours a day in lines at the Uffizi and Accademia, you can easily avoid this by making reservations (see page 39). A couple of Florence's popular sights—the Bargello and the Museum of San Marco—close at 13:50 (though the latter is open later on weekends). Other museums close early only on certain days. Before heading into Florence, especially if you'll be there for only a day or two during the crowded summer months, carefully check all the opening and closing times of your must-see museums. Set up a good itinerary in advance. Do my recommended Renaissance Walk in the morning or late afternoon to avoid heat and crowds. Stop often for gelato.

Florence in One Day

8:30   Accademia *(David)*; reserve in advance.

10:00   Renaissance Walk through town center, climb Giotto's Tower.

12:00   Bargello (best statues), lunch at Cantinetta dei Verrazzano (closed Sun) or in market neighborhood.

Florence Overview

14:00   Shop around San Lorenzo.
16:30   Uffizi Gallery (finest paintings); reserve at least a month in advance (with your hotel's help or by phone).
19:00   Dinner on/near Piazza della Signoria; hikers can take the Oltrarno Walk (best local color) and have dinner at 20:00 across the river.

Florence in Two Days
Day 1
8:30   Accademia *(David);* reserve in advance.
10:00   Museum of San Marco (art by Fra Angelico).
12:00   Medici Chapels (Michelangelo).
14:00   Lunch, market, wander, shop.
16:30   Baptistery (closes at 14:00 on Sun).
17:00   Climb Giotto's Tower.
18:00   Renaissance Walk through heart of old town.
20:00   Dinner near Piazza della Signoria.

Day 2
9:00   Bargello (greatest statues).
11:00   Duomo Museum (intriguing statues by Donatello and Michelangelo) or Science Museum.
13:00   Lunch, free to wander and shop.

15:00	Church of Santa Maria Novella (Masaccio painting) and old perfumery.
17:00	Uffizi Gallery (best paintings); reserve at least a month in advance (through your hotel or by phone).
19:00	Oltrarno Walk.
20:00	Dinner in Oltrarno.

Florence in Three (or More) Days
Day 1
8:30	Accademia *(David);* reserve in advance.
10:00	Museum of San Marco (Fra Angelico).
12:00	Markets, shop, wander.
13:00	Lunch.
14:00	Medici Chapels (Michelangelo).
15:00	Church of Santa Maria Novella and old perfumery.
16:30	Baptistery.
17:00	Giotto's Tower.
18:00	Renaissance Walk through heart of old town.
20:00	Dinner on or near Piazza della Signoria.

Day 2
9:00	Bargello (top statues).
11:00	Science Museum.
13:00	Lunch, free to wander and shop.
16:30	Uffizi Gallery (unforgettable paintings); reserve at least a month in advance (through your hotel or by phone).
19:00	Sunset at Piazzale Michelangelo (consider a dinner picnic).

Day 3
9:00	Duomo Museum.
11:00	Santa Croce Church (opens at 13:00 on Sun).
13:00	Lunch.
14:00	Pitti Palace, Boboli and Bardini Gardens.

18:00   Oltrarno Walk.
20:00   Dinner in Oltrarno.

Day 4
Side-trip to Siena (sights open daily; 1–2 hours by bus), or consider an overnight stay to enjoy the town at twilight.

Days 5, 6, and so on
Visit your pick of Pisa, Lucca, and Tuscan hill towns.

Arrival in Florence

For a rundown on Florence's train station, the bus station next door, and nearby airports, see Transportation Connections, page 223. The taxi stand in front of the train station has a fast-moving line (except on holidays). Most recommended hotels are within a 10- or 15-minute walk. Buses and the bus ticket booth are just outside the station (with your back to the tracks, they're on the left). Many of the hotels listed are in the direction of the Church of Santa Maria Novella. From the station (again, with your back to the tracks), cross the wide square to reach the church—taking care not to become bus kill—and continue to the piazza in front. The underground Galleria S.M. Novella tunnel that leads from the station under the square to the church keeps you out of the traffic (but beware of pickpockets when you emerge from the tunnel).

Tourist Information

There are three TIs in Florence: across from the train station, near Santa Croce Church, and on Via Cavour.

The TI across the square from the train station is most crowded—expect long lines (Mon–Sat 8:30–19:00, Sun 8:30–14:00; with your back to tracks, exit the station—it's across the square in wall near corner of church, Piazza Stazione 4, tel. 055-212-245). In the train station, avoid the Hotel Reservations "Tourist Information" window (marked *Informazioni Turistiche Alberghiere*) near the McDonald's; it's not a real TI, but a hotel-reservation business instead.

The TI near Santa Croce Church is pleasant, helpful, and uncrowded (Mon–Sat 9:00–19:00, Sun 9:00–14:00, shorter hours off-season, Borgo Santa Croce 29 red, tel. 055-234-0444).

Another winner is the TI three blocks north of the Duomo (Mon–Sat 8:30–18:30, Sun 8:30–13:30, closed Sun in winter, Via Cavour 1 red, tel. 055-290-832 or 055-23-320, international bookstore across street).

At any TI, pick up a free map (ask for the "APT" map and tear out the excellent center inset to keep handy in your pocket), a current museum-hours listing (extremely important, since no guidebook—

Daily Reminder

Sunday: The Duomo's dome, Museum of Precious Stones, and the Central Market are closed. These sights close early: Duomo Museum (at 13:40) and the Baptistery's interior (at 14:00). A few sights are open only in the afternoon: Duomo (13:30–16:45), Santa Croce Church (13:00–17:30), Church of San Lorenzo (13:30–17:30), and Brancacci Chapel and the Church of Santa Maria Novella (both 13:00–17:00). The Museum of San Marco, which is open on the second and fourth Sunday of the month until 19:00, closes entirely—as does the Bargello—on the first, third, and fifth Sunday. The Medici Chapels and Palazzo Davanzati close on the second and fourth Sunday. The Science Museum is generally closed (but open Oct–May on the second Sunday of the month). Need a calendar? Look in the appendix.

It's not possible to reserve tickets by phone for the major sights (Accademia, Uffizi Gallery) because the booking office is closed; try other options instead (see page 39 for details).

Monday: The biggies are closed, including Accademia *(David)* and Uffizi Gallery, as well as the Orsanmichele Church and Palatine Gallery/Royal Apartments and the Modern Art Gallery in the Pitti Palace.

The Medici Chapels close on the first, third, and fifth Monday of the month. The Museum of San Marco and the Bargello close on the second and fourth Monday. At the Pitti Palace, the Grand Ducal Treasures and the Boboli and Bardini Gardens close on the first and last Monday. Palazzo Davanzati closes on the first, third, and fifth Monday. The San Lorenzo Market is closed Monday in winter.

including this one—has ever been able to accurately predict the hours of Florence's sights for the coming year), and any information on entertainment. The free, monthly *Florence Concierge Information* magazine lists museums, plus lots that I don't: concerts, markets, sporting events, church services, shopping ideas, bus and train connections, and an entire similar section on Siena. *The Florentine,* published every other Thursday, is a free newspaper for expats and tourists (in English; news, events, kids' activities, and cultural insights, download latest issue at www.theflorentine.net). Both of these English freebies are available at TIs and hotels all over town.

Helpful Hints

Theft Alert: Florence has particularly hardworking thief gangs. They specialize in tourists and hang out where you do: near

Target these sights on Mondays: Duomo, Duomo Museum, Giotto's Tower, Baptistery, Medici-Riccardi Palace, Brancacci Chapel, Mercato Nuovo, Michelangelo's House, Science Museum, Palazzo Vecchio, and churches. Or take a walking tour.

Tuesday: All sights are open except for Michelangelo's House and the Brancacci Chapel. The Science Museum closes early (13:00).

Wednesday: All sights are open except for Medici-Riccardi Palace. The Santo Spirito Church is open only in the morning (10:00–12:00).

Thursday: All sights are open. These sights close early: Duomo (15:30) and Palazzo Vecchio (14:00).

Friday: All sights are open. The Church of Santa Maria Novella opens only in the afternoon (13:00–17:00).

Saturday: All sights are open, but the Science Museum closes at 13:00 June–Sept. These sights close early on the first Saturday of the month: Duomo (15:30) and the Duomo's dome (16:00).

Late-Hours Note: The Accademia, Uffizi, and Palatine Gallery/Royal Apartments in the Pitti Palace are open Tue–Sun until 18:50. Many other sights are open until 19:00: Museum of San Marco (Sat–Sun), Museum of Precious Stones (Thu), San Lorenzo Market (daily), Medici-Riccardi Palace (Thu–Tue), the Duomo's dome (Mon–Fri), Baptistery (Mon–Sat), Mercato Nuovo (daily), Palazzo Vecchio (Fri–Wed), and Leonardo Museum (daily). These sights are open until 19:30: Duomo Museum (Mon–Sat), Giotto's Tower (daily), the Boboli and Bardini Gardens in the Pitti Palace (daily, June–Aug only), and San Miniato Church (daily).

the train station, the station's underpass (especially where the tunnel surfaces), and major sights. Also be on guard at two squares frequented by drug pushers (Santa Maria Novella and Santo Spirito). American tourists—especially older ones—are considered easy targets.

Medical Help: To reach a doctor who speaks English, call 055-475-411 (they answer 24/7, reasonable house calls to your hotel—arriving within an hour for €130, only €50 if you go to the clinic at Via L. Magnifico 59, near Piazza della Libertà when the doctor's in: Mon–Fri 11:00–12:00 & 17:00–18:00, Sat 11:00–12:00, house calls only on Sun, no appointment necessary). The TI has a list of English-speaking doctors. There are 24-hour pharmacies at the train station and near the Duomo on Borgo San Lorenzo.

Churches: Many churches now operate like museums, charging an admission fee to see their art treasures. Modest dress for men, women, and even children is required in some churches, and recommended for all of them—no bare shoulders, short shorts, or short skirts. Be respectful of worshippers; don't use a flash. Churches usually close from 12:00 or 12:30 to 15:00 or 16:00.

Addresses: Street addresses list businesses in red and residences in black (color-coded on the actual street number and indicated by a letter following the number in printed addresses: r = red, no indication = black). *Pensioni* are usually black but can be either. The red and black numbers each appear in roughly consecutive order on streets but bear no apparent connection with each other. I'm lazy and don't concern myself with the distinction (if one number's wrong, I look for the other) and can easily find my way around.

Internet Access: Internet Train is the dominant chain, with bright and cheery rooms, speedy computers, and long hours (daily 9:30–24:00, www.internettrain.it). Find branches at the train station (downstairs), Piazza della Repubblica (Via Porta Rossa 38 red), Piazza Santa Croce (Via de Benci 36 red), and Ponte Vecchio (Borgo San Jacopo 30 red). Two other Internet cafés are in the north of Florence, between the Duomo and the Accademia, near the Medici-Riccardi Palace: **Italian Point** (daily 9:00–20:00, €2/hour with this 2007 book, Via Ricasoli 19 red) and **easyInternet** (daily 9:00–23:00, Via Ricasoli 23 red).

Bookstores: Local guidebooks (sold at kiosks) are cheap and give you a map and a decent commentary on the sights. For brand-name guidebooks in English, try **Feltrinelli International** (Mon–Sat 9:00–19:30, closed Sun, Via Cavour 20 red, a few blocks north of the Duomo and across the street from the TI and the Medici-Riccardi Palace on Via Cavour, tel. 055-219-524), **Edison Bookstore** (Mon–Sat 9:00–24:00, Sun 10:00–24:00, sells CDs and novels on Renaissance and a lot more on its four floors, facing Piazza della Repubblica, tel. 055-213-110), or **Paperback Exchange** (cheaper, all books in English, bring in your used book for a discount on a new one, Mon–Fri 9:00–19:30, Sat 10:00–19:30, closed Sun and Aug, just south of the Duomo on Via delle Oche 4 red, tel. 055-293-460).

Laundry: The **Wash & Dry Lavarapido** chain offers long hours and efficient, self-service launderettes at several locations (about €7 for wash and dry, daily 8:00–22:00, tel. 055-580-480). These are close to recommended hotels: Via dei Servi 105 (and a rival launderette at Via Guelfa 22 red, off Via Cavour; both near *David*); Via del Sole 29 red and Via della Scala 52 red (between train station and river); Via Ghibellina 143 red (Palazzo Vecchio); and Via dei Serragli 87 red (across the river in Oltrarno neighborhood).

Travel Agency: Get train tickets, reservations, and supplements at travel agencies rather than at the congested train station. The cost is often the same, though sometimes there's a minimal charge. Ask your hotel for the nearest travel agency, or try American Express.

   American Express offers all the normal services, but is most helpful as an easy place to get your train tickets, reservations, supplements (all the same price as at the station), cell phone rental, or just information on trains (Mon–Fri 9:00–17:30, closed Sat–Sun, 3 short blocks north of Palazzo Vecchio on Via Dante Alighieri 22 red, tel. 055-50-981).

Chill Out: Schedule several cool breaks into your sightseeing where you can sit, pause, and refresh yourself with a sandwich, gelato, or coffee.

Getting Around Florence

I organize my sightseeing geographically and do it all on foot.

   If you take **buses,** a €1 ticket gets you one hour (€1.80/3 hrs, €4/24 hrs, buy in *tabacchi* shops or newsstands and validate on bus, or buy 1-hour tickets sold on bus for €1.50, route map available at TI, info tel. 800-424-500). Multiday passes are also available.

   Florence requires a lot of walking. Its buses don't really cover the old center well. Fun little *elettrico* buses weave and circle around the old center from the station, and big buses rumble from the station and Piazza San Marco (near Museum of San Marco and many recommended hotels) to points beyond where most tourists go.

   Of the many bus lines here are the only ones I found helpful: *elettrico* #D (from train station to Ponte Vecchio, joyriding through Oltrarno), *elettrico* #B (up and down the Arno River from Ognissanti to Santa Croce), lines #7, #31, and #32 (connecting the station, Duomo, and Piazza San Marco with #7 continuing on to Fiesole) and lines #12 and #13 (from station to Porta Romana, up to Piazzale Michelangelo, and on to Santa Croce).

   Hop-on, hop-off bus tours stop at the major sights (see "Tours," page 29).

   The minimum cost for a **taxi** ride is €4, or €6 after 22:00 and on Sundays (rides in the center of town should be charged as tariff #1). A taxi ride from the train station to Ponte Vecchio costs about €8.50. Taxi fares and supplements (e.g., €2 extra if you call a cab) are clearly explained on signs in each taxi.

Tips for Tackling My Self-Guided Tours

Sightseeing can be hard work. My self-guided tours are designed to make your visits to Italy's finest museums meaningful, fun, fast, and painless. Make reservations for the Uffizi, Accademia *(David)*, Brancacci Chapel, and the Medici-Riccardi Palace (see page 39). You can reserve an entrance time for the Bargello, Medici Chapels, and Museum of San Marco, but it's unnecessary. To make the most of my tours, read the chapter the night before your visit.

Because of labor demands, hours of sights change without warning. Pick up the latest listing of museum hours at a TI. Don't put off visiting a must-see sight such as *David;* you never know when a place will close unexpectedly for a holiday, strike, or restoration.

When you arrive at the sight, use the overview map to get the lay of the land and the basic tour route. Expect a few changes—paintings can be on tour, on loan, out sick, or shifted at the whim of the curator. To adapt, pick up any available free floor plans as you enter. If you can't find a particular painting, just ask any museum worker. Point to the photograph in this book and ask, *"Dov'è?"* (DOH-vay; it means "Where?").

I cover the highlights at sights. You may want to supplement with an audioguide (dry-but-useful recorded descriptions in English, about €4, usually available on site).

Museums have their rules; if you're aware of them in advance, they're no big deal. Keep in mind that many sights have "last entry" times 30–60 minutes before closing. Guards usher people out before the official closing time.

Cameras are normally allowed, but no flashes or tripods (without special permission). Flashes damage oil paintings and distract others in the room. Even without a flash, a hand-held camera will take a decent picture (or buy postcards or posters at the museum bookstore). Video cameras are usually allowed.

For security reasons, you're often required to check even small bags. Many museums have a free checkroom at the entrance. They're safe. If you have something you can't bear to part with, stash it in a pocket or purse.

At the museum bookshop, thumb through the biggest guidebook to be sure you haven't overlooked something that is of particular interest to you. If there's an on-site cafeteria, it's usually a good place to rest and have a snack or light meal. Museum WCs are free and generally clean.

And finally, every sight or museum offers more than the few stops I cover. Use these tours as an introduction—not the final word.

TOURS

Note that big bus companies offer tours of Florence, but for most, the city is really best on foot. The outfits listed here are hardworking, creative, and offer a worthwhile array of organized sightseeing activities. Nearly all have guides available for private hire. Study their Web sites for details.

Walking Tours of Florence—This company offers a variety of tours (up to 12/day year-round) featuring downtown Florence, Uffizi highlights, and Tuscany day trips. Their guides are native English-speakers. The three-hour "Original Florence" walk hits the main sights but gets offbeat to weave a picture of Florentine life in medieval and Renaissance times. Tours go rain or shine with as few as two participants (€25 for 3-hour Original Florence walk daily at 9:15, office open Mon–Sat 8:00–18:00, Sun 8:30–13:30 but off-season closed on Sun and for lunch, booking necessary for all tours, Via dei Sassetti 1, second floor, above Odeon Cinema, near Piazza della Repubblica, tel. 055-264-5033 during day or mobile 329-613-2730 from 18:00–20:00, www.italy.artviva.com, staff@artviva.com). For schedule details, pick up their extensive brochure in your hotel lobby.

Florentia—Top-notch, private walking tours—geared for thoughtful, well-heeled travelers with longer than average attention spans—are led by local scholars. The tours range from introductory city walks and museum visits to in-depth thematic walks such as the Golden Age of Florence, the Medici Dynasty, and side-trips into Tuscany (tours start at €125 for 2 hours, reserve in advance, tel. 338-890-8625, US tel. 510/549-1707, www.florentia.org, info@florentia.org).

Context Florence—Started by the folks who run Context Rome in Rome, this group of graduate students and professors lead "walking seminars" as scholarly as Florentia's (above). Their tours include a three-hour Michelangelo seminar, an in-depth study of the artist's work and influence (€76/person) and a two-hour evening orientation stroll called the Florence Evening Transect (€35/person, tel. 06-482-0911, US tel. 888-467-1986, www.contextflorence.com, info@contextflorence.com, run by Lani Bevacqua and Paul Bennett).

Local Guides—Good guides include Paola Barubiani and her partners at Walks Inside Florence (tel. 335-526-6496, www.walksinsideflorence.it, pbarub@tin.it) and Alessandra Marchetti (mobile 347-386-9839, aleoberm@tin.it).

Hop-on, Hop-off Bus Tours—Around town, you'll see big double-decker sightseeing buses double-parking at major sights. Tourists on the top deck can listen to brief recorded descriptions of the sights, snap photos, and enjoy an effortless drive-by look at the major landmarks. Tickets cost €20 (good for 24 hours, first bus at 9:30, last bus at 18:00, pay as you board, tickets include two bus lines—Blue is 1 hour with a trip up to Piazzale Michelangelo, Green is 2 hours with a side-trip to Fiesole). As the name implies, you can hop off when you want and catch the next bus (every 30 min depending on the season). Hop-on stops include the train station, Duomo, and Pitti Palace (www.firenze.city-sightseeing.it).

Accidental Tourist—This tour company picks you up in a van for a day of cooking classes, hiking, biking, or wine-tasting, then drops you off back in Florence (prices vary, e.g., €85 for cooking class, 9:30–17:00, book online in advance, allow 4 days for reply to e-mails, US tel. 348/659-0040, www.accidentaltourist.com, info @accidentaltourist.com).

SIGHTS

In this chapter, Florence's most important museums have the shortest listings and are marked with a ✪ (and page number). These sights are covered in greater detail in one of the self-guided tours included in this book.

The Renaissance Walk (see page 56) connects a number of these sights, from Michelangelo's *David* to the Ponte Vecchio over the Arno River. You can book ahead to visit the major museums on this walk (Accademia and Uffizi Gallery); see page 39 for details.

Price Hike Alert: Some of Italy's museums have found a clever way to squeeze more money out of visitors. They host a special exhibit (which no tourist really cares to pay for) and require that you pay to see it along with the permanent collection. The result: Already steep admission fees jump by about €3.

North of the Duomo (Cathedral)

▲▲▲Accademia (Galleria dell'Accademia)—This museum houses Michelangelo's *David*, the consummate Renaissance statue of the buff, Biblical shepherd boy ready to take on the giant. Nearby are some of the master's other works, including his powerful (unfinished) *Prisoners*, *St. Matthew*, and a *Pietà* (possibly by one of his disciples). Florentine Michelangelo Buonarotti, who would work tirelessly through the night, believed that the sculptor was a tool of God, responsible only for chipping away at the stone until the intended sculpture emerged. Beyond the magic

marble are two floors of mildly interesting pre-Renaissance and Renaissance paintings, including a couple of lighter-than-air Botticellis.

Cost, Hours, Location: €6.50, plus €3 fee for recommended reservation, Tue–Sun 8:15–18:50, closed Mon (last entry 45 min before closing, Via Ricasoli 60, tel. 055-238-8609).

○ See page 59 of the Renaissance Walk.

Nearby: Piazza S.S. Annunziata, behind the Accademia, displays lovely Renaissance harmony. Facing the square are two fine buildings: the 15th-century Santissima Annunziata church (worth a peek) and Brunelleschi's Hospital of the Innocents (Spedale degli Innocenti, not worth going inside), with terra-cotta medallions by Luca della Robbia. Built in the 1420s, the hospital is considered the first Renaissance building. I love sleeping on this square (at Hotel Loggiato dei Serviti, see page 189) and picnicking here during the day.

▲▲**Museum of San Marco (Museo di San Marco)**—One block north of the Accademia, this 15th-century monastery houses the greatest collection anywhere of frescoes and paintings by the

early Renaissance master Fra Angelico. The ground floor features the monk's paintings, along with some works by Fra Bartolomeo. Upstairs are 43 cells decorated by Fra Angelico and his assistants. While the monk/painter was trained in the medieval religious style, he also learned and adopted Renaissance techniques and

sensibilities, producing works that blended Christian symbols and Renaissance realism. Don't miss the cell of Savonarola, the charismatic monk who rode in from the Christian right, threw out the Medicis, turned Florence into a theocracy, sponsored "bonfires of the vanities" (burning books, paintings, and so on), and was finally burned himself when Florence decided to change channels (€4, Mon–Fri 8:15–13:50, Sat–Sun 8:15–19:00, but closed first, third, and fifth Sun and second and fourth Mon of each month, on Piazza San Marco, tel. 055-238-8608). While you can reserve an entrance time here, it's entirely unnecessary.

Florence

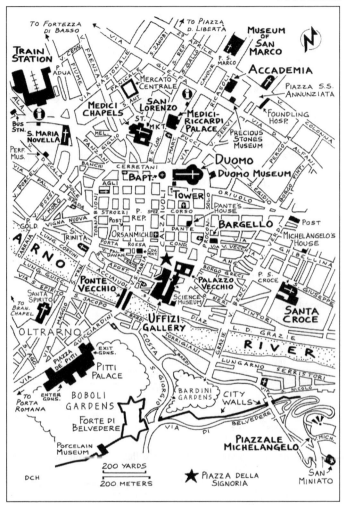

Museum of Precious Stones (Museo dell'Opificio delle Pietre Dure)—This unusual gem of a museum features mosaics of inlaid marble and stones. You'll see remnants of the Medici workshop from 1588, including 500 different precious stones, the tools used to cut and inlay them, and room after room of the sumptuous finished product. The helpful loaner booklet available next to the ticket window describes it all in English (€2, Mon–Wed and Fri–Sat 8:15–14:00, Thu 8:15–19:00, closed Sun, around corner from Accademia at Via degli Alfani 78, tel. 055-26-511).

Florence at a Glance

▲▲▲**Uffizi Gallery** Greatest collection of Italian paintings any-where—reserve at least one month in advance. **Hours:** Tue–Sun 8:15–18:50, closed Mon.

▲▲▲**Accademia** Michelangelo's *David* and powerful (unfin-ished) *Prisoners*—reserve ahead. **Hours:** Tue–Sun 8:15–18:50, closed Mon.

▲▲▲**Bargello** Underappreciated sculpture museum (Michelangelo, Donatello, Medici treasures). **Hours:** Daily 8:15–13:50; closed first, third, and fifth Sun and second and fourth Mon of each month.

▲▲**Museum of San Marco** Best collection anywhere of fres-coes and paintings by the early Renaissance master Fra Angelico. **Hours:** Mon–Fri 8:15–13:50, Sat–Sun 8:15–19:00; closed first, third, and fifth Sun and second and fourth Mon of each month.

▲▲**Medici Chapels** Tombs of Florence's great ruling family, designed and carved by Michelangelo. **Hours:** Daily 8:15–16:50; closed the second and fourth Sun and the first, third, and fifth Mon of each month.

▲▲**Church of Santa Maria Novella** 13th-century Dominican church with Masaccio's famous 3-D painting. **Hours:** Mon–Thu and Sat 9:00–17:00, Fri and Sun 13:00–17:00.

▲▲**Santa Croce Church** 14th-century Franciscan church with precious art, tombs of famous Florentines, and Brunelleschi's Pazzi Chapel. **Hours:** Mon–Sat 9:30–17:30, Sun 13:00–17:30.

▲▲**Science Museum** Fascinating collection of old clocks, tele-scopes, maps, and Galileo's finger. **Hours:** June–Sept Mon and Wed–Fri 9:30–17:00, Tue and Sat 9:30–13:00, closed Sun; Oct–May Mon and Wed–Sat 9:30–17:00, Tue 9:30–13:00, generally closed Sun but open second Sun of month 10:00–13:00.

▲▲**Pitti Palace** Three museums in lavish palace: Palatine Gallery/Royal Apartments (Raphael art), Modern Art Gallery, Grand Ducal Treasures (Medici treasure chest), plus sprawl-ing Boboli and Bardini Gardens. **Hours:** Palatine Gallery and Modern Art Gallery: Tue–Sun 8:15–18:50, closed Mon. Grand Ducal Treasures, plus Boboli and Bardini Gardens: Daily 8:15–18:30, until 19:30 June–Aug, closed first and last Mon of the month.

▲▲**Brancacci Chapel** Works of Masaccio, early Renaissance master who reinvented perspective. **Hours:** Mon and Wed–Sat 10:00–17:00, Sun 13:00–17:00, closed Tue. Reservations required.

▲▲**Duomo (Santa Maria del Fiore)** Gothic cathedral with colorful facade, long nave, and the first dome built since ancient Roman times. **Hours:** Mon–Wed and Fri–Sat 10:00–17:00 except first Sat of month 10:00–15:30, Thu 10:00–15:30, Sun 13:30–16:45.

▲▲**Duomo Museum** Underrated cathedral museum with great sculpture. **Hours:** Mon–Sat 9:00–19:30, Sun 9:00–13:40.

▲**Climbing Duomo's Dome** Grand view into the cathedral, close-up of dome architecture, and after 463 steps, a glorious Florence vista. **Hours:** Mon–Fri 8:30–19:00, Sat 8:30–17:40 except first Sat of month 8:30–16:00, closed Sun. Long and slow lines, go early, no reservations accepted.

▲**Giotto's Tower** Bell tower with views equaling Duomo's, 50 fewer steps, and fewer lines. **Hours:** Daily 8:30–19:30.

▲**Baptistery** Bronze doors fit to be the gates of Paradise. **Hours:** Doors always viewable; Baptistery open Mon–Sat 12:00–19:00, Sun 8:30–14:00.

▲**Medici-Riccardi Palace** Lorenzo the Magnificent's home, with fine art, frescoed ceilings, and a lovely Chapel of the Magi. **Hours:** Thu–Tue 9:00–19:00, closed Wed.

▲**Palazzo Vecchio** Fortified palace once the home of the Medici family, wallpapered with mediocre art. **Hours:** Fri–Wed 9:00–19:00, Thu 9:00–14:00.

▲**Ponte Vecchio** Famous bridge lined with gold and silver shops. **Hours:** Bridge always open.

▲**Michelangelo's House** Museum featuring early, lesser-known works of the master. **Hours:** Wed–Mon 9:30–14:00, closed Tue.

▲**Piazzale Michelangelo** Hilltop square in south Florence offering stunning view of city and Duomo. **Hours:** Always open.

▲**San Miniato Church** Gem of a basilica, with sumptuous Renaissance chapel and sacristy showing scenes of St. Benedict. **Hours:** Daily 8:00–19:30.

Church of San Lorenzo—This redbrick, white-ribbed dome—which looks like the Duomo's little sister—is the Medici church and the burial place of the family's founder, Giovanni di Bicci de' Medici (1360–1429). The facade is big, ugly, and unfinished because Pope Leo X (also a Medici) pulled the plug on the project due to dwindling funds—after Michelangelo had labored on it for four years (1516–1520). Inside, though, is the spirit of Florence in the 1420s, with columns and arches in perfect Renaissance symmetry and simplicity. The Brunelleschi-designed church is lit by an even, diffused light. Images of St. Lawrence, the Medici patron saint who was martyred on a grill, are everywhere.

Highlights of the church include two finely sculpted Donatello pulpits (in the nave), the Martelli Chapel with Filippo Lippi's *Annunciation* (left transept), and the Old Sacristy (far left corner), designed by Brunelleschi as a burial chapel for the Medicis. Bronze doors that flank the sacristy's small altar are by Donatello. Overhead, the dome above the small altar alcove shows the exact arrangement of the heavens on the day the chapel was finished. Along the left side of the church is a cloister (good Duomo views) and Michelangelo's staircase to the Laurentian Library. Around the back end of the church is the entrance to the Medici Chapels (see below) and the New Sacristy designed by Michelangelo for a later generation of dead Medicis (€2.50, Mon–Sat 10:00–17:30, Sun 13:30–17:30, free information brochure).

▲▲**Medici Chapels (Cappelle Medicee)**—The burial site of the ruling Medici family in the Church of San Lorenzo includes the dusky Crypt; the big, domed Chapel of Princes; and the magnificent, all-Michelangelo New Sacristy featuring the master's architecture, tombs, and statues. The Medicis made their money in textiles and banking and patronized a dream team of Renaissance artists who put Florence on the cultural map. Michelangelo, who spent his teen years living with the Medicis, was commissioned for the family's final tribute (€6, daily 8:15–16:50 but closed the second and fourth Sun and the first, third, and fifth Mon of each month, tel. 055-238-8602).

✪ See Medici Chapels Tour on page 138.

▲**San Lorenzo Market and the nearby Central Market**—Florence's vast open-air market sprawls around the Church of San Lorenzo. Most of the leather stalls are run by Iranians selling South American leather that was tailored in Italy. Prices are soft (daily 9:00–19:00, closed Mon in winter, between the Duomo and train station).

The giant iron-and-glass Central Market, a block away, is a wonderland of picturesque produce and is fun to explore. While the San Lorenzo Market—with its garment stalls in the streets—feels like a step up from a haphazard flea market, the Central Market retains a Florentine elegance. There are plenty of fun eateries in the market, sloshing out cheap and tasty pasta to locals (Mon–Sat 7:00–14:00, closed Sun).

▲**Medici-Riccardi Palace (Palazzo Medici-Riccardi)**—Lorenzo the Magnificent's home is worth a look for its art. The tiny Chapel of the Magi contains colorful Renaissance gems like the *Procession of the Magi* frescoes by Benozzo Gozzoli. The former library has a Baroque ceiling fresco by Luca Giordano, a prolific artist from Naples known as Fast Luke *(Luca fa presto)* for his ambidextrous painting abilities. While the Medicis originally occupied this 1444 house, in the 1700s it became home to the Riccardi family, who added the Baroque flourishes. As only eight people are allowed into the Chapel of the Magi every seven minutes, it's smart to call for a reservation if you want to avoid a wait (€5, Thu–Tue 9:00–19:00, closed Wed, Via Cavour 3, kitty-corner from Church of San Lorenzo, one long block north of Baptistery, tel. 055-276-0340).

○ See Medici-Riccardi Palace Tour on page 147.

Duomo and Nearby

▲▲**Duomo (Santa Maria del Fiore)**—Florence's Gothic cathedral has the third-longest nave in Christendom. The church's noisy neo-Gothic facade from the 1870s is covered with pink, green, and white Tuscan marble. Since nearly all of its great art is stored in

the Duomo Museum (behind the church), the best thing about the interior is the shade. The inside of the dome is decorated by one of the largest paintings of the Renaissance, a huge *Last Judgment* by Giorgio Vasari and Federico Zuccari. Note: The massive crowds that overwhelm the entrance in the morning clear out by afternoon (free, Mon–Wed and Fri–Sat 10:00–17:00 except first Sat of month 10:00–15:30, Thu 10:00–15:30, Sun 13:30–16:45, modest dress code enforced, tel. 055-230-2885).

The cathedral's claim to artistic fame is Brunelleschi's magnificent dome—the first Renaissance dome and the model for domes to follow.

○ See page 63 of the Renaissance Walk.

▲**Climbing the Duomo's Dome**—For a grand view into the cathedral from the base of the dome, a peek at some of the tools used in the dome's construction, a chance to see Brunelleschi's "dome-within-a-dome" construction, a glorious Florence view from the top, and the equivalent of 463 plunges on a Stairmaster, climb the dome. To avoid the long, dreadfully slow-moving line, arrive by 8:30 or drop by very late (€6, Mon–Fri 8:30–19:00, Sat

8:30–17:40 except first Sat of month 8:30–16:00, closed Sun, enter from outside church on north side, tel. 055-230-2885).

▲**Giotto's Tower (Campanile)**—The 270-foot bell tower has 50 fewer steps than the Duomo's dome, offers a faster, less-crowded climb, and has a view of the Duomo to boot, but the cage-like top makes taking good photographs difficult (€6, daily 8:30–19:30, last entry 40 min before closing).

🅞 See page 65 of the Renaissance Walk.

▲**Baptistery**—Michelangelo said its bronze doors were fit to be the gates of Paradise. Check out the gleaming copies of Lorenzo Ghiberti's bronze doors facing the Duomo. Making a breakthrough in perspective, Ghiberti used mathematical laws to create the illusion of receding distance on a basically flat surface.

The doors on the north side of the building were designed by Ghiberti when he was young; he'd won the honor and opportunity by beating Brunelleschi in a competition (the rivals' original entries are in the Duomo Museum, see below).

Inside, sit and savor the medieval mosaic ceiling where it's always Judgment Day, and Jesus is giving the ultimate thumbs-up and thumbs-down (€3, interior open Mon–Sat 12:00–19:00, Sun 8:30–14:00; bronze doors are on the outside, so always "open"; original panels are in the Bargello Museum).

🅞 See page 99 of the Bargello Tour.

▲▲**Duomo Museum (Museo dell'Opera del Duomo)**—The underrated cathedral museum, behind the church at Via del Proconsolo 9, is great if you like sculpture. On the ground floor, look for a late Michelangelo *Pietà*, the eight restored panels of Ghiberti's north doors for the Baptistery, and statues from the original Baptistery facade. Upstairs, you'll find Brunelleschi's models for his dome, as well as Donatello's anorexic *Mary Magdalene* and playful choir loft. The museum features most of Ghiberti's original "Gates of Paradise" panels; the panels on the Baptistery's doors today are copies (€6, Mon–Sat 9:00–19:30, Sun 9:00–13:40, last entry 40 min before closing, one of the few museums in Florence open on Mon, tel. 055-230-2885).

🅞 See Duomo Museum Tour on page 122.

Between the Duomo and Piazza della Signoria

▲▲▲**Bargello (Museo Nazionale)**—This under-appreciated sculpture museum is in a former police station–turned–prison

Make Reservations to Avoid Lines

Florence has a reservation system for its top five sights—Uffizi, Accademia, Bargello, Medici Chapels, and Pitti Palace. I highly

recommend getting reservations for the Accademia (Michelangelo's *David*) and the Uffizi (Renaissance paintings). While you can generally get an entry time for the Accademia within a few days, the Uffizi is often booked up a month in advance. Your best strategy is to get reservations for both as soon as you know when you'll be in town. Hotels are accustomed to offering this service free (or for a small charge) when clients make a room reservation. Just request it with your hotel booking. After learning how easy this is and seeing hundreds of bored, sweaty tourists waiting in lines without the reservation, it's hard not to be amazed at their cluelessness.

If you want to make the booking(s) yourself, dial 055-294-883 (Mon–Fri 8:30–18:30, Sat 8:30–12:30, closed Sun). An English-speaking operator walks you through the process, and two minutes later you say *grazie,* with appointments (15-min entry window) and six-digit confirmation numbers for each of the top museums and galleries. Some booking agencies offer reservations online for a hefty fee (minimum €9.50/ticket, such as www.weekendafirenze.it).

Besides these main attractions, the only other places you should book in advance are the Brancacci Chapel (reservations are mandatory to see the Masaccio frescoes) and the Medici-Riccardi Palace (for quick entry into the sumptuous Chapel of the Magi, reservations are recommended). You do this direct (phone numbers are included in the sight listings in this chapter), and spots are generally available a day in advance.

Ticket phone numbers are often busy; be persistent. The best time to call is around 14:00–15:00 or just before closing.

that looks like a mini–Palazzo Vecchio. It has Donatello's painfully beautiful *David* (the very influential first male nude to be sculpted in a thousand years), works by Michelangelo, and rooms of Medici treasures cruelly explained in Italian only (politely suggest to the staff that English descriptions would be wonderful). Moody Donatello, who embraced realism with his lifelike statues, set the personal and artistic style for many Renaissance artists to follow. The best works are in the ground-floor room at the foot of the outdoor staircase and in the room directly above (€4, daily 8:15–13:50 but closed first, third, and fifth Sun and second and fourth Mon of each month, last entry 40 min before closing, Via del Proconsolo 4, tel. 055-238-8606).

✪ See Bargello Tour on page 95.

Dante's House (Casa di Dante)—Dante's house—actually a copy built near his house—reopened after a lengthy restoration, but is painfully lacking in artifacts, many of which were destroyed by a fire while in storage. The reopening releases Dante fans from the Purgatorio of waiting, but falls short of Paradiso. The house's only valuable offering—not worth the entrance fee—is the exhibit of information panels that introduce visitors to the history of Florence within the context of Dante's life (€4, Tue–Sat 10:00–17:00, open sporadic hours on Sun, closed Mon, near the Bargello at Via S. Margherita 1, tel. 055-219-416).

Orsanmichele Church—In the ninth century, this loggia (covered courtyard) was a market used for selling grain (stored upstairs). Later, it was closed in to make a church. Outside, check out the dynamic statue-filled niches, some with accompanying symbols from the guilds that sponsored the art. Donatello's *St. Mark* and *St. George* (on the northeast and northwest corners) step out boldly in the new Renaissance style. The interior has a glorious Gothic tabernacle (1359), housing the painted wooden panel depicting *Madonna delle Grazie* (1346). The iron bars spanning the vaults were the Italian Gothic answer to the French Gothic external buttresses. Look for the rectangular holes in the piers—these were once wheat chutes that connected to the upper floors (church is free, Tue–Sun 10:00–17:00, closed Mon, niche sculptures always viewable from the outside). You can give the *Madonna della Grazie* a special thanks if you're in town when an evening concert is held inside the Orsanmichele (tickets sold on day of concert from door facing Via dei Calzaiuoli).

✪ See page 67 of the Renaissance Walk.

The museum upstairs, currently closed, holds many of the church's precious originals. Someday, tourists might be able to enjoy the fine statues by Ghiberti, Donatello, and company.

A block away, you'll find the...

▲Mercato Nuovo (a.k.a. the Straw Market)—This market *loggia* is how Orsanmichele looked before it became a church. Originally a silk and straw market, Mercato Nuovo still functions as a rustic yet touristy market today (at the intersection of Via Calimala and Via Porta Rossa). Prices are soft, but the San Lorenzo Market is much better for haggling. Notice the circled X in the center, marking the spot where people hit after being hoisted up to the top and dropped as punishment for bankruptcy. You'll also find *Porcellino* (a statue of a wild boar nicknamed "little pig"), which people rub and give coins to in order to ensure their return to Florence. This new copy, while only a few years old, already has a polished snout. Nearby, a wagon sells tripe (cow innards) sandwiches—a local favorite (daily 9:30–19:00).

▲**Piazza della Repubblica and Nearby**—This large square sits on the site of Florence's original Roman Forum. The lone column—nicknamed the belly button of Florence—once marked the intersection of the two main Roman roads. All that survives of Roman Florence is its grid street plan and this column. Look at the map (by the benches—where the old boys hang out to talk sports and politics) to see the ghost of Rome in its streets. Roman Florence was a garrison town—a rectangular fort with this square marking the intersection of the two main roads (Via Corso and Via Roma).

Today's piazza, framed by a triumphal arch, is a nationalistic statement celebrating the unification of Italy. Florence, the capital of the country (1865–1870) until Rome was liberated, lacked a square worthy of this grand new country. So the neighborhood here was razed to open up an imposing, modern forum surrounded by stately circa-1890 buildings.

Between here and the river you'll find characteristic parts of the medieval city that give a sense of what this neighborhood felt like before it was bulldozed. Back in the Middle Ages, writers described Florence as so densely built up that when it rained, pedestrians didn't get wet. Torches were used to light the lanes in midday. The city was prickly with noble families' towers (like San Gimignano) and had Romeo and Juliet–type family feuds. But with the rise of city power (c. 1300), no noble family was allowed to have an architectural ego trip taller then the City Hall, and nearly all other towers were taken down.

The fancy La Rinascente department store, facing the Piazza della Repubblica, is one of the city's finest (WC on fourth floor, go up the stairs for the pricey bar with an impressive view terrace).

▲**Palazzo Davanzati**—The first few floors of this five-story, late medieval tower house are free to visit and grant a rare look at a noble dwelling built in the 14th century (though the historic furniture ranges from the 14th–18th centuries). In 1838, the last Davanzati heir plunged to his self-inflicted death here in the courtyard. On the first floor, look at the wooden trapdoors in the floor—they offered easy access to shoot arrows or dump boiling hot oil prepped by grandma onto enemies who ventured into the public space below. The chute near the stairwell was the well receptacle. The tiny room on the side? Yes, it's a centuries-old WC (daily 8:15–13:50, closed first, third, and fifth Mon and second and fourth Sun, no English explanation, Via Porta Rossa 13, tel. 055-238-8610).

On and near Piazza della Signoria

▲▲▲Uffizi Gallery—This greatest collection of Italian paintings anywhere features works by Giotto, Leonardo, Raphael, Caravaggio, Rubens, Titian, and Michelangelo, and a roomful of Botticellis, including his *Birth of Venus*. Start with Giotto's early stabs at Renaissance-style realism, then move on through the 3-D experimentation of the early 1400s to the real thing rendered by the likes of Botticelli and Leonardo. Finish off with the High Renaissance—Michelangelo, Rubens, and Titian. Because only 600 visitors are allowed inside the building at any one time, during the day there's generally a very long wait. The good news: no Louvre-style mob scenes. The museum is nowhere near as big as it is great. Few tourists spend more than two hours inside. The paintings are displayed on one comfortable, U-shaped floor in chronological order from the 13th through 17th centuries (left wing—the best: Florentine Middle Ages to Renaissance; connecting corridor: sculpture; right wing: High Renaissance to Baroque).

Cost, Hours, Reservations: €9.50, plus €3 for recommended reservation, Tue–Sun 8:15–18:50, closed Mon (last entry 45 min before closing; after entering, take elevator or climb 4 long flights of stairs). To avoid the long lines, it's smart to get reservations at least a month ahead.

○ For details on making reservations and for a self-guided tour, see Uffizi Gallery Tour on page 74.

In the Uffizi's Courtyard: Enjoy the courtyard (free), full of artists and souvenir stalls. The surrounding statues honor earthshaking Florentines: artists (Michelangelo), philosophers (Machiavelli), scientists (Galileo), writers (Dante), explorers (Amerigo Vespucci), and the great patron of so much Renaissance thinking, Lorenzo "the Magnificent" de' Medici. ○ For more, see page 71 of the Renaissance Walk.

▲Palazzo Vecchio—With its distinctive castle turret, this fortified palace—the Town Hall—is a Florentine landmark. But if you're visiting only one palace interior in town, the Pitti Palace is better. The Palazzo Vecchio interior is worthwhile only if you're a real fan of Florentine history or of the artist Giorgio Vasari, who wallpapered the place with mediocre magnificence.

Highlights include the 13,000-square-foot Grand Hall (Sala Grande), lined with huge Vasari paintings of Florence at war. The central ceiling painting shows Cosimo I de' Medici, the patron who financed Vasari's work. In the hall stands Michelangelo's statue of *Victory* (*La Vittoria*, 1533–1534), showing a young man triumphing over an older man. This was the prototype of the many spiral-shaped statues by other artists that also line the Grand Hall.

Go upstairs from the Grand Hall and circle through a dozen richly decorated rooms to the Room of the Lilies (Sala dei Gigli), with Duomo views and Donatello's bronze statue of *Judith and Holofernes*. The statue was commissioned by the Medicis, who saw themselves as the noble Judith slaying their (drunken, sleepy) enemies. When the Medicis were driven out, the Florentines took it from the Medici-Riccardi Palace and placed it at the Palazzo Vecchio doorway (where the fake *David* stands) as a symbol of their triumph over the corrupt Medicis. A decade later, it was replaced by Michelangelo's *David* as the symbol of Florence victorious.

The adjoining Chancery Room (Cancelleria) was once Machiavelli's office. In the nearby Map Chamber (Sala delle Carte Geografiche), Southern Californians can find their hometowns on maps (far right corner, upper level) charting the known world in the 16th century.

Cost, Hours, Information: €6, €8 combo-ticket with Brancacci Chapel, Fri–Wed 9:00–19:00, Thu 9:00–14:00, ticket office closes one hour earlier (tel. 055-276-8224).

Pass on the €4.10 audioguide unless you want to know the fine details of Florentine political leaders, but take advantage of the nifty computer screens scattered through out the museum. You control which mini-documentaries to view, such as an animation of the transporting of *David* to the Piazza della Signoria or guidance on viewing sculptural highlights within the *palazzo*.

Even if you don't go to the museum, do step into the **free courtyard** behind the fake *David* just to feel the essence of the Medicis (you'll have to go through metal detectors but you don't have to pay). Until 1873, Michelangelo's *David* stood at the entrance, where the copy is today.

○ See page 69 of the Renaissance Walk.

On the Square: While the huge statues in the square are important only as the whipping boys of art critics and as rest stops for pigeons, the nearby **Loggia dei Lanzi** has several important statues. Look for Cellini's bronze statue of Perseus holding the head of Medusa. The plaque on the pavement in front of the fountain marks the spot where the monk Savonarola was burned in MCDXCVIII, or 1498 (for more on Savonarola, see ○ Museum of San Marco Tour on page 105).

▲▲Science Museum (Istituto e Museo di Storia della Scienza)—When we think of the Florentine Renaissance, we think of visual arts: painting, mosaics, architecture, and sculpture. But when the visual arts declined in the 1600s (abused and co-opted by political powers), music and science flourished in Florence. The first opera was written here. And Florence hosted many breakthroughs in science, as you'll see in this fascinating collection of Renaissance and later clocks, telescopes, maps, and ingenious gadgets. Trace the technical innovations as modern science emerges from 1000 to 1900. One of the most talked-about bottles in Florence is the one here containing Galileo's finger. The first floor features various tools for gauging the world, from a compass and thermometer to Galileo's telescopes. The second floor delves into clocks, pumps, medicine, and chemistry. Loaner English guidebooklets are available. It's friendly, comfortably cool, never crowded, and just a block east of the Uffizi on the Arno River (€6.50, June–Sept Mon and Wed–Fri 9:30–17:00, Tue and Sat 9:30–13:00, closed Sun; Oct–May Mon and Wed–Sat 9:30–17:00, Tue 9:30–13:00, generally closed Sun but open second Sun of month 10:00–13:00; Piazza dei Giudici 1, tel. 055-265-311, www.imss.fi.it).

   ✪ See Science Museum Tour on page 169.

▲**Ponte Vecchio**—Florence's most famous bridge is lined with shops that have traditionally sold gold and silver. A statue of Cellini, the master goldsmith of the Renaissance, stands in the center, ignored by the flood of tacky tourism. ✪ See page 72 of Renaissance Walk.

   Notice the "prince's passageway" above the bridge. In less secure times, the city leaders had a fortified passageway connecting the Vecchio Palace and Uffizi with the mighty Pitti Palace, to which they could flee in times of attack. This passageway, called the **Vasari Corridor,** is technically open to the public, but a visit is almost impossible to arrange, and if you do manage it, usually a disappointment (open "seasonally," try the museum reservation line, tel. 055-264-321).

Santa Croce Church and Nearby

▲▲**Santa Croce Church**—This 14th-century Franciscan church, decorated with centuries of precious art, holds the tombs of great Florentines. The loud, 19th-century Victorian Gothic facade faces a huge square ringed with tempting shops and littered with tired tourists. Escape into the church and admire its sheer height and spaciousness.

   Enter and head towards the front of the church. On your right is the **tomb of Galileo Galilei** (1564–1642), the Pisan who lived his last years under house arrest near Florence. Having defied

Floods in Florence

Summer visitors to Florence gaze at the lazy green creek called the Arno River and have a tough time imagining it being a destructive giant. But rare, powerful flooding is a part of life in Florence. The Arno River washed away the Ponte Vecchio in 1177 and 1333. And on November 4, 1966, a hard rain turned the Arno into a wall of water, inundating the city with mud stacked as high as 20 feet. Nearly 14,000 families were left homeless, and a huge amount of art was destroyed or damaged.

Almost as impressive as the flood was the huge outpouring of support, as the art-loving world came to the city's rescue. While money poured in from far and wide, volunteers nicknamed "mud angels" mopped up things. After the flood, scientists made great gains in restoration techniques as they cleaned and repaired masterpieces from medieval and Renaissance times.

Today you'll see plaques around town showing the high-water marks (about 6 feet high at the Duomo). Now that a dam has tamed the Arno, kayakers glide peacefully on the river, sightseers enjoy the great art with no thought of a flood, and locals...still get nervous after every heavy rain.

---

the Church by saying that the Earth revolved around the sun, his heretical remains were only allowed in the church long after his death.

Directly opposite is the **tomb of Michelangelo Buonarroti** (1475–1564). Santa Croce was Michelangelo's childhood church, as he grew up a block east of here at Via dei Bentaccordi 15 (where nothing but a plaque marks the spot). The tomb, with the allegorical figures of painting, architecture, and sculpture, was designed by Michelangelo's great admirer, the artist/biographer Vasari. Vasari also did the series of paintings that line the left side of the nave, using the twisting poses and bulky muscles that Michelangelo pioneered.

You'll find several sights along the right side of the nave, including a memorial to the poet **Dante Alighieri** (1265–1321). There's no body inside—Dante was banished by his hometown because of his politics. Exiled Dante looks weary, the Muse of Poetry mourns, and Lady Florence gestures to say, "Look what we missed out on."

The **tomb of Niccolò Machiavelli** (1469–1527), which lies two tombs over in the direction of the apse, features Lady Justice presenting a medallion with his portrait on it. Macchiavelli, a champion of democratic Florence, opposed the Medicis as tyrants.

When they returned to power, he was arrested and tortured. He retired to his farm to write *The Prince*, a how-to manual on hardball politics.

Next, a carved gray and gold **relief by Donatello** of the Annunciation shows a kneeling angel gently breaking the news to an astonished Mary. Notable for its unprecedented realism, the wispy Mary (on the right) is considered one of the artistic breakthroughs that marked the beginning of the long-awaited Renaissance.

Two tombs up is **Gioachino Rossini** (1792–1868), composer of many operas and the *William Tell Overture* (a.k.a. the *Lone Ranger* theme). Rossini died in Paris but his body was later moved here to his homeland during a wave of Italian nationalism in the late 19th century. (If you'd like to extend your tour of tombs, a gallery below the church and accessible from the courtyard is chock-full of tombs and sepulchres of lesser-knowns.)

The first chapel to the right of the main altar features the famous fresco by Giotto of the *Death of Saint Francis*. With simple but eloquent gestures, Francis' brothers bid him a sad farewell, one of the first expressions of human emotion in modern painting.

At the end of the right transept, a door leads into the sacristy, where you'll find a rumpled bit of St. Francis' tunic *(Parte di Tunica)* and old sheets of music. In the bookshop, notice the photos of the devastating flood of 1966 high on the wall. Beyond that is the mildly interesting "leather school" that's really more of a touristy leather store. Exit between the Rossini and Machiavelli tombs into the cloisters.

Enter Brunelleschi's **Pazzi Chapel** (on the left), considered one of the finest pieces of Florentine Renaissance architecture. Notice

how the color scheme accentuates the architectural lines—no decoration needed. The circle-in-square design was inspired by the Pantheon in Rome and reflects the ancient Romans' belief in the unity and harmony of perfect shapes. While originally used as a monk's chapter house, it later became the Pazzi family's private chapel. Imagine how modern this chapel must have seemed when it was built in the mid-1400s.

Cost, Hours, Information: Church entry-€5, Mon–Sat 9:30–17:30, Sun 13:00–17:30. A modest dress code is enforced. The free museum is worthwhile only for historians. The €4 audioguide is slow-talking. Tel. 055-246-6105.

▲**Michelangelo's House (Casa Buonarroti)**—Fans enjoy a house standing on property once owned by Michelangelo. The house was built by the artist's grand-nephew, who turned it into a little museum honoring his famous relative. You'll see some of Michelangelo's early, less-than-monumental statues and a few sketches. Be warned: Michelangelo's descendants attributed everything they could to their famous relative, but very little here (beyond two marble relief panels and a couple of sketches) is actually by Michelangelo (€6.50, Wed–Mon 9:30–14:00, closed Tue, English descriptions, Via Ghibellina 70, tel. 055-241-752).

The highlights are on the first floor, in rooms that adjoin the first-floor landing. Climb the stairs to the landing, where you come face-to-face with portraits of 60-year-old Michelangelo (by his contemporaries), the Buonarroti family sword, and some leather shoes thought to be Michelangelo's. The room to the right displays small clay and wax models—some by Michelangelo, some by pupils—that the artist used to sketch out ideas for his statues.

The room to the left of the landing displays two relief panels, Michelangelo's earliest-known sculptures. Teenage Michelangelo carved every inch of the *Battle of the Centaurs* (1490–1492). This squirming tangle of battling nudes shows Michelangelo's fascination with anatomy. He kept this in his personal collection all his life. *The Madonna of the Stairs* (c. 1490) is as contemplative as the *Centaurs* is dramatic. Throughout his long career,  bipolar Michelangelo veered between these two styles—moving or still, emotional or thoughtful, pagan or Christian.

The small, darkened room adjoining the landing is for the museum's vast collection of Michelangelo's sketches. Unfortunately, only a handful of works are displayed at a time. Vasari claims that Michelangelo wanted to burn his preliminary sketches, lest anyone think him less than perfect.

And finally, true Michelangemaniacs can complete their visit by exiting outside to gaze at Via Ghibellina 67 (next door to a *farmacia*). This humble doorway, lined with gray-green stone, was once the entrance to Michelangelo's actual residence, circa 1520.

Leonardo Museum—This small, entrepreneurial venture is overpriced but fun for anyone who wants to crank the shaft and spin the ball bearings of Leonardo's genius inventions. While this exhibit has no actual historic artifacts, it shows about 30 of Leonardo's inventions made into models, each described in English. What makes this exhibit special is that you're encouraged to touch and play with the models—it's great for kids (€6, daily 10:00–19:00, Via dei Servi 66 red).

Near the Train Station

▲▲**Church of Santa Maria Novella**—This 13th-century Dominican church is rich in art. Along with crucifixes by Giotto and Brunelleschi, there's every textbook's example of the early Renaissance mastery of perspective: *The Holy Trinity* by Masaccio. The exquisite chapels trace art in Florence from medieval times to early Baroque. The outside of the church features a dash of Romanesque (horizontal stripes), Gothic (pointed arches), Renaissance (geometric shapes), and Baroque (scrolls). Step in and look down the 330-foot nave for a 14th-century optical illusion (€2.50, Mon–Thu and Sat 9:00–17:00, Fri and Sun 13:00–17:00).

✪ See Santa Maria Novella Tour on page 151.

Nearby: A palatial **perfumery** (Farmacia di Santa Maria Novella) is around the corner 100 yards down Via della Scala at #16 (free but shopping encouraged, Mon–Sat 9:30–19:30, Sun 10:30–18:30, tel. 055-216-276). Thick with the lingering aroma of centuries of spritzes, it started as the herb garden of the Santa Maria Novella monks. Well-known even today for its top-quality products, it is extremely Florentine. Pick up the history sheet at the desk, and wander deep into the shop. From the back room, you can peek at one of Santa Maria Novella's cloisters with its dreamy frescoes and imagine a time before Vespas and tourists.

South of the Arno River

▲▲**Pitti Palace**—The palace, several blocks southwest of the Ponte Vecchio, has three separate museums and two gardens. While reservations by phone are possible (tel. 055-294-883), they are not necessary. If there happens to be a long line at the palace, you can bypass it (and the line at the metal detector) for a fee: Head up to the front of the line to the quick reservations window (at the right-hand side of the facade), ask to enter immediately, and buy a ticket with the €3 reservation fee.

The **Palatine Gallery/Royal Apartments (Galleria Palatina)** is the biggie, featuring palatial room after chandeliered room, its walls sagging with masterpieces by 16th- and 17th-century masters including Rubens, Titian, and Rembrandt. Its Raphael collection is the second biggest anywhere—the Vatican beats them by one. Included in the ticket is the **Modern Art Gallery,** which features Romantic, Neoclassical, and Impressionist works by 19th- and 20th-century Tuscan painters (€8.50, Tue–Sun 8:15–18:50, closed Mon, tel. 055-238-8614).

The **Grand Ducal Treasures (Museo degli Argenti)** is the Medici treasure chest, with jeweled crucifixes, exotic porcelain,

Oltrarno, South of the Arno River

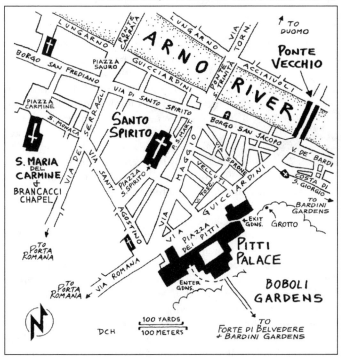

gilded ostrich eggs, and so on, made to entertain fans of applied arts (€8, includes the mildly interesting Costume Museum, Porcelain Museum, Boboli Gardens, and Bardini Gardens, daily 8:15–18:30, open 1 hour later June–Aug, closed first and last Mon of month).

Behind the palace, the huge, landscaped **Boboli Gardens** and **Bardini Gardens** offer a shady refuge from the city heat (both gardens covered by Grand Ducal Treasures ticket, see previous entry). The recently reopened Bardini Gardens offer a belvedere with lovely panoramic city views. You can enter the Bardini Gardens at two different places: 1) When you exit the Boboli Gardens, head uphill, going around Forte di Belvedere, and then left down Costa di San Giorgio to the Bardini entrance on your right at #4 (it's a 10–15 minute walk from the Pitti Palace). After visiting the garden, you can walk downhill and exit at what also serves as the lower entrance. 2) You can enter—or exit—the Bardini Gardens at Via de' Bardi 1 red, near Piazza de' Mozzi and the bridge called Ponte alle Grazie.

▲▲**Brancacci Chapel**—For the best look at Masaccio's works (he's the early Renaissance master who re-invented perspective),

see his restored frescoes here. Instead of medieval religious symbols, Masaccio's paintings feature simple, strong human figures with facial expressions that reflect their emotions. The accompanying works of Masolino and Filippino Lippi provide illuminating contrasts (€4, free reservations required—it's very easy…just call, €8 combo-ticket with Palazzo Vecchio, limit of 30 visitors every 15 minutes, Mon and Wed–Sat 10:00–17:00, Sun 13:00–17:00, closed Tue, ticket office closes at 16:30, cross Ponte Vecchio and turn right and hike to Piazza del Carmine, tel. 055-276-8224).

○ See Brancacci Chapel Tour on page 160.

The neighborhoods around the church are considered the last surviving bits of old Florence.

Santo Spirito Church—This church has a classic Brunelleschi interior and a painted, carved wooden crucifix attributed to Michelangelo. The sculptor donated this early work to the monastery in appreciation for allowing him to dissect and learn about bodies. Pop in for a delightful Renaissance space and a chance to marvel at a Michelangelo all alone (free, Thu–Sat and Mon–Tue 10:00–12:00 & 16:00–17:30, Wed 10:00–12:00, closed Sun to sightseers, Piazza Santo Spirito, tel. 055-210-030).

▲**Piazzale Michelangelo**—Overlooking the city from across the river (look for the huge statue of *David*), this square is worth the 30-minute hike, drive (free parking), or bus ride (either #12 or #13 from the train station) for the view of Florence and the stunning dome of the Duomo (see photo on page 22 of Orientation). Off the west side of the piazza is a somewhat hidden terrace, an excellent place to retreat from the mobs. After dark, the square is packed with local school kids licking ice cream and each other. About 200 yards beyond all the tour groups and teenagers is the stark, beautiful, crowd-free, Romanesque San Miniato Church.

▲**San Miniato Church**—This church was dedicated to a martyred saint who died on this hill. Imagine it all alone, without any nearby buildings or fancy stairs, a peaceful refuge for white-robed Benedictine monks to pray and work. (The church remains part of a functioning monastery today.) Its green-and-white marble facade is classic Florentine Romanesque, while the eagle on top—with bags of wool in his talons—symbolizes the wool guild that paid for the church. The little Renaissance chapel front and center was built in response to the splendid altar (left side of the nave) for Jacopo of Portugal. Jacopo died in Florence in about 1450, when he was 26. His very wealthy family mourned him by hiring the best artists of the day to decorate this sumptuous chapel (made by cutting a hole in the wall). It's a resume of the best of Renaissance humanism, with wonderfully 3-D paintings and a plush ceiling of glazed  terra-cotta panels by della Robbia. For me, though, the highlight is the brilliantly preserved art in the sacristy (behind altar in the room on right) showing scenes from the life of St. Benedict (c. 1350) by a follower of Giotto. Drop a euro into the box to light the room for five minutes. Stroll through the cemetery behind the church to marvel at the showy crypts and headstones of Florentine hotshots from the last two centuries (free, daily 8:00–19:30, 200 yards above Piazzale Michelangelo, bus #12 or #13 from train station, tel. 055-266-181).

Oltrarno Walk—If you never leave the touristy center, you won't really see Florence. There's more to the city than tourism. Most of its people live and work outside of the touristy zone. While tourism has crept into the Oltrarno neighborhood, south of the Arno River, you can still feel the rustic, old Florence in this area. To keep things easy, I've limited this self-guided tour to a perfectly straight line (you can't get lost). But be sure to venture down inviting side streets. Cross the Ponte Vecchio, turn right, and walk west on the busy, noisy road toward Pisa—it changes names, from Borgo San Jacopo and Via di Santo Spirito to Borgo San Frediano—until you reach the city wall at Porta San Frediano. Along this route, you can check out several recommended restaurants (see Eating, page 209). As you walk, consider these points:

After one block, at the fancy **Hotel Lungarno,** step up to the Arno River viewpoint for a great look at the Ponte Vecchio. Recall the story of Kesserling, the Nazi commander-in-chief of Italy who happened to be an art-lover. As the Nazis retreated in 1944, he was commanded to blow up all the bridges. Rather than destroy the venerable Ponte Vecchio, he disabled it by blowing up the surrounding neighborhood. Turn around and cross the street to see the ivy-covered nub of a medieval tower—ruined August 6, 1944.

Along this walk, you'll see plenty of artisans at work and lots of inviting little **shops.** You're welcome to drop in, but remember, it's polite to say *"Buon giorno"* and *"Ciao." "Can I take a look?"* is *"Posso guardare?"* (POH-soh gwahr-DAH-ray).

The streets are busy with *motorini* (Vespas and other motor bikes). While these are allowed in the city, nonresident cars are not (unless they are electric). Notice that parked cars have a *residente* permit on their dash. You might see a police officer (likely a woman) later on the walk, keeping out traffic.

Look for little architectural details. Tiny shrines protect the corners of many blocks. Once upon a time, the iron spikes on the walls impaled huge candles, which provided a little light. Electricity changed all that, but notice that there are no electric wires visible. They're under the streets.

This street is lined with apartment buildings punctuated by the occasional *palazzo*. The skyline and architecture are typical of the 13th to 16th centuries. Huge *palazzi* (recognized by their immense doors, lush courtyards, and grand stonework) were for big-shot merchants. Many have small wooden doors designed to look like stones (like those at #3b on Borgo San Frediano). While originally for one family, these buildings are now subdivided, as evidenced by the huge banks of doorbells at the door. Hooks high on the building facades are reminders of the 13th- and 14th-century textile trade, when newly dyed fabrics were hung out to dry.

The **Church of Santa Maria del Carmine,** with its famous Brancacci Chapel and Masaccio frescoes, is a short detour off Borgo San Frediano (see ✪ Brancacci Chapel Tour on page 160).

A couple of blocks up, before Porta San Frediano (and its tower), look left up towards Piazza dei Nerli. The bold, yellow schoolhouse was built during Mussolini's rule—grandly proclaiming the resurrection of the Italian empire.

Porta San Frediano, built about 1300, is part of Florence's medieval wall, which stretches impressively from here to the river. In medieval times, a three-quarter-mile-wide strip outside the wall was cleared to deny attackers any cover. The tower was originally twice as high, built when gravity ruled warfare. During the Renaissance, when gunpowder dominated warfare, the tower—now just an easy target—was lopped. Notice the original doors—immense and studded with fat iron nails to withstand battering rams. Got a horse? Lash it to a ring.

Tour over. You passed several fun eateries, and the colorful Trattoria Sabatino is just outside the wall (all described in Eating, page 196). *Ciao.*

Near Florence: Fiesole

Perched on a hill overlooking the Arno valley, Fiesole gives weary travelers a break in the action and, during the heat of summer, a breezy location from which to admire the city below. The ancient Etruscans knew a good spot when they saw one, and chose to settle here, establishing Fiesole about 400 years before the Romans founded Florence. Wealthy Renaissance families in pre-air-conditioning days also chose Fiesole as a preferred vacation spot and built villas in the surrounding hillsides. Later, 19th-century Romantics spent part of the Grand Tour admiring the vistas, much like the hordes of tourists do today. Most come here for the view—the actual sights pale in comparison to those in Florence.

Getting to Fiesole: From the Florence train station, take bus #7—enjoying a peek at gardens, vineyards, orchards, and villas—to the last stop, Piazza Mino (€1, 4/hr, fewer after 20:00, 20 min, departs Florence from the line of bus stops just out of the east exit of train station, and also from south side of Piazza San Marco). Taxis from Florence cost about €20 (take taxi to highest point you want to visit—La Reggia Ristorante for view terrace, or Church of San Francesco—then explore downhill). Drivers will have difficulty finding parking in Fiesole; if staying overnight, arrange a spot with your hotel. Rare, free street parking is scattered throughout the city, designated by a *P* sign (on Via della Mura Etrusche, for example). If you see a meter, you need to pay (€1/hr).

At the Florence bus station, you can buy a €7.20 Fiesole Pass, which includes round-trip bus fare and the €7 combo-ticket for the Roman Theater, Archaeological Park, Civic Museum, and Bandini Museum. Buy it from the bus ticket booth, immediately outside the station's east exit.

Tourist Information: To reach Fiesole's TI from the bus stop, face the cathedral, turn right and take the first left. The TI is immediately to the right of the Roman Archaeological Park. Pick up a free map (Mon–Sat 9:00–18:00, Sun 10:00–13:00 & 14:00–18:00, closes one hour earlier in winter, Via Portigiani 3, tel. 055-598-720). **Market day** is Saturday, when a modest selection of food and household items fills Piazza Mino (8:00–13:00).

SIGHTS

▲▲Terrace with a View—Catch the sunset (and your breath) from the view terrace just below La Reggia Ristorante. It's a steep hike from the Fiesole bus stop (face bell tower, take Via San Francesco on left).

Church of San Francesco—For even more hill-climbing, continue up from the view terrace to this charming little church. Several colorful altar paintings and an intimate scale make this church more enjoyable than Fiesole's Duomo (free, Mon–Sat 7:30–12:00 & 15:00–19:00, Sun 9:00–11:00 & 15:00–19:00, Via San Francesco 13).

The eclectic collection at the **Ethnographic Missionary Museum,** tiny and hidden beneath the church, includes an Egyptian mummy, ancient coins, Chinese buddhas, and the *in situ* ruins of a third-century Etruscan wall (donation suggested, irregular hours, unmarked door inside church leads to cloisters and museum).

Duomo—While this church has a drab, 19th-century exterior, the interior is worth a look, if only for the blue- and white-glazed Giovanni della Robbia statue of St. Romulus over the entry door (free, daily 7:30–12:00 & 15:00–18:00, across Piazza Mino from the bus stop).

Roman Theater and Archaeological Park—Occasionally used today for plays, this well-preserved theater held up to 2,000 people. The site's other ruins are, well, ruined, and lacking in explanation. But the valley view and peaceful setting are lovely (€7 combo-ticket includes the Civic and Bandini museums, daily 9:30–19:00, from the bus stop, cross Piazza Mino toward the back of the Duomo).

Civic Museum—Located within the Archaeological Park, the museum imparts insight into Fiesole's Etruscan and Roman roots with well-displayed artifacts, sans English descriptions (€7 combo-ticket, daily 9:30–19:00).

Bandini Museum—This petite museum displays the wooden panels of lesser-known Gothic and Renaissance painters as well as the glazed terra-cotta figures of Andrea della Robbia (€7 combo-ticket, daily 9:30–19:00, behind Duomo, Via Dupre 1).

SLEEPING

(€1 = about $1.20, country code: 39)
For the Sleep Code, see page 186.

$ Hotel Villa Bonelli has three stars, 20 dim, outdated rooms, an abandoned ambience, and an unbeatable price (Sb-€60, Db-€90, Tb-€120, air-con, 250 yards from bus stop up Via Gramsci, right on Via Poeti to #1, tel. 055-59-513, fax 055-598-942, www.hotelvillabonelli.com, info@hotelvillabonelli.com).

EATING

These two restaurants are on Piazza Mino, where the bus stops from Florence.

Ristorante Perseus, a local favorite, serves authentic Tuscan dishes at a fair price in a rambling interior. Specials are scrawled on a scrap of paper (daily 12:00–15:00 & 19:00–23:30, Piazza Mino 9, tel. 055-59-143, friendly Ago speaks English).

Ristorante Aurora is an upscale alternative with a view terrace overlooking the city of Florence (daily 12:00–14:30 & 19:00–22:30, next to bus stop on Piazza Mino, tel. 055-599-020).

Picnics: Fiesole is made to order for a scenic and breezy picnic. Grab a pastry at Fiesole's best *pasticceria,* **Alcedo** (Via Gramsci 29), then round out your goodies at the **Co-Op** supermarket on Via Gramsci before walking to the panoramic terrace. Or, for more convenience and less view, picnic at the shaded park on the way to the view terrace (walk up Via San Francesco about halfway to the terrace, and climb the stairs to the right).

RENAISSANCE WALK

From David *to the Arno River*

After centuries of labor, Florence gave birth to the Renaissance. We'll start with the Renaissance poster boy, Michelangelo's *David*. A short walk away are the Baptistery doors that opened the Renaissance, and the dome that captured its soaring spirit. Finally, we'll reach Florence's political center, dotted with monuments of that proud time. Great and rich as this city is, it's easily covered on foot. This walk through the top sights is less than a mile long, running from the Accademia (home of *David*), past the Duomo to the Arno River.

ORIENTATION

Accademia (Michelangelo's *David*): €6.50 (plus €3 fee for recommended reservation), Tue–Sun 8:15–18:50, closed Mon (last entry 45 min before closing, Via Ricasoli 60, tel. 055-238-8609). No photos or videos are allowed. The museum is most crowded on Sun, Tue, and right when it opens. It's smart to reserve ahead; see page 39 for details.

    Getting There: It's a 15-minute walk from the train station or a 10-minute walk from the Duomo (head northeast on Via Ricasoli). Taxis are reasonable.

Medici-Riccardi Palace: €5, Thu–Tue 9:00–19:00, closed Wed, Via Cavour 3. Reservations are recommended for the palace's Chapel of the Magi (call ahead, tel. 055-276-0340).

Duomo (Cathedral): Free, Mon–Wed and Fri–Sat 10:00–17:00 (except first Sat of month 10:00–15:30), Thu 10:00–15:30, Sun 13:30–16:45. Tel. 055-230-2885. Climbing the **dome** costs €6 (Mon–Fri 8:30–19:00, Sat 8:30–17:40 except first Sat of month 8:30–16:00, closed Sun; enter from outside church on north side, arrive by 8:30 or drop by very late to avoid a long wait in line).

Giotto's Tower: €6, daily 8:30–19:30, last entry 40 min before closing.

Baptistery: €3, Mon–Sat 12:00–19:00, Sun 8:30–14:00. The famous bronze doors are on the outside so they're always "open" (viewable) and free. The original panels are in the Duomo Museum.

Orsanmichele Church: Free, Tue–Sun 10:00–17:00, closed Mon. Niche sculptures are always viewable from the outside. The church hosts evening concerts; tickets are sold on the day of the concert from the door facing Via dei Calzaiuoli.

Information and Services: The nearest TI is on Via Cavour, two blocks from the Accademia (pick up update of current museum hours). WCs are in the Accademia basement and in cafés along the walk.

Length of This Tour: Allow three hours.

Photography: Photos are prohibited in the Accademia. In churches and other museums, photos without a flash are generally OK.

Cuisine Art: You'll find cafés, self-service cafeterias, bars, and gelato shops along the route. Many good eateries along this route are described in the Eating chapter.

Starring: Michelangelo, Brunelleschi, and Ghiberti.

THE TOUR BEGINS

The Duomo, the cathedral with the distinctive red dome, is the center of Florence and the orientation point for this walk. If you ever get lost, home's the dome.

We'll start at the Accademia (2.5 long blocks north of the Duomo), though you could easily start at the Duomo and visit the Accademia later.

• *Head to the Accademia. If you're shuffling slowly in line once you enter the building, notice the perspective tricks on the walls of the ticket room.*

The Florentine Renaissance (1400–1550)

In the 13th and 14th centuries, Florence was a powerful center of banking, trading, and textile manufacturing. The resulting wealth fertilized the cultural soil. Then came the Black Death in 1348. Nearly half of the population died, but the infrastructure remained strong, and the city rebuilt better than ever. Led by Florence's chief family, the art-crazy Medicis, and with the naturally aggressive and creative spirit of the Florentines, it's no wonder the long-awaited Renaissance finally took root here.

The Renaissance—the "rebirth" of Greek and Roman culture that swept across Europe—started around 1400 and lasted about 150 years. In politics, the Renaissance meant democracy; in science,

Renaissance Walk

200 YARDS
200 METERS

MUSEUM OF SAN MARCO

P. S. MARCO

START
ACCADEMIA

P. S. S. ANNUNZ.

V. GUELFA

CAVOUR

RICASOLI

MEDICI CHAPELS

SAN LORENZO

MEDICI-RICCARDI PALACE

FOUNDLING HOSP.

V. ALF.

TO TRAIN STN.

MKT.

B. S. LOR.

VIA

VIA

PUCCI

V. SERVI

PANZ.

CERRETANI

DUOMO

DUOMO MUSEUM

BAPT.

AGLI

TOWER

ORIUOLO

S. MARIA RICCI

STROZZI

CORSO

DANTE'S HOUSE

CALZAIUOLI

REP.

P. SPEZ.

SOLO

BARGELLO

MICHEL. HOUSE

ORSAN-MICHELE

TAV. DANTE

VIA

VERD

GHIB.

PORTA ROSSA

COND.

PROCO

V. G. VECCHIA

V. PAL. DAVAN.

TERME

MARIA

COV. MKT.

V. ANG.

B. S. APOST.

BORGO GRECI

P. S. CROCE

L. ACCIAIUOLI

EXIT

PALAZZO VECCHIO

BENCI

SCIENCE MUSEUM

V. D. NERI

SANTA CROCE

S. JAC.

LUNG. DIAZ

TINTORI

GUICC.

UFFIZI GALLERY

ARNO

PONTE VECCHIO
FINISH

OLTRARNO

DCH

★ PIAZZA DELLA SIGNORIA

a renewed interest in exploring nature. The general mood was optimistic and "humanistic," with a confidence in the power of the individual.

In medieval times, poverty and ignorance had made life "nasty, brutish, and short" (for lack of a better cliché). The church was the people's opiate, and their lives were only a preparation for a happier time in heaven after leaving this miserable vale of tears.

Medieval art was the church's servant. The noblest art form was architecture—churches themselves—and other arts were considered most worthwhile if they embellished the house of God. Painting and sculpture were narrative and symbolic, to tell Bible stories to the devout and illiterate masses.

As prosperity rose in Florence, so did people's confidence in life and themselves. Middle-class craftsmen, merchants, and bankers felt they could control their own destinies, rather than being at the whim of nature. They found much in common with the ancient Greeks and Romans, who valued logic and reason above superstition and blind faith.

Renaissance art was a return to the realism and balance of Greek and Roman sculpture and architecture. Domes and round arches replaced Gothic spires and pointed arches. In painting and sculpture, Renaissance artists strove for realism. Merging art and science, they used mathematics, the laws of perspective, and direct observation of nature to paint the world on a flat surface.

This was not an anti-Christian movement, though it was a logical and scientific age. Artists saw themselves as an extension of God's creative powers. At times, the church even supported the Renaissance and commissioned many of its greatest works. Raphael frescoed Plato and Aristotle on the walls of the Vatican. But for the first time in Europe since Roman times, we also find rich laymen who wanted art simply for art's sake.

After 1,000 years of waiting, the smoldering fires of Europe's classical heritage burst into flame in Florence.

The Accademia—Michelangelo's *David*

Start with the ultimate. When you look into the eyes of Michelangelo's *David,* you're looking into the eyes of Renaissance Man. This 14-foot-tall symbol of divine victory over evil represents a new century and a whole new Renaissance outlook. This is the age of Columbus and classicism, Galileo and Gutenberg, Luther and Leonardo—of Florence and the Renaissance.

In 1501, Michelangelo Buonarotti, a 26-year-old Florentine, was commissioned to carve a large-scale work for the Duomo. He was given a block of marble that other sculptors had rejected as too tall, shallow, and flawed to be of any value. But Michelangelo picked up his hammer and chisel, knocked a knot off what became

David's heart, and started to work.

The figure comes from a Bible story. The Israelites, God's chosen people, are surrounded by barbarian warriors led by a brutish giant named Goliath. The giant challenges the Israelites to send out someone to fight him. Everyone is afraid except one young shepherd boy—David. Armed only with a sling, which he's thrown over his shoulder, David cradles a stone in the pouch of the sling and faces Goliath.

The statue captures David as he's sizing up his enemy. He stands relaxed but alert, leaning on one leg in a classical pose. In his powerful right hand, he fondles the stone he'll fling at the giant. His gaze is steady—searching with intense concentration, but also with extreme confidence. Michelangelo has caught the precise moment when David is saying to himself, "I can take this guy."

Note that while the label on *David* indicates that he's already slain the giant, the current director of the Accademia believes, as I do, that Michelangelo has portrayed David facing the giant.

David is a symbol of Renaissance optimism. He's no brute but a civilized, thinking individual who can grapple with and overcome problems. He needs no armor, only his God-given body and wits. Look at his right hand, with the raised veins and strong, relaxed fingers. Many complained that it was too big and overdeveloped. But this is the hand of a man with the strength of God. No mere boy could slay the giant. But David, powered by God, could...and did.

Originally, the statue was commissioned to go on top of the Duomo, but the people loved it so much they put it next to the Palazzo Vecchio on the main square, where a copy stands today. (If the relationship between the head and body seems a bit out of proportion, it's because Michelangelo designed it to be seen "correctly" from far below the rooftop of the church.) Note the crack in *David*'s left arm where it was broken off during a riot near the Palazzo Vecchio.

Florentines could identify with David. Like him, they considered themselves God-blessed underdogs fighting their city-state rivals. In a deeper sense, they were civilized Renaissance people slaying the ugly giant of medieval superstition, pessimism, and oppression.

• *Hang around awhile. Eavesdrop on tour guides.* David *stands under a wonderful Renaissance-style dome. Lining the hall leading up to* David *are other statues by Michelangelo—his* Prisoners (Prigioni), St. Matthew, *and a* Pietà.

More Michelangelo

If you're a fan of Earth's greatest sculptor, you won't leave Florence until there's a check next to each of these:

- **Bargello Museum:** Several Michelangelo sculptures (see tour on page 95).
- **Duomo Museum:** Another moving *Pietà* (see tour on page 122).

- **Medici Chapels:** The *Night* and *Day* statues, plus others done for the Medici tomb, located at Church of San Lorenzo (see tour on page 138).
- **Laurentian Library:** Michelangelo designed the entrance staircase, located at Church of San Lorenzo.
- **Palazzo Vecchio:** His *Victory* statue.
- **Uffizi:** A rare Michelangelo painting (see tour on page 74).
- **Michelangelo's House:** Built on property the artist once owned, at Via Ghibellina 70, containing some early works.
- **Church of Santa Croce:** Michelangelo's tomb.
- **Santa Spirito Church:** Wooden crucifix.

Prisoners

These unfinished figures seem to be fighting to free themselves from the stone. Michelangelo believed the sculptor was a tool of God, not creating but simply revealing the powerful and beautiful

figures he put in the marble. Michelangelo's job was to chip away the excess, to reveal. He needed to be in tune with God's will, and whenever the spirit came upon him, Michelangelo worked in a frenzy, often for days on end without sleep.

The *Prisoners* gives us a glimpse of this fitful process, showing the restless energy of someone possessed, struggling against the rock that binds him. Michelangelo himself fought to create the image he saw in his mind's eye. You can still see the grooves from the chisel, and you can picture Michelangelo hacking away in a cloud of dust. Unlike most sculptors, who built a model and then marked up their block of marble to know where to chip, Michelangelo always worked freehand, starting from the front and working back. These figures emerge from the stone (as his colleague Vasari put it) "as though surfacing from a pool of water."

The *Prisoners* was designed for the never-completed tomb of Pope Julius II (who also commissioned the Sistine Chapel ceiling). Michelangelo may have abandoned them simply because the project itself petered out, but he may have deliberately left them unfinished. Having satisfied himself that he'd accomplished what he set out to do, and seeing no point in polishing them into their shiny, finished state, he went on to a new project.

As you study the *Prisoners,* notice Michelangelo's love and understanding of the human body. His greatest days were spent sketching the muscular, tanned, and sweating bodies of the workers in the Carrara marble quarries. Here, the prisoners' heads and faces are the least-developed part—they "speak" with their poses. Comparing the restless, claustrophobic *Prisoners* with the serene and confident *David* gives an idea of the sheer emotional range in Michelangelo's work.

Pietà (by Michelangelo or, more likely, by his followers)

In the unfinished *Pietà* (the threesome closest to *David*), they struggle to hold up the sagging body of Christ. Michelangelo emphasizes the heaviness of Jesus' dead body, driving home the point that this divine being suffered a very human death. Christ's massive arm is almost the size of his bent and broken legs. By stretching his body—if he stood up he'd be over seven feet tall—its weight is exaggerated.

• *Leaving the Accademia (possibly after a look at its paintings, including two Botticellis), turn left and walk toward the Duomo down Via Ricasoli. About halfway to the big church, turn right on Via dei Pucci. Directly ahead is the bustling San Lorenzo street market. Just before that (on the first corner) is the imposing Medici-Riccardi Palace.*

Medici-Riccardi Palace

Renaissance Florence was ruled by the rich banking family, the Medicis, who lived here. Studying this grand Florentine palace, you'll notice fortified lower walls and elegance limited to the upper fancy stories. The Medici family may have been the local Rockefellers but, having self-made wealth rather than actual noble blood, they were always a bit defensive. The Greek motifs along the eaves highlight the palace's Renaissance roots. Back then, rather than having parking spots, grand buildings came with iron rings to which you'd tether your horse.

The interior shows off a quintessential Florentine *palazzo* with a courtyard and a couple of impressive rooms, most notably the sumptuous little Chapel of the Magi (€5 palace entry, Thu–Tue 9:00–19:00, closed Wed). ✪ See Medici-Riccardi Palace Tour on page 147.

• *From the palace, head for the Duomo—down Via Martelli, with a possible detour to explore the San Lorenzo street market and, perhaps, the Church of San Lorenzo (page 36) and neighboring Medici Chapels (✪ See Medici Chapels Tour, page 138). The dome of the Duomo is best viewed just to the right of the facade on the corner of the pedestrian-only street.*

The Duomo—Florence's Cathedral

The dome of Florence's cathedral—visible from all over the city—inspired Florentines to do great things. The big but unremarkable

church itself (called the Duomo) is Gothic, built in the Middle Ages by architects who left it unfinished.

Think of the confidence of the age: The Duomo was built with a big hole in its roof awaiting a dome. This was before the technology to span it with a dome

was available. *No problema.* They knew that someone soon could handle the challenge. In the 1400s, the architect Brunelleschi was called on to finish the job. Brunelleschi capped the church Roman-style—with a tall, self-supporting dome as grand as the ancient Pantheon, which he had studied.

He used a dome within a dome. First, he built the grand white skeletal ribs, which you can see, then filled them in with interlocking bricks in a herringbone pattern. The dome grew upward like an igloo, supporting itself as it proceeded from the base. When they reached the top, Brunelleschi arched the ribs in and fixed them in place with the lantern. His dome, built in only 14 years, was the largest since Rome's Pantheon.

Brunelleschi's dome was the wonder of the age, the model for many domes to follow, from St. Peter's to the US Capitol. People gave it the ultimate compliment, saying, "Not even the ancients could have done it." Michelangelo, setting out to construct the dome of St. Peter's, drew inspiration from the dome of Florence. He said, "I'll make its sister...bigger, but not more beautiful."

The church's facade looks old, but is actually neo-Gothic—only from 1870. The facade was rushed to completion (about 600 years after the building began) to celebrate Italian unity, here in the city that for a few years served as the young country's capital. Its "retro" look captures the feel of the original medieval

The Duomo and Nearby

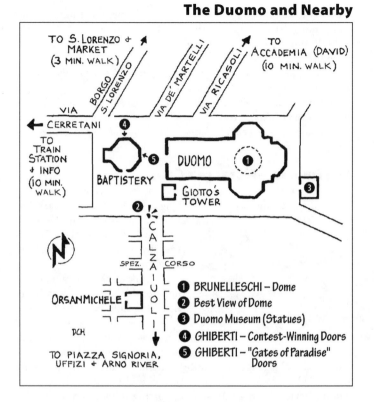

TO S. LORENZO & MARKET (3 MIN. WALK)

TO ACCADEMIA (DAVID) (10 MIN. WALK)

BORGO S. LORENZO

VIA DE' MARTELLI

VIA RICASOLI

VIA CERRETANI

TO TRAIN STATION + INFO (10 MIN. WALK)

4

5

BAPTISTERY

DUOMO **1**

3

GIOTTO'S TOWER

2

CALZAIUOLI

N

SPEZ. CORSO

ORSANMICHELE

DCH

TO PIAZZA SIGNORIA, UFFIZI + ARNO RIVER

1 BRUNELLESCHI – Dome
2 Best View of Dome
3 Duomo Museum (Statues)
4 GHIBERTI – Contest-Winning Doors
5 GHIBERTI – "Gates of Paradise" Doors

facade—green, white, and pink marble sheets that cover the brick construction; Gothic (pointed) arches; and three horizontal stories decorated with mosaics and statues. Still, the facade is generally ridiculed. (While one of this book's authors thinks it's the most beautiful church facade this side of heaven, the other one naively agrees with those who call it "the cathedral in pajamas.")

Still feeling bare after being cleaned out during the Neoclassical age and by the terrible flood of 1966, the inside is a bit disappointing (free, but not worth a long wait). Walk to the base of the dome. Notice how the crossing expands to include half the transepts, making the hole they needed to cover even larger. The dome is decorated by a vast Vasari fresco from the late 1570s. Look back to notice the structural elements in gray and the cream-colored filling. Step into the crypt to see the floor of the previous church and tomb of Brunelleschi (€3, but it's free to peek at the tomb from the bookshop down the stairs).

Giotto's Tower (Campanile)

The bell tower (to the right of the facade) offers an easier, less crowded, and faster climb than the Duomo's dome, though the

unobstructed views from the Duomo are better. Giotto, like any good Renaissance genius, wore several artistic hats. Considered the father of modern painting, he designed this 270-foot-tall bell tower for the Duomo two centuries before the age of Michelangelo. In his day, Giotto was called the ugliest man to ever walk the streets of Florence, but he left the city what, in our day, many call the most beautiful bell tower in all of Europe.

The bell tower served as a sculpture gallery for Renaissance artists—notice Donatello's four prophets on the side that faces out (west). These are copies, but the originals are at the wonderful Duomo Museum, just behind the church (❍ see Duomo Museum Tour on page 122). In the museum you'll also get a close-up look at Brunelleschi's wooden model of his dome, Ghiberti's doors (described next), and a late *Pietà* by Michelangelo.

• *The Baptistery is the small octagonal building in front of the church.*

Baptistery and Ghiberti's Bronze Doors

Florence's Baptistery is dear to the soul of the city. In medieval and Renaissance times, the locals—eager to link themselves to the classical past—believed (wrongly) that this was a Roman building. It is, however, Florence's oldest building (11th century). Most festivals and parades either started or ended here. Go inside (for a modest €3 fee) for a fine example of pre-Renaissance mosaic art (1200s–1300s) in the Byzantine style. Workers from St. Mark's in Venice came here to make the remarkable ceiling mosaics (of Venetian glass) in the late 1200s.

The Last Judgment on the ceiling gives us a glimpse of the medieval worldview. Life was a preparation for the afterlife, when you

would be judged good or bad, black or white, with no in-between. Christ, peaceful and reassuring, would bless you with heaven (on his right hand, thumbs up) or send you to hell (below Christ's ultimate thumbs down) to be tortured by demons and gnashed between the teeth of monsters. This hellish scene looks like something right out of the *Inferno* by Dante...who was dipped into the baptismal waters right here.

The Baptistery's bronze doors bring us out of the Middle Ages and into the Renaissance. Florence had great civic spirit, with different guilds and merchant groups embellishing their city with great art. The city staged a competition in 1401 for the commission of the Baptistery's north doors (on the right side as you face the Baptistery with the Duomo at your back). All the greats entered, and 25-year-old Lorenzo Ghiberti won easily, beating out heavyweights such as Brunelleschi (who, having lost the Baptistery gig, was free to go to Rome, study the Pantheon, and later design the Duomo's dome). The original entries of Brunelleschi and Ghiberti are in the Bargello, where you can judge them for yourself.

Later, in 1425, Ghiberti was given another commission, for the east doors (facing the church), and this time there was literally no contest. The bronze panels of these doors (the ones with the

crowd of tourists looking on) added a whole new dimension to art—depth. Michelangelo said these doors were fit to be the gates of paradise. (These panels are copies. The originals are in the nearby Duomo Museum. ✪ For more detailed descriptions of the panels, see page 126 of the Duomo Museum Tour.) Here we see how the Renaissance was a merging of art and science. Realism was in, and Renaissance artists used math, illusion, and dissection to get it.

In the "Jacob and Esau" panel (just above eye level on the left), receding arches, floor tiles, and banisters create a background for a realistic scene. The figures in the foreground stand and move like real people, telling the Bible story with human details. Amazingly, this spacious, three-dimensional scene is made from bronze only a few inches deep.

Ghiberti spent 27 years (1425–1452) working on these panels. That's him in the center of the door frame, atop the second row of panels—the head on the left with the shiny male pattern baldness.

• *Facing the Duomo, turn right onto the pedestrian-only street that runs south from here toward the Arno River.*

Via dei Calzaiuoli

The pedestrian-only Via dei Calzaiuoli (kahlts-ay-WOH-lee) was part of the ancient Roman grid plan that became Florence. Throughout the city's history, this street has connected the religious center (where we are now) with the political center (where we're heading), a five-minute walk away. In the last decade, traffic jams have been replaced by potted plants, and this is a pleasant place to stroll, people-watch, window-shop, catch the drips on your gelato cone, and wonder why American cities can't become pedestrian-friendly.

And speaking of gelato. . .Grom, which keeps its *gelati* in covered metal bins, the old-fashioned way, is just a one-block detour away (daily 11:00–23:00, take your first left to Via delle Oche 24a; see tips on page 212). Or you could drop by any of the several nearby *gelati* parlors. *Perchè no?* (Why not?)

On Via dei Calzaiuoli, two blocks down from the Baptistery, look right on Via degli Speziali to see a triumphal arch celebrating the unification of Italy. In ancient Roman times, the Piazza della Repubblica, where the arch stands, was the city center.

Orsanmichele Church—
Florence's Medieval Roots

The Orsanmichele Church (on the right at the intersection with Via Orsanmichele) provides an interesting look at Florentine values. It's a combo church/granary. Originally

this was an open loggia (covered porch) with a huge warehouse upstairs to store grain to feed the city during sieges. The arches of the loggia were artfully filled in (14th century) and the building gained a new purpose—as a church.

Circle the church. Each niche was filled with an important statue. In earlier Gothic times, statues were set deeply in the niches, simply embellishing the house of God. Here we see statues (as restless as man on the verge of the Renaissance) stepping out from the protection of the church.

Donatello's *St. George* (at the northwest corner of church) is alert, perched on the edge of his niche, scanning the horizon for dragons, and announcing the new age with its new outlook. (The original statue is in the Bargello.) Compare this Renaissance-style *St. George* with Nanni's smaller-scale, deeply set, and less sophisticated *Four Saints* statue to its left (pictured on page 68).

Below some of the niches, you'll find the symbols of the various guilds and groups that paid for the art. The relief below

Orsanmichele Church

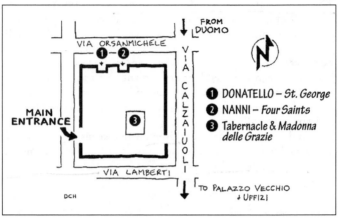

FROM DUOMO

VIA ORSANMICHELE

❶ ❷

VIA CALZAIUOLI

MAIN ENTRANCE

❸

❶ DONATELLO – *St. George*
❷ NANNI – *Four Saints*
❸ Tabernacle & *Madonna delle Grazie*

VIA LAMBERTI

TO PALAZZO VECCHIO & UFFIZI

DCH

the *Four Saints* is a good example. Art historians differ here. It was commissioned either by the carpenters' and masons' guild or by the guys who do discount circumcisions.

The entrance to the church is on the opposite side of Via dei Calzaiuoli. Inside, look for the pillars with rectangular holes in them (three feet off the ground), used for delivering grain from the storage rooms upstairs. Look up to see the rings hanging from the ceiling, which were likely used to make pulleys for lifting grain, and the iron bars spanning the vaults for support.

Notice the Gothic tabernacle's medieval elegance. What it lacks in depth and realism, it makes up for in color, with an intricate assemblage of marble, glass, gold, and expensive lapis lazuli. It was built to display Orcagna's *Madonna delle Grazie*, which received plague survivors' grateful prayers. Normally a tabernacle would be placed in the center of a church's apse, but in this case the shrine was in the granary, and it's never been moved since its glory days.

This is a wonderful scene—Florence in 1350. Remember the candlelit medieval atmosphere that surrounds this altarpiece as you view similar altarpieces out of context in the Uffizi Gallery. Consider returning for one of the church's evening concerts.

• *Florence's best collection of sculpture, the Bargello (see page 95), is a few blocks east down Via dei Tavolini. But let's continue down the mall 50 more yards, to the huge and historic square.*

Palazzo Vecchio—Florence's Political Center

The main civic center of Florence is dominated by the Palazzo Vecchio, the Uffizi Gallery, and the marble greatness of old Florence littering the cobbles. This square still vibrates with the echoes of Florence's past—executions, riots, and great celebrations. There's even Roman history—look for the chart showing the ancient city (on a waist-high, freestanding display to your right as you enter the square). Today, it's a tourist's world with pigeons, postcards, horse buggies, and tired hubbies. And, if it would make your tired hubby happy, the ritzy Café Rivoire—with the best view seats in town—is famous for

its fine desserts and pudding-thick hot chocolate (closed Sun).

Before you towers the Palazzo Vecchio, the Medicis' palatial City Hall—a fortress designed to contain riches and survive the many riots that went with local politics. The windows are just beyond the reach of angry stones, the tower was a handy lookout post, and justice was doled out sternly on this square. Michelangelo's *David* once stood (until 1873) where the replica stands today. The original *David*, damaged in a 1527 riot (when a bench thrown out of a palace window knocked its left arm off), was moved indoors for its own protection.

While the palace interior is not worth touring on a short visit, be sure to step past the replica *David* through the front door into the Palazzo Vecchio's courtyard (free). This palace was Florence's

civic center. You're surrounded by art for art's sake—a statue frivolously marking the courtyard's center, and ornate walls and columns. Such luxury was a big change 500 years ago. The squiggly wall painting is called *grotteschi*, inspired by the art that decorated the walls of ancient Roman villas being excavated at the time (c. 1500, named for "grotto" because the ancient villas were actually well below 15th-century Roman street level).

• *Back outside, check out the statue-filled Loggia.*

The Loggia, once a forum for public debate, was perfect for a city that prided itself on its democratic traditions. But later, when the Medicis figured that good art was more desirable than free speech, it was turned into an outdoor sculpture gallery. Notice the

squirming Florentine themes—conquest, dominance, rapes, and severed heads. The statues lining the back are Roman originals brought back to Florence by a Medici when he moved home after living in Rome. Two statues in the front deserve a closer look.

Benvenuto Cellini's *Perseus,* the Loggia's most noteworthy piece, shows the Greek hero who decapitated the snake-headed Medusa. They say Medusa was so ugly she turned humans who looked at her to stone—though one of this book's authors thinks she's kinda cute.

The Rape of the Sabines, with its pulse-quickening rhythm of muscles, is Mannerist, from the restless period following the stately and confident Renaissance (c. 1560). The sculptor, Giambologna, proved his mastery of the medium by sculpting three entangled bodies from one piece of marble. The composition is best viewed from below and in front. The relief panel below shows a wider view of the terrible scene.

Note what looks like an IV tube on the arm of the horrified husband. It's an electrified wire that effectively keeps the pigeons away.

• *Cross the square to the big fountain of Neptune by Ammanati that Florentines (including Michelangelo) consider a huge waste of marble—though one of this book's authors.... Find the round bronze plaque on the ground 10 steps in front of the fountain.*

Savonarola

The Medici family was briefly thrown from power by an austere monk named Savonarola, who made Florence a constitutional republic. He organized huge rallies lit by roaring bonfires here on the square where he preached. While children sang hymns, the devout brought their rich "vanities" (such as paintings, musical instruments, and playing cards) and threw them into the flames.

But not everyone wanted a return to the medieval past. Encouraged by the pope, the Florentines fought back and arrested Savonarola. For two days, they tortured him, trying unsuccessfully to persuade him to see their side of things. Finally, on the very

Palazzo Vecchio and Nearby

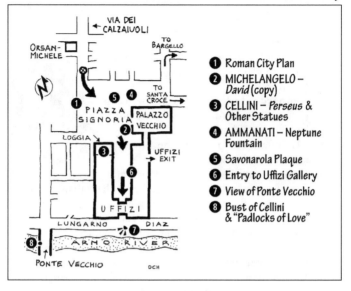

VIA DEI CALZAIUOLI

ORSAN-MICHELE

TO BARGELLO

TO SANTA CROCE

PIAZZA SIGNORIA

PALAZZO VECCHIO

LOGGIA

UFFIZI EXIT

UFFIZI

LUNGARNO   DIAZ

ARNO RIVER

PONTE VECCHIO

DCH

1 Roman City Plan

2 MICHELANGELO – David (copy)

3 CELLINI – *Perseus* & Other Statues

4 AMMANATI – Neptune Fountain

5 Savonarola Plaque

6 Entry to Uffizi Gallery

7 View of Ponte Vecchio

8 Bust of Cellini & "Padlocks of Love"

spot where Savonarola's followers had built bonfires of vanities, the monk was burned. The bronze plaque, engraved in Italian *("Qui dove…"),* reads: "Here, Girolamo Savonarola and his Dominican brothers were hanged and burned" in the year "MCCCCXCVIII" (1498). For help in deciphering Roman numerals, see page 377 in the appendix.

• *Stay cool, we have 100 yards to go. Follow the gaze of the fake David into the courtyard of the two-toned horseshoe-shaped building…*

Uffizi Courtyard—The Renaissance Hall of Fame

The top floor of this building, known as the *uffizi* ("offices") during Medici days, is filled with the greatest collection of Florentine painting anywhere. It's one of Europe's top four or five art galleries (see next chapter).

The Uffizi courtyard, filled with merchants and hustling young artists, is watched over by 19th-century statues of the great figures of the Renaissance. Tourists zero in on the visual accomplishments of the era—not realizing that it was many-faceted. Let's pay tribute to the nonvisual Renaissance as well, as we wander through Florence's Hall of Fame.

• *Stroll down the left side of the courtyard from Palazzo Vecchio to the river, noticing…*

1. **Lorenzo the Magnificent** was a great art patron and cunning power broker. Excelling in everything except modesty, he set the tone for the Renaissance.

2. **Giotto,** an architect (he holds the plan to the city's great bell tower—named for him), was the first great modern painter.
3. **Donatello,** the sculptor who served as a role model for Michelangelo, holds a hammer and chisel.
4. **Leonardo da Vinci** was a scientist, sculptor, musician, engineer...and not a bad painter either.
5. **Michelangelo** ponders the universe and/or stifles a belch.

6. **Dante,** with the laurel-leaf crown and lyre of a poet, says, "I am the father of the Italian language." He was the first Italian to write a popular work *(The Divine Comedy)* in non-Latin, using the Florentine dialect, which soon became "Italian" throughout the country.
7. The poet **Petrarch** wears laurel leaves from Greece, a robe from Rome, and a belt from Wal-Mart.
8. **Boccaccio** wrote *The Decameron,* stories told to pass the time during the 1348 Black Death.
9. The devious-looking **Machiavelli** is hatching a plot—his book *The Prince* taught that the end justifies the means, paving the way for the slick and cunning "Machiavellian" politics of today.
10. **Vespucci** (in the corner) was an explorer who gave his name to a fledgling New World.
11. **Galileo** (in the other corner) holds the humble telescope he used to spot the moons of Jupiter.

• *Finish your walk at the Arno River, overlooking the Ponte Vecchio.*

Ponte Vecchio

Before you is the Ponte Vecchio (Old Bridge). A bridge has spanned

this narrowest part of the Arno since Roman times. While Rome "fell," Florence really didn't, remaining a bustling trade center along the river. To get into the exclusive little park below, you'll need to join the Florence rowing club.

• *Finish by hiking to the center of the bridge.*

A fine bust of the great goldsmith, Cellini, graces the central point of the bridge. This statue is a reminder that, in the 1500s, the Medicis booted out the bridge's butchers and tanners and installed

the gold- and silversmiths who still tempt visitors to this day. This is a very romantic spot late at night. In fact, look at the piles of padlocks. Guys demonstrate the enduring quality of their love by ceremonially taking their girls here, locking a lock, and throwing the key into the Arno. (But what's with the combination lock?)

Notice the Medicis' protected and elevated passageway that led from the Palazzo Vecchio through the Uffizi, across the Ponte Vecchio, and up to the immense Pitti Palace, four blocks beyond the bridge.

During World War II, the local German commander was instructed to blow the bridge up. But even some Nazis appreciate history—he blew up the buildings at either end, leaving the bridge impassable but intact. *Grazie.*

UFFIZI GALLERY TOUR

(Galleria degli Uffizi)

In the Renaissance, Florentine artists rediscovered the beauty of the natural world. Medieval art had been symbolic, telling Bible stories. Realism didn't matter. But Renaissance people saw the beauty of God in nature and the human body. They used math and science to capture the natural world on canvas as realistically as possible.

The Uffizi Gallery (oo-FEET-zee) has the greatest overall collection anywhere of Italian painting. We'll trace the rise of realism and savor the optimistic spirit that marked the Renaissance.

My eyes love things that are fair,
and my soul for salvation cries.
But neither will to Heaven rise
unless the sight of Beauty lifts them there.
　　—Michelangelo Buonarroti, sculptor, painter, poet

ORIENTATION

Cost: €9.50, plus €3 fee for optional but highly recommended reservation.

Reservations: As only 600 are allowed into the museum at a time, there are infamously long lines to get in. Avoid the three-hour peak-season wait by getting a reservation. The reserved spots can get booked up over a month in advance. The simplest solution: When you book your hotel room, ask your hotelier to get you a time. You'll still pay the reservation fee. Sometimes hoteliers buy the reservations en masse, and will ask you to pay up front for a voucher that includes the reservation fee and possibly also an extra service fee (€3–5). Or you reserve a time on your own; it's an easy and slick process if you can

Uffizi Gallery Overview

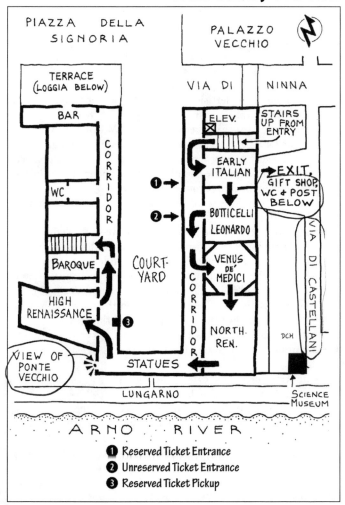

PIAZZA DELLA SIGNORIA

PALAZZO VECCHIO

TERRACE (LOGGIA BELOW)

VIA DI NINNA

BAR

ELEV.

STAIRS UP FROM ENTRY

CORRIDOR

EARLY ITALIAN

EXIT, GIFT SHOP, WC & POST BELOW

WC

❶→

❷→

BOTTICELLI LEONARDO

VIA DI CASTELLANI

BAROQUE

COURT-YARD

VENUS DE' MEDICI

HIGH RENAISSANCE

CORRIDOR

❸

NORTH. REN.

DCH

VIEW OF PONTE VECCHIO

STATUES

LUNGARNO

SCIENCE MUSEUM

A R N O   R I V E R

❶ Reserved Ticket Entrance
❷ Unreserved Ticket Entrance
❸ Reserved Ticket Pickup

get through the often busy reservation line. Dial 055-294-883 during office hours (Mon–Fri 8:30–18:30, Sat 8:30–12:30, closed Sun). With the help of an English-speaking operator, you'll get an entry slot (15-min window) and a six-digit confirmation number.

After you have your reservation (or voucher), go to the Uffizi 10 minutes before your appointed time. Walk briskly past the 200-yard-long line—pondering the IQ of this gang—to the special ticket office marked #3 (across the courtyard from the entry—see map) for those with reservations (labeled in English "Entrance for Reservations Only"), give your number (or voucher), pay (cash only), and scoot right in through door #1, on the opposite side and closer to the Piazza della Signoria.

If you haven't called ahead, there are other ways to make an Uffizi reservation—sometimes for the same day, depending on luck and availability: Try booking directly at the Uffizi (enter the left side of door #2, pay for ticket up front, 8:00–17:00); take a tour of the museum with Walking Tours of Florence (booking required, see "Walking Tours," page 29); or for a hefty fee, you can reserve online through various agencies such as www.weekendafirenze.it or www.florenceart .it. Sometimes, by the end of the day (an hour before closing), there are no lines and you can just walk right in.

Hours: Tue–Sun 8:15–18:50 (last entry 45 min before closing), closed Mon.

Getting There: It's on the Arno River between Palazzo Vecchio and Ponte Vecchio, a 15-minute walk from the train station.

Information: You can buy cheap Uffizi guidebooks from street vendors. The Uffizi (www.arca.net/uffizi) has a gift shop (at exit on ground floor, has public entrance and WC). The only WC accessible from the museum is on the top floor, near the snack bar and the stairs leading down to the exit.

Length of This Tour: Allow two hours.

Cloakroom: At the start, far from the finish.

Cuisine Art: The simple café at the end of the gallery has reasonably priced salads, desserts, fruit cups, and a terrace with a Duomo/Palazzo Vecchio view. A cappuccino here is one of Europe's great treats. Also see page 207 for nearby restaurants.

Photography: Cameras not allowed.

Starring: Botticelli, Venus, Raphael, Giotto, Titian, Leonardo, and Michelangelo.

THE TOUR BEGINS

The Ascent

• *Buy your ticket, then walk up the four long flights of the monumental staircase to the top floor (or take the elevator). Your brain should be fully aerated from the hike up. Past the ticket-taker, look out the window.*

The Uffizi is U-shaped, running around the courtyard. Except for a little Baroque spill-over, the entire collection is on this one floor, displayed chronologically. This left wing contains Florentine painting from medieval to Renaissance times. The right wing (which you can see across the courtyard) has art from the Roman and Venetian High Renaissance, works from the Baroque period that followed, and a café terrace facing the Duomo. A short hallway with sculpture connects the two wings. We'll concentrate on the Uffizi's forte, the Florentine section, then get a taste of the art it inspired.

• *Down the hall, enter the first door on the left and face Giotto's giant* Madonna and Child.

Medieval—When Art Was As Flat As the World (1200–1400)

Giotto (c. 1266–1337)—*Madonna and Child (Madonna col Bambino Gesu, Santi e Angeli)*

Mary and baby Jesus sit on a throne in a golden never-never land symbolizing heaven. It's as if medieval Christians couldn't imagine holy people inhabiting our dreary material world. It took Renaissance painters to bring Mary down to Earth and give her human realism. For the Florentines, "realism" meant "three-dimensional." In this room, pre-Renaissance paintings show the slow process of learning to paint a 3-D world on a 2-D surface.

Before concentrating on the Giotto, look at some others in the room. The **crucifixion** (on your right as you face the Giotto) was medieval 3-D—paint a crude two-dimensional work...then physically tilt the head forward. Nice try.

The three similar-looking Madonna-and-Bambinos in this room—all painted within a few decades of each other around the year 1300—show baby steps in the march to realism. **Duccio**'s piece (on the left as you face Giotto) is the most medieval and two-dimensional. There's no background. The angels are just stacked one on top of the other, floating in the golden atmosphere. Mary's throne is crudely drawn—the left side is at a three-quarters angle while the right is practically straight on. Mary herself is a wispy cardboard-cutout figure seemingly floating just above the throne.

On the opposite wall, the work of **Cimabue**—mixing the iconic Byzantine style with budding Italian realism—is an improvement. The large throne creates an illusion of depth. Mary's foot actually sticks out over the lip of the throne. Still, the angels are stacked totem pole-style, serving as heavenly bookends.

Giotto (JOT-oh) employed realism to make his theological points. He creates a space and fills it. Like a set designer, he builds a three-dimensional "stage"—the canopied throne—then peoples it with real beings. The throne has angels in front, prophets behind, and a canopy over the top, clearly defining the throne's three dimensions. The steps leading up to it lead from our space to

Medieval Art

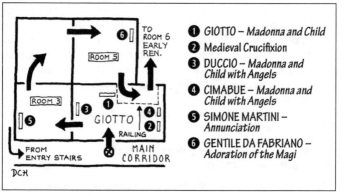

❶ GIOTTO – *Madonna and Child*
❷ Medieval Crucifixion
❸ DUCCIO – *Madonna and Child with Angels*
❹ CIMABUE – *Madonna and Child with Angels*
❺ SIMONE MARTINI – *Annunciation*
❻ GENTILE DA FABRIANO – *Adoration of the Magi*

Mary's, making the scene an extension of our world. But the real triumph here is Mary herself—big and monumental, like a Roman statue. Beneath her robe, she has a real live body, with knees and breasts that stick out at us. This three-dimensionality was revolutionary in its day, a taste of the Renaissance a century before it began.

Giotto was one of the first "famous" artists. In the Middle Ages, artists were mostly unglamorous craftsmen, like carpenters or cable-TV repairmen. They cranked out generic art and could have signed their work with a bar code. But Giotto was recognized as a genius, a unique individual. He died in a plague that devastated Florence. If there had been no plague, would the Renaissance have started 100 years earlier?

• *Enter Room 3, to the left of Giotto.*

Simone Martini (c. 1285–1344)—*Annunciation*
(*Annunciazione con i Santi Ansano e Giulitta*)

Simone Martini boils things down to the basic figures needed to get the message across: 1) The angel appears to sternly tell 2) Mary that she'll be the mother of Jesus. In the center is 3) a vase of lilies, a symbol of purity. Above is 4) the Holy Spirit as a dove about to descend on her. If the symbols aren't enough to get the message across, Simone Martini has spelled it right out for us in Latin: "*Ave Gratia Plena*...Hail, favored one, the Lord is with you." Mary doesn't look exactly pleased as punch.

This is not a three-dimensional work. The point was not to recreate reality but to teach religion, especially to the illiterate

masses. This isn't a beautiful Mary or even a real Mary. She's a generic woman without distinctive features. We know she's pure—not from her face but only because of the halo and symbolic flowers. Before the Renaissance, artists didn't care about the beauty of individual people.

Simone Martini's *Annunciation* has medieval features you'll see in many of the paintings in the next few rooms: 1) religious subject, 2) gold background, 3) two-dimensionality, and 4) meticulous detail.

• *Pass through Room 4, full of golden altarpieces, stopping at the far end of Room 5.*

Gentile da Fabriano (c. 1370–1427)—*Adoration of the Magi (Adorazione dei Magi)*

Look at the incredible detail of the Three Kings' costumes, the fine horses, and the cow in the cave. The canvas is filled from top to bottom with realistic details—but it's far from realistic. While the Magi worship Jesus in the foreground, their return trip home dangles over their heads in the "background."

This is a textbook example of the International Gothic style popular with Europe's aristocrats in the early 1400s: well-dressed, elegant people in a colorful, design-oriented setting. The religious subject is just an excuse to paint secular luxuries like brocade-pattern clothes and jewelry. And the scene's background and foreground are compressed together to create an overall design that's pleasing to the eye.

Such exquisite detail work raises the question: Was Renaissance three-dimensionality truly an improvement over Gothic, or simply a different style?

• *Exit to your right and hang a U-turn left into Room 7.*

Early Renaissance (mid-1400s)

Paolo Uccello (1397–1475)—*The Battle of San Romano (La Battaglia di S. Romano)*

In the 1400s, painters worked out the problems of painting realistically, using mathematics to create the illusion of three-dimensionality. This colorful battle scene is not so much a piece of art as an exercise in perspective. Paolo Uccello (oo-CHEL-loh)

Early Renaissance

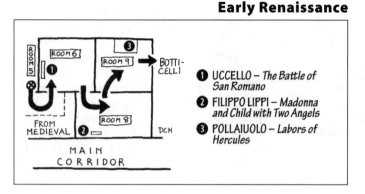

1 UCCELLO – *The Battle of San Romano*

2 FILIPPO LIPPI – *Madonna and Child with Two Angels*

3 POLLAIUOLO – *Labors of Hercules*

has challenged himself with every possible problem.

The broken lances at left set up a 3-D "grid" in which to place this crowded scene. The fallen horses and soldiers are experiments in "foreshortening"—shortening the things that are farther away from us (which appear smaller) to create the illusion of distance. Some of the figures are definitely A-plus material, like the fallen  gray horse in the center and the white horse at the far right walking away. But some are more like B-minus work—the kicking red horse's legs look like ham hocks at this angle, and the fallen soldier at far right would only be child-sized if he stood up.

And then there's the D-minus "Are you on drugs?" work. The converging hedges in the background create a nice illusion of a distant hillside maybe 250 feet away. So what are those soldiers the size of the foreground figures doing there? And jumping the hedge, is that rabbit 40 feet tall?

Paolo Uccello almost literally went crazy trying to master the three dimensions (thank God he was born before Einstein discovered one more). Uccello got so wrapped up in it he kind of lost... perspective.

• *Enter Room 8.*

Fra Filippo Lippi (1406–1469)—*Madonna and Child with Two Angels (Madonna col Bambino e Due Angeli)*

Compare this Mary with the generic female in Simone Martini's *Annunciation*. We don't need the wispy halo over her head to tell us she's holy—she radiates sweetness and light from her divine face. Heavenly beauty is expressed by a physically beautiful woman.

Fra (Brother) Lippi, an orphan raised as a monk, lived a less-than-monkish life. He lived with a nun who bore him two children. He spent his entire life searching for the perfect Virgin.

Through his studio passed Florence's prettiest girls, many of whom decorate the walls here in this room.

Lippi painted idealized beauty, but his models were real flesh-and-blood human beings. You could look through all the thousands of paintings from the Middle Ages and not find anything so human as the mischievous face of one of Lippi's little angel boys.

• *Enter Room 9, with two small works by Pollaiuolo in the glass case between the windows.*

Antonio Pollaiuolo (c. 1431–1498)—*Labors of Hercules (Fatiche di Ercole)*

Hercules gets a workout in these two small panels showing the human form at odd angles. The poses are the wildest imaginable, to show how each muscle twists and tightens. While Uccello worked on perspective, Pollaiuolo studied anatomy. In medieval times, dissection of corpses was a sin and a crime (the two were one then). Dissecting was a desecration of the human body, the temple of God. But Pollaiuolo was willing to sell his soul to the devil for artistic knowledge. He dissected.

There's something funny about this room that I can't put my finger on...I've got it—no Madonnas. Not one.

We've seen how Early Renaissance artists worked to conquer reality. Now let's see the fruits of their work, the flowering of Florence's Renaissance.

• *Enter the large Botticelli room and take a seat.*

Florence—The Renaissance Blossoms (1450–1500)

Florence in 1450 was in a Firenz-y of activity. There was a can-do spirit of optimism in the air, led by prosperous merchants and bankers and a strong middle class. The government was reasonably democratic, and Florentines saw themselves as citizens of a strong Republic—like ancient Rome. Their civic pride showed in the public monuments and artworks they built. Man was leaving

The Renaissance Blossoms

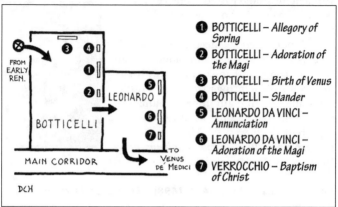

1. BOTTICELLI – *Allegory of Spring*
2. BOTTICELLI – *Adoration of the Magi*
3. BOTTICELLI – *Birth of Venus*
4. BOTTICELLI – *Slander*
5. LEONARDO DA VINCI – *Annunciation*
6. LEONARDO DA VINCI – *Adoration of the Magi*
7. VERROCCHIO – *Baptism of Christ*

the protection of the church to stand on his own two feet.

Lorenzo de' Medici, head of the powerful Medici family, epitomized this new humanistic spirit. Strong, decisive, handsome, poetic, athletic, sensitive, charismatic, intelligent, brave, clean, and reverent, Lorenzo was a true Renaissance Man, deserving of the nickname he went by—the Magnificent. He gathered Florence's best and brightest around him for evening wine and discussions of great ideas. One of this circle was the painter Botticelli (bot-i-CHEL-ee).

Sandro Botticelli (1445–1510)—*Allegory of Spring (Allegoria della Primavera)*

It's springtime in a citrus grove. The winds of spring blow in (Mr. Blue, at right), causing the woman on the right to sprout flowers from her lips as she morphs into Flora, or Spring—who walks by, spreading flowers from her dress. At the left are Mercury and the Three Graces, dancing a delicate maypole dance. The Graces may be symbolic of the three forms of love—love of beauty, love of people, and sexual love, suggested by the  raised intertwined fingers. (They forgot love of peanut butter on toast.) In the center stands Venus, the Greek goddess of love. Above her flies a blindfolded Cupid, happily shooting his arrows of love without worrying whom they'll hit.

Here is the Renaissance in its first bloom, its "springtime" of innocence. Madonna is out, Venus is in. Adam and Eve hiding their nakedness are out, glorious flesh is in. This is a return to the pre-Christian pagan world of classical Greece, where things of the flesh are not sinful. But this is certainly no orgy—just fresh-faced innocence and playfulness.

Botticelli emphasizes pristine beauty over gritty realism. The lines of the bodies, especially of the Graces in their see-through nighties, have pleasing, S-like curves. The faces are idealized but have real human features. There's a look of thoughtfulness and even melancholy in the faces—as though everyone knows that the innocence of spring will not last forever.

• *Look at the next painting to the right.*

Botticelli—*Adoration of the Magi (Adorazione dei Magi)*

Here's the rat pack of confident young Florentines who reveled in the optimistic pagan spirit—even in a religious scene. Botticelli included himself among the adorers, looking vain in the yellow robe at far right. Lorenzo's the Magnificent-looking guy at the far left.

Botticelli—*Birth of Venus (Nascita di Venere)*

According to myth, Venus was born from the foam of a wave. Still only half awake, this fragile, newborn beauty floats ashore on a clam shell, blown by the winds, where her maid waits to dress her. The pose is the same S-curve of classical statues (as we'll soon see). Botticelli's pastel colors make the world itself seem fresh and newly born.

This is the purest expression of Renaissance beauty. Venus' naked body is not sensual but innocent. Botticelli thought that

physical beauty was a way of appreciating God. Remember Michelangelo's poem: Souls will never ascend to heaven "...until the sight of Beauty lifts them there."

Botticelli finds God in the details—Venus' wind-blown hair, the translucent skin, the maid's braided hair, the slight ripple of the wind's abs, and the flowers tumbling in the slowest of slow motions, suspended like musical notes, caught at the peak of their brief life.

Mr. and Mrs. Wind intertwine—notice her hands clasped around his body. Their hair, wings, and robes mingle like the wind. But what happened to those splayed toes?

• *"Venus on the Half-Shell" (as many tourists call this) is one of the masterpieces of Western art. Take some time with it. Then find the small canvas on the wall to the right, near the* Allegory of Spring.

Botticelli—*Slander (La Calunnia)*

The spring of Florence's Renaissance had to end. Lorenzo died young. The economy faltered. Into town rode the monk Savonarola,

preaching medieval hellfire and damnation for those who embraced the "pagan" Renaissance spirit. "Down, down with all gold and decoration," he roared. "Down where the body is food for the worms." He presided over huge bonfires, where the people threw in their fine clothes, jewelry, pagan books...and paintings.

Slander spells the end of the Florentine Renaissance. The setting is classic Brunelleschian architecture, but look what's taking place beneath those stately arches. These aren't proud Renaissance Men and Women but a ragtag, medieval-looking bunch, a Court of Thieves in an abandoned hall of justice. The accusations fly and everyone is condemned. The naked man pleads for mercy but the hooded black figure, a symbol of his execution, turns away. The figure of Truth (naked Truth)—straight out of *The Birth of Venus*—looks up to heaven as if to ask, "What has happened to us?" The classical statues in their niches look on in disbelief.

Botticelli listened to Savonarola. He burned some of his own paintings and changed his tune. The last works of his life were darker, more somber, and pessimistic of humanity.

The German poet Heine said, "When they start by burning books, they'll end by burning people." Savonarola, after four short years of power, was burned on his own bonfire in the Piazza della Signoria, but by then the city was in shambles. The first flowering of the Renaissance was over.

• *Enter the next room.*

Leonardo da Vinci (1452–1519)—*Annunciation*

A scientist, architect, engineer, musician, and painter, Leonardo was a true Renaissance Man. He worked at his own pace rather than to please an employer, so he often left works unfinished. The two in this room aren't his best, but even a lesser Leonardo is enough to put a museum on the map, and they're definitely worth a look.

Gabriel has walked up to Mary and now kneels on one knee like an ambassador, saluting her. See how relaxed his other hand is, draped over his knee. Mary, who's been reading, looks up with a gesture of surprise and curiosity.

Leonardo constructs a beautifully landscaped "stage" and puts his characters in it. Look at the bricks on the right wall. If you extended lines from them, the lines would all converge at the center of the painting, the distant blue mountain. Same with the edge of the sarcophagus and the railing. Subconsciously, this subtle touch creates a feeling of balance, order, and spaciousness.

Think back to Simone Martini's *Annunciation* to realize how much more natural, relaxed, and realistic Leonardo's version is. He's taken a miraculous event—an angel appearing out of the blue—and presented it in a very human way.

Leonardo da Vinci—*Adoration of the Magi*

Leonardo's human insight is even more apparent here, in this unfinished work. The poor kings are amazed at the Christ child—even afraid of him. They scurry around like chimps around fire. This work is as agitated as the *Annunciation* is calm, giving us an idea of Leonardo's range. Leonardo was pioneering a new era of painting, showing not just the outer features but the inner personality.

The next painting to the right, *Baptism of Christ,* is by Verrocchio, Leonardo's teacher. Leonardo painted the angel on the far left when he was only 14 years old. Legend has it that when Verrocchio saw that some kid had painted an angel better than he ever would... he hung up his brush for good.

Florence saw the first blossoming of the Renaissance. But when the cultural climate turned chilly, artists flew south to warmer climes. The Renaissance shifted to Rome.

• *Exit into the main hallway. Breathe. Sit. Admire the ceiling. Look out the window. See you in five.*

Back already? Now continue down the hallway and turn left into the octagonal Venus de' Medici *room (they only allow 25 people in at a time). If you skip this because there's a line, you'll also be missing the*

Classical Sculpture and Northern Renaissance

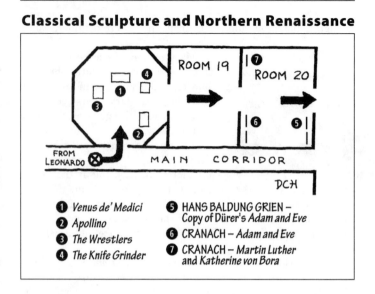

ROOM 19
ROOM 20

7

4
1
6
5

3

2

FROM LEONARDO ⊗   **MAIN   CORRIDOR**

DCH

❶ *Venus de' Medici*
❷ *Apollino*
❸ *The Wrestlers*
❹ *The Knife Grinder*

❺ HANS BALDUNG GRIEN –
Copy of Dürer's *Adam and Eve*
❻ CRANACH – *Adam and Eve*
❼ CRANACH – *Martin Luther and Katherine von Bora*

next five rooms, which include works by Cranach, Dürer, Memling, Holbein, Giorgione, and others.

Classical Sculpture

If the Renaissance was the foundation of the modern world, the foundation of the Renaissance was classical sculpture. Sculptors, painters, and poets alike turned for inspiration to these ancient Greek and Roman works as the epitome of balance, 3-D perspective, human anatomy, and beauty.

The *Venus de' Medici,* or *Medici Venus* (*Venere de' Medici,* Ancient Greece)

Is this pose familiar? Botticelli's *Birth of Venus* has the same posi-

tion of the arms, the same S-curved body, and the same lifting of the right leg. A copy of this statue stood in Lorenzo the Magnificent's garden, where Botticelli used to hang out. This one is a Roman copy of the lost original by the great Greek sculptor Praxiteles. The *Venus de' Medici* is a balanced, harmonious, serene statue from Greece's "Golden Age," when balance was admired in every aspect of life.

Perhaps more than any other work of art, this statue has been the epitome of both ideal beauty and sexuality. In the 18th and 19th centuries, sex was "dirty," so the sex drive of cultured aristocrats was channeled into a love of pure beauty. Wealthy sons and daughters of Europe's aristocrats made the pilgrimage to the Uffizi to complete their classical education...where they swooned in ecstasy before the cold beauty of this goddess of love.

Louis XIV had a bronze copy made. Napoleon stole her away to Paris for himself. And in Philadelphia in the 1800s, a copy had to be kept under lock and key to prevent the innocent from catching the Venere-al disease. At first, it may be difficult for us to appreciate such passionate love of art, but if any generation knows the power of sex to sell something—be it art or underarm deodorant—it's ours.

The Other Statues
Venus de' Medici's male counterpart is on the right, facing Venus. *Apollino* (a.k.a. "Venus with a Penis") is also by the master of smooth, cool lines: Praxiteles.

The other works are later Greek (Hellenistic), when quiet balance was replaced by violent motion and emotion. *The Wrestlers*, to the left of Venus, is a study in anatomy and twisted limbs—like Pollaiuolo's paintings a thousand years later.

The drama of *The Knife Grinder* to the right of Venus stems from the off-stage action—he's sharpening the knife to flay a man alive.

This fine room was a showroom, or a "cabinet of wonders," back when this building still functioned as the Medici offices. Filled with family portraits, it's a holistic statement that symbolically links the Medici family with the four basic elements: air (weathervane in the lantern), water (inlaid mother of pearl), fire (red wall), and earth (inlaid stone floor).

• *Exit the octagonal room and pass through Room 19 into Room 20.*

Northern Renaissance
Hans Baldung Grien (c.1404–1545)
Copy of Dürer's *Adam and Eve*

The warm spirit of the Renaissance blew north into Germany. Albrecht Dürer (1471–1528), the famous German painter and engraver, traveled to Venice, where he fell in love with all things Italian. Returning home, he painted the First Couple in the Italian style—full-bodied, muscular (check out Adam's abs and Eve's knees), "carved" with strong shading, fresh-faced, and innocent in their earthly Paradise.

This copy, by Hans Baldung Grien, of Dürer's original (now in the Prado) was a training exercise. Like many of Europe's artists—including Michelangelo and Raphael—Baldung Grien learned technique by studying Dürer's meticulous engravings, spread by the newly invented printing press.

Lucas Cranach (1472–1553)—*Adam and Eve*

Eve sashays forward, with heavy-lidded eyes, to offer the forbidden fruit. Adam stretches to display himself and his foliage to Eve. The

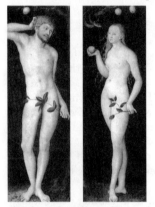

two panels are linked by smoldering eye contact, as Man and Woman awaken to their own nakedness. The Garden of Eden is about to be rocked by new ideas that are both liberating and troubling.

Though the German Lucas Cranach occasionally dabbled in the "Italian style," he chose to portray his Adam and Eve in the now-retro look of International Gothic.

They are slimmer than Dürer's, smoother, more S-shaped, elegant, graceful, shapely, and erotic, with the dainty pinkies of the refined aristocrats signing Cranach's paycheck.

Though life-sized, Adam and Eve are not lifelike, not monumental, not full-bodied or muscular, and are not placed in a real-world landscape with distant perspectives. Even so, Cranach was very much a man of the Renaissance, a friend of Martin Luther, and a champion of humanism.

Cranach—*Martin Luther*

Martin Luther—German monk, fiery orator, and religious whistle-blower—sparked a century of European wars by speaking out against the Catholic Church.

Luther (1483–1546) lived a turbulent life. In early adulthood, the newly ordained priest suffered a severe personal crisis of faith, before finally emerging "born again." In 1517, he openly protested against church corruption and was excommunicated. Defying both the pope and the emperor, he lived on the run as an outlaw, watching as his ideas sparked peasant riots. He still found time to translate the New Testament from Latin to modern German, write hymns such as "A Mighty Fortress," and spar with the humanist Erasmus and fellow-Reformer Zwingli.

Now 46 years old, Martin Luther is easing out of the fast lane. Recently married to an ex-nun, he has traded his monk's habit for street clothes, bought a house, had several kids...and has clearly been enjoying his wife's home cooking and home-brewed beer.

Cranach—*Katherine von Bora* (Luther's wife)

When "Katie" decided to leave her convent, the famous Martin Luther agreed to help find her a husband. She rejected his nominees, saying she'd marry no one... except Luther himself. In 1525 the 42-year-old ex-priest married the 26-year-old ex-nun "to please my father and annoy the pope." Martin turned his checkbook over to "my lord Katie," who also ran the family farm, raised their six children and 11 adopted orphans, and hosted Martin's circle of friends (including Cranach) at loud, chatty dinner parties.

• *Pass through the next couple of rooms, exiting to a great view of the Arno and Ponte Vecchio. Stroll through the hall with sculpture.*

The Sculpture Hall

A hundred years ago, no one even looked at Botticelli—they came to the Uffizi to see the sculpture collection. And today, these 2,000-year-old Roman copies of 2,500-year-old Greek originals are hardly noticed...but they should be.

As you wander, pay attention to the Medicis' collection. It's arranged chronologically, from the time of Julius Caesar to the era of Constantine (the first Christian emperor). Look up as you go. Along the ceiling are portraits of leading citizens, as well as an ornate patterned ceiling décor in the "grotesque" style inspired by frescoes discovered in Nero's Golden House (in Rome). The entire Greek and Roman pantheon were present here—a design meant to humble visiting dignitaries and diplomats.

• *Grab a seat at one of the benches scattered throughout the hall for a...*

View of the Arno

Enjoy Florence's best view of the Arno and Ponte Vecchio. You can also see the red-tiled roof of the Vasari Corridor, the "secret" passage connecting the Palazzo Vecchio, Uffizi, Ponte Vecchio, and Pitti Palace on the other side of the river—a half-mile in all. This was a private walkway, wallpapered in great art, for the Medici

High Renaissance

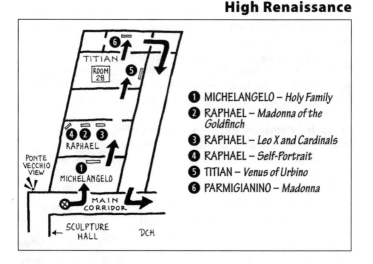

1. MICHELANGELO – *Holy Family*
2. RAPHAEL – *Madonna of the Goldfinch*
3. RAPHAEL – *Leo X and Cardinals*
4. RAPHAEL – *Self-Portrait*
5. TITIAN – *Venus of Urbino*
6. PARMIGIANINO – *Madonna*

family's commute from home to work.

As you appreciate the view (best at sunset), remember that it's this sort of pleasure that Renaissance painters wanted you to get from their paintings. For them, a canvas was a window you looked through to see the wide world.

We're headed down the home stretch now. If your little U-feetsies are killing you and it feels like torture, remind your-

self it's a pleasant torture and smile...like the statue next to you.

• *In the far hallway, turn left into the first room (#25) and grab a blast of cold from the air-conditioner vent on the floor to the left.*

High Renaissance (1500–1550)— Michelangelo, Raphael, Titian

Michelangelo Buonarroti (1475–1564)—*Holy Family (Sacra Famiglia)*

This is the only completed easel painting by the greatest sculptor in history. Florentine painters were sculptors with brushes. This shows it. Instead of a painting, it's more like three clusters of statues with some clothes painted on.

The main subject is the holy family—Mary, Joseph, and baby Jesus—and in the background are two groups of nudes looking like classical statues. The background represents the old pagan world, while Jesus in the foreground is the new age of Christianity. The figure of young John the Baptist at right is the link between the two.

This is a "peasant" Mary, with a plain face and sunburned arms. Michelangelo shows her from a very unflattering angle—we're looking up her nostrils. But Michelangelo himself was an ugly man, and he was among the first artists to recognize the beauty in everyday people.

Michelangelo was a Florentine—in fact, he was like an adopted son of the Medicis, who recognized his talent—but much of his greatest work was done in Rome as part of the Pope's face-lift of the city. We can see here some of the techniques he used on the Sistine Chapel ceiling that revolutionized painting—monumental figures; dramatic angles (we're looking up Mary's nose); accentuated, rippling muscles; and bright, clashing colors (all the more apparent since both this work and the Sistine have been recently cleaned). These added an element of dramatic tension that was lacking in the graceful work of Leonardo and Botticelli.

Michelangelo painted this for Angelo Doni for 70 ducats. (Michelangelo designed, but didn't carve, the elaborate frame.) When the painting was delivered, Doni tried to talk Michelangelo down to 40. Proud Michelangelo took the painting away and would not sell it until the man finally agreed to pay double...140 ducats.

• *Enter Room 26.*

Raphael (Raffaello Sanzio, 1483–1520)— *Madonna of the Goldfinch (La Madonna del Cardellino)*

Raphael (roff-eye-ELL) brings Mary and Bambino down from heaven and into the real world of trees, water, and sky. He gives baby Jesus (right) and John the Baptist a realistic, human playfulness. It's a tender scene painted with warm colors and a hazy background that matches the golden skin of the children.

Raphael perfected his craft in Florence, following the graceful style of Leonardo. In typical Leonardo fashion, this group of Mary, John the Baptist, and Jesus is arranged in the shape of a pyramid, with Mary's head at the peak.

The two halves of the painting balance perfectly. Draw a line down the middle, through Mary's nose and down through her knee. John the Baptist on the left is balanced by Jesus on the right. Even the trees in the

Six Degrees of Leo X

This sophisticated, luxury-loving pope was at the center of an international, Renaissance world that spread across Europe. He crossed paths with many of the Renaissance Men of his generation. Based on the theory that any two people are linked by only "six degrees of separation," let's link Leo X with the actor Kevin Bacon:

- Leo X's father was Lorenzo the Magnificent, patron of Botticelli and Leonardo.
- When Leo X was age 13, his family took in 13-year-old Michelangelo.
- Michelangelo inspired Raphael, who was later hired by Leo X.
- Raphael exchanged masterpieces with fellow genius Albrecht Dürer, who was personally converted by Martin Luther (who was friends with Lucas Cranach), who was excommunicated by...Leo X.
- Leo X was portrayed in the movie *The Agony and the Ecstasy,* which starred Charlton Heston, who was in *Planet of the Apes* with Burgess Meredith, who was in *Rocky* with Sylvester Stallone, who was in *Cop Land* with Robert De Niro, who was in *Sleepers* with...Kevin Bacon.

background balance each other, left and right. These things aren't immediately noticeable, but they help create the subconscious feelings of balance and order that reinforce the atmosphere of maternal security in this domestic scene—pure Renaissance.

Raphael—*Leo X and Cardinals (Leone X con i Cardinali)*

Raphael was called to Rome at the same time as Michelangelo, working next door while Michelangelo did the Sistine ceiling. Raphael peeked in from time to time, learning from Michelangelo's monumental, dramatic figures. His later work is grittier and more realistic than the idealized, graceful, and "Leonardoesque" Madonna.

Pope Leo is big, like a Michelangelo statue. And Raphael captures some of the seamier side of Vatican life in the cardinals' eyes—shrewd, suspicious, and somewhat cynical. With Raphael, the photographic realism pursued by painters ever since Giotto was finally achieved.

The Florentine Renaissance ended in 1520 with the death of Raphael. Raphael (see his self-portrait to the left of the Madonna) is considered both the culmination and conclusion of the Renaissance. The realism, balance, and humanism we associate with the Renaissance are all found in Raphael's work. He combined the grace of Leonardo with the power of Michelangelo. With his death, the Renaissance shifted again—to Venice.

• *Pass through the next room and enter Room 28.*

Titian (Tiziano Vecelli, c. 1490–1576)—*Venus of Urbino (La Venere di Urbino)*

Compare this *Venus* with Botticelli's newly hatched *Venus* and you get a good idea of the difference between the Florentine and Venetian

 Renaissance. Botticelli's was pure, innocent, and otherworldly. Titian's should have a staple in her belly button. This isn't a Venus, it's a centerfold— with no purpose but to please the eye and other organs. While Botticelli's allegorical Venus is a message, this is a massage. The bed is used.

Titian and his fellow Venetians took the pagan spirit pioneered in Florence and carried it to its logical hedonistic conclusion. Using bright, rich colors, they captured the luxurious life of happy-go-lucky Venice.

While Raphael's *Madonna of the Goldfinch* was balanced with a figure on the left and one on the right, Titian balances his painting in a different way—with color. The canvas is split down the middle by the curtain. The left half is dark, the right half warmer. The two halves are connected by a diagonal slash of luminous gold—the nude woman. The girl in the background is trying to find her some clothes.

By the way, visitors from centuries past also panted in front of this Venus. The poet Byron called it "*the* Venus." With her sensual skin, hey-sailor look, and suggestively placed hand, she must have left them blithering idiots.

• *Find the n-n-n-next painting...in Room 29.*

Parmigianino (1503–1540)—*Madonna of the Long Neck (Madonna dal Collo Lungo)*

Raphael, Michelangelo, Leonardo, and Titian mastered reality. They could place any scene onto a canvas with photographic accuracy. How could future artists top that?

Mannerists such as Parmigianino tried by going beyond realism, exaggerating it for effect. Using brighter colors and twisting poses (two techniques explored by Michelangelo), they created scenes more elegant and more exciting than real life.

By stretching the neck of his Madonna, Parmigianino (like the cheese) gives her an unnatural, swanlike beauty. She has the same

pose and position of hands as Botticelli's *Venus* and the *Venus de' Medici*. Her body forms an arcing S-curve—down her neck as far as her elbow, then back the other way along Jesus' body to her knee, then down to her foot. The baby Jesus seems to be blissfully gliding down this slippery slide of sheer beauty.

In the Uffizi, we've seen many images of female beauty: from ancient goddesses to medieval Madonnas to wicked Eves, from Botticelli's pristine nymphs to Michelangelo's peasant Mary, from Raphael's Madonna-and-baby to Titian's babe. Their physical beauty expresses different aspects of the human spirit.

• *Pass through several rooms, returning to the main hallway.*

The Rest of the Uffizi

As art moved into the Baroque period, artists took Renaissance realism and exaggerated it still more—more beauty, more emotion, or more drama. There's lots of great stuff in the following rooms, and I'd especially recommend the enormous canvases of Rubens, Rembrandt's *Self-Portrait*, and the shocking ultra-realism of Caravaggio's *Bacchus* and *Abraham Sacrificing Isaac* (downstairs on the way out). Note that when there are newly restored paintings, the Uffizi shows them off in Room 38 (near the exit stairs) with an English description of the work done.

• *But first, head to the end of the hallway (WCs en route) for a true aesthetic experience.*

The Little Cappuccin Monk (Cappuccino)

This drinkable art form, born in Italy, is now enjoyed all over

the world. It's called *The Little Cappuccin Monk* because the coffee's frothy light-and-dark-brown foam looks like the two-toned cowls of the Cappuccin order. Sip it on the terrace in the shadow of the towering Palazzo Vecchio, and be glad we live in an age where you don't need to be a Medici to enjoy all this fine art. *Salute.*

BARGELLO
TOUR

The Renaissance began with sculpture. The great Florentine paint-ers were "sculptors with brushes." You can see the birth of this rev-olution of 3-D in the Bargello (bar-JEL-oh), which boasts the best collection of Florentine sculpture. It's a small, uncrowded museum and a pleasant break from the intensity of the rest of Florence.

ORIENTATION

Cost: €4 (more if a special exhibition is offered).

Hours: Daily 8:15–13:50 but closed first, third, and fifth Sun and second and fourth Mon of each month. Last entry 40 minutes before closing.

Getting There: It's located at Via del Proconsolo 4, a three-minute walk northeast of the Uffizi. Facing the Palazzo Vecchio, go behind the Palazzo and turn left. Look for a rustic brick building with a spire that looks like a baby Palazzo Vecchio. If lost ask, "DOH-vay bar-JEL-oh?"

Information: Nothing in English. Tel. 055-238-8606.

Length of This Tour: Allow one hour.

Cuisine Art: Inexpensive bars and cafés await in the surrounding streets. See recommended eateries on page 207.

Photography: Permitted only in the courtyard.

Starring: Michelangelo, Donatello, Brunelleschi, Ghiberti, and four different *David*s.

THE TOUR BEGINS

Sculpture in Florence

• *Buy your ticket and take a seat in the courtyard.*

The Bargello, built in 1255, was an early Florence police station *(bargello)* and then a prison. The heavy fortifications tell us that politics in medieval Florence had its occupational hazards.

The Bargello, a three-story rectangular building, surrounds this cool and peaceful courtyard. The best statues are found in two rooms—one on the ground floor at the foot of the outdoor staircase, and another one flight up, directly above. We'll proceed logically, in a chrono kind of way, from Donatello to Verrocchio to Michelangelo.

But first, meander around this courtyard and get a feel for sculpture in general and rocks in particular. Sculpture is a much more robust art form than painting. Think of the engineering problems alone of the sculpting process: quarrying and cutting the stone, transporting the block to the artist's studio, all the hours of chiseling chips away, then the painstaking process of sanding the final product by hand. A sculptor must be strong enough to gouge into the stone but delicate enough to groove out the smallest details. Think of Michelangelo's approach to sculpting—he wasn't creating a figure; he was liberating it from the rock that surrounded it.

If the Renaissance is humanism, then sculpture is the perfect medium with which to express it. It shows the human form, standing alone, independent of church, state, or society, ready to create itself.

Finally, a viewing note. Every sculpture has an invisible "frame" around it—the stone block it was cut from. Visualizing this frame helps you find the center of the composition.

• *Climb the courtyard staircase to the next floor up and turn right into the large Donatello Room. Pause at Donatello's painted bust of Niccolo da Uzzanò.*

Donatello—*Niccolo da Uzzanò* (c. 1420)

Not an emperor, not a king, not a pope or prince, this is one of Florence's leading businessmen in a toga, portrayed in the style of an ancient Roman bust. In the 1400s, when Florence was inventing the Renaissance that all Europe would soon follow, there was an optimistic spirit of democracy that gloried in everyday people. With wrinkles, quizzical look, and bags under the eyes, Donatello has portrayed this man literally wart (left cheek) and all.

Donatello—An early *David* (marble, 1408)

This is the first of several *David*s we'll see in the Bargello. His dainty pose makes him a little unsteady on his feet. He's dressed like a medieval knight (fully clothed but showing some leg through

Bargello—Donatello Room

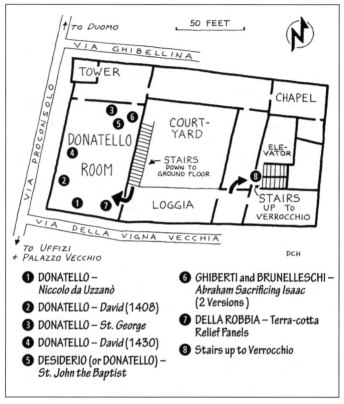

TO DUOMO

50 FEET

VIA GHIBELLINA

VIA PROCONSOLO

TOWER

CHAPEL

❸ ❻
❺

COURT-YARD

DONATELLO

❹

ROOM

← STAIRS
DOWN TO
GROUND FLOOR

ELE-VATOR

❷

❽

❶ ❼

LOGGIA

STAIRS
UP TO
VERROCCHIO

VIA DELLA VIGNA VECCHIA

TO UFFIZI
& PALAZZO VECCHIO

DCH

❶ DONATELLO –
Niccolo da Uzzanò

❷ DONATELLO – David (1408)

❸ DONATELLO – St. George

❹ DONATELLO – David (1430)

❺ DESIDERIO (or DONATELLO) –
St. John the Baptist

❻ GHIBERTI and BRUNELLESCHI –
Abraham Sacrificing Isaac
(2 Versions)

❼ DELLA ROBBIA – Terra-cotta
Relief Panels

❽ Stairs up to Verrocchio

the slit skirt). The generic face and blank, vacant eyes give him the look not of a real man but of an anonymous decoration on a church facade. At age 22, Donatello still had one foot in the old Gothic style. To tell the story of David, Donatello plants a huge rock right in the middle of Goliath's forehead.

• *At the far end of the room,* St. George *stands in a niche in the wall.*

Donatello—*St. George* (*S. Giorgio,* 1416)

The proud warrior has both feet planted firmly on the ground. He stands on the edge of his niche looking out alertly. He tenses his powerful right hand as he prepares to attack. George, the Christian slayer of dragons, was just the sort of righteous warrior whom proud Renaissance Florentines could rally around in their struggles with nearby cities. Nearly a century later, Michelangelo's

Donatello
(1386–1466)

Donatello was the first great Renaissance genius, a model for Michelangelo and others. He mastered realism, creating the first truly lifelike statues of people since ancient times. Donatello's work is highly personal. Unlike the ancient Greeks—but like the ancient Romans—he often sculpted real people, not idealized versions of pretty gods and goddesses. Some of these people are downright ugly. In the true spirit of Renaissance humanism, Donatello appreciated the beauty of flesh-and-blood human beings.

Donatello's personality was also a model for later artists. He was moody and irascible, purposely setting himself apart from others in order to concentrate on his sculpting. He developed the role of the "mad genius" that Michelangelo would later perfect.

David replaced *George* as the unofficial symbol of Florence, but *David* was clearly inspired by *George's* relaxed intensity and determination. (This is the original marble statue. A bronze version stands in its original niche at Orsanmichele Church.)

The relief panel below shows George doing what he's been pondering. To *George's* right, the sketchy arches and trees create the illusion of a distant landscape. Donatello, who apprenticed in Ghiberti's studio, is credited with teaching his master how to create 3-D illusions like this.

• *On the floor to your left, you'll find...*

Donatello—*David* (bronze, c. 1430)

He's naked. Donatello, who never married, sees David as a teenage

boy wearing only a helmet, boots, and sword. The smooth-skinned warrior sways gracefully, poking his sword playfully at the severed head of the giant Goliath. His *contrapposto* stance is similar to Michelangelo's *David,* resting his weight on one leg in the classical style, but it gives him a feminine rather than masculine look. Gazing into his coy eyes and at his bulging belly is a very different experience from confronting Michelangelo's older and sturdier Renaissance Man.

This *David* paved the way for Michelangelo's. Europe hadn't seen a free-standing male nude like this in a thousand years. In the Middle Ages, the human body was considered a dirty thing, a symbol of man's weakness, something to be covered up in shame. The church prohibited exhibitions of nudity like this one and certainly would never decorate a church with it. But in the Renaissance, a new class of rich and powerful merchants appeared who bought art for personal enjoyment. Reading Plato's *Symposium*, they saw the ideal of Beauty in the form of a young man. This particular statue stood in the Medicis' palace...where Michelangelo, practically an adopted son, grew up admiring it.

As we see the different *David*s in the Bargello, compare and contrast the artists' styles. How many ways can you slay a giant?
• St. John the Baptist, *done by Donatello or his student, is to the right of the boyish, naked* David.

Desiderio da Settignano (or Donatello)—*St. John the Baptist (S. Giovanni Battista)*

John the Baptist was the wild-eyed, wildcat prophet who lived in the desert preaching, living on bugs 'n' honey, and baptizing Saviors of the world. Donatello, the mad prophet of the coming Renaissance, might have identified with this original eccentric.
• *On the wall next to* George, *you'll find some bronze relief panels. Don't look at the labels just yet.*

Ghiberti and Brunelleschi— Baptistery Door Competition Entries (two different relief panels, titled *Il Sacrificio di Abramo*)

Some would say these two panels are the first works of the Renaissance. These two versions of *Abraham Sacrificing Isaac* were finalists in the contest held in 1401 to decide who would do the bronze doors of the Baptistery. The contest sparked citywide excitement that evolved into the Renaissance spirit. Lorenzo Ghiberti won, and later did the doors known as the Gates of Paradise. Filippo Brunelleschi lost—fortunately for us—freeing him to design the Duomo's dome.

Both artists catch the crucial moment when Abraham, obeying God's orders, prepares to slaughter and burn his only son as a sacrifice. At the last moment—after Abraham passed this test of faith—an angel of God appears to stop the bloodshed.

Is one panel clearly better than the other?

You be the judge. Here are the two finalists for the Baptistery door competition—Ghiberti's and Brunelleschi's. Which do you like best?

Ghiberti's, on the left, won.

Let's look at composition: One is integrated and cohesive; the other is a balanced knickknack shelf of segments. Human drama: One has bodies and faces that speak. The boy's body is a fine classical nude in itself, so real and vulnerable. Abraham's face is intense and ready to follow God's will. Perspective: An angel zooms in from out of nowhere to save the boy in the nick of time. Detail: One lamb's ram's wool is curlier than the other, one altar is more intricate.

It was obviously a tough call, but Ghiberti's was chosen, perhaps because his goldsmith training made him better suited for the technical end.

• *Along the walls, you'll find several colorful terra-cotta reliefs.*

Luca della Robbia—Terra-Cotta Relief Panels

Mary and baby Jesus with accompanying angels look their most serene in these panels by the master of painted, glazed porcelain. Polished blue, white, green, and yellow, they have a gentle and feminine look that softens the rough masculine stone of this room. Luca was just one of a family of della Robbias who pioneered art in terra-cotta.

• *Exit the Donatello room through the same door you entered. Cross to the rooms on the other side of the courtyard. Take your first left, then immediately turn right and climb the carpeted stairs to the next floor. At the top of the stairs, turn left, then left again. Verrocchio's David stands (when not out for restoration) in the center of the room.*

Verrocchio—*David* (c. 1470)

Andrea del Verrocchio (1435–1488) is best known as the teacher of Leonardo da Vinci, but he was also the premier sculptor of

the generation between Donatello and Michelangelo. This saucy, impertinent *David* is younger and more masculine than Donatello's, but a far cry from Michelangelo's monumental version. He's definitely the shepherd "boy" described in the Bible. He leans on one leg, not with a firm, commanding stance but a nimble one (especially noticeable from behind). Compare the smug smile of the victor with Goliath's "Oh, have I got a headache" expression.

• *Go back through the doorway you entered in, and head straight to a room of glass cases filled with small statues. In the center of the room, you'll find...*

Pollaiuolo—*Hercules and Antaeus (Ercole e Anteo,* 1498)

Antaeus was invincible as long as he was in contact with the Earth, his mother. So Hercules just picked him up like "The Rock" of the Renaissance and crushed him to death.

More than any early artist from this period, Antonio Pollaiuolo studied the human body in motion. These figures are not dignified Renaissance Men. Yet, in this tangled pose of flailing arms and legs, there still is a Renaissance sense of balance—all the motion spins around the center of gravity where their bodies grind together.

• *In the nearby glass cases are small-scale, alternate versions of the* Mercury *that we'll soon see.*

The Rest of the Bargello

Before we lose elevation to visit the final room downstairs, browse around the upper floors. On this floor, you'll likely find ivories, jewelry, and terra-cotta Mary-baby-and-angel panels by other members of the della Robbia clan (unless some of the art has been moved downstairs). The top floor has armor and medallions.

• *Now descend back to the courtyard on the ground floor. The final room we'll visit is through the door to your left at the bottom of the stairs. We'll begin with three lesser Michelangelos.*

Michelangelo—*Bacchus (Baccho,* c. 1497)

Bacchus, the god of wine and revelry, raises another cup to his lips, while his little companion goes straight for the grapes.

Bargello—Ground Floor

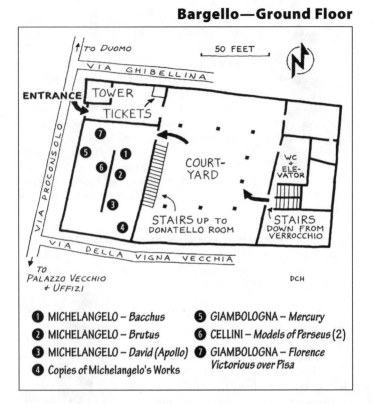

1 MICHELANGELO – *Bacchus*

2 MICHELANGELO – *Brutus*

3 MICHELANGELO – *David (Apollo)*

4 Copies of Michelangelo's Works

5 GIAMBOLOGNA – *Mercury*

6 CELLINI – *Models of Perseus* (2)

7 GIAMBOLOGNA – *Florence Victorious over Pisa*

Maybe Michelangelo had a sense of humor after all. Compare this tipsy Greek god of wine with his sturdy, sober *David,* begun a few years later. *Bacchus* isn't nearly so muscular, so monumental...or so sure on his feet. Hope he's not driving. The pose, the smooth muscles, the beer belly, and swaying hips look more like Donatello's boyish *David.*

This was Michelangelo's first major commission. He often vacillated between showing man as strong and noble, and as weak and perverse. This isn't the nobility of the classical world, but the decadent side of orgies and indulgence.

• *Just to the left, you'll find...*

Michelangelo—*Brutus* (*Bruto,* 1540)

Another example of the influence of Donatello is this so-ugly-he's-beautiful bust by Michelangelo. His rough intensity gives him the look of a man who has succeeded against all odds, a dignity and heroic quality that would be missing if he were too pretty.

The subject is Brutus, the Roman who, for the love of liberty, murdered his friend and dictator, Julius Caesar *(Et tu...?).*

Michelangelo could understand this man's dilemma. He himself was torn between his love of the democratic tradition of Florence and loyalty to his friends the Medicis, who had become dictators.

So he gives us two sides of a political assassin. The right profile (the front view) is heroic. But the hidden side, with the drooping mouth and squinting eye, makes him more cunning, sneering, and ominous.

Michelangelo—*David* (also known as *Apollo,* 1530–1532)

This restless, twisting man is either David or Apollo. (Is he reaching for a sling or a quiver?) As the last of the *David*s in the Bargello, it's a good time to think back on

those we've seen: Donatello's generic warrior and girlish, gloating *David;* Verrocchio's boyish, impish version; and now this unfinished one by Michelangelo. Michelangelo certainly learned from these earlier versions, even copying certain elements, but what's truly amazing is that his famous *David* in the Accademia is so completely different from the others, so much larger than life in every way.

In the glass cases in the corner are small-scale copies of some of Michelangelo's most famous works. Back near the entrance there's a bust of Michelangelo by his fellow sculptor da Volterra, capturing Michelangelo's broken nose and brooding nature.
• *On the other side of the room...*

Giambologna—*Mercury*

Catch this statue while you can—he's got flowers waiting to be delivered. Despite all the bustle and motion, *Mercury* has a solid Renaissance core: the line of balance that runs straight up the center, from toes to hip to fingertip. He's caught in mid-stride. His top half leans forward, counterbalanced by his right leg in back, while the center of gravity rests firmly at the hip-bone. Down at the toes, notice the cupid practicing up for the circus.

Cellini—*Models of Perseus (Perseo)*

The life-size statue of Perseus slaying Medusa, located in the open-air loggia next to Palazzo Vecchio, is cast bronze. Benvenuto Cellini started with these smaller models in wax and bronze to get the difficult process down. When it came time to cast the full-size work, everything was going fine...until he realized he didn't have enough metal! He ran around the studio, gathering up pewterware and throwing it in, narrowly avoiding a messterpiece.

Giambologna— *Florence Victorious over Pisa (Firenze Vittoriosa su Pisa)*

This shows the fierce Florentine chauvinism born in an era when Italy's cities struggled for economic and political dominance...and Florence won.

MUSEUM OF SAN MARCO TOUR

(Museo di San Marco)

Two of Florence's brightest lights lived in the San Marco Monastery, a reminder that the Renaissance was not just a secular phenomenon. At the Museum of San Marco, you'll find these two different expressions of 15th-century Christianity—Fra Angelico's radiant paintings, fusing medieval faith with Renaissance realism, and Savonarola's moral reforms, fusing medieval faith with modern politics.

ORIENTATION

Cost: €4.

Dress Code: None.

Hours: Mon–Fri 8:15–13:50, Sat–Sun 8:15–19:00, but closed the first, third, and fifth Sun and the second and fourth Mon of each month.

Getting There: It's on Piazza San Marco, around the corner from the Accademia, and several long blocks northeast of the Duomo (head up Via Ricasoli or Via Cavour).

Information: Tel. 055-238-8608. Reservations available but unnecessary.

Length of This Tour: Allow one hour.

Cuisine Art: See page 206 in Eating chapter.

Photography: Not allowed.

Starring: Fra Angelico's paintings and Savonarola's living quarters.

THE TOUR BEGINS

Overview

Ground Floor: The world's best collection of Fra Angelico paintings.

Upstairs: The monks' cells (living quarters), decorated by Fra Angelico, and the cell of the most famous resident, Savonarola.

• *Buy ticket and enter the courtyard/cloister.*

GROUND FLOOR

The Courtyard/Cloister

Stepping into the cloister, you can feel the spirituality of this place, a respite from the hubbub of modern Florence. The first view at the end of the corridor is of St. Dominic (the founder of this order) worshipping Christ. In this one scene, we learn what this house is all about. Monks spent their lives here meditating on the gift of salvation. Across the courtyard, the lunette (crescent-shaped painting) above the door of the refectory (dining hall) features Christ dead in a coffin. Symbolic of the Eucharist, this scene reminded the monks that you need both physical and spiritual nourishment. Another door from this cloister leads to the hospice wing. It's introduced by a lunette that shows two monks welcoming Christ. (Jesus said, "As you welcome the least among men, you also welcome me.") With this reminder, monks were encouraged to treat a visitor as if that stranger were Christ himself.

You'll see Renaissance arches framing Gothic cross-vaulting—an apt introduction to a monastery built during an optimistic time (1439), when Renaissance humanism dovetailed with medieval spirituality. Fra Angelico considered painting to be a form of prayer. He worked to bridge the gap between the infinite (Christ) and the finite (a mortal's ability to relate to God) by injecting an ethereal atmosphere into his frescoes.

Fra Angelico—*Fresco of St. Dominic and Crucifixion*

The fresco by Fra Angelico (in the corner of the cloister, straight

ahead from the entrance) shows Dominic, the founder of the order, hugging the bloody cross like a groupie adoring a rock star. Monks who lived here—including Fra Angelico, Savonarola, and Fra Bartolomeo—renounced money, sex, ego, and rock music to follow a simple, regimented life, meditating on Christ's ultimate sacrifice.

• *We'll tour the rooms around the courtyard moving counterclockwise. The first one, by the entrance, is the Hospice (Ospizio).*

Museum of San Marco—Ground Floor

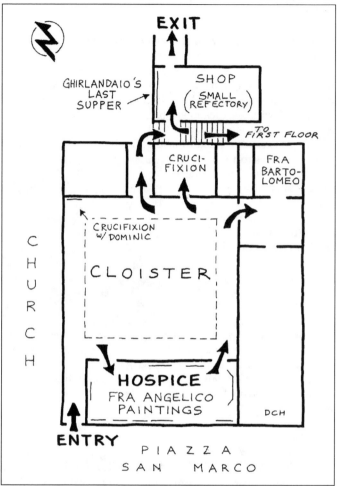

EXIT

GHIRLANDAIO'S
LAST
SUPPER

SHOP
(SMALL
REFECTORY)

TO
FIRST FLOOR

CRUCI-
FIXION

FRA
BARTO-
LOMEO

CRUCIFIXION
W/ DOMINIC

CLOISTER

CHURCH

HOSPICE
FRA ANGELICO
PAINTINGS

DCH

ENTRY

PIAZZA
SAN MARCO

The Hospice (Ospizio), with Paintings by Fra Angelico (Beato Angelico)

Fra Angelico (c. 1400–1455)—equal parts monk and painter—fused early-Renaissance technique with medieval spirituality. His works can be admired for their beauty or contemplated as spiritual visions. Browse the room, and you'll find serene-faced Marys, Christs, and saints wearing gold halos (often painted on altarpieces), bright primary colors (red-blue-yellow/gold), evenly lit scenes, and meticulous detail—all creating a mystical world of their own, glowing from within like stained-glass windows.

• *Start with the large altarpiece—showing the* Deposition *at the near end of the room.*

Fra Angelico—*Deposition of Christ from the Cross* (*Pala di Santa Trinità*)

Christ's body is lowered from the cross, mourned by haloed women (on the left) and contemporary Florentines (right). There's a clearly defined foreground (the kneeling, curly-headed man and the woman with her back to us), background (the distant city and hills), and middle distance (the trees).

Fra Angelico, trained in medieval religious painting, never closed his eyes to the innovations of the budding Renaissance, using both styles all his life. There are Gothic elements, such as the altarpiece frame, inherited from his former teacher (who painted the pinnacles on top). The holy wear halos, and the stretched-out "body of Christ" is symbolically "displayed" like the communion bread.

But it's truly a Renaissance work. The man in green lowering Christ bends forward at a strongly foreshortened (difficult to draw) angle. Christ's toes, kissed by Mary Magdalene, cross the triptych wall, ignoring the frame's traditional three-arch divisions. Fra Angelico was boldly "coloring outside the lines" to create a single, realistic scene.

And the holy scene has been removed from its golden heaven and placed in the first great Renaissance landscape—on a lawn, among flowers, trees, cloud masses, real people, and the hillsides of Fiesole overlooking Florence. Fra Angelico, the ascetic monk, refused to renounce one pleasure—his joy in the natural beauty of God's creation.

• *Working counterclockwise around the room, you'll find the following works (among others).*

Fra Angelico—*Triptych of St. Peter the Martyr* (*Trittico di San Pietro Martire*)

In this early, more "medieval" work, Fra Angelico sets (big) Mary and Child in a gold background flanked by (small) saints standing obediently in their niches. Having recently joined the Dominican community in Fiesole, young Brother Giovanni (as he was known in his lifetime) now dressed like these famous Dominicans—white robe, blue cape, and tonsured haircut.

Peter the Martyr (next to Mary, with bloody head) exemplified the unbending Dominican spirit. Attacked by heretics (see the scene above Peter), he was hacked in the head with a dagger but died still preaching, writing with his own blood: *"Credo in Deum"* ("I believe in God").

• *Continuing counterclockwise...*

Fra Angelico—Two Panels: *Wedding and Funeral of the Virgin (Sposalizio e Funerali della Vergine)*

Fra Angelico's teenage training was as a miniaturist, so even these small *predella* panels (part of a larger altarpiece) are surprisingly realistic—the folds in the clothes, the gold-brocade hemlines, and the precisely outlined people, as though etched in glass. Notice the Renaissance perspective tricks he was exploring, setting the wedding in front of receding buildings and the funeral among candles that get shorter at the back of the scene.

Fra Angelico—*Last Judgment (Giudizio Universale)*

Despite the Renaissance, Florence in the 1420s was still a city in the Christian universe described by Dante. Hell (to the right) is

a hierarchical barbecue where sinners are burned, boiled, and tortured by a minotaur-like Satan, who rules the bottom of the pit. The blessed in heaven (left) play ring-around-the-rosy with angels. In the center, a row of open tombs creates a 3-D highway to hell, stretching ominously to that final Judgment Day.

Fra Angelico (and assistants)—*Thirty-Five Scenes Painted on Doors of a Silverware Storeroom (Panelli dell'Armadio degli Argenti)*

The first nine scenes in this life of Christ are by Fra Angelico himself (the rest by assistants). Like storyboards for a movie, these

natural, realistic, and straightfor-
ward panels "show" through action,
they don't just "tell" through
symbols. (The Latin inscription
beneath each panel is redundant.)
The miraculous is presented as an
everyday occurrence.

1. The Wheel of Ezekiel (OK,
   that's medieval symbolism)
   prophesies Christ's coming.
2. In the Annunciation, the
   angel gestures to tell Mary
   that she'll give birth.
3. Newborn Jesus glows, amazing his parents, while timid shepherds sneak a peek.
4. Precocious Jesus splays himself and says, "Cut me."
5. One of the Magi kneels to kiss the babe's foot.
6. In the temple, the tiny baby is dwarfed by elongated priests
   and columns.
7. Mary and the baby ride, while Joseph carries the luggage.
8. Meanwhile, babies are slaughtered in a jumble of gore, dramatic poses, and agonized faces.
9. The commotion contrasts with the serenity of child Jesus in
   the temple.

This work by 50-year-old Fra Angelico—master of many styles,
famous in Italy, recently returned from a gig in the Vatican—has
the fresh, simple, spontaneous storytelling of a children's book.

Fra Angelico—*Lamentation (Compianto sul Cristo Morto)*
This painting of the executed Christ being mourned silently by
loved ones was the last thing many condemned prisoners saw during their final hours. It once hung in a church where the soon-to-
be executed were incarcerated.

The melancholy mood is understated, suggested by a series
of horizontal layers—Christ's body, the line of mourners, the city

walls, landscape hori-
zon, layered clouds,
and the crossbar. It's as
though Christ is being
welcomed into peaceful
rest, a comforting mes-
sage from Fra Angelico
to the condemned.
        "Fra Angelico"
(Angelic Brother) is a nickname that describes his reputation for
sweetness, humility, and compassion. It's said he couldn't paint a

crucifixion without crying. In 1984, he was beatified by Pope John Paul II and made patron of artists.

• *At the far end of the room hangs the...*

Fra Angelico—*Altarpiece of the Linen-Drapers (Tabernacolo dei Linaioli)*

The impressive size and marble frame (by Ghiberti) attest to Fra Angelico's worldly success and collaboration with Renaissance

greats. The monumental Mary and Child and the saints on the doors are gold-backed and elegant to please conservative patrons. In the three *predella* panels below, Fra Angelico gets to display his Renaissance chops, showing haloed saints mingling with well-dressed Florentines amid local city- and landscapes. (Find Ghiberti in the left panel, kneeling, in blue.)

• *On the long wall are three similar-looking altarpieces. These are examples of a scene known as a* sacra conversazione.

Evolution of the *Sacra Conversazione*

Fra Angelico (largely) invented what became a common Renaissance theme: Mary and Child surrounded by saints "conversing" informally about holy matters. Four examples in this room show how Fra Angelico, exploring Renaissance techniques, developed the idea over his lifetime.

The *Triptych of St. Peter the Martyr,* shown on page 109, is not a true *sacra conversazione,* even though it shows Mary and saints. But Mary is unnaturally big, flanked by smaller saints in a line. The gold background gives no hint that they inhabit the same space, and there is no eye contact between them and no "conversation."

• *Going from left to right along the long wall, you'll find the following three altarpieces in the* sacra conversazione *style.*

Fra Angelico—*Annalena Altarpiece (Pala d'Annalena)*

In the *Annalena Altarpiece*—considered Florence's first true *sacra conversazione*—the saints emerge from their niches, gather cautiously in a semicircle, and tentatively acknowledge each other

with eyes and gestures. The background is traditional gold, but now in the form of a curtain hanging behind the throne.

Still, everyone's either facing out or in profile—not the natural poses of a true crowd. Mary and Jesus direct our eye to Mary's brooch, the first in a series of circles radiating out from the center: brooch, halo, canopy arch, circle of saints. Set in a square frame, this painting has the circle-in-a-square composition that marks many *sacra conversazioni*.

Fra Angelico—*San Marco Altarpiece (Pala di San Marco)*

In 1439, Cosimo de' Medici built this monastery, inviting Fra Angelico's Dominican community to move here from Fiesole. Fra Angelico soon became prior (head monk), turning down an offer to be archbishop of Florence.

Cosimo commissioned this painting as the centerpiece of the new church (next door). For the dedication Mass, Fra Angelico theatrically "opens the curtain," revealing a stage set with a distant backdrop of trees, kneeling saints in the foreground, and a crowd gathered around Mary and Child at center stage on a raised, canopied throne. The altarpiece was like a window onto a marvelous world where holies mill about on Earth as naturally as mortals.

The *San Marco Altarpiece* places the holy saints clearly in the 3-D world we inhabit. The carpet makes a "chessboard" pattern to establish 3-D space. To show just how far we've come from Gothic, Fra Angelico gives us a painting-in-a-painting—a crude, gold-backed crucifixion.

Fra Angelico—*Bosco ai Frati Altarpiece (Pala di Bosco ai Frati)*

This altarpiece is Fra Angelico's last great work, and he uses every stylistic arrow in his quiver: detailed friezes of the miniaturist; medieval halos and gold backdrop; monumental, naturally posed figures in the style of Masaccio (especially St. Francis, on the left, with his relaxed *contrapposto*); 3-D perspective established by the floor tiles; and Renaissance love of natural beauty (the trees and sky).

Fra Angelico's bright colors are eye-catching. The gold backdrop sets off the red-pink handmaidens, which set off Jesus' pale skin. The deep blue of Mary's dress, frosted with a precious gold hem, turns out at her feet to show a swath of the green inner lining, suggesting the 3-D body within.

Despite Renaissance realism, Fra Angelico creates a world of his own—perfectly lit, with no moody shadows, dirt, frayed clothing, or imperfection. The faces are certainly realistic, but they express no human emotion. These mortals, through sacrifice and meditation, have risen above the petty passions celebrated by humanist painters to achieve a serenity that lights them from within.

• *Exit the Hospice back into the court-yard. Continue counterclockwise and enter the next set of rooms (marked* Lavabo e Refettorio*). The small room on the left has paintings and fresco fragments by Fra Bartolomeo. Working clockwise around the room, you'll find these works by...*

Fra Bartolomeo (1473–1517)

Fra Bartolomeo lived and worked in this monastery a generation after the "Angelic" brother. *Ecce Homo* shows the kind of Christ that young, idealistic Dominican monks (like Fra Bartolomeo) adored in their meditations—curly-haired, creamy-faced, dreamy-eyed, bearing the torments of the secular world with humble serenity.

Fra Bartolomeo—*St. Dominic (San Domenico)*

St. Dominic holds a finger to his lips—"Shh! We have strict rules in my order." Dominic (c. 1170–1221), a friend of St. Francis of Assisi, formed his rules after seeing the austere *perfetti* (perfect ones) of the heretical Cathar sect of southern France. He figured they could only be converted by someone just as extreme, following Christ's simple, possession-free lifestyle. Nearing 50, Dominic made a 3,400-mile preaching tour—on foot, carrying his luggage—from Rome to Spain to Paris and back. Dominic is often portrayed with the star of revelation over his head.

Fra Bartolomeo—*St. Thomas Aquinas (San Tommaso d'Aquino)*

St. Thomas Aquinas (c. 1225–1274), the intellectual giant of the U. of Paris, used logic and Aristotelian models to defend and explain

Christianity (building the hierarchical belief system known as Scholasticism). He's often shown with a heavy build and the sun of knowledge burning in his chest.

Fra Bartolomeo—*Portrait of Savonarola* (*Ritratto di Fra Girolamo Savonarola*)

This is the famous portrait—in profile, hooded, with big nose and clear eyes, gazing intently into the darkness—of the man reviled as the evil opponent of Renaissance goodness. Would it surprise you to learn that it was Savonarola who inspired Fra Bartolomeo's art? Bartolomeo was so moved by Savonarola's sermons that he burned his early nude paintings (and back issues of *Penthouse*), became a monk, gave up painting for a few years...then resurfaced to paint the simple, sweet frescoes we see here.

• *Leaving the world of Fra Bartolomeo, return to the courtyard and continue to the next room (Capitolo), which contains the large wall fresco...*

Fra Angelico—*Crucifixion with Saints* (*Crocifissione dell'Angelico*)

Shortly after the Fiesole monks moved into their new digs here (c. 1440), Fra Angelico began decorating the walls with frescoes. This

crucifixion, against a bleak background, is one of more than 20 versions in the monastery of Christ's torture/execution. It was in this room that naughty monks were examined and judged.

Among the group of hermits, martyrs, and religious extremists who surround the cross, locate Dominic (kneeling at the foot of the cross, in Dominican white robe, blue cape, and tonsured hair, with star on head), Peter the Martyr (kneeling in right corner, with bloody head), and Thomas Aquinas (standing behind Peter, with jowls and sun on chest).

The bell in the room is the original church bell, the one that rang a warning to Savonarola the night he was arrested. (The mob was so enraged that they exiled the bell for 10 years.)

• *Return to the courtyard and head upstairs to the first floor.*

FIRST FLOOR

Notice the general lay of the monastic land here (see map). This floor is lined with the cells (bedrooms) of those who lived in the monastery. Each room was frescoed by Fra Angelico or his assistants. The building has three wings: for the novice monks (way around on the left), for more senior monks (to the immediate left), and for lay support people (to the right). As you head down the halls, you'll see that each cell has a fresco of a crucifix and St. Dominic, but each shows Dominic in a different position. (There was even a book explaining how different gestures heighten the various states of worship.)

Novice monks—those in their first year of study—hadn't yet taken their lifelong vows. The frescoes decorating their cells were simple, as appropriate for beginners. Cells of the clerics befitted more learned theologians—those who had taken permanent vows. Their cells have complex religious imagery for meditation. In monastic life, everything is a form of prayer, from the Fra Angelico paintings to eating to posture. Pondering these scenes, monks trained in the physical posture of worship: humility, adoration, flagellation, reflection, and so on. The laymen's wing (to the right of the welcoming Annunciation fresco) is where the janitors, cooks, gardeners, and support staff slept. This art is narrative; it's less demanding intellectually, with sparser symbolism. (There are even names written on the halos.) At the end of the left wing is Savonarola's cell.

• *Now study the fresco (pictured on page 117) that greets everyone at the top of the stairs...*

Fra Angelico—*The Annunciation*

Monks gathered in this corner for common prayers, contemplating Christ's life from beginning *(The Annunciation)* to end (the *Crucifixion with St. Dominic,* over your shoulder).

The angel Gabriel is the light (accentuated by light coming in from the real window and the glitter mixed into the fresco). Sway back and forth and watch the angel's wings sparkle as he brings "the good news" to the very humble and accepting virgin. Mary is under an arcade remarkably similar to the one in the monastery courtyard. Fra Angelico literally brings this scene home to the monks. It was paintings such as this that made Fra Angelico so famous that the pope would call him to paint the Vatican. Yet this, like the other frescoes here, was meant only for the private eyes of humble monks. The caption reads: Remember to say your Hail Marys.

Museum of San Marco—First Floor

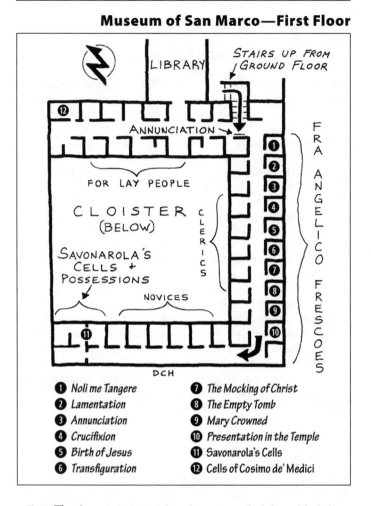

STAIRS UP FROM GROUND FLOOR

LIBRARY

ANNUNCIATION →

FOR LAY PEOPLE

CLOISTER (BELOW)

SAVONAROLA'S CELLS + POSSESSIONS

CLERICS

NOVICES

DCH

FRA ANGELICO FRESCOES

❶ Noli me Tangere
❷ Lamentation
❸ Annunciation
❹ Crucifixion
❺ Birth of Jesus
❻ Transfiguration
❼ The Mocking of Christ
❽ The Empty Tomb
❾ Mary Crowned
❿ Presentation in the Temple
⓫ Savonarola's Cells
⓬ Cells of Cosimo de' Medici

• *From* The Annunciation, *take a few steps to the left, and look down the (east) corridor lined with cells.*

Fra Angelico's Frescoes (in monks' cells of the east corridor)

After a long day of prayer, meditation, reading, frugal meals, chopping wood, hauling water, translating Greek, attending Mass, and more prayer—a monk retired to one of these small, bare, lamplit rooms. His "late-night TV" was programmed by the prior—Fra Angelico—in the form of a fresco to meditate on before sleep.

All in all, 43 cells were decorated in the early 1440s under Fra Angelico's direction, but many were executed by assistants. Some of Fra Angelico's best work is found in the 10 cells along the left-hand side.

Cell ❶—Noli me Tangere (the first of 10 rooms on the left-hand side of the corridor): The resurrected Jesus, appearing as a hoe-carrying gardener, says, "Don't touch me" and gingerly sidesteps Mary Magdalene's grasp. The flowers and trees represent the blossoming of new life, and they're about the last we'll see. Most scenes have stark, bare backgrounds, to concentrate the monk's focus on just the essential subject.

Cell ❷—Lamentation: Christ and mourners are a reverse image of the Lamentation downstairs. Christ levitates, not really supported by the ladies' laps. The colors are muted grays, browns, and pinks. Dominic (star on head) stands contemplating, just as the monk should do by mentally transporting himself to the scene.

Cell ❸—Annunciation: The painting's arches echo the room's real arch. (And they, in turn, harmoniously "frame" the "arch" of Mary and the angel bending toward each other to talk.) Peter the Martyr (bloody head) looks on.

You can't call these cells a wrap until you've found at least six crosses, three Dominics, three Peters, and a Thomas Aquinas. Ready, go.

Cell ❹—Crucifixion: That's one. And another Dominic.

Cell ❺—Birth of Jesus: And there's your second Peter.

Cell ❻—Transfiguration: Forsaking Renaissance realism, Fra Angelico emphasizes the miraculous. In an aura of blinding light, Christ spreads his arms cross-like, dazzling the three witnesses at the bottom of the "mountain." He's joined by disembodied heads of prophets, all spinning in a circle echoed by the room's arch.

Cell ❼—*The Mocking of Christ:*
From Renaissance realism to Dalí surrealism. Dominic, while reading the Passion, conjures an image of Christ—the true king, on a throne with globe and scepter—now blindfolded, spit upon, slapped, and clubbed by...a painting of medieval symbols of torment. This must have been a puzzling riddle from the Master to a novice monk.

Cell ❽—*The Empty Tomb:* The worried women are reassured by an angel that "He is risen." Jesus, far away in the clouds, seems annoyed that they didn't listen to him.

Cell ❾—*Mary Crowned:* ...triumphantly in Heaven, while Dominic, Peter, Aquinas, Francis, and others prepare to celebrate with high-fives.

Cell ❿—*Presentation in the Temple:* Baby Jesus is swaddled like a mummy. And there's your final Peter.
• *Continue around the bend—Savonarola's three rooms are at the far end of the corridor. Stop at the last room on the right in the corridor.*

Girolamo Savonarola (1452–1498)—His Rooms and Possessions (Celle del Savonarola)

⓫—Savonarola's Cells
You'll find a number of Savonarola's possessions scattered about this room and the adjacent cluster of three rooms, his living quarters. Browse around while reading about his life.

Last Room in the Corridor
The room displays Savonarola's **blue cloak** and personal **crucifix.** Home-schooled by his Scholastic grandfather, the 22-year-old had his life changed by hearing a sermon on repentance. He traded his scholar's robes for the blue cloak of a simple Dominican monk. He quickly became known for his asceticism, devotion, and knowledge of the Bible.
• *Now enter the Celle del Savonarola.*

First Room of Savonarola's Living Quarters

The **portrait bust** shows the hooded monk whose personal charisma and prophetic fervor led him from humble scholar to
celebrity preacher to prior of San Marco to leader of Florence to
controversial martyrdom. The **relief** under the portrait bust shows
Savonarola at his greatest moment. He stands before the Florence
city council and pledges allegiance to Florence's constitution,
assuming control of the city after the exile of the Medici (1494).
Reviled as a fanatical, regressive tyrant and praised as a saint,
reformer, and champion of democracy, Savonarola was a complex
man in turbulent times.

Various **paintings** depict Savonarola in action, including one
by Federico Andreotti showing the powerful monk reproaching
two troublemakers in his study.

• *The next room is...*

Savonarola's Study (Studiolo)

Seated at this **desk,** in his ecclesiastical folding **chair (La sedia
del Savonarola),** Savonarola scoured his **Bible** for clues to solve
Florence's civic strife.

In 1482 at age 30, the monk had come to San Marco as a lec-
turer. He was bright, humble...and boring. Then, after experiencing divine revelations, he spiced his sermons with prophecies of
future events...which started coming true. His sermons on Ezekiel,
Amos, Exodus, and the Apocalypse predicted doom for the Medici
family. He made brazen references to the pope's embezzling and
stable of mistresses and preached hope for a glorious future after
city and church were cleansed.

Packed houses heard him rail against the "prostitute church...
the monster of abomination." Witnesses wrote that "the church
echoed with weeping and wailing," and afterward "everyone wan-
dered the city streets dazed and speechless." From this humble
desk, he corresponded with the worldly pope, the humanist Pico
della Mirandola, and fans, such as Lorenzo the Magnificent, who
begrudgingly admired his courage.

Lorenzo died, the bankrupt Medicis were exiled, and
Florence was invaded by France...as Savonarola had prophesied. In
the power vacuum, Savonarola was seen as a moderate voice who
championed a return to Florence's traditional constitution. He was
made head of a Christian commonwealth.

Room with Savonarola's Possessions
(Le Reliquie di Savonarola)

Savonarola's personal moral authority was unquestioned, as his
simple **wool clothes** and **rosary** attest.

At first, his rule was just. He cut taxes, reduced street crime, shifted power from rich Medicis to citizens, and even boldly proposed banning Vespas from tourist zones.

However, Savonarola had an uncompromising and fanatical side, as his **hair-shirt girdle** attests. His government passed strict morality laws against swearing, blasphemy, gambling, and ostentatious clothes, which were enforced by gangs of thuggish teenagers. At the height of the Christian Republic, during Lent of 1497, followers built a huge "bonfire of vanities" on the Piazza della Signoria where they threw wigs, carnival masks, dice, playing cards, musical instruments, and discredited books and paintings.

In 1498 several forces undermined Savonarola's Republic: scheming Medicis, crop failure, rival cities, a pissed-off pope threatening excommunication for Savonarola and political isolation for Florence, and a public tiring of puritanism. Gangs of opponents (called Arrabbiati, "Rabid Dogs") battled Savonarola's supporters (the "Weepers"). Meanwhile, Savonarola was slowly easing out of public life, refusing to embroil the church in a lengthy trial, retiring to his routine of study, prayer, and personal austerity.

During Lent, a Franciscan monk challenged a Dominican to a public ordeal by fire to prove Savonarola right or wrong. (The righteous one would supposedly survive.) The Franciscan chickened out, but a bloodthirsty mob—with the blessing of city leaders and the pope—marched on San Marco to arrest Savonarola. Arrabbiati fought monks with clubs (imagine it in the **courtyard** out the window), while the church bells clanged and the monks shouted, *"Salvum fac populum tuum, Domine!"* ("Save thy people, Lord!"). The Arrabbiati stormed up the stairs to this floor, and Savonarola was handed over to the authorities in the library doorway (back near Fra Angelico's *Annunciation,* where you can also see the appropriate *Kiss of Judas* fresco in the cell nearby). He was taken to Palazzo Vecchio, tortured, tried, and sentenced.

On May 23, 1498 (see the **painting** *Suplizio del Savonarola in Piazza della Signoria*), before a huge crowd in the square in front

of the Palazzo Vecchio (where today there's a memorial plaque embedded in the pavement in front of the Neptune fountain), Savonarola was publicly defrocked, then publicly forgiven by a papal emissary. Then he was hanged—not American execution-style, where the neck snaps, but slowly strangled, dangling from a rope, while  teenage boys hooted and threw rocks.

The crowd looked on the lifeless body of this man who had once captivated their minds, as they lit a pyre under the scaffold—see the **stick** *(palo)* from the fire. The flames rose up, engulfing the body, when suddenly...his arm shot upward!—like a final blessing or curse—and the terrified crowd stampeded, killing several. His ashes were thrown in the Arno.

The Rest of the Museum

The corridor near Fra Angelico's *Annunciation* has the Library, with music and other manuscripts. In a cell across the hall is Fra Angelico's *Kiss of Judas* fresco. At the end of the corridor (right side) are the Cells of Cosimo de' Medici (**⓬**), the founder of the Medici ruling dynasty and builder of this monastery. Inside, the painting of the Magi includes a kneeling Magus kissing the baby's feet—a portrait of Cosimo.

• *To exit, return to the stairway and descend. Take a right at the bottom into a bookshop decorated with a fine Ghirlandaio* Last Supper *fresco (are you as tired as John is?), then through corridors filled with a hodgepodge of architectural fragments and on to the exit. On the street, turn right, then right again, and you'll see the Duomo.*

DUOMO MUSEUM TOUR

(Museo dell'Opera del Duomo)

Brunelleschi's dome, Ghiberti's bronze doors, and Donatello's statues—these creations define the 1400s (the "Quattrocento") in Florence, when the city blossomed and classical arts were reborn. All are featured at the Duomo Museum, plus a Michelangelo *Pietà* intended as his sculptural epitaph. While copies now decorate the exteriors of the cathedral, Baptistery, and bell tower, the original sculptured masterpieces of the complex are now restored and displayed safely indoors, filling the Duomo Museum. This recently refurbished museum is a delight, though it's overlooked by most visitors to Florence. There's never a line.

ORIENTATION

Cost: €6.

Hours: Mon–Sat 9:00–19:30, Sun 9:00–13:40, last entry 40 minutes before closing, closed on holidays. Note that this is one of the few museums in Florence open on Monday.

Getting There: The museum is across the street from the Duomo on the east side, at Via del Proconsolo 9.

Information: Tel. 055-230-2885. If you find all this church art intriguing, look through the open doorway of the Duomo art studio, which has been making and restoring church art since the days of Brunelleschi (a block toward the river from the Duomo at Via dello Studio 23a).

Length of This Tour: Allow 90 minutes.

Photography: Prohibited.

Starring: Brunelleschi, Ghiberti, Donatello, and Michelangelo.

THE TOUR BEGINS

Ghiberti's doors are on the ground floor, while Donatello's statues are on the first floor. The *Pietà* is on a landing halfway between floors.

GROUND FLOOR

The Medieval Cathedral

• *Browse the first few small rooms.*

Roman sarcophagi, Etruscan fragments, a chronological chart,

and broken **Baptistery statues** attest to the 2,000-year history of Florence's cathedral, Baptistery, and campanile (bell tower, called Giotto's Tower). The Baptistery was likely built on the site of a pagan Roman temple. It was flanked by a humble church that, by the 1200s, was not big enough to contain the exuberant spirit of a city growing rich from the wool trade and banking. In 1296, the cornerstone was laid for a huge church—today's cathedral, or Duomo—intended to be the biggest in Christendom.

• *The first large room (with a pope sitting at one end) is lined with statues from the original facade. On the long wall you'll find...*

Madonna with the Glass Eyes (Madonna col Bambino)

The church was dedicated to Mary—starry-eyed over the birth of baby Jesus. She sits, crowned like a chess-set queen, above the main door, framed with a dazzling mosaic halo. She's accompanied (to our right) by St. Zenobius,

Florence's first bishop during Roman times, whose raised hand consecrates the former pagan ground as Christian.

This room displays the statues that sat in niches on the original facade (1296–1587), designed by the church's architect, Arnolfo di Cambio. Had it been completed, the three-story facade would have looked much like today's colorful, neo-Gothic version, with pointed arches and white, pink, and green marble, studded with statues and gleaming with gold mosaics.

Duomo Museum—Ground Floor

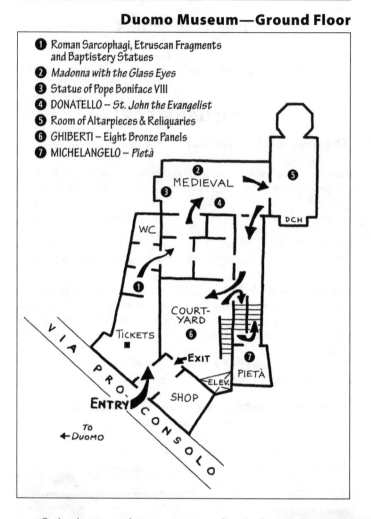

1. Roman Sarcophagi, Etruscan Fragments and Baptistery Statues
2. *Madonna with the Glass Eyes*
3. Statue of Pope Boniface VIII
4. DONATELLO – *St. John the Evangelist*
5. Room of Altarpieces & Reliquaries
6. GHIBERTI – Eight Bronze Panels
7. MICHELANGELO – *Pietà*

MEDIEVAL

WC

DCH

COURT-YARD

TICKETS

EXIT

ELEV.

PIETÀ

SHOP

ENTRY

VIA PRO CONSOLO

TO ← DUOMO

Only the ground story was ever finished, the work stalled by the plague, stylistic debates, and the construction of the cathedral itself. The upper two-thirds remained bare, brown brick all through medieval and Renaissance times, until 1587, when the still-incomplete facade was torn down.

Large, Seated Statue of Pope Boniface VIII

Despised by Dante for meddling in politics, this pope paid 3,000 florins to get his image in a box seat on the facade. His XL shirt size made him

look correct when viewed from below. Though the statue is styl-
ized, Arnolfo di Cambio realistically shows the pope's custom-
made, extra-tall hat and bony face. (Most of the room's statues are
straight-backed to hang on the facade.)

• *On the long wall opposite the Madonna, find...*

Donatello—*St. John the Evangelist (San Giovanni Evangelista)*

A hundred years later, di Cambio's medieval facade became a
showcase for Renaissance sculptors.

John sits gazing at a distant horizon,
his tall head rising high above his massive
body. This visionary foresees a new age...
and the coming Renaissance. The right
hand is massive—as relaxed as though it
were dangling over the back of a chair, but
full of powerful tension. With the mighty
right hand of Michelangelo's *David,* and
the beard of Michelangelo's *Moses,* this
work is a hundred years ahead of its time.

At 22 years old, Donatello (c. 1386–
1466) sculpted this just before becoming a
celebrity for his inspiring statue of *St. George* (original in Bargello,
copy on the exterior of the Orsanmichele Church). Donatello, like
most early Renaissance artists, was a blue-collar worker, raised as
a workshop apprentice among knuckle-dragging musclemen. He
proudly combined physical skill with technical know-how to create beauty (Art + Science = Renaissance Beauty). His statues are
thinkers with big hands who can put theory into practice.

• *Up a few steps at the end of the room is a...*

Room of Altarpieces and Reliquaries

These medieval altarpieces, which once adorned chapels and
altars inside the Duomo, show saints and angels suspended in a

gold never-never land. In the adjoining room,
the ornate reliquaries hold bones and objects
of the saints (Peter's chains, Jerome's jawbone,
and so on), many bought from a single, slick
14th-century con artist preying on medieval
superstition.

In the 1400s, tastes changed, and these
symbols of crude medievalism were purged
from the Duomo and stacked in storage. Soon
artists replaced the golden heavenly scenes
with flesh-and-blood humans who inhabited
the physical world of rocks, trees, and sky...the
Renaissance.

• *In the ground-floor courtyard, you'll find...*

Ghiberti—Eight Bronze Panels from the Baptistery Doors Called the "Gates of Paradise" (1425–1452)

The Renaissance began in 1401 with a citywide competition to build new doors for the Baptistery. Lorenzo Ghiberti (c. 1378–1455) won the job and built the doors (now on the Baptistery's north side), which everyone loved. He then was hired to make another set of doors—these panels—for the main entrance facing the Duomo. These Gates of Paradise revolutionized the way Renaissance people saw the world around them.

Of the 10 panels from the Gates of Paradise, the museum displays eight, as the rest are still being cleaned. (Copies now adorn the Baptistery itself.) Restoration is difficult, because the corrosive oxides gather inside, between the bronze panel and gilding. (Even these cleaned panels are pitted and blotched.) The panels are under glass to protect against natural light, and gassed with nitrogen against oxygen and humidity.

Joseph (Storie di Giuseppe e Beniamino)

With just the depth of a thumbnail, Ghiberti creates a temple in the round inhabited by workers. This round temple wowed Florence. Armed with the rules of perspective, Ghiberti rendered reality with a mathematical precision we don't normally notice in everyday life, when our eyes and mind settle for ballpark estimates. For Florentines, suddenly the world acquired a whole new dimension—depth.

Adam and Eve (La Creazione e Storie di Adamo ed Eva)

Ghiberti tells several stories in one panel—a common medieval technique—using different thickness in the relief. In the sketchy background (very low relief), God in a bubble conducts the Creation. In the center (a little thicker), Eve springs from Adam's side. Finally, in the lower left (in high relief), an elegantly robed

God pulls Adam, as naked as the day he was born, from the mud.

Ghiberti welcomed the innovations of other artists. See the angel flying through an arch (right side). This arch is in very low relief but still looks fully 3-D because it's rendered sideways, using painters'-perspective tricks—a relief technique Ghiberti learned from one of his employees, the young Donatello.

Jacob and Esau (Storie di Giacobbe ed Esau)

The "background" arches and the space they create are as interesting as the scenes themselves. At the center is the "vanishing

point" on the distant horizon, where all the arches and floor tiles converge. This calm center gives us an eye-level reference point for all the figures. Those closest to us are big, clearly defined, and at the bottom of the panel. Distant figures are smaller, fuzzier, and higher up.

Ghiberti has placed us about 20 feet away from the scene, part of this casual crowd of holy people—some with their backs to us—milling around an arcade.

Labors of Adam, and Cain and Abel
(Il lavoro dei progenitori e Storie di Caino e Abele)

On one mountain, we see Cain and Abel offering a sacrifice at the top, Adam waving at the bottom, and the first murder in between. In early panels such as this one, Ghiberti used only a sketchy landscape as a backdrop for human activities.

Ghiberti, the illegitimate son of a goldsmith, labored all his working life (over 50 years) on the two Baptistery doors. These were major manufacturing jobs, employing a large workshop of artists and artisans for each stage of the process: making the door frames that hold the panels, designing and making models of the panels (forming them in wax in order to cast them in bronze), gilding the panels (by bathing them in powdered gold dissolved in mercury, then heating until the gold and bronze blended), polishing the panels, mounting them, installing the doors...and signing paychecks for everyone along the way. Ghiberti was as much businessman as artist.

Solomon and the Queen of Sheba

The receding arches stretch into infinity, giving the airy feeling that we could see forever. All of the arches and stair steps con-

verge at the center of the panel, where the two monarchs meet, uniting their respective peoples. Ghiberti's subject was likely influenced by the warm ecumenical breeze blowing through Florence in 1439, as religious leaders convened here in an attempt to reunite the eastern (Constantinople) and western (Rome) realms of Christendom.

If the Renaissance began in 1401 with Ghiberti's doors, it ended in 1555 with Michelangelo's *Pietà*.

• *In the courtyard are two staircases almost side by side. Ascend the old (not new) staircase to the first landing.*

Michelangelo—*Pietà* (1547–1555)

Aging Michelangelo (1475–1564) was designing his own tomb, with this as the centerpiece. He was depressed by old age, the recent death of his soul mate, and the grim reality that by sculpting this statue he was writing his own obituary. It was done without a commission. As Michelangelo envisioned this for his own tomb, it's fair to consider it an introspective and very personal work.

Three mourners tend the broken body of the crucified Christ. We see Mary, his mother (the shadowy figure on our right); Mary

Magdalene (on the left, polished up by a pupil); and Nicodemus, the converted Pharisee, whose face is clearly that of Michelangelo himself. The polished body of Christ stands out from the unfinished background. Michelangelo (as Nicodemus), who spent a lifetime bringing statues to life by "freeing" them from the stone, looks down at what could be his final creation, the once-perfect body of Renaissance Man that is now twisted, disfigured, and dead.

Seen face-on, the four figures form a powerful geometric shape of a circle inside a triangle, split down the middle by Christ's massive, but very dead, arm. Seen from the right side, they seem to interact with each other, their sketchy faces changing emotions from grief to melancholy to peaceful acceptance.

Fifty years earlier, a confident Michelangelo had worked here on these very premises, skillfully carving *David* from an imperfect block. But he hated this marble for the *Pietà*; it was hard and grainy and gave off sparks when hit wrong. (The chisel grooves in the base remind us of the sheer physical effort of a senior citizen sculpting.) Worst of all, his housekeeper kept bugging him with the same question that Pope Julius II used to ask about the Sistine Chapel—"When will you finish?" Pushed to the edge, Michelangelo grabbed a hammer and attacked the statue, hacking away and breaking off limbs, then turned to the servant and said, "There! It's finished!" (An assistant later repaired some of the damage, but cracks are still visible in Christ's left arm and only leg.)

• *Continue upstairs to the first floor, entering a large room lined with statues and two balconies. Donatello's four prophets are at the far end.*

FIRST FLOOR

Room of the Cantorie (Le Cantorie)— Donatello's Prophets

The room displays the original 16 statues (by several sculptors) that ring the bell tower's third story (where copies stand today). Donatello did five of them, plus some others in collaboration.

Donatello ("Little Donato") invented the Renaissance style that Michelangelo would later perfect—powerful statues that are ultra-realistic, even ugly, sculpted in an "unfinished" style by an artist known for experimentation and his prickly, brooding personality. Both men were famous but lived like peasants, married only to their work.

Donatello—*Habakkuk (Abacuc)*

Donatello's signature piece shows us the wiry man beneath the heavy mantle of a prophet. His rumpled cloak falls down the front,

dividing the body lengthwise. From the deep furrows emerges a bare arm with well-defined tendons and that powerful right hand. His long, muscled neck leads to a bald, pumpkin-like head (the Italians call the statue *Lo Zuccone*).

The ugly face, with several days' growth of beard, crossed eyes, and tongue-tied mouth, looks crazed. This is no confident Charlton Heston prophet, but a man who's spent too much time alone, fasting in the wilderness, searching for his calling, and who now returns to babble his vision on a street corner.

Duomo Museum—First Floor

- **⑧ DONATELLO** – *Habakkuk* and *Jeremiah*
- **⑨ PISANO** – *Four Prophets*
- **⑩ DELLA ROBBIA** – *Cantoria*
- **⑪** "Lamb of God" Panel
- **⑫ DONATELLO** – *Cantoria*
- **⑬ DONATELLO** – *Mary Magdalene*
- **⑭** Medieval Crucifix
- **⑮** John the Baptist's Finger
- **⑯ PISANO (& Others)** – *The Campanile Panels*
- **⑰ BRUNELLESCHI** – Dome Model, Scaffolding, Tools & Death Mask
- **⑱** Wooden Balcony Models
- **⑲** Facade Models
- **⑳** Laying of 1860 Facade
- **㉑** Emilio de Fabris & Designs

COURT-
YARD
(BELOW)

PIETÀ

ELEV.

VIA PROCONSOLO

TO
←DUOMO

PCH

Donatello, the eccentric prophet of a new style, identified with this statue, talking to it, swearing at it, yelling at it: "Speak!"
• *Nearby, look for...*

Donatello—*Jeremiah (Geremia)*

Watching Jerusalem burn in the distance, the ignored prophet reflects on why the Israelites wouldn't listen to his warning. He purses his lips bitterly, and his downturned mouth is accentuated by his plunging neck muscle and sagging shoulders. The folds in

the clothes are very deep, suggesting the anger, sorrow, and disgust that Jeremiah feels but cannot share, as it is too late.

Movement, realism, and human drama were Donatello's great contributions to sculpture.
• *Along the long, left-hand wall are four dark-stained statues.*

Andrea and Nino Pisano's *Four Prophets*

Pisano's prophets are elegant but smaller and two-dimensional, with flat backs to stand obediently in their niches. The faces are generic and calm. Little wonder that these stuffy prophets were replaced on the bell tower by Donatello's younger and more energetic *Habakkuk* and *Jeremiah*.
• *The two balconies in Room 12 are two* cantorie—*Donatello's on the right (from the entrance), della Robbia's on the left. Della Robbia's is a reconstruction from casts, with the original 10 panels below.*

Luca della Robbia—*Cantoria* (1431–1438)

After almost 150 years of construction, the cathedral was nearly done, and they began preparing the interior for the celebration.

Brunelleschi hired a little-known sculptor, 30-year-old Luca della Robbia, to make this choir box—a balcony for singers next to the organ in the cathedral—and it summed up the exuberance of the Quattrocento. The panels are a celebration of music, song, and dance performed by toddlers, children, and teenagers.

The *cantoria* brings Psalm 150 to life like an MTV video. Latin speakers can read the text, while the rest can follow along with the pictures. Start in the upper left:

"Praise the Lord," *(Laudate D.N.M.)* reads the banner along the top. "Praise him in his holy place, in the firmament *(Firmamento)* for his mighty deeds *(Virtu)* and greatness *(Magnitudinus)*." Then come the panels:

1. (Upper left panel): Teenagers laugh and dance to the sound of trumpets, as the text reads "Praise with the sound of trumpets" *(sono Tubae)*.

2. and 3. Babysitters put down infants and pick up guitars and autoharps ("Praise him with psalter and zither," *Psaltero et Cythera*).

4. "... Praise him with tambourines..." *(Timpano)*

5. "...and dancing" *(Choro)*. Seven kids dance ring-around-the-rosy as della Robbia sculpts a scene in the round on an almost-flat surface, showing front, back, and in-between poses.

6. "...with pipes and strings" *(Organo)*. A child Apollo pumps a hand organ.

7. "...and with jubilant cymbals" *(Cimbales)*. The kids make a joyful racket. "Everybody praise the Lord!"

Della Robbia's choir box was a triumph, a celebration of Florence's youthful boom time. Perhaps sensing he could never top it, the young sculptor hung up his hammer and chisel and concentrated on the colorful glazed terra-cotta for which he's best known. (Find the **round "Lamb of God" panel** over your left shoulder, above a doorway nearby, by Luca's nephew, who took over the workshop.)

Donatello—*Cantoria*

If della Robbia's balcony looks like afternoon recess, Donatello's looks like an all-night rave. Donatello's figures are sketchier, murky, and filled with frenetic activity, as the dancing kids hurl themselves around the balcony. Imagine candles lighting this as they seem to come to life. If the dance feels almost pagan, there's a reason.

Recently returned from a trip to Rome, Donatello carved in the style of classical friezes of dancing *putti* (chubby, playful toddlers). This choir box stood in a dark area of the Duomo, so Donatello chose colorful mosaics and marbles to catch the eye, while purposely leaving the dancers unfinished and shadowy, tangled figures flitting inside the columns. In the dim light, worshippers swore they saw them move.

• *Enter an adjoining room to the left of the entrance to see bishops' robes, a half-ton silver altarpiece, and...*

Donatello—*Mary Magdalene (Maddalena)*

Carved out of white poplar, originally painted with realistic colors (like the **medieval crucifix** displayed nearby), this statue is less

a Renaissance work of beauty than a medieval object of intense devotion.

Mary Magdalene—the legendary prostitute rescued from the streets by Jesus—folds her hands in humble prayer. Her once-beautiful face and body have been scarred by the fires of her own remorse, fasting, and repentance. The matted hair sticks to her face; veins and tendons line the anorexic arms and neck. The rippling hair suggests emotional turmoil within. But from her hollow, tired eyes, a new beauty shines, an enlightened soul that doesn't rely on the external beauty of human flesh.

The man who helped re-birth the classical style now shocked Florence by turning his back on it. Picking up a knife, he experimented in the difficult medium of wood carving, where subtlety can get lost when the wood splits off in larger-than-wanted slivers.

Sixty-five-year-old Donatello had just returned to Florence, after years away. His city had changed. Friends were dying (Brunelleschi died before they could reconcile after a bitter fight), favorite pubs were overrun with frat boys, and Florence was gaga over Greek gods in pretty, gleaming marble. Donatello fell into a five-year funk, completing only two statues, including this one.

• *In the display case to the left of* Mary, *you'll find...*

John the Baptist's Finger in a Reliquary *(Artista fiorentino: Reliquario di un osso di dito di S. Giovanni Battista)*

The severed index finger of the beheaded prophet is the most revered relic of all the holy body parts in this museum.

• *Pass back through the large room of the* cantorie *and into the next room. Work clockwise from the entrance.*

Andrea Pisano (and others)—
The Campanile Panels
(c. 1334–1359)

These 28 hexagonal and 28 diamond-shaped, blue-glazed panels decorated Giotto's Tower, seven per side (where copies stand today). The original design scheme was perhaps Giotto's, but most were executed by his successor, Andrea Pisano, and assistants.

The panels celebrate technology, showing workers, inventors,

Pop. 100,000... but Still a Small Town

Ghiberti won the bronze-door competition. Brunelleschi lost and took teenage Donatello with him to Rome. Donatello returned to join Ghiberti's workshop. Ghiberti helped Brunelleschi with dome plans. Brunelleschi, Donatello, and Luca della Robbia collaborated on the Pazzi Chapel. And so on, and so on.

---

and thinkers. Allegorically, they depict man's long march to "civilization"—a blend of art and science, brain and brawn. But realistically, they're snapshots of that industrious generation that helped Florence bounce back ferociously from the Black Death of 1348.

The lower, **hexagonal panels** (reading clockwise from the entrance) show God starting the chain of creation by inventing (1) man and (2) woman, then (3) Adam and Eve continuing the work, (4) Jabal learning to domesticate sheep, (5) Jubal blowing a horn, inventing music...

• *Continuing along the next wall...*

(6) Tubalcain the blacksmith, and (7) Noah inventing wine and Miller Time. (8) An astronomer sights along a quadrant to chart the heavens and the (round, tilted-on-axis, pre-Columbian) earth, (9) a master builder supervises his little apprentices building a brick wall, (10) a doctor holds a flask of urine to the light for analysis, etc.

• *On the fourth wall, check out...*

(20) The invention of sculpture, as a man chisels a figure to life.

The upper **diamond-shaped panels,** of marble on blue majolica (tin-glazed pottery tinged blue with copper sulfate), add religion (sacraments and virtues) to the civilization equation.

• *Enter the next, narrow room to find tools, scaffolding, and, at the end of the corridor, a wooden model of the cathedral dome's lantern.*

Brunelleschi's Dome—
Model of the Lantern
(Cupola di S. Maria del Fiore)

Brunelleschi's dome (look at this model of the dome, or out the window at the real thing) put mathematics in stone, a feat of engineering that was functional and beautiful. It rises 330 feet from the ground, with eight white, pointed-arch ribs, filled in with red brick and capped with a "lantern" to hold it all in place.

The dome had to cover a gaping 140-foot hole in the roof of the church (a drag on rainy Sundays), a hole too wide to be spanned by the wooden scaffolding traditionally used to support a dome while it was being built. (An earlier architect suggested supporting the dome with a great mound of dirt inside the church...filled with coins, so peasants would later cart it away for free.) In addition, the eight-sided "drum" that the dome was to rest on was too  weak to support a heavy dome, and there were no side buildings on the church on which to attach Gothic-style buttresses.

The solution was a dome within a dome, leaving a hollow space between to make it lighter. And the dome had to be self-supporting, both while being built and when finished, so as not to require buttresses.

Brunelleschi used wooden models such as these to demonstrate his ideas to skeptical approval committees.

• *In the display cases are scaffolding and tools.*

Scaffolding

Although no scaffolding supported the dome, they needed exterior scaffolding for the stone and brick masons. The support timbers were stuck into postholes in the drum (some are visible on the church today).

The dome rose in rings. First, they'd stack a few blocks of white marble to create part of the ribs, then connect the ribs with horizontal crosspieces, then fill in the space with red brick in a herringbone pattern. When the ring was complete and self-supporting, they'd move the scaffolding up and do another section.

Tools

The dome weighs 80 million pounds—as much as the entire population of Florence—so Brunelleschi had to design special tools and machines to lift and work all that stone. (The lantern alone—which caps the dome—is a marble building nearly as tall as the Baptistery.) You'll see sun-dried bricks, brick molds, rope, a tool belt, compasses, stone pincers, and various pulleys for lifting. Brunelleschi also designed a machine (not on display) where horses turned a shaft that reeled in rope, lifting heavy loads.

The dome was completed in 16 short years, capping 150 years of construction on the church. Brunelleschi enjoyed the dedication ceremonies, but he died before the lantern was completed. His legacy is a dome that stands as a proud symbol of man's ingenuity, proving that art and science can unite to make beauty.

• *Next to the lantern model, find...*

Brunelleschi's Death Mask *(Anonimo: Maschera funebre)*

Filippo Brunelleschi (1377–1446) was uniquely qualified to create the dome. Trained in sculpture, he gave it up in disgust after losing the Baptistery gig. In Rome, he visualized placing the Pantheon on top of the Duomo, and dissected its mathematics and engineering.

Back home, he astounded Florence with a super-realistic painting of the Baptistery, as seen from the Duomo's front steps. Florentines lined up to see the painting (now lost) displayed side by side with the real thing, marveling at the 3-D realism. (Brunelleschi's mathematics of linear perspective were later expanded and popularized by Alberti.)

In 1420 Brunelleschi was declared *capomaestro* of the dome project. He was a jack-of-all-trades and now master of all as well, overseeing every aspect of the dome, the lantern, and the machinery to build them. Despite all his planning, it's clear from documentary evidence that he was making it up as he went along, exuding confidence to workers and city officials while privately improvising.

• *In the next room, behind glass, you'll see...*

Two Wooden Models for the Duomo's Balcony

But the church wasn't done. Even today, there's bare brick on much of the drum at the base of the dome. In 1507, a competition was held to cover that brick with a marble balustrade. Baccio d'Agnolo won and covered part of the southeast section before others with better taste stopped him. (Look out the window to see the real McCoy.)

• *The next room deals with...*

Facade from the 16th to the 19th Centuries

In 1587, the medieval facade by di Cambio was considered hopelessly outdated and was torn down like so much old linoleum. But work on a replacement never got off the ground, and the front of the church sat bare for nearly 300 years while they debated proposal after proposal (like the models in this room) by many famous architects. Most versions champion the Renaissance style to match

Brunelleschi's dome, rather than Gothic to fit the church.
• *Enter the next room.*

Laying of the First Stone of the Facade in 1860
In the 1800s, the Romantic movement led to a renaissance of the Gothic style (so to speak). In 1860, a ceremonial first stone was laid—using the hammer and trowel displayed here—by King Vittorio Emmanuel II, the future leader of a newly unified modern Italy.
• *In the last room on this floor...*

The 19th-Century Facade
Emilio de Fabris (portrait) won the competition with a neo-Gothic facade that echoed the original work of di Cambio. The new-old facade was dedicated in 1887. Notice that even de Fabris changed designs as he went—the spikes along the roofline in some of the designs are not there today. For a clearer look at the proposals up high on the wall, head upstairs to the sparse third-floor landing.

Critics may charge that Fabris' facade is too retro, but it was the style of the church beloved by Ghiberti, Donatello, Brunelleschi, and the industrious citizens of Florence's Quattrocento, who saw it as Florence's finest art gallery.

MEDICI CHAPELS TOUR

(Cappelle Medicee)

The Medici (MED-ee-chee) Chapels contain tombs of Florence's great ruling family, from Lorenzo the Magnificent to those less so. The highlight is a chapel designed by Michelangelo at the height of his creative powers. This is the Renaissance Man's greatest "installation," a room completely under his artistic control, featuring innovative architecture, tombs, and sculpture. His statues are a middle-aged man's brooding meditation on mortality, the fall of the Medici Golden Age, and the relentless passage of time—from *Dawn* to *Day* to *Dusk* to *Night*.

ORIENTATION

Cost: €6.

Dress Code: No tank tops or short shorts or short skirts.

Hours: Daily 8:15–16:50 but closed the second and fourth Sun and the first, third, and fifth Mon of each month.

Getting There: It's in the Church of San Lorenzo—the one with the smaller dome on Florence's skyline (5-min walk northwest of Duomo). The bustling outdoor market almost obscures the chapel entrance at the back (west end) of the church. See page 36 for more about the Church of San Lorenzo and the open-air market.

Information: Tel. 055-238-8602.

Length of This Tour: Allow one hour.

Photography: Prohibited.

Starring: Michelangelo's statues *Day, Night, Dawn,* and *Dusk.*

THE TOUR BEGINS

Overview

The Medici Chapels consist of three burial places: the unimpressive Crypt, the large and gaudy Chapel of Princes, and—the highlight—Michelangelo's New Sacristy, a room completely designed by him, with architecture, tombs, and statues to honor four Medicis.

• *Enter the Chapel and buy tickets. Immediately after you show your ticket, you're in…*

The Crypt

This gloomy, low-ceilinged room with gravestones underfoot reminds us that these "chapels" are really tombs. You'll see lots of "Lorenzos" here (the family's patron saint)…but none that is "Magnificent" (he's later). The collection of ornate silver and gold reliquaries are appropriately macabre and worth a quick look.

• *Head upstairs via the staircase on the right into the large, domed, multicolored…*

Chapel of Princes (La Cappella dei Principi, 1602–1743)

The impressive **dome** overhead (seen from outside, it's the big, red-brick "mini-Duomo") tops an octagonal room that echoes the Baptistery and Duomo drum. It's lined with six tombs of Medici rulers. It's decorated everywhere with the **Medici coat of arms**—a shield with six balls representing the pills of doctors *(medici)*, their original occupation. Along with many different colored marbles, geologists will recognize jasper, porphyry, quartz, alabaster, coral, mother-of-pearl, and lapis lazuli.

Sixteen shields ring the room at eye level, the Tuscan cities ("Civitas") ruled by Florence's dukes. Find Florence, with its fleur-de-lis ("Florentiae"), and Pisa ("Pisarum"), both just left of the altar.

The bronze **statues** honor two of the "later" Medicis, the cultured but oppressive dukes who ruled Florence after the city's glorious Renaissance. Ferdinando I (ruled 1587–1609), in ermine cape and jewels, started the work on this Chapel of Princes and tore down the Duomo's medieval facade. His son, Cosimo II (ruled 1609–1621, to the right), appointed Galileo "first professor" of science at Pisa U., inspiring him to label the moons of Jupiter "the Medici Stars."

Apart from the **altar**, finished in 1939 for a visit from Hitler and Mussolini, there is no Christian symbolism in this spacious but stifling temple to power, wealth, and mediocre Medicis.

• *Continue down the hall, passing statues of Roman armor with worms sprouting out, to Michelangelo's New Sacristy.*

New Sacristy (Sagrestia Nuova)—Michelangelo

The entire room—architecture, tombs, and statues—was designed by Michelangelo over a 14-year period (1520–1534) to house the bodies of four of the Medici family. Michelangelo, who spent his teen years in the Medici household and personally knew three of the four buried here, was emotionally attached to the project. This is the work of a middle-aged man (age 45–59) reflecting on his contemporaries dying around him, and on his own mortality.

• *There are tombs decorated with statues against three of the walls, and an altar on the fourth. Start with the tomb on the left wall (as you enter and face the altar).*

Tomb of Lorenzo II, Duke of Urbino

Lorenzo II—the grandson of Lorenzo the Magnificent—is shown as a Roman general, seated, arm resting on a Medici-bank money box, and bowing his head in contemplation. He had been the model for Machiavelli's *The Prince,* and when he died without a male heir at 27 (of tuberculosis and syphilis), the line of great princes stretching back to Cosimo the Elder died with him.

His sarcophagus, with a curved, scrolled lid, bears the reclining statues that Michelangelo named *Dusk* and *Dawn.* **Dusk** (the man), worn out after a long day, slumps his chin on his chest and reflects on the day's events. **Dawn** (the woman) stirs restlessly after a long night, with an anguished face, as though waking from a bad dream. *Dusk* and *Dawn,* with their counterparts *Day* and *Night* (opposite wall), represented to Michelangelo the swift passage of time, which kills everyone and causes our glorious deeds on earth to quickly fade.

During the years he worked here, Michelangelo suffered the deaths of his father, his favorite brother, and his unofficial step-brother, Pope Leo X Medici. In addition, plagues in 1522 and 1527 killed thousands in Florence. In 1527 his adoptive city of Rome was looted by mercenaries. Michelangelo's letters reveal that, turning 50, he was feeling old, tired ("If I work one day, I need four to recuperate"), and depressed (he called it *mio pazzo,* "my madness"), facing the sad fact that the masterpiece of his youth—the grand tomb of Pope Julius II—was never going to be completed.

Overachievers in severe midlife crises may wish to avoid the Medici Chapels.

• *On the opposite wall...*

Tomb of Giuliano, Duke of Nemours

Overshadowed by his famous father (Lorenzo the Magnificent) and big brother (Pope Leo X), **Giuliano** led a wine-women-and-song life, dying young without a male heir. His statue as a Roman general, with scepter, powerful Moses-esque pose, and alert, intelligent face, looks in the direction of the Madonna statue, as though asking forgiveness for a wasted life. The likeness is not at all accurate. Michelangelo said, "In a thousand years, no one will know how they looked."

Giuliano's "active" pose complements the "contemplative" one of Lorenzo, showing the two elements (thought + action) that Plato and Michelangelo believed made up the soul of man.

Night (the woman) does a crossover sit-up in her sleep, toning the fleshy abs that look marvelously supple and waxlike,

The Medicis in a Minute and a Half

The Medici family—part *Sopranos,* part Kennedys, part John-D-and-Catherine-T art patrons—dominated Florentine politics for 300 years (c. 1434–1737). Originally a hardworking, middle-class family in the cloth, silk, and banking businesses, they used their wealth, blue-collar popularity, and philanthropy to rise into Europe's nobility, producing popes and queens.

1400s: The Princes
Lorenzo the Magnificent (ruled 1469–1492), Cosimo's grandson, epitomized the Medici ruling style: publicly praising Florence's constitution while privately holding the purse strings. A true Renaissance Man, Lorenzo's personal charisma, public festivals, and support of da Vinci, Botticelli, and teenage Michelangelo made Florence Europe's most enlightened city.

1494–1532: Exile in Rome
After Lorenzo's early death, the family was exiled by the Florentines. The Medicis became victims of bank failure, Savonarola's reforms, and the Florentine tradition of democracy. They built a power base in Rome under Lorenzo's son (Pope Leo X, who made forays into Florence) and nephew (Pope Clement VII, who finally invaded Florence and crushed the republic).

1537–1737: The Grand Duchy—Mediocre Medicis
Backed by Europe's popes and kings, the "later" Medicis—descendants of Cosimo the Elder's brother—ruled Florence and Tuscany as just another duchy. Politically repressive but generous patrons of the arts and sciences (the Uffizi, Pitti Palace, Cellini, Galileo), they married into Europe's royal families (Catherine and Marie de' Medici were queens of France) while Florence declined as a political and economic power.

not like hard stone. She's highly polished, shimmering, and finished with minute details. Michelangelo's females—musclemen with coconut-shell breasts—are generally more complete and (some think) less interesting than his men.

Theories abound that Michelangelo was homosexual. While his private sex life (or lack thereof) ultimately remains a mystery, his public expressions of affection were clearly weighted toward men. Some say he was less interested in female bodies and felt he could easily sum them up in a statue.

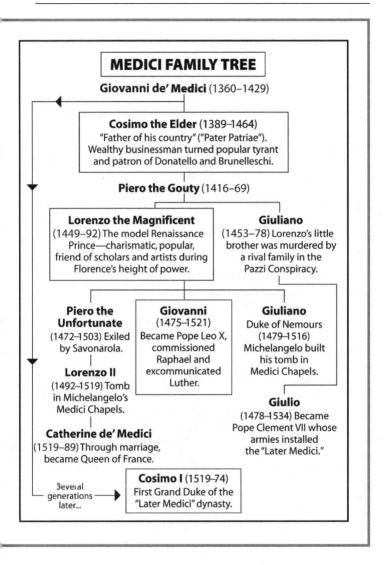

MEDICI FAMILY TREE

Giovanni de' Medici (1360–1429)

Cosimo the Elder (1389–1464)
"Father of his country" ("Pater Patriae").
Wealthy businessman turned popular tyrant
and patron of Donatello and Brunelleschi.

Piero the Gouty (1416–69)

Lorenzo the Magnificent
(1449–92) The model Renaissance
Prince—charismatic, popular,
friend of scholars and artists during
Florence's height of power.

Giuliano
(1453–78) Lorenzo's little
brother was murdered by
a rival family in the
Pazzi Conspiracy.

Piero the Unfortunate
(1472–1503) Exiled
by Savonarola.

Lorenzo II
(1492–1519) Tomb
in Michelangelo's
Medici Chapels.

Catherine de' Medici
(1519–89) Through marriage,
became Queen of France.

Giovanni
(1475–1521)
Became Pope Leo X,
commissioned
Raphael and
excommunicated
Luther.

Giuliano
Duke of Nemours
(1479–1516)
Michelangelo built
his tomb in
Medici Chapels.

Giulio
(1478–1534) Became
Pope Clement VII whose
armies installed
the "Later Medici."

Several
generations
later...

Cosimo I (1519–74)
First Grand Duke of the
"Later Medici" dynasty.

Day (the man) works out a crick in his back, each limb twisting a different direction, turning away from us. He looks over his shoulder with an expression (suspicious? angry? arrogant?) forever veiled behind chisel marks suggestive of Impressionist brush strokes. In fact, none of the four reclining statues' faces expresses a clear emotion, as all are turned inward, letting body language speak.

If, as some say, Michelangelo purposely left these statues "unfinished" while liberating them from their stone prison, it certainly adds mystery and a contrast in color and texture. *Night*'s moonlit clarity and *Day*'s rough-hewn grogginess may also reflect Michelangelo's own work schedule—a notorious day-sleeper and guilt-ridden layabout ("Dear to me is sleep") who, when inspired (as a friend wrote), "works much, eats little, and sleeps less."

Among *Night*'s symbols (the crescent moon on her forehead, owl under knee, and poppies underfoot) is a grotesque **mask** with, perhaps, a self-portrait. Michelangelo, a serious poet (so much so he almost considered sculpting his "day job"), has *Night* say in one of his poems: "As long as shame and sorrow exist/I'd rather not see or hear/So speak softly and let me sleep."

Day, *Night*, *Dawn*, and *Dusk*—brought to life in this room where Michelangelo had his workshop, and where they've been ever since—meditate eternally on Death, squirming restlessly, unable to come to terms with it.

• On *the entrance wall is the...*

Tomb of Lorenzo the Magnificent and his Brother Giuliano

As the tomb was never completed, all that really marks where The Magnificent One's body lies is the marble base that the Madonna and saints stand on. Perhaps Michelangelo was work-ing up to the grand finale to honor the man who not only was the greatest Medici but who also plucked a poor 13-year-old Michelangelo from an obscure apprenticeship to dine at the Medici table with cardinals and kings.

Lorenzo's beloved younger brother, Giuliano, died in 1478 in a "hit" by a rival family, stabbed to death before the altar of the Duomo during Easter Mass. (Lorenzo, wounded, drew his sword and backpedaled to safety. Enraged supporters grabbed the assassins—including two priests planted there by the pope—and literally tore them apart.)

The **Medici Madonna,** unlike many Michelangelo women, is thin, vertical, and elegant, her sad face veiled under chisel marks. She tolerates the squirming, two-year-old Jesus, who still seems to want to breast-feed, aware of the hard life her son has ahead of him. Mary's right foot is still buried in stone, so this unfin-ished statue was certainly meant to be worked on more. The saints **Cosmas** and **Damian** were done by assistants.

The Unfinished Project

The Chapel project (1520–1534) was plagued by delays: design changes, late shipments of Carrara marble, the death of patrons, Michelangelo's other obligations (including the Laurentian Library next door), his own depression, and...revolution.

In 1527, Florence rose up against the Medici pope and declared itself an independent republic. Michelangelo, torn between his love of Florence and loyalty to the Medicis of his youth, walked a fine line. He continued to work for the pope while simultaneously designing fortified city walls to defend Florence from the pope's troops. In 1530, the besieged city fell, republicans were rounded up and executed, and Michelangelo went into hiding (perhaps in the chapel basement, down the steps to the left of the altar). Fortunately, his status both as artist and staunch Florentine spared him from reprisals.

In 1534, a new pope enticed Michelangelo to come back to Rome with a challenging new project: painting the *Last Judgment* over the altar in the Sistine Chapel. Michelangelo left, never to return to the Medici Chapels. Assistants gathered up statues and fragments from the chapel floor (and the Madonna from Michelangelo's house) and did their best to assemble the pieces according to Michelangelo's designs.

• *The apse is the area behind the altar. This has the best view of the chapel as a whole.*

Sketches on the Walls of the Apse

Michelangelo's many design changes and improvisational style come to life in these (dimly lit and hard to see behind Plexiglas) black chalk and charcoal doodles, presumably by Michelangelo and assistants.

• *Starting on the left wall and working clockwise at about eye level...*

I think I saw hash marks counting off days worked, a window frame for the Laurentian Library, scribbles, a face, an arch, a bearded face, and (on the right wall) squares, a nude figure crouching in a doorway, a twisting female nude with her dog, and a tiny, wacky, cartoon Roman soldier with shield and spurs. You really do get a sense of Michelangelo and staff working, sweating, arguing, and just goofing off as the hammers pound and dust flies.

The Whole Ensemble—Michelangelo's Vision

The New Sacristy was the first chance for Michelangelo, the quintessential well-rounded Renaissance Man, to use his arsenal of talents—as sculptor, architect, and Thinker of Big Ideas—on a single, multimedia project. The resulting "installation" (a 20th-century term) produces a powerful overall effect that's different for everyone—"somber," "meditative," "redemptive," "ugly."

The room is a cube topped with a Pantheon-style dome, with three distinct stories—the heavy tombs at ground level, upper-level windows with simpler wall decoration, and the dome, better lit and simpler still. The whole effect draws the eye upward, from dark and "busy" to light and airy. (It's intensified by an optical illusion—Michelangelo made the dome's coffers, the upper windows, and round lunettes all taper imperceptibly at the top to make them look taller and higher.)

The white walls are lined in gray-brown-green stone. The half columns, arches, and triangular pediments are traditional Renaissance forms, but with no regard for the traditional "orders" of the time (matching the right capital with the right base, the correct width-to-height ratio of columns, upper story taller than lower, etc.). Michelangelo had Baroque-en the rules, baffling his contemporaries and pointing the way to a new, more-ornate style that used old forms as mere decoration.

Finally, Michelangelo, a serious neo-Platonist, wanted this room to symbolize the big philosophical questions that death presents to the survivors. Summing up these capital-letter concepts (far, far more crudely than was ever intended), the room might say:

Time (the four reclining statues) kills Mortal Men (statues of Lorenzo and Giuliano) and mocks their Glory (Roman power symbols). But if we Focus (Lorenzo and Giuliano's gaze) on God's Grace (Madonna and Child), our Souls (both Active and Contemplative parts) can be Resurrected (the Chapel was consecrated to this) and rise from this drab Earth (the dark, heavy ground floor) up into the Light (the windows and lantern) of Heaven (the geometrically perfect dome) where God and Plato's Ideas are forever Immortal.

And that, folks, is a Mouthful.

MEDICI-RICCARDI PALACE TOUR

Cosimo (the Elder) de' Medici, the founder of the ruling family dynasty, lived here with his upwardly mobile clan, including Lorenzo the Magnificent. Besides the immediate family, the palace also hosted many famous Florentines: teenage Michelangelo, who lived almost as an adopted son; Leonardo da Vinci, who played lute for Medici parties; and Botticelli, who studied the classical sculpture that dotted the gardens. The historical ambience is captured in a few well-preserved rooms and in a 15th-century fresco that brings the colorful Medici world to life.

ORIENTATION

Cost: €5.

Hours: Thu–Tue 9:00–19:00, closed Wed. To avoid a wait to see the lavish Chapel of the Magi, call a day in advance to make a reservation (tel. 055-276-0340).

Dress Code: None.

Getting There: Via Cavour 3, kitty-corner from the Church of San Lorenzo, one long block north of the Baptistery.

Information: The €1 informational brochure details the visual artistry of the building's architecture, along with the works covered in this tour.

Length of This Tour: Allow less than an hour.

Photography: Not allowed.

Starring: Cosimo de' Medici and Lorenzo the Magnificent.

THE TOUR BEGINS

Exterior

Cosimo de' Medici hired the architect Michelozzo to build the palace (1444), whose three-story facade set the tone throughout Florence—rough stones at bottom, rising to smooth and elegant on top. Two generations later, Michelangelo added the distinctive "kneeling windows" (with scrolls), an innovation that cropped up on palaces the world over. In the 1700s the palace was extended northward (keeping the same style) by the next owners, the Riccardi family.

Courtyard

As with many Italian homes, the courtyard served as an open-air meeting point and "living room" for the extended family. The

statue of Orpheus (who calmed wild animals with his harp) reminded visitors that the Medici family calmed wild Florence with smart and soothing politics. Find the family shield above the arches, with the six pills of these doctors *(medici)* turned cloth merchants turned international bankers. The Riccardi family later gilded this Renaissance lily with Baroque decor and adorned this courtyard with their collection of classical sculpture.

One of the rooms that opens onto the courtyard was Lorenzo the Magnificent's public office. Today the palace is a functioning county government building. As you wander around, notice the bureaucrats at work.

Garden

Pop out into the fragrant garden with its greenhouse for lemon trees. The tiny garden is a mere fraction of the once-spacious gardens that stretched for a city block to the north. The grounds were studded with fountains and statues, including the *Venus de' Medici* (Uffizi). Donatello's *David* (Bargello) likely stood in the courtyard. Teenage Michelangelo studied sculpture and the liberal arts in the family school located in the gardens.

• *Coming back into the courtyard from the garden, take a left into the…*

Multimedia Room

This "Star Wars meets art history" setup allows you to navigate through details of Gozzoli's Magi frescoes by pointing at a large video screen. You point at the image, it zooms into it, and a narrator explains the fresco's story and the historical context. An attendant can assist you with the system. Two smaller plasma screens take you through 1) a re-creation of this room as Lorenzo's workshop would have been in 1492 (think pilgrims), and 2) visual directions on how to control the pointing screens.

• *From the courtyard, a stairway leads to the Chapel of the Magi. The other stairway, just off the courtyard, goes to the Luca Giordano–decorated library. Both are on the first floor.*

Chapel of the Magi (Cappella di Gozzoli)

This sumptuous little room was the nuclear family's private chapel, where they could kneel at the altar and pray to a *Madonna and Child* by Filippo Lippi (where a copy stands now). At the time, it was rare and highly prestigious for a family to have a private chapel (this is one of only three in Florence). But Cosimo was the pope's banker—he even bankrolled one of the Crusades. He could afford it.

The three walls around the altar display *The Journey of the Magi,* or three kings—one king per wall—by Benozzo Gozzoli (1459).

On the biggest wall, a curly-haired young king on a white horse leads a parade of men through a rocky landscape. But the scene

takes you not to Bethlehem but to 15th-century, Medici-populated Tuscany. Riding behind the king are Cosimo (in red hat, riding modest brown donkey) and his son Piero (red hat, gray-white horse), who succeeded Cosimo as ruler of Florence. In the line of red-hatted young men behind them, find Piero's 10-year-old son and future ruler—Lorenzo the Magnificent (sixth in from the left, in red cap, with scoop nose, brown bowl-cut hair, and intense gaze). Ask the attendant (with the red-tipped pointer) where the others are: *"Dov'è* (DOH-vay) *Benozzo Gozzoli? Dov'è Cosimo? Dov'è Lorenzo?"*

The next wall (working clockwise) sets the king and his entourage in a green, spacious, and obviously Tuscan landscape. The men wear colorful clothes that set trends throughout Europe.

Every year on Epiphany (January 6), the Medici men would actually dress up like this and parade down Via Larga to celebrate the holiday of the three kings.

On the last wall, notice that the white-bearded king on his white donkey (far left) got cut off when the room was later remodeled. But the fresco was preserved—find the horse's ass on the other side of the doorway.

Gozzoli's crystal-clear, shadowless scenes reflect the style of his teacher, Fra Angelico. Pristine red, white, and green predominate—the Medici family colors. The portraits are realistic, showing the leading characters of 1459 Florence.

The room itself functioned both as a chapel and as an audience chamber for Cosimo. Notice how it's cleverly designed to have parallel themes. On Sunday morning, the art seemed religious...but on a normal workday it could be all political. Rather than trying to wow his guests with a "Wizard of Oz" show of might, Cosimo made a classy display of cool power and sophistication. When learned rival powers came here, they thought, "Damn, these Medicis are good."

• *Return to the courtyard and find the other staircase to the reception hall, decorated by Luca Giordano.*

Luca Giordano "Gallery"

This Baroque, Versailles-like former reception hall is part of a later extension added by the Riccardi family. The ceiling (*Allegory of Divine Wisdom,* frescoed in 1685 by the Naples artist Luca Giordano) honors Medici bigshots through the ages. They're the guys with starbursts over their heads frolicking with Greek gods. The blue-robed woman over the entrance is Florence, immersed in the nobility of the classical world. Also on display is Filippo Lippi's cheek-to-cheek *Madonna and Child.*

SANTA MARIA NOVELLA TOUR

The Church of Santa Maria Novella, chock-full of groundbreaking paintings and statues, is a reminder that the Renaissance was not simply a secular phenomenon. Many wealthy families paid for chapels inside the church that today are appreciated for their fine art.

Masaccio's fresco *The Trinity*, the first painting of modern times to portray three-dimensional space (1427), blew a "hole in the wall" of this church. From then on, a painting wasn't just a decorated panel, but a window into the spacious 3-D world of light and color. With Masaccio's *Trinity* as the centerpiece, the church traces Florentine art from the medieval to the Quattrocento (1400s) to the onset of Baroque.

ORIENTATION

Cost: €2.50.

Hours: Mon–Thu and Sat 9:00–17:00, Fri and Sun 13:00–17:00.

Dress Code: No bare shoulders or short skirts or short shorts for adults. Your clothing must cover your knees. Free poncho-like coverings are available.

Getting There: It's on Piazza Santa Maria Novella, a block south of the train station.

Notes: Art lovers can seek out the adjacent **cloisters** (€2.70, includes meager church museum, entry to the left of the church's facade); the Chapel of the Spaniards is notable for Bonaiuto's fresco *Allegory of the Dominican Order*.

Around the corner from the church is a fancy **perfumery** that's free and fun to visit (Mon–Sat 9:30–19:30, Sun 10:30–18:30, Via della Scala 16, tel. 055-216-276); see page 48 for details.

Length of This Tour: Allow one hour.

Santa Maria Novella

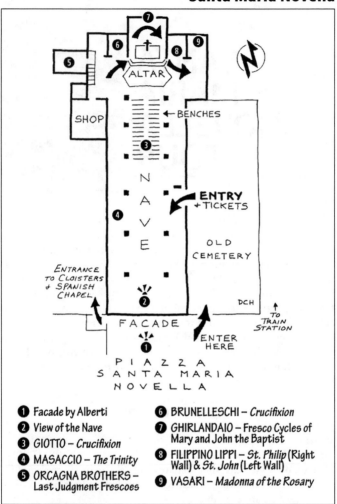

1. Facade by Alberti
2. View of the Nave
3. GIOTTO – *Crucifixion*
4. MASACCIO – *The Trinity*
5. ORCAGNA BROTHERS – Last Judgment Frescoes
6. BRUNELLESCHI – *Crucifixion*
7. GHIRLANDAIO – Fresco Cycles of Mary and John the Baptist
8. FILIPPINO LIPPI – *St. Philip* (Right Wall) & *St. John* (Left Wall)
9. VASARI – *Madonna of the Rosary*

Photography: Prohibited.

Starring: Masaccio, Giotto, Brunelleschi, Ghirlandaio, and Filippino Lippi.

THE TOUR BEGINS

❶ Exterior—The Facade

The green-and-white marble facade by Leon Battista Alberti (1456–1470) contains elements of Florence's whole history: Romanesque (horizontal stripes, like the Baptistery), Gothic (pointed arches on the bottom level), and Renaissance (geometric squares and circles on the upper level).

The church itself is cross-shaped, with a high central nave and low-ceilinged side aisles—the scrolls on the facade help bridge the two levels.

• *Enter the courtyard to the right of the main door, passing through the cemetery, where you'll pay to enter. Masaccio's* Trinity *is on the opposite wall from the entrance. But we'll start our tour at the central doorway in the facade, looking down the long nave to the altar.*

❷ Interior—View down the Nave from the Main Entrance
The long, 330-foot nave looks even longer, thanks to a 14th-century

perspective illusion. The columns converge as you approach the altar, their number increases, the arches get lower, and the floor gets higher, creating a tunnel effect. Gothic architects were aware of the rules of perspective, just not how to render it on a two-dimensional canvas.
• *Hanging from the ceiling in the middle of the nave is...*

❸ Giotto (c. 1266–1337)—*Crucifixion*
Giotto's altarpiece originally stood on the main altar. Stately and understated, it avoids the gruesome excesses of many medieval crucifixes. The tragic tilt of Christ's head, the parted lips, and the

stretched rib cage tell more about human suffering than the excessive spurting of blood.

On either side of the crossbar, Mary and John sit in a golden iconic heaven, but they are fully human, turned at a three-quarter angle, with knowing, sympathetic expressions. Giotto, the proto-Renaissance experimenter in perspective, creates the illusion that Christ's hands are actually turned out, palms down, not hammered flat against the cross.
• *Masaccio's* Trinity *is on the left wall, about midway along the nave (opposite the entrance). For the best perspective, stand about 20 feet from it, then take four steps to your left. Masaccio positioned it to be seen*

by the faithful as they dipped fingers into a (missing) font and crossed themselves—"Father, Son, and Holy Ghost."

❹ Masaccio (1401–1428)—*The Trinity* (1425–1427)

In his short but influential five-year career, Masaccio was the first painter since ancient times to portray Man in Nature—real

humans with real emotions, in a spacious three-dimensional world. (Unfortunately for tourists, he did the best 3-D space here, and the best humans in the Brancacci Chapel across the river.)

With simple pinks and blues (now faded), Masaccio creates the illusion that we're looking into a raised, cube-shaped chapel (about nine feet tall) topped with an arched ceiling and framed at the entrance with classical columns. Inside the chapel, God the Father stands on an altar, holding up the cross of Christ. (Where's the dove of the Holy Spirit? Why is God's "white collar" crooked?) John looks up at Christ while Mary looks down at us. Two donors (husband and wife, most likely) kneel on the front step outside the chapel, their cloaks spilling out of the niche. Below this fake chapel sits a fake tomb with the skeleton of Adam; compare it with the real tomb and niche to the right.

The checkerboard-coffered ceiling creates a 3-D tunnel effect, with rows of panels that appear to converge at the back, the panels getting smaller, lower, and closer together. Earlier painters had played with tricks like this, but Masaccio went further. He gave such thought to the proper perspective that we, as viewers, know right where we stand in relation to this virtual chapel.

He knew that, in real life, the rows of coffers would, if extended, stretch to the distant horizon. Lay a mental ruler along them, and you'll find the "vanishing point"—where all the lines intersect—all the way down below the foot of the cross. Masaccio places us there, with that at eye level, looking "up" into the chapel.

Having fixed where the distant horizon is and where the viewer is, Masaccio draws a checkerboard grid in between, then places the figures on it (actually underneath it) like chess pieces. What's truly amazing is that young Masaccio seemed to grasp this stuff intuitively—a "natural," eyeballing it and sketching freehand what later artists would have to work out with a pencil and paper.

What Masaccio learned intuitively, Brunelleschi analyzed mathematically and Alberti (who did the facade) codified in his famous 1435 treatise, *On Painting*. Soon, artists everywhere were drawing Alberti checkerboards on the ground, creating spacious,

perfectly lit, 3-D scenes filled with chess-piece humans.
• *The Orcagna Chapel is at the far end of the left transept. As you approach, view the chapel from a distance. This is the illusion that Masaccio tried to create—of a raised chapel set in a wall—using only paint on a flat surface. Climb the steps to see...*

❺ Orcagna Brothers (a.k.a. the di Cione Brothers)—Frescoes of the Last Judgment: *Inferno, Purgatorio, and Paradiso* (1340–1357)

In 1347–1348, Florence was hit with the terrible Black Death (bubonic plague) that killed half the population. Here, in the

Orcagna Chapel, the fading frescoes from that grim time show hundreds of figures, and not a single smile.

It's the Day of Judgment (center wall), and God (above the stained-glass window) spreads his hands to divide the good and evil. God has selected Dante as the interior decorator for heaven and hell. (Find Dante all in white, with his ear-flap cap, among the crowd to the left of the window, about a third of the way up.) Notice that God is bigger than the angels, who dwarf the hallowed saints, who are bigger than ordinary souls such as Dante, mirroring the feudal hierarchy of king, nobles, knights, and serfs.

In *Heaven* (left wall), Hotel Paradiso is *completo,* stacked with gold-haloed saints. *Hell* (faded right wall) is a series of layers, the descending rings of Dante's *Inferno.* A river of fire runs through it, dividing *Purgatory* (above) and *Hell* (below). At the bottom of the pit, where dogs and winged demons run wild, naked souls in caves beg for mercy and get none.

• *In a chapel to the left of the church's main altar, you'll find...*

❻ Filippo Brunelleschi—*Crucifixion*

Filippo Brunelleschi (1377–1446)—architect, painter, sculptor—used his skills as an analyst of nature to carve (in wood) a perfectly realistic *Crucifixion,* neither prettified nor with the grotesque exaggeration of medieval religious objects. His Christ is buck naked,

not particularly muscular or handsome, with bulging veins, armpit hair, tensed leg muscles, and bent feet. The tilt of Christ's head frees a tendril of hair that directs our eye down to the wound and the dripping blood, dropping straight from his side to his thigh to his calf—a strong vertical line that sets off the curve of Christ's body. Brunelleschi carved this to outdo his friend Donatello's crucifix in Santa Croce. Donatello's is an agonized peasant; Brunelleschi's a dignified noble.

• *In the choir area behind the main altar are Ghirlandaio's 21 frescoes, stacked seven to a wall. We'll concentrate on just the six panels on the bottom.*

❼ Domenico Ghirlandaio—Fresco Cycles of Mary and John the Baptist (1485–1490)

At the peak of Florence's power, wealth, and confidence, Domenico Ghirlandaio (1449–1494) painted portraits of his fellow Florentines in their Sunday best, inhabiting video-game landscapes of mixed classical and contemporary buildings, rubbing shoulders with saints and angels. The religious subjects get lost in the colorful scenes of everyday life—perhaps a metaphor for how Renaissance humanism was marginalizing religion.

• *Start with the left wall and work clockwise along the bottom. The first scene is...*

Expulsion of Joachim from the Temple

Proud, young Florentine men (the group at left) seem oblivious to bearded, robed saints rushing from the arcade. There's Ghirlandaio

himself (in the group on the right) looking out at us, with one hand proudly on his hip and the other gesturing, "I did this." The scene is perfectly lit, almost shadow-free, allowing us to look deep into the receding arches.

• *The next scene, on the right is...*

Birth of the Virgin

Five beautiful young women, led by the pregnant daughter of Ghirlandaio's patron, parade up to newborn Mary. The pregnant girl's brocade dress is a microcosm of the room's decorations.

Dancing babies in the room's classical frieze celebrate Mary's birth, obviously echoing Donatello's beloved *cantoria* in Florence's Duomo Museum.

True, Ghirlandaio's works are "busy"—each scene crammed with portraits, designs, fantasy architecture, and great costumes—but if you mentally frame off small sections, you discover a collection of mini-masterpieces.

• *On the lowest part of the center wall, flanking the stained-glass window, are two matching panels.*

Giovanni Tornabuoni Kneeling and *Francesca Tornabuoni* (his wife) *Kneeling*

Giovanni Tornabuoni, who paid for these frescoes, was a successful executive in the Medici Company (and Lorenzo the Magnificent's uncle). However, by the time these frescoes were being finished, the Medici bank was slipping seriously into the red, and soon the family had to flee Florence, creditors on their heels.

• *On the right wall...*

Mary Meets Elizabeth

In a spacious, airy landscape (with the pointed steeple of Santa Maria Novella in the distance), Mary and Elizabeth embrace,

uniting their respective entourages. The parade of ladies in contemporary dress echoes the one on the opposite wall. This panel celebrates youth, beauty, the city, trees, rocks, and life.

A generation after Brunelleschi and Alberti, all artists—including the near-genius Ghirlandaio—had mastered perspective tricks. Here, Alberti's famed checkerboard is laid on its side, making a sharply receding wall to create the illusion of great distance.

Ghirlandaio employed many assistants in his productive workshop: "Johnson, you do the ladies' dresses. Anderson, you're great at birds and trees. And Michelangelo...you do young men's butts." The three small figures leaning over the wall (above Mary and Elizabeth) were likely done by 13-year-old Michelangelo, an apprentice here before being "discovered" by Lorenzo the

Magnificent. Relaxed and natural, they cast real shadows, as true to life as anyone in Ghirlandaio's perfect-posture, face-the-camera world.

Ghirlandaio was reportedly jealous (and talented Michelangelo contemptuous), but, before they parted ways, Michelangelo learned how to lay fresco from the man who did it as well as anyone in Florence.

• *Above, on the far right...*

The Birth of John the Baptist
Set in a typical (rich) Florentine bedroom, John's birth is attended by none other than Lorenzo de' Medici's mom (second figure from right), with the broad face, thin lips, and scooped nose Lorenzo would inherit.

• *In the chapel to the right of the altar, Filippino Lippi did the frescoes on the left and right walls. Look first at the right wall, lower level (there's a decent view from the altar steps)...*

❽ Filippino Lippi

St. Philip at the Temple of Mars
In an elaborate shrine, a statue of the angry god Mars waves his broken lance menacingly. The Christian Philip points back up and says, "I'm not afraid of him—that's a false god." To prove it, he opens a hole in the base of the altar, letting out a little dragon, who promptly farts (believe it when you see it), causing the pagan king's son to swoon and die. The overcome spectators clutch their foreheads and noses.

If Ghirlandaio was "busy," Lippi is downright hyperactive, filling every square inch with something frilly—rumpled hair, folds in clothes, dramatic gestures, twisting friezes, wind-blown flags, and gassy dragons.

• *On the left wall, lower level...*

St. John the Evangelist Raising Drusiana from the Dead
The miracle takes place in a spacious 3-D architectural setting, but Lippi has all his actors in a chorus line across the front of the stage. Filippino Lippi (1457–1504, the son of the more famous Fra Filippo Lippi) was apprenticed to Botticelli

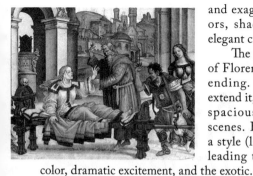

and exaggerated his bright colors, shadowless lighting, and elegant curves.

The sober, dignified realism of Florence's Quattrocento was ending. Michelangelo would extend it, building on Masaccio's spacious, solemn, dimly lit scenes. But Lippi championed a style (later called Mannerism, leading to Baroque) that loved color, dramatic excitement, and the exotic.

• *In the next chapel to the right of the altar, on the central wall, find...*

❾ Giorgio Vasari—*Madonna of the Rosary*

The picture-plane is saturated with images from top to bottom. Saints and angels twist and squirm around Mary (the red patch in the center), but their body language is gibberish, just an excuse for Vasari to exhibit his technique.

Giorgio Vasari (1511–1574), best known as the writer of *The Lives of the Artists*, was a prolific artist himself. As a Mannerist, he copied the "manner" of, say, a twisting Michelangelo statue, but violated the sober spirit, multiplying by 100 and cramming the canvas. I've tried to defend Vasari from the art critics who unanimously call his art superficial and garish...but doggone it, they're right.

With Vasari, who immortalized the Florentine Renaissance with his writing, that Renaissance ended.

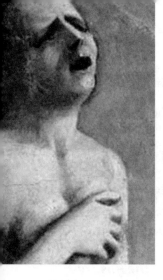

BRANCACCI CHAPEL TOUR

(Cappella Brancacci)

In the Brancacci (bran-KAH-chee) Chapel, Masaccio created a world in paint that looked like the world we inhabit. For the first time in a thousand years, Man and Nature were frozen for inspection. Masaccio's painting techniques were copied by many Renaissance artists, and his people—sturdy, intelligent, and dignified, with an expression of understated astonishment—helped shape Renaissance Men and Women's own self-images.

ORIENTATION

Cost: €4, or €8 combo-ticket with Palazzo Vecchio.

Dress Code: Shorts and bare shoulders are OK in the chapel, but modest dress is requested when visiting the rest of the church.

Reservations: Call the chapel for free, mandatory reservations in English, often available for the same day (dial 055-276-8224; it's frequently busy, but keep trying—the best time to call is around 14:00–15:00). Reservation times begin every 15 minutes, with a maximum of 30 visitors per time slot. You have 15 minutes in the actual chapel.

Video: Visits on the top of each hour include a free 40-minute English video on the history of the frescoes and the Biblical stories they represent. The doors close promptly when the video starts (first door on left past the ticket office/chapel entrance).

Hours: Mon and Wed–Sat 10:00–17:00, Sun 13:00–17:00, closed Tue; ticket office closes at 16:30. The chapel is accessible only through the paid entrance to the right of the church.

Getting There: The Brancacci Chapel is in the Church of Santa Maria del Carmine, on Piazza del Carmine, in the Oltrarno

Brancacci Chapel

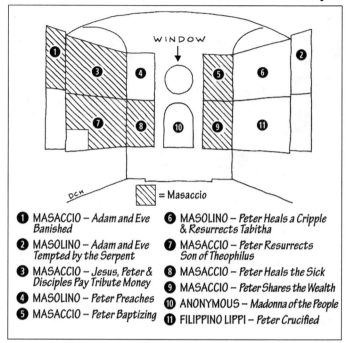

● MASACCIO – *Adam and Eve Banished*

❷ MASOLINO – *Adam and Eve Tempted by the Serpent*

❸ MASACCIO – *Jesus, Peter & Disciples Pay Tribute Money*

❹ MASOLINO – *Peter Preaches*

❺ MASACCIO – *Peter Baptizing*

❻ MASOLINO – *Peter Heals a Cripple & Resurrects Tabitha*

❼ MASACCIO – *Peter Resurrects Son of Theophilus*

❽ MASACCIO – *Peter Heals the Sick*

❾ MASACCIO – *Peter Shares the Wealth*

❿ ANONYMOUS – *Madonna of the People*

⓫ FILIPPINO LIPPI – *Peter Crucified*

neighborhood south of the Arno River. It's about a 15-minute walk or short taxi ride (about €8.50) from downtown Florence (e.g., Palazzo Vecchio).

Length of This Tour: Allow 30 minutes.

Photography: Allowed without a flash.

Starring: Masaccio, Masolino, and Filippino Lippi.

THE TOUR BEGINS

Overview

The chapel has frescoes that tell the story of Peter—half are by Masaccio and half by Masolino or Filippino Lippi (the son of Filippo Lippi). Although Masaccio is the star, the panels by his colleagues are interesting and a good contrast in styles. Masaccio's works are sprinkled among the others, mostly on the left and center walls.

We'll see them roughly in the order they were painted, from upper left to lower right—the upper six by Masaccio and Masolino (1424–1425), the lower ones by Masaccio (1426–1427) and Filippino Lippi (1481–1485).

• *Start with the left wall, the small panel in the upper left.*

Masaccio—*Adam and Eve Banished from Eden*

Renaissance Man and Woman—as nude as they can be—turn their backs on the skinny, unrealistic, medieval Gate of Paradise

and take their first step as mortal humans in the real world. For the first time in a thousand years of painting, these figures cast a realistic shadow, seemingly lit by the same light we are—the natural light through the Brancacci Chapel's window.

Eve wails from deep within. (The first time I saw her, I thought Eve's gaping mouth was way over the top, until I saw the very same expression on someone dealing with a brother's death.) Adam buries his face in shame. These simple human gestures speak louder than the religious symbols of medieval art.

• *Compare Masaccio's* Adam and Eve *with the one on the opposite wall, by his colleague Masolino.*

Masolino—*Adam and Eve Tempted by the Serpent*

Masolino's elegant, innocent First Couple float in an ethereal Garden of Eden with no clear foreground or background (Eve hugs a tree or she'd float away). Their bodies are lit evenly by a pristine, all-encompassing, morning-in-springtime light that casts no shadows.

In 1424, Masolino da Pani-cale (1383–1435) was hired by the Brancacci family to decorate this chapel with the story of Peter (beginning with the Original Sin that Peter's "Good News" saves man from). Masolino, a 40-year-old contractor with too many other commitments, invited 23-year-old Masaccio (1401–1428) to help him. The

two set up scaffolding and worked side by side—the older, work-manlike master and the young, intuitive genius—in a harmonious collaboration. They just divvied up the panels, never (or rarely) working together on the same scene.

• *Return to the left wall, upper level. From here, we'll work clockwise around the chapel. After* Adam and Eve, *the second panel is...*

Masaccio—*Jesus, Peter, and the Disciples Pay the Tribute Money*

The tax collector (in red miniskirt, with his back to us) tells Jesus that he must pay a temple tax. Jesus gestures to say, "OK, but the

money's over there." Peter, his right-hand man (gray hair and beard, brown robe), says, "Yeah, over there." Peter goes over there to the lake (left side of panel), takes off his robe, stoops down at an odd angle, and miraculously pulls a coin from the mouth of a fish. He puts his robe back on and (right side of panel) pays the man.

Some consider this the first modern painting, placing real humans in a real setting, seen from a single viewpoint—ours. Earlier painters had done far more detailed landscapes than Masaccio's sketchy mountains, lake, trees, clouds, and buildings, but they never fixed where the viewer was in relation to these things.

Masaccio tells us exactly where we stand—near the crowd, farther from the trees, with the sun to our right casting late-afternoon shadows. We're no longer detached spectators, but an extension of the scene. Masaccio lets us stand in the presence of the human Jesus. While a good attempt at three-dimensionality, Masaccio's work is far from perfect. Later artists would perfect mathematically what Masaccio eyeballed intuitively.

The disciples all have strong, broad-shouldered bodies, but each face is unique. Blonde, curly-haired, clean-shaven John is as handsome as the head on a Roman coin (Masaccio had just returned from Rome). Thomas (far right, with a five o'clock shadow) is intense. Their different reactions—with faces half in shadow, half in light—tell us they're divided over paying the tax.

Masaccio's people have one thing in common—a faraway look in the eye, as though hit with a spiritual two-by-four. They're deep in thought, reflective, and awestruck, aware they've just experienced something miraculous. But they're also dazzled, glazed over, and a bit disoriented, like tourists at the Brancacci Chapel.

• *Continuing clockwise, we move to the next panel, on the center wall.*

Masolino—*Peter Preaches to a Crowd*

Masolino and Masaccio, different in so many ways, were both fans of Giotto (c. 1266–1337), who told stories with simple gestures and minimal acting, adding the human drama by showing the reaction of bystanders. Here, the miraculous power of the sermon is not

evident in Peter (who just raises his hand) but in the faces of the crowd. The lady in the front row is riveted, while others close their eyes to meditate. The big nun (far right) finds it interesting enough to come a little closer, while the tonsured monk's mouth slips open in awe. The gentleman to the left is skeptical but wants to hear more.

Masolino never mastered 3-D space like Masaccio. Peter's extreme profile is a cardboard cutout, his left leg stands too high to plant him realistically on flat ground, the people in the back have their gazes fixed somewhere above Peter, and the "Masacciesque" mountains in the background remain just that, background.

• *Continuing clockwise to the other side of the window...*

Masaccio—*Peter Baptizing Converts*

A muscular man kneels in the stream to join the cult of Jesus. On the bank (far right), another young man waits his turn, shivering in his jockstrap. Among the crowd, a just-baptized man wrestles with his robe, while the man in blue, his hair still dripping, buttons up.

The body language is eloquent: the strongman's humility, the shivering youth's uncertainty, and the bowed heads of the just-baptized, reflecting on the life-altering choice they've just made.

Masaccio builds these bodies with patches of color (an especially effective technique in fresco, where colors can bleed together). He knew that a kneeling man's body, when lit from the left (the direction of the chapel window), would look like a patchwork of bright hills (his pecs) and dark crevasses (his sternum). He assembles the pieces into a sculptural, 3-D figure, "modeled" by light and shade.

Again, Masaccio was the first artist to paint real humans—with 3-D bodies and individual faces, reflecting inner emotions—in a real-world setting.

• *Continue clockwise to the right wall.*

Masolino—*Peter Heals a Cripple* (left side) and *Resurrects Tabitha* (right side)

Masolino takes a crack at the 3-D style of his young partner, setting two separate stories in a single Florentine square, defined by an arcade on the left and a porch on the right. Crude elements of the future Renaissance style abound—the receding buildings establish the viewer's point of reference; the rocks scattered through the square define 3-D space; there are secular details in the background (mother and child, laundry on a balcony, a monkey on a ledge); and the cripple (left) is shown at an odd angle (foreshortening). Masaccio may have helped on this panel.

But there's no denying that the stars of the work are the two sharply dressed gentlemen strolling across the square, who help to divide (and unite) the two stories of Peter. The patterned coat is a textbook example of the International Gothic style that was the rage in Florence—elegant, refined, graceful, with curvy lines creating a complex, pleasing pattern. The man walking is shown at a three-quarters angle, but Masolino shows the coat from the front to catch the full display. The picture is evenly lit, with only a hint of shadow, accentuating the colorful clothes and cheerful atmosphere.

In mid-project (1426), Masolino took another job in Hungary, leaving Masaccio to finish the lower half of the chapel. Masolino never again explored the Renaissance style, building a successful career with the eternal springtime of International Gothic.

• *We move to the lower level. Start on the left wall with the second panel and work clockwise.*

Masaccio—*Peter Resurrects the Son of Theophilus*

Peter (in that same brown robe...like Masaccio, who was careless about his appearance) raises the boy from the world of bones, winning his freedom from stern Theophilus (seated in niche to the left).

The courtyard setting is fully 3-D, Masaccio having recently learned a bit of perspective mathematics from his (older) friends Brunelleschi and Donatello. At the far right of the painting, there are three of the Quattrocento (1400s) giants who invented painting perspective (from right to left): Brunelleschi, who broke down reality mathematically; Alberti, who popularized the math with his book, *On Painting;* and Masaccio himself (looking out at us), who opened everyone's eyes to the psychologically powerful possibilities.

Little is known of Masaccio's short life. "Masaccio" is a nickname (often translated as "Big, Clumsy Thomas") describing his personality—stumbling through life with careless abandon, not worrying about money, clothes, or fame...a lovable doofus.

Next to Masaccio's self-portrait is a painting within a painting of Peter on a throne. On a flat surface with a blank background, Masaccio has created a hovering hologram, a human more 3-D than even a statue made in medieval times.

"Wow," said Brother Philip, a 20-year-old Carmelite monk stationed here when Masaccio painted this. Fra Filippo ("Brother Philip") Lippi was inspired by these frescoes and went on to become a famous painter himself. At age 50, while painting in a convent, he fell in love with a young nun, and they eloped. Nine months later, "Little Philip" was born, and he too grew to be a famous painter—Filippino Lippi...who, in 1481, was chosen to complete the Brancacci Chapel.

Filippino Lippi painted substantial portions of this fresco, including the group in the far left (five heads but only eight legs).

• *Moving clockwise to the center wall...*

Masaccio—*Peter Heals the Sick with his Shadow*

Peter is a powerful Donatello statue come to life, walking toward us along a Florentine street. Next to him, in the red cap, is bearded

Donatello, Masaccio's friend and mentor.

Masaccio inspired more than painters. He gave ordinary people a new self-image of what it is to be human. Masaccio's people are individuals, not generic Greek gods, not always pretty (like the old bald guy) but still robust and handsome in their own way. They exude a seriousness that makes them very adult. Compare these street people with Masolino's two well-dressed dandies, and you see the difference between Florence's working-class, urban, "democratic" spirit (Guelphs) and the courtly grace of Europe's landed gentry (Ghibellines).

• *The next panel, on the other side of the altar, is...*

Masaccio—*Peter Shares the Wealth with the Poor*

Early Christians practiced a form of communal sharing. The wealthy Ananias lies about his contribution, and he drops dead at Peter's feet. Peter takes the missing share and gives it to a poor lady who can't even afford baby pants. The shy baby, the grateful woman, and the admiring man on crutches show Masaccio's blue-collar sympathies.

The scene reflects an actual event in Florence—a tax-reform measure to make things equal for everyone. Florentines were championing a new form of government where, if we all contribute our fair share through taxes, we don't need kings and nobles.

• *The altar under the window holds a painting that is not by Masaccio, Masolino, or Lippi.*

Anonymous (possibly Coppo di Marcovaldo)— *The Madonna of the People*

This medieval altarpiece replaces the now-destroyed fresco by Masaccio that was the centerpiece of the whole design—Peter's

crucifixion.

With several panels still unfinished, Masaccio traveled to Rome to meet up with Masolino. Masaccio died there (possibly poisoned) in 1428, at age 27. After his death, the political and artistic climate changed, the chapel was left unfinished (the lower right wall), and some of his frescoes were scraped off whole (his *Crucifixion of Peter*) or in part—we saw in *Peter Resurrects the Son of Theophilus* that several exiled Brancaccis were erased from history, later to be replaced.

Finally, in 1481, new funding arrived and Filippino Lippi, the son of the monk-turned-painter, was hired to complete the blank panels and retouch some destroyed frescoes.

• *The right wall, lower section, contains two panels by Filippino Lippi. The first and biggest is...*

Filippino Lippi—*Peter Crucified*

Lippi completes the story of Peter with his upside-down crucifixion. Lippi tried to match the solemn style of Masaccio, but his

figures are less statuesque, more colorful, and more detailed, and the compositions are busier. Still, compared with Lippi's other, more hyperactive works found elsewhere, he's reined himself in admirably to honor the great pioneer.

In fact, while Masaccio's perspective techniques were enormously influential, learned by every Tuscan artist, his sober style was not terribly popular. Another strain of Tuscan painting diverged from Masaccio—from the adult Fra Filippo Lippi to Botticelli, Ghirlandaio, and Filippino Lippi—mixing in the bright colors, line patterns, and even lighting of International Gothic. But Masaccio's legacy remained strong, emerging in the grave, statuesque, harsh-shadow creations of two Florentine giants—Leonardo da Vinci and Michelangelo.

SCIENCE MUSEUM TOUR

(Istituto e Museo di Storia della Scienza)

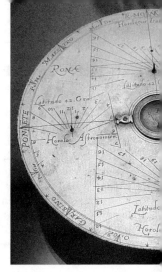

Enough art, already! Forget the Madonnas and Venuses for a while to ponder weird contraptions from the birth of modern science. The same spirit of discovery that fueled the artistic Renaissance helped free the sciences from medieval mumbo jumbo. The Institute and Museum of the History of Science is a historical overview of technical innovations from roughly A.D. 1000 to 1900, featuring early telescopes, clocks, experiments, and Galileo's finger in a jar.

English majors will enjoy expanding their knowledge. Art lovers can admire the sheer beauty of functional devices. Engineers will be in hog heaven among endless arrays of gadgets. Everyone will be fully amused by my feeble attempts to explain technical concepts.

ORIENTATION

Cost: €6.50.

Hours: June–Sept Mon and Wed–Fri 9:30–17:00, Tue and Sat 9:30–13:00, closed Sun; Oct–May Mon and Wed–Sat 9:30–17:00, Tue 9:30–13:00, generally closed Sun but open second Sun of month 10:00–13:00.

Getting There: It's at Piazza dei Giudici 1, one block east of the Uffizi, on the north bank of the Arno River.

Information: Tel. 055-265-311, www.imss.fi.it.

Length of This Tour: Allow 90 minutes.

Photography: Prohibited.

Starring: Galileo's telescopes, experiment models, and finger.

THE TOUR BEGINS

Overview

There are two floors of rooms. The collection is not really chronological, but if you follow the rooms in order, you get a good overview. Find the displays by their room number (I, II, III, etc.) and exhibit number (I.1, I.2, I.3, etc.). Pick up the helpful English-language pamphlets when you buy your tickets, and chat up the English-speaking docents as you go. They're eager to demonstrate how some of these scientific gadgets work. In fact, the staff is happy that you're there to see this museum, and not just lost on your way to the nearby Uffizi.

• *Buy your ticket on the ground floor, then climb stairs to the first floor. Before entering Room I, pick up a free loaner guidebook in English; it gives an in-depth explanation of the mechanisms and how they affected people's daily lives.*

FIRST FLOOR

The objects displayed in the first three rooms measured the world around us—the height of distant mountains, the length of a man's arm, the movement of the stars across the sky. This was the bold, first step in science, to observe nature and measure it. What they found is that nature—apparently so ever-changing and chaotic—actually behaves in an orderly way, mirroring rather simple mathematical formulas.

Room I: Mathematical Instruments

• *In the center of Room I, you'll find...*

Exhibit I.1—Arabic Celestial Globe (*Globo Celeste Arabo,* 1085)

Looking down on this map of the heavens, you have a God's-eye view of the night sky. Find familiar constellations such as the fish, hunter, snake, and bear (our "Big Dipper"). Arab traders mapped the dome of heaven that arches overhead to help them navigate by the stars. During this era, Muslim scholars were rapidly advancing the fields of astronomy and navigation, using their mathematical knowledge to also discover the principles of algebra.

The universe only got bigger with each new bit of knowledge.

• *In the first glass case to the left, on the middle shelf, find...*

Exhibit I.10—Quadrant (*Quadrante Solare*)

You'd grab this wedge-shaped quadrant by its curved edge, point it away from you, and sight along the top edge toward, say, a distant tower or star. Then you'd read the scale etched along the curved edge to find how many degrees above the horizon the object is.

A quadrant measures the triangle formed by you, the horizon, and a distant object. Once you know some of the triangle's six variables (three angles and three sides), you can figure the others. (That's trigonometry.)

Armed with this knowledge, you could use the quadrant to measure all kinds of things. On land, you could calculate how high or how far away a building is. At sea, you could figure your position in relation to the sun and stars.

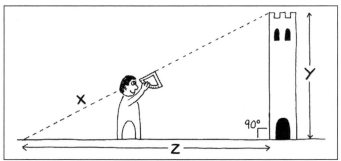

Most of the instruments in Rooms I, II, and III are variations on the earliest, simplest device—the quadrant. (A *quad*-rant is one-*fourth* of a 360-degree circle, or 90 degrees.)
• *Just above the quadrant, find...*

Exhibits I.2 Through I.9—Arabic Astrolabes *(Astrolabi Arabi)*

Astrolabes, invented by the ancient Greeks and pioneered by medieval Arab sailors, combined a quadrant with a map of the sky (a star chart), allowing you to calculate your position against the stars without doing all the math. You'd hang the metal disk from your thumb and sight along the central crossbeam, locate a star, then read its altitude above the horizon on the measuring scale etched around the rim.

Next, you entered in this information by turning the little handle on the astrolabe's face. This set the wheels-within-wheels into motion, and you'd watch the constellations spin across a backdrop of coordinates. You kept turning until the astrolabe mirrored the current heavens. With your known coordinates dialed in, the astrolabe calculated the unknowns, and you could read out your position along the rim.

In addition, knowing the position of the stars and sun told you the current time of day (see the 24-hour clock around the rim), which was especially useful for Muslims in their daily prayers.

• *In the glass case in the far right corner of the room, on the middle shelf, look for...*

Exhibit I.102—Michelangelo's Compass (*Compasso detto di Michelangelo*)

Maybe Michelangelo once used this (it's said to have been his), and I suppose it's even conceivable that he used it to measure, say, *David*'s hand or to draw a circle on the Sistine ceiling. Regardless, dividers like this were a common way for Renaissance Men and Women to measure the world and marvel at its harmonious proportions.

• *Enter the next room...*

Room II: More Quadrants and Various Combinations

In the 1500s, improvements were made on the relatively crude quadrants and astrolabes, spurred by the need to navigate the open oceans.

• *Straight ahead, just to the left of the exit doorway, see...*

Exhibit II.27—Quadrant (*Quadrante Universale,* 1608)

Like a Popeil's Pocket-Navigator, this all-purpose unit has 1,001 uses. The quadrant measures angles. A magnetic compass points to north. A sundial (in the compass's removable cap) tells the time of day, as the sun casts a shadow from the vertical piece onto a scale of hours.

On the backside of the quadrant, a big half-dial arcs across rows of numbers, allowing even non-trig majors to calculate the trajectory of cannon balls. The movable arm even passed through a table of zodiac signs to cast your horoscope—how the stars' alignment affects you personally.

• *On the bottom shelf of the glass case back by the entrance doorway, is...*

Exhibit II.88—Calculator (*Macchina Calcolatrice,* 1664)

This calculator (mechanical, of course, not electrical) could add and subtract. Enter the numbers you're adding on the dials, and the dials turn gears inside that spin a tube marked with numbers in concentric rings. The answer appears in the digital readout.

• *Pass through Room III to...*

Rooms IV and V: Galileo

Galileo Galilei (1564–1642) is known as the father of modern science. His discoveries pioneered many scientific fields, and he was among the first to blend mathematics with hands-on observation of nature to find practical applications. Raised in Pisa, he achieved fame teaching at the University of Padua before retiring to Florence. The museum displays several of his actual possessions (lens, two telescopes, compass, and thermometer), models illustrating his early experiments, and his finger.

• *Preserved in a jar in the glass case is...*

Exhibit IV.10—Galileo's Finger
(Dito Medio della Mano Destra di Galileo)

Galileo is, perhaps, best known as a martyr for science. He popularized the belief (conceived by the Polish astronomer, Nicolaus Copernicus, in the early 1500s) that the Earth orbits around the sun. At the time, the Catholic Church preached an Earth-centered universe, and, at the age of 70, Galileo was hauled before the Inquisition in Rome and forced to kneel and publicly proclaim that the Earth did not move around the sun. As he walked away, legend has it, he whispered to his followers, "But it does move!"

His students preserved this finger bone, displayed on a marble pedestal, as a kind of sacred relic in this shrine to science. Galileo's beliefs eventually triumphed over the Inquisition, and, appropriately, we have his middle finger raised upward for all those blind to science.

• *Also in the glass case, displayed in an ivory frame, is...*

Exhibit IV.1—Galileo's Telescope Lens
(Lente obiettiva di Galileo)

Galileo was the first earthling to see the moons of Jupiter. With a **homemade telescope** (in Room V), he looked through this lens (it wasn't cracked then) and saw three moons lined up next to Jupiter. This discovery also irked the Church, which insisted that only Earth had a satellite. You could see Jupiter's moons with your own eyes if you simply looked through the telescope, but few church scholars bothered to do so, content to believe what they'd read in ancient books.

Exhibit IV.5—Pendulum Clock Model
(Modello dell'Applicazione del Pendolo all'Orologio)
It's said that during a church service in Pisa, Galileo looked up to see the cathedral's chandelier swaying slowly back and forth, like a pendulum. He noticed that a wide-but-fast arc took the same amount of time as a narrow-but-slow arc. "Hmmm. Maybe that regular pendulum motion could be used to time things...."

Exhibit IV.7—Thermometer (*Termoscopio,* 19th century)
Galileo also invented the thermometer (similar to this one), though his glass tube filled with air would later be replaced by thermometers of mercury.
• *The big wooden ramp in Room IV is...*

Exhibit IV.13—Inclined Plane
Legend has it that Galileo dropped cannonballs from the Leaning Tower of Pisa to see whether heavier objects fall faster than lighter ones, as the ancient philosopher Aristotle (and most people) believed. In fact, Galileo probably did not drop objects from the Leaning Tower, but he likely rolled them down a wooden ramp like this reconstructed one. If a docent is nearby, ask for a demonstration.

Rolling balls of different weights down the ramp, he timed them as they rang the bells posted along the way. (The bells are spaced increasingly farther apart, but a ball—accelerating as it drops—will ring them in a regular time.) What Galileo found is that—if you discount air resistance—all objects fall at the same rate, regardless of their weight. (It's the air resistance that makes a feather fall more slowly than a cannonball, not the weight.)

He also found that falling objects accelerate (speed up) at a regular rate (9.8 meters per second faster every second) summed up in a mathematical formula (distance is proportional to the time squared).

Exhibit IV.15—Model of Water-Lifting Device
(Macchina da Alzare Acqua)
The horses walk in a circle, rocking the two crossbars back and forth. The crossbars alternately lift and lower buckets in wells, allowing two horses to draw water from four wells. Galileo was among the first research scientists to suggest practical applications of his principles.

• *Enter Room V, filled with telescopes. Galileo's two telescopes are in the first glass case on the right-hand wall.*

Room V: Galileo's Telescopes

Galileo built these **telescopes** (Exhibits V.1 and V.2), based on reports he'd read from Holland. He was the first person to seriously study the heavens with telescopes. Though these only magnified the image about 30 times ("30 power," which is less than today's binoculars), he saw Jupiter's moons, Saturn's rings, the craters of the moon (which he named "seas"), and blemishes (sunspots) on the supposedly perfect sun.

A telescope is essentially two "magnifying glasses" (convex lenses) in a tube, one at either end. The farther apart the lenses, the greater the magnification, prompting the 15-foot **telescope hanging on the wall** (V.51). (The longest ever built was 160 feet, but the slightest movement jiggled the image.)

Room VI: Lenses and Prisms

A curved glass lens can bend light, magnifying an image. A **lens-grinding machine** (Exhibit VI.55) could make higher-quality lenses than human hands could.

The study of optics in the 1600s initially had few practical applications beyond optical illusions for the amusement of nobles. Party guests could look at a reflection and see a **man and woman switching genders** (Exhibit VI.53) or walk from side to side to see **Christ become Mary become a saint** (VI.54).

Room VII: Mapping the Cosmos

• *The large contraption in the center of Room VII is...*

Exhibit VII.30—Armillary Sphere
(*Sfera Armillare Tolemaica,* c. 1590)

This is a 10-foot-high, gilded-wood model of the universe as conceived by ancient Greeks and medieval Europeans. You'd turn a crank (which is now missing), and watch the stars and planets orbit around the Earth in the  center. (The map of North America is pretty accurate, but you're on your own past Reno.) This Earth-centered view of the universe—which matches our common-sense observations of the night sky—was codified by Ptolemy, a Greek-speaking Egyptian of the second century A.D.

Ptolemy (silent P) summed up Aristotle's knowledge of the heavens and worked out the mathematics explaining its movements. His math was complex, especially when trying to explain the planets, which occasionally lag behind the stars in their paths across the night sky. (We now know it's because fast-orbiting Earth passes the outer planets in their longer, more time-consuming orbits around the sun.)

Ptolemy's system dominated Europe for 1,400 years. It worked most of the time and fit well with medieval Christianity's human-centered theology. But, finally, Nicolaus Copernicus (and Galileo) made the mental leap to a sun-centered system. This simplified the math, explained the movement of planets, and—most importantly—changed earthlings' conception of themselves forever.

• *On the wall near the entrance, find the large, round...*

Exhibit VII.40—Map of the World (Fra Mauro—*Mappamondo*, 15th century)

With Columbus' voyages, the Europeans' world suddenly got bigger and rounder. This map portrays the spherical world on a flat surface. South is up. At the bottom, find *Europa, Norvegia* (Norway), and Russia. Africa's tip is on top, with India and China to the left.

Room VIII: Microscopes

The inner world was expanding, too. One day, a Dutchman picked something from his teeth, looked at it under his crude microscope, and discovered a mini-universe, crawling with thousands of "very little animalcules, very prettily a-moving" (i.e., bacteria and protozoa). Antoni van Leeuwenhoek (1632–1723) popularized the microscope, finding that fleas have fleas, semen contains sperm, and one-celled creatures are our fellow animals.

This room displays **simple *(semplice)*** and **compound *(composto)* microscopes.** A

simple one is just a single convex lens—what we'd call a magnifying glass. A compound is two (or more) lenses in a tube, working like a telescope, where one lens magnifies the object, and the eyepiece lens magnifies the magnified image.

Van Leeuwenhoek opted for a simple microscope, since early compound ones often blurred and colored things around the edges. His glass bead–size lens could make a flea look 275 times bigger.

Room IX: Thermometers

Even nature's most changeable force—the weather—was analyzed by human reason.

You'll see many interesting **thermometers** *(termometri)*—spiral ones, tall ones, and skinny ones on distinctive bases. All operate on the basic principle that heat expands things. So, a liquid in a closed glass tube will expand and rise upward as the temperature rises.

Galileo's early thermometer held air, which is too easily affected by changing air pressure. So they experimented with various liquids in a vacuum tube—first water, then alcohol. Finally, Gabriel Fahrenheit (1656–1736) tried mercury, the densest liquid, which expands evenly. He set his scale to the freezing point (32 degrees) and boiling point (212 degrees) of water. Anders Celsius (1701–1744) also used water as the standard but called the freezing point 0 and the boiling point 100.

• *Left of the entrance is...*

Room X: Meteorology

Exhibits X.1–25—Column Barometers

To make a barometer, take a long, skinny glass tube like the one in the wood frame, fill it with liquid mercury, then turn it upside down and put the open end into a bowlful of more mercury. The column of mercury keeps standing as the air in the room "pushes back," pressing down on the surface of the bowl of mercury.

Changing air pressure signals a change in the weather. Hot air expands, pressing down harder on the bowl of mercury, pushing the mercury column up above 30 inches, "pushing away" clouds, and pointing to good, dry weather (called *Gran Secco* on this device). Low pressure lets the mercury drop, warning of "big rains" *(Gran Pioggia)*. Your home barometer probably has a round dial with a needle, but it operates on a similar principle.

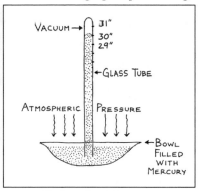

• *To the right of the entrance...*

Exhibit X.54—Hygrometer

When it's humid (lots of water vapor in the air), your hair gets limp. When it's dry, it frizzes. In various humidity gauges displayed here, when it's humid, the thread or paper absorbs moisture, getting heavier and tilting the scale that measures the humidity.

Room XI: Reflecting Telescopes

The telescopes we saw in Room V were "refracting telescopes," made with lenses that bend (refract) light. The big ones in this room—thick-barreled, often with the eyepiece on the side—are

more modern **reflecting telescopes.** They use mirrors to bounce the light rays back and forth through several (refracting) lenses to increase the magnification, thus avoiding the long tubes and distortion of refractors.

Finally, the big double-lensed contraption, *Grande Lente Ustoria* (Exhibit XI.5) was owned by the Medici Grand Duke of Florence, who, I believe, used it to burn bugs.

• *Take a break before heading upstairs.*

SECOND FLOOR

Room XII: Clocks

In an ever-changing universe, what is constant enough to measure the passage of time? The sun and stars passing over every 24 hours work for calendar time, but not for hours, minutes, or seconds. Medieval man used sundials, or the steady flow of water or sand through an opening, but these were only approximate.

By the 1600s, with overseas trade booming, there was a crying need for an accurate and durable clock to help in navigation. Sighting by the stars told you your latitude but was less certain on whether you were near Florence, Italy (latitude 44), or Portland, Maine (also latitude 44). You needed a way to time Earth's 24-hour rotation, to know exactly where you were on that daily journey—i.e., your longitude. Reward money was offered for a good clock that could be taken to sea, and science sprang into action.

• *The big clock to the left of the entrance is a...*

Exhibit XII.38—Planetary Clock

Tick. Tock.

This clock is powered by the big, suspended weights that slowly "fall." The energy turns a series of cogwheels that slowly move the clock hands around the dial. The whole thing is regulated by a horizontal ring (at the top) rocking back and forth, once a second. Though big and crude, this "grandfather"-type clock has the three essentials:

1. Power (falling weights).
2. An "escapement" (the cogs that transform the "falling" power into turning power).
3. A regulator that keeps the gears turning evenly. (This one has a rocking ring, while others used a swinging pendulum.)

• *In the glass case ahead in the left corner, find a...*

Exhibit XII.1—Spring Clock

A clock run by dangling weights won't work on a rocking ship. This clock is powered by a metal spring that slowly uncoils. (The spring is also the power behind most **watches.**) The power is regulated by a pendulum—Galileo's contribution. Unfortunately, a rocking pendulum on a rocking ship won't work either.

The longitude problem was finally solved—and a £20,000 prize won—by John Harrison of England (1693–1776), whose "chronometer" (not in this museum) was a spring-driven clock in a suspension device to keep it horizontal. It was accurate within three seconds a day, far better than any in this room.

• *In the glass case along the right wall...*

Exhibit XII.33—The Writing Hand *(La Mano che Scrive)*

A clockwork mechanism powers this mechanical hand that writes profundities in Latin (It begins *Huic Domui Deus...* and means, "For this house, God limits neither time nor space") The hand gets an A for ingenuity and a B-minus for penmanship.

During the so-called Age of Reason (1600s) and Age of Enlightenment (1700s), the clock was the perfect metaphor for the orderly workings of God's well-crafted universe.

• *To the left of the glass case, find the big, black...*

Exhibit XII.28—"Perpetual Motion" Clock

This big, black clock rolls a ball down a spiral ramp, powering the very device that will launch it back up again. And so on, and so on, ad infinitum...or so hoped those pursuing the elusive machine that could power itself. In fact, in every energy exchange (as stated in the second law of thermodynamics), a certain amount is transformed into nonrecyclable heat, meaning a perpetual motion machine is impossible. This principle of entropy (the trend toward dissipation of energy) leads philosophers to ponder the eventual cold, lifeless fate of the universe itself.

• *Head to the large Room XIV.*

Room XIV: Electricity
(or, more precisely, Electromagnetism)

Lightning, magnets, and static cling mystified humans for millennia. Little did they know that these quite different phenomena are

all generated by the same invisible force—electromagnetism.

In the 1700s, electricity began to be studied, harnessed...and played with. The big **static electricity–generating machine** (in the center of the room) was a popular party amusement. You turned a (missing) crank to spin the glass disk, which rubbed against cloth, generating static electricity. The electricity could be stored in the glass Leyden Jar (a jar coated with metal and filled with water). The metal rod sticking out the top of the jar gave off a small charge when touched, enough to create a spark, shock a party guest, or tenderize a turkey (as Ben Franklin attempted one Thanksgiving). But a static generator like this could never produce enough electricity for practical use.

• *In the glass case to the left of the entrance are several early batteries.*

Alessandro Volta (1745–1827) built the first **battery** in Europe (XIV.114 and XIV.117 are similar), which generates electricity from a chemical reaction. He stacked metal disks of zinc and copper between disks of cardboard soaked with salt water. The zinc slowly dissolves, releasing electrons into the liquid. Hook a wire to each end of the battery, and the current flows. When the zinc is gone, your battery is dead.

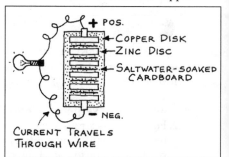

The **electric motor,** *Motore elettrico* (XIV.132, located near the doorway where you entered this room), generates electricity by moving a magnet through a coil of copper wire, a principle perfected by England's Michael Faraday in 1831. This invention soon led to the production of electricity on a large scale.

Room XV: Pneumatic (Air) and Hydraulic (Water) Pumps

Exhibits XV.21–22—Archimedes Screw Models (*Modelo di Vite d'Archimede*)

Back in third-century-B.C. Greece, Archimedes—the man who gave

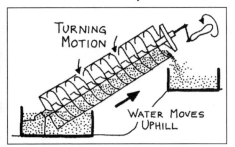

us the phrase "Eureka!" ("I've found it!")—invented a way to pump water that's still occasionally used today. It's a screw in a cylinder. Simply turn the handle and the screw spins, channeling the water up in a spiral path. Dutch windmills powered big Archimedes screws to push water over dikes, to reclaim land from the sea.

Rooms XVI and XVII: Models for Demonstrating Newton's Mechanics

Isaac Newton (1642–1727) explained all of the universe's motion ("mechanics")—from spinning planets to rolling rocks—in a few simple mathematical formulas.

Exhibit XVI.6—Double Rising Cone (*Doppio Cono Saliente*)

The double cone rolls up the incline, seemingly defying gravity and Newton's laws. Ah, but Newton would remind us, the cone's center of gravity is always descending.

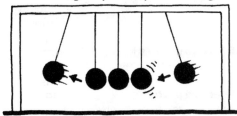

The **collision balls** in Room XVII (the big wooden frame with hanging balls), a popular desktop toy in the 1970s, demonstrate Newton's three famous laws.

1. **Inertia.** The balls just sit there unless something moves them, and once they're set in motion, they'll keep moving the same way until something stops them.
2. **Force = Mass times Acceleration.** The harder you strike the balls, the farther they go. Use two balls to strike with, and you pack twice the punch.
3. **For every action, there's an equal and opposite reaction.** When one ball swings in and strikes the rest, one ball at the other end swings out, then returns and strikes back.

Room XVIII: Medicine

Back when the same guy who cut your hair removed your appendix, surgery was crude. In the 1700s, there were no anesthetics beyond a bottle of wine, and there was no knowledge of antiseptics.

The almost life-size wax **obstetrics models**—showing various breech-style complications—are a pregnant woman's nightmare.

Room XIX: Pharmacy

Exhibit XIX.1—Pharmaceutical Jars (late 1700s)

Read the labels on the jars to see what was considered therapeutic in the 1700s: cocaine *(Coca Boliviana)*, anise, poisonous plants *(Belladonna)*, tea *(The)*, ipecac *(Ipecacuana)*, and something I believe translates as "flies' nuts" *(Noci Mosca)*.

Room XX: Chemistry

• *On the wall, find the...*

Exhibit XX.34—Affinity Table (*Tabula Affinitatum,* 18th century)

This is a precursor of modern periodic tables of the elements. Antoine Lavoisier (1743–1794) was the Galileo of chemistry, introducing sound methodology and transforming the mumbo jumbo of medieval alchemy into hard science. He used the standardized terminology of suffixes that describe the different forms a single element can take (sulfur, sulf-ide, sulf-ate, sulf-uric, etc.).

Room XXI: Weights and Measures

• *In the glass case ahead, bottom shelf, find the...*

Exhibit XXI.28—One-Meter Rod *(Metro)*

Much of the purpose of science is to use constants to measure an ever-changing universe. Here's one constant: the meter, established in 1790 as the fundamental unit by which all distances are measured.

The rod is exactly one meter. Or 39.37 inches. Or 1/1,000th of the distance from the Science Museum to *David*. Or 1/10,000,000th of the distance from the equator to the North Pole. Or, according to the updated definition of 1960, a meter is the length of 1,650,763.73 wavelengths in a vacuum of the orange-red radiation of krypton 86.

Ain't science wonderful?

SLEEPING

For hassle-free efficiency, I favor hotels and restaurants that are handy to your sightseeing activities. Nearly all of my recommended accommodations are located in Florence's downtown core.

The accommodations scene varies wildly with the season. Spring and fall are very tight and expensive, while mid-July through August is wide open and discounted. November through February is also generally empty. I've listed prices for peak season: April, May, June, September, and October.

With good information and an e-mail or phone call beforehand, you can find a stark, clean, and comfortable double with breakfast and a private bath for around €100 (less at the smaller places, such as the *soggiorni*). You get elegance in peak season for €160. Virtually all of the accommodations are within minutes of the great sights. Some places listed are old and rickety, and I've described them as such. I like places that are clean, small, central, relatively quiet at night, traditional, inexpensive, and friendly and not listed in other guidebooks. (In Florence, six out of eight means it's a keeper.)

Book ahead, especially for weekends and holidays (see page 185). Hotels often fill up in advance on Easter (April 8 in 2007), April 25, May 1, June 24 (Florence's patron saint day), November 1, and on Fridays and Saturdays all year. Places will hold a room until early afternoon. If they say they're full, mention that you're using this book. If you're traveling off-season, you can show up without reservations and find huge discounts.

Book direct—not through a tourist agency or Web site. These room-finding services cannot give opinions on quality and they generally take a commission (up to 20 percent) from the hotel. A major advantage of this book is its extensive listing of good-value rooms offered at discounted "net prices." These prices assume (and require) that you book direct so the hotel gets the full room fee, and can pass along their savings to you.

Museum-goers take note: When you book your room, you can usually ask your hotelier to book entry times for you to visit the popular Uffizi Gallery and the Accademia (Michelangelo's *David*). This service is fast, easy, and offered free (or at a small charge) by your hotel—the only requirement is advance notice. Ask them to make appointments for you any time the day after your arrival for the Uffizi and the Accademia. For details, see page 74.

TYPES OF ACCOMMODATIONS

Hotels

Most rooms cluster around €90–150 (with private bathrooms). Three or four people economize by sharing larger rooms. Solo travelers find that the cost of a *camera singola* is often only 25 percent less than a *camera doppia*. Most listed hotels have rooms for anywhere from one to five people. If there's room for an extra cot, they'll cram it in for you.

You normally get close to what you pay for. Prices are fairly standard. Shopping around earns you a better location and more character, but rarely a cheaper price.

However, prices at nearly any hotel can get soft if you do any of the following: arrive direct (without using a pricey middleman like the TI or a Web booking service), offer to pay cash, stay at least three nights, mention this book, or visit off-season. Offer to skip breakfast for a better price. If you're on a budget, ask for a cheaper room or a discount. Always ask.

You'll save €30 if you request a room without a shower and just use the shower down the hall. Generally rooms with a bath or shower also have a toilet and a bidet (which Italians use for quick sponge baths). The cord that dangles over the tub or shower is not a clothesline. You pull it when you've fallen and can't get up (though, oddly, they're often bundled up out of reach to keep them out of the way).

Double beds are called *matrimoniale,* even though hotels aren't interested in your marital status. Twins are *due letti singoli.* Convents offer cheap accommodation but only *letti singoli.*

Air-conditioning sometimes costs an extra per-day charge, is worth seeking out in summer, and is rarely available from fall through spring. Fancier hotels usually come with air-conditioning (included in the price), a little safe, and a small stocked fridge called a *frigo bar* (FREE-goh bar; pay for what you use). Many hotel rooms have a TV and phone.

If you arrive on an overnight train, your room may not be ready. Drop your bag at the hotel and dive right into Florence. When you check in, the receptionist will normally ask for your passport and keep it for a couple of hours. Hotels are legally required to register each guest with the local police. Relax. Americans are notorious for making this chore more difficult than it needs to be.

Assume that breakfast is included in the prices I've listed, unless otherwise noted. If breakfast is included but optional, you might want to skip it. While convenient, it's often a bad value— €10 for a simple continental buffet with unlimited *caffè latte*. You can sometimes request cheese or salami (about €3 extra). I enjoy taking breakfast at the corner café. It's OK to supplement what you order with a few picnic goodies.

Rooms are safe. Still, zip camera bags and keep money out of sight. More pillows and blankets are usually in the closet or available on request. In Italy, towels and linen aren't always replaced every day. Hang your towel up to dry.

Your hotelier, a good source of advice, can direct you to the nearest launderette and Internet café.

To avoid the time-wasting line at the reception desk in the morning, settle up your bill the evening before you leave.

PRACTICALITIES

Phoning

To call Italy from the US or Canada, dial 011-39 (the country code) and then the local number. If calling Italy from another European country, dial 00-39-local number.

Making Reservations

To reserve from home, e-mail, fax, or phone your request. You'll find a handy reservation form in the appendix (online at www .ricksteves.com/reservation). Europeans prefer e-mail to pricey faxing. If you don't get an answer to a faxed request, consider that a "no." (Many little places get 20 faxes a day after they're full and can't afford to respond.) It's also easy to reserve by phone. (For details, see "Telephones" in this book's Introduction—page 12.)

Most hotels listed are accustomed to English-speaking tourists. Simple English is usually fine. A two-night stay for the nights of August 16 and 17 would be "2 nights, 16/8/07 to 18/8/07." (Europeans write the date day/month/year, and hotel jargon uses your day of departure.) You'll often receive a response back requesting one night's deposit.

Your credit card number will usually be accepted as the deposit. Be sure to fax your card number (rather than e-mail it) to keep it private, safer, and out of cyberspace. You can pay with your card or cash when you arrive; if you don't show up, you'll be billed for one night.

Sleep Code

(€1 = about $1.20)
To help you easily sort through these listings, I've divided the rooms into three categories based on the price for a standard double room with bath during high season:

$$$ Higher Priced—Most rooms €165 or more.
  $$ Moderately Priced—Most rooms between €110–165.
    $ Lower Priced—Most rooms €110 or less.

To give maximum information in a minimum of space, I use the following code to describe the recommended accommodations. Prices listed are per room, not per person.

  S = Single room (or price for one person in a double).
  D = Double or Twin room. "Double beds" are often two twins sheeted together and are usually big enough for nonromantic couples.
  T = Triple (generally a double bed with a single).
  Q = Quad (usually two double beds).
  b = Private bathroom with toilet and shower or tub.
  s = Private shower or tub only (the toilet is down the hall).

  According to this code, a couple staying at a "Db-€140" hotel would pay a total of €140 (about $170) for a double room with a private bathroom. You can assume a hotel takes credit cards unless you see "cash only" in the listing. Unless otherwise noted, hotel staff speak basic English and breakfast is included.

Always reconfirm your reservations several days in advance by phone. On the small chance the hotel loses track of your reservation, bring along your faxed confirmations, or hard copies of your confirmations by e-mail.

Honor your reservations, or cancel them by phone or e-mail. Long distance is cheap from public phone booths.

ACCOMMODATIONS IN FLORENCE

Between the Station and Duomo

$$ Hotel Accademia is an elegant place with marble stairs, parquet floors, attractive public areas, 21 pleasant but pricey rooms, and a floor plan that defies logic (Db-€145, Tb-€175, prices promised through 2007 with this book, 5 percent additional discount with cash, air-con, tiny courtyard, Via Faenza 7, tel. 055-293-451, fax 055-219-771, www.hotelaccademiafirenze.com, info@hotelaccademiafirenze.com).

$$ Residenza dei Pucci, a block north of the Duomo, has 12 tastefully decorated rooms—in soothing earth tones—with aristocratic furniture and tweed carpeting. It's fresh and bright (Sb-€130, Db-€145, Tb-€165, Db suite with grand Duomo view-€207, €233 for four, 10 percent discount through 2007 with cash and this book, Via dei Pucci 9, tel. 055-281-886, fax 055-264-314, www .residenzadeipucci.com, residenzadeipucci@residenzadeipucci.com).

$$ Hotel Centrale, with 20 spacious and recently renovated rooms, is indeed central (Db-€140, Tb-€172, 5 percent discount with this book through 2007, air-con, elevator, Via dei Conti 3, tel. 055-215-761, fax 055-215-216, www.hotelcentralefirenze.it, info @hotelcentralefirenze.it).

$ Hotel Aldobrandini, a budget choice in a cheaply remodeled old palazzo, has 15 basic, clean rooms, with the San Lorenzo market at its doorstep and the entrance to the Medici Chapels a few steps away (Ss-€40, Sb-€50, D-€65, Db-€80 with this book in 2007, €75 with cash, lots of night noise but has double-paned windows, fans, behind market stalls at Piazza Madonna degli Aldobrandini 8, tel. 055-211-866, fax 055-267-6281, www.hotelaldobrandini .it, info@hotelaldobrandini.it, Ignazio).

Near the Central Market

$$ Hotel Basilea has predictable three-star, air-conditioned comfort in its 38 modern rooms (Sb-€84, Db-€114, Tb-€160, 5 percent discount and breakfast included with this book in 2007, elevator, terrace, Via Guelfa 41, near intersection with Via Nazionale—a busy street, ask for a room in the back, tel. 055-214-587, fax 055-268-350, www.hotelbasilea.net, basilea@dada.it).

$$ Florence Dream Domus B&B, with six precious little rooms, is well-run and appropriately named—you'll feel like a Medici princess settling into its doily world of aristocratic pastels (Db-€140, Tb-€175, pricier bigger rooms, 2-night minimum, air-con, Via de Ginori 26, tel. 055-295-346, fax 055-267-5643, www .florencedream.it, info@florencedream.it).

$ Hotel Enza, which is basic, quirky, and hard-working, rents 19 decent rooms for a great value (S-€40, Sb-€50, D-€60, Db-€80, 10 percent discount in 2007 with this book and cash, breakfast-€5, air-con except in doubles without bath, Via San Zanobi 45, tel. 055-490-990, fax 055-473-672, www.hotelenza.it, info@hotelenza.it).

$ Casa Rabatti is the ultimate if you always wanted to be a part of a Florentine family. Its four simple, clean rooms are run with motherly warmth by Marcella, who speaks minimal English. Seeing 10 years of my family Christmas cards on their walls, I'm reminded how long she has been keeping budget travelers happy (D-€50, Db-€60, €25 per bed in shared quad or quint, prices good

Florence Hotels

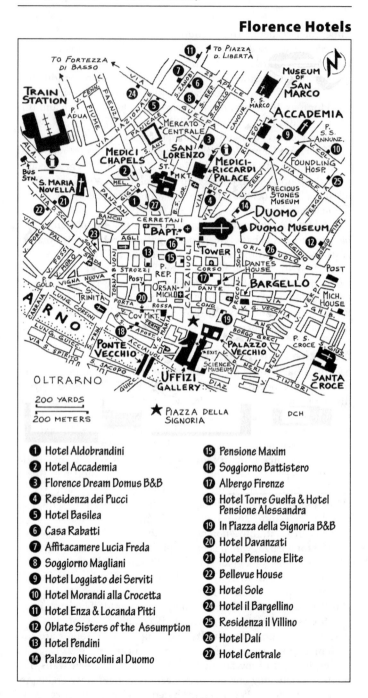

200 YARDS
200 METERS

★ PIAZZA DELLA SIGNORIA

DCH

1. Hotel Aldobrandini
2. Hotel Accademia
3. Florence Dream Domus B&B
4. Residenza dei Pucci
5. Hotel Basilea
6. Casa Rabatti
7. Affitacamere Lucia Freda
8. Soggiorno Magliani
9. Hotel Loggiato dei Serviti
10. Hotel Morandi alla Crocetta
11. Hotel Enza & Locanda Pitti
12. Oblate Sisters of the Assumption
13. Hotel Pendini
14. Palazzo Niccolini al Duomo
15. Pensione Maxim
16. Soggiorno Battistero
17. Albergo Firenze
18. Hotel Torre Guelfa & Hotel Pensione Alessandra
19. In Piazza della Signoria B&B
20. Hotel Davanzati
21. Hotel Pensione Elite
22. Bellevue House
23. Hotel Sole
24. Hotel il Bargellino
25. Residenza il Villino
26. Hotel Dalí
27. Hotel Centrale

with this book in 2007, cash only, no breakfast, has fans, 5 blocks from station, Via San Zanobi 48 black, tel. 055-212-393, casarabatti @inwind.it).

If booked up, Marcella will put you up in her daughter's place nearby at Via Nazionale 20 (five big, airy rooms with fans, no breakfast, closer to the station). While daughter Patricia works, her mom runs the B&Bs. Getting bumped to Patricia's gives you slightly more comfort and slightly less personality...certainly not a net negative.

$ Affitacamere Lucia Freda is basic, clean, and cheap. Its four ground floor-yet-quiet rooms share two bathrooms, a kitchenette, and a leafy garden terrace (S-€45, D-€50, T-€70, cash only, no breakfast, Via San Zanobi 76, but ring at #31, tel. 055-487-533, mobile 380-546-2386, luciafreda@libero.it, run by kind Lucia and son Claudio).

$ Locanda Pitti, tiny and funky with simple rooms, is run by a young couple (Db-€60 with this book and cash in 2007, Tb-€90, air-con-€5, no breakfast, next to Hotel Enza at Via San Zanobi 43, tel. 055-462-7327, mobile 348-597-2670, www.roomsinflorence.it, info@roomsinflorence.it, Isabella and Marco).

$ Soggiorno Magliani is central and humble, with seven rooms that feel and smell like a great-grandmother's home (S-€39, D-€49, T-€65, cash only but secure reservation with credit card, no breakfast, a little traffic noise but has double-paned windows, near Via Guelfa at Via Santa Reparata 1, tel. 055-287-378, hotel -magliani@libero.it, run by the friendly duo Vincenza and her English-speaking daughter, Cristina).

East of the Duomo

$$$ Hotel Loggiato dei Serviti, at the most prestigious address in Florence on the most Renaissance square in town, gives you Old World romance with hair dryers. Stone stairways lead you under open-beam ceilings through this 16th-century monastery's classy

public rooms. The 33 cells—with air-conditioning, TVs, mini-bars, and telephones—wouldn't be recognized by their original inhabitants. The hotel staff is both professional and warm (Sb-€120, Db-€180 promised with this book in 2007, family suites from €263, elevator, Piazza S.S. Annunziata 3, tel. 055-289-592, fax 055-289-595, www.loggiatodeiservitihotel.it, info @loggiatodeiservitihotel.it, Chiara and Simonetta). Ask for a room in the back to avoid piazza noise at night. When full, they rent five spacious and elegant rooms in a 17th-century annex a block away. While it lacks the monastic mystique, the rooms are bigger and gorgeous.

$$$ Hotel Morandi alla Crocetta, another former convent, envelops you in a 16th-century cocoon. Located on a quiet street, with 10 rooms, period furnishings, parquet floors, and wood-beamed ceilings, it takes you back a few centuries (Sb-€100, Db-€177, breakfast not worth €11, a block off Piazza S.S. Annunziata at Via Laura 50, tel. 055-234-4747, fax 055-248-0954, www.hotelmorandi .it, welcome@hotelmorandi.it). The hotel is well run by a terrific team: Claudio, Maurizio, Rolando, Paolo, and Frank.

$$$ Palazzo Niccolini al Duomo is one of five elite Historic Residence Hotels in Florence. The lady of the house, Ginevra Niccolini di Camugliano, actually greets the guests. The lounge is palatial and the 10 rooms are big and splendid, with original 16th-century frescos. If you have the money and want a Florentine palace to call home, this is a very good bet. Opened in 2003, it's just one block from the Duomo (Db-€300, prices vary on the luxuriousness of the room, check online for last-minute deals, Via dei Servi 2, tel. 055-282-412, fax 055-290-979, www.niccolinidomepalace.com, info@niccolinidomepalace.com).

$$ Residenza il Villino is popular and friendly, with 10 rooms and a pleasant, peaceful little courtyard (Db-€120, 5 percent discount in 2007 with cash and this book, Qb apartment-€150, air-con, just north of Via degli Alfani at Via della Pergola 53, tel. 055-200-1116, fax 055-200-1101, www.ilvillino.it, info@ilvillino.it, Sergio, Elisabetta, and son Lorenzo).

$ Hotel Dalí (in all the guidebooks) has 10 decent, basic rooms in a nice location for a great price. Rare in this area and price range, the hotel has plenty of free parking (S-€40, D-€65, Db-€80, extra bed-€20, no breakfast, has fans, great for singles, 2 blocks behind the Duomo at Via dell'Oriuolo 17, tel. and fax 055-234-0706, hoteldali@tin.it, Marco).

$ Oblate Sisters of the Assumption run an institutional 20-room hotel in a Renaissance building with a dreamy garden, fine (if simple) rooms, and a quiet, prayerful ambience. The staff doesn't speak English; it's best to reserve by fax, using simple English that God only knows how they translate (S-€40, D-€76, T-€114, Q-€152, cash only, single beds only, elevator, Borgo Pinti 15, tel. 055-248-0582, fax 055-234-6291).

Near Piazza della Repubblica

These are the most central of my accommodations recommendations (and therefore a little overpriced). While worth the extra cost for many, given Florence's walkable core, nearly every hotel can be considered central.

$$ Hotel Pendini, a three-star hotel overlooking Piazza della Repubblica, has Old World tiles, chandeliers, 42 rooms, and high prices (Sb-€110, Db-€150, air-con, elevator, fine lounge and breakfast room, Via Strozzi 2, tel. 055-211-170, fax 055-281-807, www.hotelpendini.net, pendini@florenceitaly.net, Barbara).

$ Pensione Maxim, right on Via dei Calzaiuoli, is a big, institutional-feeling place as close to the sights as possible. Its halls are narrow, but the 26 basic rooms are comfortable and well-maintained. Their newer and even more sterile hotel is downstairs (Sb-€80, Db-€108, Tb-€138, Qb-€155, 5 percent discount with cash and this book in 2007, air-con, elevator, Via dei Calzaiuoli 11, tel. 055-217-474, fax 055-283-729, www.hotelmaximfirenze.it, hotmaxim@tin.it, father Paolo and daughters Nicola and Chiara).

$ Soggiorno Battistero, literally next door to the Baptistery, has seven simple, airy rooms, most with great views, overlooking the Baptistery and square (Sb-€75, Db-€98, Tb-€135, Qb-€145, prices good through 2007 with this book, 5 percent cash discount, breakfast served in room, air-con, double-paned windows, Wi-Fi, Piazza San Giovanni 1, third floor, no elevator, tel. 055-295-143, fax 055-268-189, www.soggiornobattistero.it, battistero@dada.it, lovingly run by Italian Luca and his American wife Kelly).

$ Albergo Firenze, a big, efficient place, offers 58 modern, basic rooms in a central locale two blocks behind the Duomo (Sb-€78, Db-€98, Tb-€132, Qb-€162, air-con, elevator, noisy, at Piazza Donati 4 across from Via del Corso 8, tel. 055-214-203, fax 055-212-370, www.hotelfirenze-fi.it, firenze.albergo@tiscali.it).

Near Piazza della Signoria and Ponte Vecchio

$$$ Hotel Torre Guelfa is topped by a fun medieval tower with a panoramic rooftop terrace and a huge living room. Its 29 pricey rooms vary wildly in size. Room #15, with a private terrace (€240), is worth reserving several months in advance (Sb-€120, standard Db-€185, Db junior suite-€230, family deals, 5 percent discount with cash in 2007, air-con, elevator, a couple blocks northwest of Ponte Vecchio, Borgo S.S. Apostoli 8, tel. 055-239-6338, fax 055-239-8577, www.hoteltorreguelfa.com, info@hoteltorreguelfa.com; Sabina, Giancarlo, Carlo, and Sandro).

$$$ In Piazza della Signoria B&B, overlooking Piazza della Signoria, is peaceful, classy, and homey at the same time. It comes with all the special touches and little extras you'd expect in a top-end American B&B (viewless Db-€200, view Db-€260, Tb-€280, family apartments, lavish bathrooms, air-con, tiny elevator, Via dei Magazzini 2, tel. 055-239-9546, mobile 348-321-0565, fax 055-267-6616, www.inpiazzadellasignoria.com, info@inpiazzadellasignoria.com, Sonia and Alessandro).

$$ Hotel Pensione Alessandra is 16th-century, tranquil, and sprawling, with 27 big, modern rooms (S-€67, Sb-€113, D-€113, Db-€150, T-€150, Tb-€196, Q-€165, Qb-€217, 5 percent discount with cash, air-con, Borgo S.S. Apostoli 17, tel. 055-283-438, fax 055-210-619, www.hotelalessandra.com, info@hotelalessandra .com, Andrea).

$$ Hotel Davanzati, bright and shiny with artistic touches, has 21 cheery rooms with all the comforts. A family affair, friendly Tomasso and father Fabrizio also book dinners, museums, and excursions (Sb-€100, Db-€160, Tb-€215, prices good in 2007 with this book, 5 percent discount for payment in cash, PlayStation 2 and DVD player in every room, air-con, elevator, Via Porta Rossa 5, tel. 055-286-666, fax 055-265-8252, www.hoteldavanzati.it, info@hoteldavanzati.it).

Near the Train Station

As with any big Italian city, the area around the train station is a magnet for hardworking pickpockets on alert for lost, vulnerable tourists with bulging money belts hanging out of their khakis.

$ Hotel Pensione Elite is run with warmth by sunny Nadia. It has 10 comfortable, if plainly furnished, rooms that can be slightly smoky (Ss-€70, Sb-€80, Ds-€75, Db-€90, Tb-€110, Qb-€130, breakfast-€6, air-con, fans, Via della Scala 12, second floor, tel. & fax 055-215-395, hotelelitefi@libero.it).

$ Bellevue House is a fourth-floor oasis (no elevator) with six spacious rooms flanking a long, mellow yellow lobby. It's a peaceful time-warp thoughtfully run by Rosanna and Antonio di Grazia (Db-€95 in April–June, Sept, and Oct, Db-€75 in off-season, prices promised through 2007 with this book, 5 percent cash discount, includes breakfast in a street level bar, Via della Scala 21, tel. 055-260-8932, mobile 333-612-5973, fax 055-265-5315, www .bellevuehouse.it, info@bellevuehouse.it).

$ Hotel Sole, a clean, cozy, non-English-speaking family-run place with eight bright, modern rooms, feels like a mini-hotel (Sb-€50, Db-€80, Tb-€110, 5 percent cash discount, no breakfast, air-con, elevator, 1:00 curfew, a block toward river from Piazza Santa Maria Novella at Via del Sole 8, tel. & fax 055-239-6094, htlsole @tiscali.it).

$ Hotel il Bargellino, run by Bostonian Carmel and her Italian husband Pino, has 10 summery rooms decorated with funky antique furniture and Pino's modern paintings, just a few blocks north of the train station. Guests are welcome to relax with Carmel on her big, breezy terrace (S-€45, D-€75, Db-€85, extra bed-€25, no breakfast, Via Guelfa 87, tel. 055-238-2658, www .ilbargellino.com, carmel@ilbargellino.com).

Oltrarno Hotels

1 Hotel la Scaletta
2 To Hotel Silla
3 Pensione Sorelle Bandini
4 Soggiorno Alessandra
5 Istituto Gould
6 Ostello Santa Monaca
7 Casa Santo Nome di Gesù

Oltrarno, South of the River

Across the river in the Oltrarno area, between the Pitti Palace and Ponte Vecchio, you'll still find small traditional crafts shops, neighborly piazzas, and family eateries. The following places are an easy walk from the Ponte Vecchio.

$$$ Hotel Silla, a classic three-star hotel with 35 cheery, spacious, pastel, and modern rooms, is a good value. It faces the river and overlooks a park opposite the Santa Croce Church (Db-€170, Tb-€210, discount in 2007 with this book, air-con, Via dei Renai 5, tel. 055-234-2888, fax 055-234-1437, www.hotelsilla.it, hotelsilla @hotelsilla.it, Laura, Chiara, and Stefano).

$$ Hotel la Scaletta, ramshackle and brimming in character, is a dark, cool place with 14 rooms, a narrow labyrinthine floor plan, senseless stairs, lots of Old World lounges, and a romantic, panoramic roof terrace (Sb-€100, Db-€140, Tb-€160, €10/day discount in 2007 with this book, air-con, Via Guicciardini 13 black, 150 yards south of Ponte Vecchio, tel. 055-283-028, fax 055-283-013, www.lascaletta.com, info@lascaletta.com, Giovanna, Paolo, Andrea, and Fabrizio). To fully enjoy their wonderful roof terrace, consider their light "Taste of Tuscany" meal—fine cold cuts, bread, and wine—for €10 per person.

$$ Pensione Sorelle Bandini, a rickety 500-year-old palace on a perfectly Florentine square, has 12 cavernous rooms, museum-warehouse interiors, a musty youthfulness, a Renaissance balcony lounge-loggia with a view, and an ambience that—for romantic bohemians—can be a highlight of Florence (D-€115, Db-€139, T-€158, Tb-€190, cash only, Mimmo or Sr. Romeo give a 10 percent discount with this book in 2007, elevator, Piazza Santo Spirito 9, tel. 055-215-308, fax 055-282-761, pensionebandini@tiscali.it).

$ Istituto Gould is a Protestant Church–run place with 41 clean and spartan rooms with twin beds and modern facilities (S-€36, Sb-€41, D-€50, Db-€58, Tb-€72, Qb-€84, no breakfast, quieter rooms in back, Via dei Serragli 49, tel. 055-212-576, fax 055-280-274, www.istitutogould.it, gould.reception@dada.it). You must arrive when the office is open (Mon–Fri 8:45–13:00 & 15:00–19:30, Sat 9:00–13:00 & 14:30–18:00, no check-in Sun or holidays).

$ Soggiorno Alessandra has five bright, comfy, and small-ish rooms. With double-paned windows, you'll hardly notice the traffic noise (D-€70, Db-€75, Tb-€95, Qb-€125, air-con-€8 extra, just past the Carraia Bridge at Via Borgo San Frediano 6, tel. 055-290-424, fax 055-218-464, www.soggiornoalessandra.it, info @soggiornoalessandra.it, Alessandra).

$ Casa Santo Nome di Gesu is a grand 29-room convent whose sisters—Franciscan Missionaries of Mary—are thankful to rent rooms to tourists. Staying in this 15th-century palace, you'll be immersed in the tranquil atmosphere created by a huge peaceful garden, generous prayerful public spaces, and smiling nuns (D-€70, Db-€85, twin beds only, authentic breakfast room, cheap dinners, Piazza del Carmine 21, tel. 055-213-856, fax 055-281-835, www.fmmfirenze.it, info@fmmfirenze.it).

$ Ostello Santa Monaca, a cheap, well-run hostel, is a long block south of the Brancacci Chapel and attracts a young back-packing crowd (€17 beds with sheets, 4- to 20-bed rooms, 2:00 curfew, Via Santa Monaca 6, tel. 055-268-338, fax 055-280-185, www.ostello.it, info@ostello.it).

Away from the Center
$ Hotel Ungherese is good for drivers. It's northeast of the city center (near *stadio*, en route to Fiesole), with a nice backyard garden, easy, €8/day street parking and quick bus access (#11 and #17)

into central Florence (Sb-€55, Db-€100, extra bed-€20, prices good through 2007 with this book, air-con, Via G. B. Amici 8, tel. & fax 055-573-474, www.hotelungherese.it, info@hotelungherese .it). Ask for a room on the garden. They can recommend good eateries nearby.

$ **Villa Camerata,** classy for an IYHF hostel, is in a pretty villa on the outskirts of Florence (€17.50 per bed with breakfast, 4- to 12-bed rooms, must have hostel membership card, ride bus #17 to Salviatino stop, Via Righi 2, tel. 055-601-451, fax 055-610-300, firenze@hostelinfo.org).

EATING

Italians are masters of the art of fine living. That means eating... long and well. Lengthy, multi-course lunches and dinners and endless hours sitting in outdoor cafés are the norm. Americans eat on their way to an evening event and complain if the check is slow in coming. For Italians, dining is an end in itself, and only rude waiters rush you. When you want the bill, mime-scribble on your raised palm or ask for it: *"Il conto?"*

Even those of us who liked dorm food will find that the local cafés, cuisine, and wines become a highlight of our Italian adventure. This is sightseeing for your palate, and even if the rest of you is sleeping in cheap hotels, your taste buds will relish an occasional first-class splurge. You can eat well without going broke. But be careful; you're just as likely to blow a small fortune on a disappointing meal as you are to dine wonderfully for €20.

Be warned: My readers fill many of the mom-and-pop eateries listed here. But even when packed with travelers, these personality-driven places are a fine value and offer high quality. If you want to steer away from my readers, grab another place. If it's in the center, it'll probably have less value and just as many tourists. To really escape from the crowds, you need to get away from the town center...though I'd rather stick around. You may have the best luck finding a local ambience at lunch, since that's when many places in the center cater to office workers. For dinner, the locals flee, and those same places fill with tourists.

To save money and time for sights, keep lunches fast and simple, eating in one of the countless pizzerias and self-service cafeterias (or picnicking, see page 200). For dessert, it's gelato (see page 202).

Tipping

Tipping is an issue only at restaurants that have waiters and waitresses. If you order your food at a counter, don't tip.

If the menu states that service is included *(servizio incluso)*, Italians generally don't tip any extra. (Many Italians don't ever tip.) But if you like to tip and you're pleased with the service, you could throw in €1 to €2 euros per person at your table.

If service is not included, tip 5 to 10 percent by rounding up or leaving the change from your bill. Leave the tip on the table or hand it to your server. It's best to tip in cash even if you pay with your credit card. Otherwise the money may never reach your server.

Restaurants

Good restaurants don't open before 19:00 for dinner. Restaurants parked on famous squares generally serve bad food at high prices to tourists. Locals eat better at lower-rent locales. Family-run places operate without hired help and can offer cheaper meals. The words *trattoria* and *osteria* (normally simple local-style restaurants) make me salivate. Any place called *ristorante* is generally more formal, with prices to match. While set menus can be cheap and easy, galloping gourmets order à la carte with the help of a menu translator. The *Marling Italian Menu Master* is excellent. *Rick Steves' Italian Phrase Book* has enough phrases for intermediate eaters.

A full meal consists of an appetizer (antipasto, €3–6), a first course (*primo piatto,* pasta or soup, €4–8), and a second course (*secondo piatto,* expensive meat and fish dishes, €6–14). Vegetables *(contorni, verdure)* may come with the *secondo* or cost extra (€3–4) as a side dish. Restaurants normally pad the bill with a cover charge (*pane e coperto*—"bread and cover charge," around €2–3) and a service charge (*servizio,* 15 percent); these charges are listed on the menu.

The euros can add up in a hurry. Light and budget eaters get by with a *primo piatto* each and sharing an antipasto. Italians admit that the *secondo* is the least interesting aspect of the local cuisine.

Delis, Cafeterias, Pizza Shops, and *Tavola Calda* (Hot Table) Bars

Florence offers many cheap alternatives to restaurants. Stop by a *rosticceria* for great cooked deli food; a self-service cafeteria for the basics without the add-ons; a *tavola calda* bar for an assortment of veggies; or a Pizza Rustica shop for stand-up or take-out pizza.

Pizza is cheap and everywhere. Key pizza vocabulary: *capricciosa* (generally ham, mushrooms, olives, and artichokes), *funghi* (mushrooms), *marinara* (tomato sauce, oregano, garlic, no cheese), *quattro formaggi* (4 different cheeses), and *quattro stagioni* (different toppings on each of the 4 quarters for those who can't choose just one menu item). If you ask for *peperoni* on your pizza, you'll get green or red peppers, not sausage. Kids like spicy *diavola* (the closest thing in Italy to American "pepperoni") or bland *margherita* (tomato and cheese) pizzas. At Pizza Rustica take-out shops, slices are sold by weight (100 grams, or *un etto,* is a hot, cheap snack; 200 grams, or *due etti,* makes a light meal).

For a fast, cheap, and healthy lunch, find a *tavola calda* bar with a buffet spread of meat and vegetables and ask for a mixed plate of vegetables with a hunk of mozzarella *(piatto misto di verdure con mozzarella).* Don't be limited by what's displayed. If you'd like a salad with a slice of cantaloupe and a hunk of cheese, they'll whip that up for you in a snap. Step up to the bar and, with a pointing finger and key words from the chart in this chapter, you can get a fine plate of mixed vegetables. If something's a mystery, ask for *un assaggio* (oon ah-SAH-joh) to get a little taste.

Italian Bars/Cafés

Italian "bars" are not taverns but cafés. These local hangouts serve coffee, mini-pizzas, sandwiches, and drinks from the cooler. Many dish up plates of fried cheese and vegetables from under the glass counter, ready to reheat.

For quick meals, bars usually have trays of cheap, ready-made sandwiches *(panini* or *tramezzini)*—some kinds are delightful grilled. To save time for sightseeing and room for dinner, my favorite lunch is a ham and cheese *panino* at a bar (called toast, have it grilled twice if you want it really hot). To get food "to go," say, *"Da portare via"* (for the road). All bars have a WC *(toilette, bagno)* in the back, and customers—and the discreet public—can use it.

Bars serve great drinks: hot, cold, sweet, or alcoholic. Chilled bottled water *(naturale* or *frizzante)* is sold cheap to go.

Coffee: If you ask for *"un caffè,"* you'll get espresso. Cappuccino is served to locals before noon and to tourists any time of day. (To an Italian, cappuccino is a breakfast drink and a travesty after anything with tomatoes.) Italians like it only warm. To get it hot, request *"Molto caldo"* (very hot) or *"Più caldo, per favore"* ("Hotter, please"; pew KAHL-doh, pehr fah-VOH-ray).

Experiment with a few of the options...
- *caffè freddo:* sweet and iced espresso
- cappuccino *freddo:* iced cappuccino
- *caffè hag:* instant decaf (any coffee drink is available decaffeinated; ask for it *decaffeinato:* day-kah-fay-een-AH-toh)
- *macchiato:* with only a little milk
- *caffè latte:* coffee with lots of hot milk, no foam. Note that

Ordering Food at *Tavola Caldas*

plate of mixed veggies	*piatto misto di verdure*	pee-AH-toh MEES-toh dee vehr-DOO-ray
"Heated, please."	*"Scaldare, per favore."*	skahl-DAH-ray pehr fah-VOH-ray
"A taste, please."	*"Un assaggio, per favore."*	oon ah-SAH-joh pehr fah-VOH-ray
artichokes	*carciofi*	kar-CHOH-fee
asparagus	*asparagi*	ah-spah-RAH-jee
beans	*fagioli*	fah-JOH-lee
breadsticks	*grissini*	gree-SEE-nee
green beans	*fagiolini*	fah-joh-LEE-nee
broccoli	*broccoli*	BROK-oh-lee
cantaloupe	*melone*	may-LOH-nay
carrots	*carote*	kah-ROT-ay
ham	*prosciutto*	proh-SHOO-toh
mushrooms	*funghi*	FOONG-ghee
potatoes	*patate*	pah-TAH-tay
rice	*riso*	REE-zoh
spinach	*spinaci*	speen-AH-chee
tomatoes	*pomodori*	poh-moh-DOH-ree
zucchini	*zucchine*	zoo-KEE-nay

(Excerpted from *Rick Steves' Italian Phrase Book*)

ordering a latte gets you only milk.

- *caffè Americano:* espresso diluted with hot water
- *caffè corretto:* espresso with a shot of liqueur (normally grappa, amaro, or Sambuca)

Beer: Beer on tap is *"alla spina."* Get it *piccola* (33 cl or 1.4 cups), *media* (50 cl or about a pint), or *grande* (a liter, about 2 pints).

Wine: To order a glass (*bicchiere*; bee-kee-AY-ray) of red *(rosso)* or white *(bianco)* wine, say, *"Un bicchiere di vino rosso/bianco."* *Corposo* means full-bodied. House wine often comes in a quarter-liter carafe *(un quarto).*

Prices: You'll notice a two-tiered price system. Drinking a cup of coffee while standing at the bar is cheaper than drinking it at a table. If you're on a budget, don't sit without first checking out the financial consequences. Ask "Same price if I sit or stand?" by saying, *"Costa uguale al tavolo o al banco?"* (KOH-stah oo-GWAH-lay ahl TAH-voh-loh oh ahl BAHN-koh).

If the bar isn't busy, you'll often just order and pay when you leave. Otherwise, 1) decide what you want; 2) find out the price by checking the price list on the wall, the prices posted near the food, or by asking the barman; 3) pay the cashier; and 4) give the receipt to the barman (whose clean fingers handle no dirty euros) and tell him what you want.

Picnics

In Florence, picnicking saves lots of euros and is a great way to sample local specialties. For a colorful experience, gather your ingredients in the morning at Florence's Central Market (near the Church of San Lorenzo); you'll probably visit several market stalls to put together a complete meal. A local *alimentari* is your one-stop corner grocery store (most will slice and stuff your sandwich for you if you buy the ingredients there). The rare *supermercato* gives you more efficiency with less color for less cost.

Juice-lovers can get a liter of O.J. for the price of a Coke or coffee. Look for "100% *succo*" (juice) on the label. Hang onto the half-liter mineral-water bottles (sold everywhere for about €1). Buy juice in cheap liter boxes, drink some, and store the extra in your water bottle. (I drink tap water—*acqua del rubinetto*.)

Picnics can be an adventure in high cuisine. Be daring. Try the fresh mozzarella, *presto* pesto, shriveled olives, and any UFOs the locals are excited about. In supermarkets, weigh your produce on the scale with the photo ID chart and print a price tag. In markets and small shops, you're expected to let the shopkeeper choose the produce for you. To get fruit that's ripe and ready "to eat today," say *"per mangiare oggi"* (pehr mahn-JAH-ray OH-jee). Shopkeepers are happy to sell small quantities of produce.

A typical picnic for two might be fresh rolls, 100 grams of cheese, 100 grams of meat (100 grams = about a quarter pound, called *un etto* in Italy), two tomatoes, three carrots, two apples, yogurt, and a liter box of juice. Total cost—about €10.

FLORENTINE CUISINE

While many Florentine restaurants serve your basic Italian fare—pasta and pizza, veal cutlets, and mixed salad—there are a few local specialties you'll find without looking too hard. In general, Florentine cuisine is hearty, simple, farmers' food: grilled meats, high-quality seasonal vegetables, fresh herbs, prized olive oil, and rustic bread. Tuscans are frugal, not wasting a single breadcrumb. They are also known as *mangiafagioli* (bean-eaters)—and sorting through the many beans on Florentine menus you'll learn why.

Note that steak and seafood are often sold by weight (priced by the kilo—1,000 grams, or just over 2 pounds; or by the *etto*—

100 grams). Sometimes, especially for steak, restaurants require a minimum order of four or five *etti*. Beware, or be shell-shocked by €50 entrées.

Here are some typical foods you'll encounter in Florence:

Appetizers *(Antipasti)*

Tuscan bread: Rustic-style breads (not baguettes) with a thick crust and chewy interior. It's a type of sourdough bread, unsalted and nearly flavorless, used almost like a utensil to sop up the heartier-flavored cuisine. Slathered with olive oil and salt, it is a popular afternoon snack. Locals describe the action of dipping their crust repeatedly into the treasured olive oil as "making the *scarpetta* (little shoe)."

Bruschetta: Toasted bread slices brushed with olive oil and rubbed with garlic, topped with chopped tomato, or a variety of spreads.

Crostini: Small toasted bread rounds topped with meat or vegetable pastes. *Alla Toscana* generally means with liver paste. *Lardo* (animal fat) is also a favorite traditional spread.

Panzanella: A simple Tuscan salad, served only in the summer, that's made of chunks of day-old bread and chopped tomatoes, onion, and basil, tossed in a light vinaigrette.

Pecorino cheese: Fresh *(fresco)* or aged *(stagionato),* from ewe's milk.

Porcini mushrooms: Harvested in the fall and used in pasta and soups.

Finocchiona sbriciolona: A soft salami flavored with fennel seed.

First Course *(Primo Piatto)*

Ribollita: "Reboiled" soup traditionally made with leftovers, including white beans *(fagioli),* seasonal vegetables, and olive oil, with layers of day-old Tuscan bread slices.

Pappardelle sulla lepre: This broad noodle is served with a rich sauce made from wild hare.

Pici al ragù: A fat, spaghetti-like pasta served most often with a meat-tomato sauce.

Main Course *(Secondo Piatto)*

Bistecca alla fiorentina: A thick T-bone steak, grilled and lightly seasoned. (The best is from the white Chiana breed of cattle you'll see grazing throughout Tuscany.) This dish is often sold by weight (per *etto,* or 100 grams), not per portion; ask what the minimum amount costs.

Cinghiale: Wild boar, served grilled or in soups, stews, and pasta. It is also made into many varieties of sausage.

Arrosto misto: Mixed roast meats, or meats on a skewer *(spiedino).*

Various game birds: Squab, pheasant, and guinea hen.

Eating with the Seasons

Italian cooks love to serve you fresh produce and seafood at its tastiest. If you must have porcini mushrooms outside of October and November, they'll be frozen. To get the freshest veggies at a fine restaurant, request *"Il piatto di verdure della stagione, per favore"* ("A plate of seasonal vegetables, please").

Here are a few examples of what's fresh when:

April–May:	Squid, green beans, asparagus, artichokes, and zucchini flowers
April, May, Sept, Oct:	Black truffles
May–June:	Asparagus, zucchini, cantaloupe, and strawberries
May–Aug:	Eggplant
Oct–Nov:	Mushrooms and white truffles
Fresh year-round:	Clams, meats, and cheese

Trippa alla fiorentina: Tripe (intestines) and vegetables sautéed in a tomato sauce, sometimes baked with parmesan cheese.

...alla fiorentina: Anything cooked "in the Florentine style." Can mean almost anything, but often means it's cooked with vegetables, especially spinach.

Dessert (Dolci)

Panforte: Dense, dark, clove-and-cinnamon-spiced cake from Siena. *Panforte* makes a good, enduring gift.

Gelato: The Florentines claim they invented Italian-style ice cream. Many think they serve some of the world's best. Consider skipping dessert at the restaurant and stretching your legs before finding a good *gelateria.*

Cantucci and Vin Santo: Florentines love this simple way to end a meal, by dipping the crunchy almond *biscotti* in *vin santo* (literally "holy wine"), a sweet, golden dessert wine.

Wines (Vini)

Brunello di Montalcino: One of Italy's greatest red wines, made from Sangiovese *grosso* grapes, comes from the slopes of Montalcino south of Siena. This full-bodied wine is aged at least four years in wooden casks, resulting in a bold, smooth character. Called "the brunette," it is a dark, brownish red and has a rich, robust, complex aroma that is suitable to pair with hearty, meaty food. Really savor this one; bottles typically start at €25.

Rosso di Montalcino: This lower-priced, younger version of Brunello—a.k.a. "baby Brunello"—is also made in Montalcino from Sangiovese grapes. It lacks the Brunello's depth of flavor and complexity, but it's still a great wine at a bargain price, usually €8–15.

Chianti: The hearty red from the Chianti region (20 miles south of Florence), made mostly from the Sangiovese grape, is world-famous. "Chianti Classico," with a black rooster symbol on the bottle neck, is usually the best. Cheap, €2 Chiantis are acidic, while better ones, starting at €8, can be flavorful, sometimes earthy or fruity.

Vino Nobile di Montepulciano: This high-quality, ruby red, dry wine—also made of Sangiovese grapes—goes well with meat dishes, especially chicken. Don't confuse this one with the inferior (but drinkable) Montepulciano wine available in most US grocery stores.

Super Tuscans: Ultra-expensive and rivaling the Brunello in taste, this newer breed of Italian wine is a creative mix of locally grown non-Italian grapes (usually from French grapes like Cabernet and Merlot), so the Italian regulating body does not rate them. Ask for help in choosing one of these at an *enoteca.* There are many choices, and at these prices, you don't want to be disappointed. Reliable brands are Sassicaia and Tignanello.

Vernaccia di San Gimignano: In Tuscany, this is the only choice for white wine–lovers, but even finicky red wine fans will be able to down a glass of this medium-dry white, which pairs well with pasta and salad.

RESTAURANTS

North of the River

Near Santa Maria Novella and the Train Station

Trattoria al Trebbio serves traditional food with simple Florentine elegance at excellent prices in its candle-lit interior. Tables spill out onto a romantic little square—an oasis of Roman Trastevere-like charm (Wed–Mon 12:00–15:00 & 19:00–23:00, Tue 12:00–15:00 only, reserve for outdoor seating, half a block off of Piazza Santa Maria Novella at Via delle Belle Donne 47, tel. 055-287-089).

At **Osteria Belledonne,** you'll feel like you're eating dinner in a crowded terrarium piled high with decorative knickknacks. Old-fashioned Tuscan food is served on tight tables—a few tables hunker on the street. They take few reservations; arrive early or wait (daily 12:00–15:00 & 19:00–23:00, Via delle Belle Donne 16 red, tel. 055-238-2609, run by sprightly Giacinto).

Trattoria Marione serves sincerely home-cooked-style meals to a mixed crowd of tourists and locals in a happy, food-loving, and steamy ambience. Dinners run about €15 plus wine (daily

Florence Restaurants

★ PIAZZA DELLA SIGNORIA

DCH

200 YARDS
200 METERS

1 Osteria Belledonne
2 Trattoria al Trebbio
3 Trattoria Marione
4 Trattoria Sostanza-Troia
5 Trattoria 13 Gobbi
6 Trattoria Zà-Zà & Trattoria Mario's
7 Central Market & Trattoria la Burrasca
8 Osteria la Congrega
9 Gran Caffè San Marco
10 Self-Service Rist. Leonardo
11 Antico Ristorante il Sasso di Dante
12 Ristorante il Ritrovo
13 Casa del Vino
14 Osteria Vini e Vecchi Sapori
15 Cantinetta dei Verrazzano & Ristorante Paoli
16 I Fratellini Wine & Sandwiches
17 Trattoria Icche C'è C'è
18 Osteria del Porcellino
19 Trattoria Nella
20 Café Rivoire
21 Osteria Vineria i'Brincello
22 Trattoria Nerone Pizzeria
23 Pasticceria Robiglio
24 Gelateria Carrozze
25 Gelateria dei Neri
26 Gelateria Carabè
27 Gelateria Grom
28 Vivoli's Gelateria
29 Il Centro Supermarcati

10:00–15:00 & 19:00–22:30, Via della Spada 27 red, tel. 055-214-756).

Trattoria Sostanza-Troia, characteristic and well-established, is famous for its beef. Hearty steaks and pastas are splittable. Whirling ceiling fans and walls strewn with old photos evoke earlier times, while the artichoke pies remind locals of grandma's cooking. Crowded, shared tables with paper tablecloths lend a bistro feel. They offer two dinner seatings, requiring reservations: one at 19:30 and one at 21:00 (dinners for about €30 plus wine, lunch Mon–Sat 12:30–14:00, closed Sun, closed Sat in off-season, Via del Porcellana 25 red, tel. 055-212-691).

Trattoria 13 Gobbi (13 Hunchbacks) is a trendy favorite, glowing with candles around a tiny garden. It serves beautifully presented, surprisingly reasonable Tuscan food on big, fancy plates to a dressy, local crowd (daily 12:15–15:00 & 19:30–23:00, Via del Porcellana 9 red, tel. 055-284-015).

Near the Central and San Lorenzo Markets

For piles of picnic produce, people-watching, or just a rustic sandwich, try the huge **Central Market** (Mercato Centrale, Mon–Sat 7:00–14:00, closed Sun, a block north of San Lorenzo street market). The cheap eateries within the market can be more colorful than sanitary. Buy a picnic of fresh mozzarella cheese, olives, fruit, and crunchy bread to munch on the steps of the nearby Church of San Lorenzo, overlooking the bustling street market.

Each of the following market neighborhood eateries is distinct and within a hundred yards of each other. Scout about and choose your favorite.

At **Casa del Vino,** Florence's oldest operating wine shop, you can order a glass of wine from among 25 open bottles, and sip it alongside local workers on break. Owner Gianni (pronounced "Johnny"), whose family has owned the Casa for 70 years, also serves interesting *panini* (Mon–Fri 9:30–19:00, closed Sat–Sun, hidden behind stalls of the San Lorenzo Market on Via dell'Ariento 16 red).

Trattoria Zà-Zà is a fun, old, characteristic high-energy place facing the Central Market. Locals lament the invasion of tourists, but everyone's happy, and the food is still great. *Ribollita,* a Tuscan soup, is their specialty. Arrive early or make a reservation, especially for the wonderful outdoor piazza seating. Consider cobbling together a meal of different *antipasti* plates (daily 11:30–23:00, Piazza del Mercato Centrale 26 red, tel. 055-215-411).

Trattoria Mario's, next to Zà-Zà, has been serving market-goers hearty lunches since 1953. Their simple formula: bustling service, old-fashioned good value, a lunch-only menu, and shared tables. It's *cucina casalinga*—home cooking. Mario's is extremely popular, so go early. If there's a line, put your name on the list

(€4 pastas, €7 *secondi*, Mon–Sat 12:00–15:30, closed Sun, cash only, no reservations, Via Rosina 2, tel. 055-218-550).

Trattoria la Burrasca is Flintstone-chic, family-run, and ideal for Tuscan home cooking. It's small—10 tables—and often filled with our readers. Anna and Antonio Genzano have cooked and served here with passion since 1982. If Andy Capp were Italian, he'd eat here for special nights out. Everything is home-made except the desserts. And if you want good wine cheap, this is the place (Fri–Wed 12:00–15:00 & 19:00–22:30, closed Thu, Via Panicale 6 black, at north corner of Central Market, tel. 055-215-827, very little English spoken).

Osteria la Congrega brags it's "a Tuscan wine bar designed to help you lose track of time." In a fresh, romantic two-level setting, chef/owner Mahyar takes pride in his fun, easy menu featuring modern Tuscan cuisine, with top-notch meat and seasonal produce. He offers quality vegetarian dishes, creative salads, and an inexpensive but excellent house wine. With just 10 uncramped tables, reservations are required for dinner (€6 pastas, €12 nightly specials, daily 12:00–15:00 & 19:00–23:00, Via Panicale 43 red, tel. 055-264-5027). Mahyar offers fine wines by the glass (see list on blackboard).

Osteria Vineria i'Brincello is a bright, happy, no-frills diner with lots of spirit, friendly service, and few tourists during lunchtime. Notice the Tuscan daily specials on the blackboard hanging from the ceiling (daily 12:00–15:00 & 18:30–22:30, corner of Via Nazionale and Via Chaira at Via Nazionale 110 red, tel. 055-282-645).

Trattoria Nerone Pizzeria serves up cheap, hearty Tuscan dishes and just-OK pizzas. The lively, flamboyantly outfitted space was once the garden courtyard of a convent (€5 pastas, €10 *secondi*, daily 11:30–23:00, just north of Via Nazionale at Via Faenza 95–97 red, tel. 055-291-217).

Near the Accademia and Museum of San Marco

Pasticceria Robiglio, a classy little café, opens up its stately dining area for lunch on workdays. They have a small menu of daily pasta and *secondi* specials and seem determined to do things like they did in the elegant pre-tourism days (generous €8 plates, pretty pastries, good wines by the glass, smiling service, Mon–Fri 12:00–15:00, longer hours as a café, open Sat but no meals, closed Sun, a block towards the Duomo off Piazza S.S. Annunziata at Via dei Servi 112 red, tel. 055-212-784).

Gran Caffè San Marco, located on Piazza San Marco across from the entrance of the Museum of San Marco, might tempt you with its convenience and outdoor seating, but it churns out horrible cafeteria fare to cheap but tired tourists. Your best bet is to grab a *panino*—of which there are several vegetarian options—from their bar on the corner (no cover charge, self-service bar and restaurant, Piazza San Marco 11, entrance around the corner on Via Cavour near #50, tel. 055-215-833).

Picnic on the Ultimate Renaissance Square: There's a handy supermarket across from the Accademia *(David)* which happily makes sandwiches to your specs (Il Centro Supermarcati, Mon–Sat 8:00–20:00, Sun 9:00–19:00, Via Ricasoli 109). Choose your fresh bread and tasty meat and cheese (assembled and sold by the weight); embellish with some veggies, milk, yogurt, or juice; and hike around the block to Piazza S. S. Annunziata, the first Renaissance square in Florence. There's a fountain for washing fruit on the square. Grab a stony seat anywhere you like and savor one of my favorite cheap Florence eating experiences. (Or, drop by Pasticceria Robiglio, half a block from the square—see the beginning of this section—for a sandwich and juice to go.)

Near the Duomo
Self-Service Ristorante Leonardo is fast, cheap, air-conditioned, and handy, just a block from the Duomo, southwest of the Baptistery (€3.50 pastas, €5 main courses, Sun–Fri 11:45–14:45 & 18:45–21:45, closed Sat, upstairs at Via Pecori 5, tel. 055-284-446). Luciano (like Pavarotti) runs the place with enthusiasm.

Antico Ristorante il Sasso di Dante serves standard Tuscan fare in a surprisingly pleasant indoor/outdoor setting in the shadow of the Duomo (€18 two-course meals, always good vegetarian dishes and special menu of the day, daily 12:00–14:30 & 19:00–22:30, come early to snag front-row seats, Piazza delle Pallottole 6, tel. 055-282-113).

Ristorante il Ritrovo, hiding down some nondescript stairs off a boring street, offers a bright, dressy setting with a homey welcome. Its meaty Tuscan cuisine, cooked with family pride, is popular for lunch with local office workers (menù €10 lunch with pasta and *secondo,* Tue–Sat 12:30–14:30 & 19:00–22:30, closed Sun–Mon, 12 tables, air-con, a block north of the Duomo at Via dei Pucci 4, tel. 055-281-688).

Near Palazzo Vecchio
Piazza della Signoria, the square facing Palazzo Vecchio, is ringed by beautifully situated yet touristy eateries. Don't waste a meal on probably microwaved food. The square's saving grace is dessert at the famous **Café Rivoire,** with its fancy desserts and thick hot chocolate. It has the top seating, service, and edibles on the square (Mon–Sat 7:40–24:00, closed Sun).

Osteria Vini e Vecchi Sapori, half a block north of Palazzo Vecchio, is a colorful hole-in-the-wall serving traditional food, including plates of mixed crostini (less than €1 each—step right up and choose at the bar) and €10 daily specials (Tue–Sat 12:30–3:00 & 19:30–22:00, Sun 12:30–3:00, closed Mon, Via dei Magazzini 3 red, facing the bronze equestrian statue in Piazza della Signoria, go behind its tail into the corner and to your left, run by Mario and Thomas).

Cantinetta dei Verrazzano is a long-established bakery/café/wine bar, serving delightful sandwich plates in an elegant old-time setting, and hot focaccia sandwiches to go. Their *Specialità Verrazzano* is a fine plate of four little crostini (like mini bruschetta) featuring different local breads, cheeses, and meats (€7.50). The *Tagliere di Focacce* (confirm the €6 per person price), a sampler plate of mini-focaccia sandwiches, is also fun. Either of these dishes with a glass of Chianti makes a fine light meal. As office workers pop in for a quick bite, it's traditional to share tables at lunchtime (Mon–Sat 8:00–21:00, closed Sun, just off Via dei Calzaiuoli on a side street across from Orsanmichele Church at Via dei Tavolini 18, tel. 055-268-590).

I Fratellini is a rustic little eatery where the "little brothers" have served peasants 27 different kinds of sandwiches and cheap glasses of Chianti wine (see list on wall) since 1875. Join the local crowd, then sit on a nearby curb or windowsill to munch, placing your glass on the wall rack before you leave (€4 for sandwich and wine, Mon–Sat 8:00–20:00, closed Sun, 20 yards in front of Orsanmichele Church on Via dei Cimatori). Be adventurous with the menu (easy-order by number). Consider *Finocchiona* (the special local salami), *Lardo di Colonnata* (lard aged in Carrara marble), and *Cinghiale Piccante* (spicy wild boar) sandwiches. Order the most expensive wine they've corked (Brunello for €4). Bottles are labeled.

Ristorante Paoli serves wonderful local cuisine to loads of cheerful eaters under a richly frescoed Gothic vault. Because of its fame and central location, it's filled mostly with tourists, but for a classy, traditional splurge meal, this is my choice (Wed–Mon 12:00–14:30 & 19:00–22:30, closed Tue, reserve for dinner, €21 tourist menù, à la carte is pricier, midway between Piazza della Signoria and the Duomo at Via dei Tavolini 12 red, tel. 055-216-215). Salads are flamboyantly cut and mixed from a trolley right at your table. The walls are sweaty with memories that go back to 1824, and the service is flamboyant and fun-loving—but don't get taken. Confirm prices. Woodrow Wilson slurped spaghetti here (his bust looks down on you as you eat).

Trattoria Icche C'è C'è (ee-kay chay chay; dialect for "whatever is, is") is a small, family-style eatery where fun-loving Gino serves quality traditional meals (three-course €11 meals, not too touristy, Tue–Sun 12:30–14:30 & 19:00–24:00, closed Mon, midway between Bargello and river at Via Magalotti 11 red, tel. 055-216-589).

Osteria del Porcellino offers a romantic setting and a seasonal menu of Tuscan classics with a creative flair. This dark, dense, candlelit place is packed with a mix of locals and tourists and run with style and enthusiasm by friendly chef Enzo. In summer, they also have inviting outdoor seating in a secretive setting out back (€8 pastas, €18 *secondi*, daily 12:00–14:30 & 19:00–24:00, reserve for dinner, Via Val di Lamona 7 red, half a block behind Mercato Nuovo, tel. 055-264-148).

Trattoria Nella serves good, typical Tuscan cuisine at affordable prices. Arrive early or be disappointed—it's understandably popular. Save room for the *panna cotta* cooked cream dessert (€22 meals, Mon–Sat 12:00–15:00 & 19:00–22:00, Sun 19:00–22:00, 3 blocks northwest of Ponte Vecchio, Via delle Terme 19 red, tel. 055-218-925). Twin brothers Federico and Lorenzo carry on their dad's tradition of keeping their clientele well-fed and happy.

Oltrarno, South of the River
Near Ponte Vecchio

Ristorante Bibo serves *"cucina tipica Fiorentina"* with a pink-table-cloth-and-black-bow-tie dressiness, and leafy, candlelit outdoor seating. It's quiet and romantic, though the food can be bland (€15 three-course meal, leave this book face up on the edge of the table for a 15 percent discount, daily 12:00–14:30 & 19:00–22:30, Piazza Santa Felicita 6 red, tel. 055-239-8554, enthusiastic Tonino).

Golden View Open Bar is a lively, trendy place, good for a salad, pizza, or pasta with fine wine and a fine view of Ponte Vecchio and the Arno River. Reservations for window tables are recommended (reasonable prices, €10 pizzas and huge salads, daily 11:30–24:00, pizza and wine served even later, impressive wine bar, 50 yards upstream from Ponte Vecchio at Via dei Bardi 58, tel. 055-214-502, run by Francesco, Marco, and Tomaso). They have three zones: a river-side pizza place, a classier restaurant, and a jazzy lounge plus a wine bar. The live jazz (Sun, Mon, and Wed at 21:00) makes for a wonderful evening.

Via di Santo Spirito and Borgo San Jacopo

Several good and colorful restaurants line this multi-named street a block off the river in Oltrarno. I'd survey the scene (perhaps following the self-guided Oltrarno Walk described on page 51) before making a choice.

Trattoria Cammillo was formerly run by Cammillo, who is now slurping spaghetti in heaven. His granddaughter Chiara carries on the legacy, mixing traditional Tuscan and creative, modern cuisine. With a charcoal grill and a team of white-aproned waiters cranking out terrific food in a fun, noisy, dressy-but-down-to-earth ambience, this place is a hit (full dinners about €36 plus

Oltrarno Restaurants

1 Ristorante Bibo

2 Golden View Open Bar

3 Trattoria Cammillo

4 Trattoria Angiolino

5 To Trattoria Sabatino & Trattoria da Sergio

6 Borgo Antico, Osteria Santo Spirito, Ricchi Caffè & Café Cabiria

7 Trattoria Casalinga

8 Olio & Convivium Gastronomia Restaurant

wine, Thu–Mon 12:00–14:30 & 19:30–22:30, closed Tue–Wed, reservations smart, Borgo San Jacopo 57 red, tel. 055-212-427).

Trattoria Angiolino serves good, old-fashioned local cuisine. Sit in the main hall rather than the stuffy side rooms (€20 for dinner plus wine, Tue–Sun 12:00–14:30 & 19:30–22:30, closed Mon, Via di Santo Spirito 36 red, tel. 055-239-8976).

Olio & Convivium Gastronomia Restaurant started as an elegant deli whose refined oil-tasting room has morphed into a romantic, aristocratic restaurant. Their three intimate rooms are surrounded by fine *prosciutti*, cheeses, and wine shelves. It's a gentle, friendly place with a quiet atmosphere and fine wines by the glass—a foodie's delight (€10 pastas, €15 *secondi*, Mon 10:00–15:00,

Tue–Sat 10:00–15:00 & 17:30–22:30, Via di Santo Spirito 4, tel. 055-265-8198).

Trattoria Sabatino, farthest away and least touristy, is spacious and disturbingly cheap, with family character, red-checkered tablecloths, and a simple menu. A super place to watch locals munch, it's just outside the Porta San Frediano (medieval gate), a 15-minute walk from Ponte Vecchio (Mon–Fri 12:00–14:30 & 19:20–22:00, closed Sat–Sun, Via Pisana 2 red, tel. 055-225-955, little English spoken). If you eat here, let it be your reward after following my self-guided Oltrarno Walk (on page 51).

Trattoria da Sergio, a tiny eatery about a block before Porta San Frediano, has homey charm and a strong local following. The food is on the gourmet side of home-cooking and therefore a bit more expensive but worth the little splurge (€9 pastas, €14 *secondi*, Tue–Sun 12:00–14:30 & 19:30–22:30, closed Mon, reservations smart for dinner, Borgo San Frediano 145 red, tel. 055-223-449).

Piazza Santo Spirito

This classic Florentine square (a bit seedy-feeling but favored by locals) has several popular little restaurants and bars that are open nightly. They offer good local cuisine, moderate prices, and impersonal service, with a choice of indoor or romantic on-the-square seating (reservations smart).

Lively **Borgo Antico** is the hit of the square, with enticing pizzas, big deluxe plates of pasta, a delightful setting, and a trendy and boisterous young local crowd (daily 12:00–24:00, best to reserve for a seat on the square, Piazza Santo Spirito 6 red, tel. 055-210-437). The quieter **Osteria Santo Spirito** has good seating on the square, a hip, eclectic interior, and cheap grub (Piazza Santo Spirito 16 red, tel. 055-238-2383).

Ricchi Caffè, next to Borgo Antico, has fine gelato, homemade desserts, shaded outdoor tables, and best of all, €3.50 pasta dishes at lunchtime (Mon–Sat 7:00–24:00, closed Sun, tel 055-215-864). After noting the plain facade of the Brunelleschi church facing the square, step inside the café and pick your favorite picture of the many ways it might be finished.

Café Cabiria, on the other side of Borgo Antico, is a trendy local hangout with good, light meals, noisy 21st-century music, and a cozy Florentine-funky room in back (Wed–Mon 10:30–1:30, closed Tue, tel. 055-215-732).

Trattoria Casalinga, an inexpensive standby, comes with aproned women bustling around the kitchen. It's probably been too popular for too long, as the service has gone a bit surly and it feels like every student group, backpacker, and Florentine artisan ends up here. But people seem to leave full and happy, with euros to spare for gelato (Mon–Sat 12:00–14:30 & 19:00–21:45, after 20:00 reserve or wait, closed Sun and all of Aug, just off Piazza Santo Spirito, near the church at Via dei Michelozzi 9 red, tel. 055-218-624).

Gelato

Gelato is an edible art form. Italy's best ice cream is in Florence—one souvenir that can't break and won't clutter your luggage. But

beware of scams at touristy joints on busy streets that turn a simple request for a cone into a €10 "tourist special" rip-off.

A key to gelato appreciation is sampling liberally and choosing flavors that go well together. Ask, as the locals do, for *"Un assaggio, per favore?"* (A taste, please?; oon ah-SAH-joh pehr fah-VOH-ray) and *"Che si sposano bene?"* (What marries well?; kay see spoh-ZAH-noh BEN-ay). *Artiginale, Nostra Produzione,* and *Produzione Propia* mean gelato is made on the premises. Also, gelato displayed in metal tins, rather than the normal white plastic, indicates it's likely to be homemade.

Gelateria Carrozze is very good (daily 11:00–24:30, closes at 20:00 in winter; on riverfront 30 yards from Ponte Vecchio toward the Uffizi, Via del Pesce 3).

Gelateria dei Neri is a favorite worth tracking down (daily 11:00–24:00, try the *crostata*—a strawberry pie flavor, 2 blocks east of Palazzo Vecchio at Via dei Neri 20/22 red).

Gelateria Carabè, a stellar choice on a tourist thoroughfare, also serves up several flavors of luscious *granita,* Italian ices made with fresh fruit (daily 9:00–2:00 in the morning, between the Duomo and Accademia, Via Ricasoli 60 red). **Grom,** another *gelateria,* uses organic ingredients and only seasonal fresh fruit (daily 11:00–23:00, Via delle Oche 24a).

Vivoli's, which serves "only today's production" is the most famous (Tue–Sun 8:00–1:00; closed Mon, closed Aug and Jan; opposite the Church of Santa Croce, go down Via Torta a block, turn right on Via Stinche). Before ordering, try a free sample of their rice flavor—*riso.*

If you want an excuse to check out the little village-like neighborhood across the river from Santa Croce, enjoy a gelato at the tiny no-name *gelateria* at Via San Miniato 5 red (just before Porta San Miniato).

FLORENCE WITH CHILDREN

Florence with kids: not ideal. But it's certainly good for them! Here are a few thoughts on family fun in the art capital of Europe.

- Be certain to call ahead to get admission appointments whenever possible. (Booking ahead is especially important for the Uffizi and to see *David* at the Accademia. You can book a museum visit when reserving a hotel room—see page 184 for more info.) Long museum lines add insult to injury for the preteen dragged into another old building filled with old paintings.

- Avoid the midday heat by planning on a cool break such as an air-conditioned, kid-friendly place for lunch.

- Eat dinner early (around 19:00), and you'll miss the romantic crowd. Skip the famous places. Look instead for self-serve cafeterias, bars (kids are welcome), or even fast-food restaurants where kids can move around without bothering others. Picnic lunches and dinners work well. For ready-made picnics, drop by the *rosticcerie* (delis) and Pizza Rustica shops (cheap take-out pizza; *diavola* is the closest thing on the menu to kid-friendly pepperoni).

- Public WCs are hard to find: Try museums, bars, gelato shops, and fast-food restaurants.

- The smart tour guide/parent incorporates the child's interests into each day's plans. When a child is unhappy, no one has fun.

- Guidebooks can make history more accessible for kids. Try *Florence: A Young Traveller's Guide* (ages 6–9) or *Florence: Just Add Water* (age 10 to adults), both easy to find in Florence. (See bookstores listed under "Helpful Hints," page 26.)

SIGHTS AND ACTIVITIES

The **Science Museum** has cool old telescopes and early chemical and science lab stuff. But the case with Galileo's finger will likely be the main highlight here (closed most Sun; see Science Museum Tour, page 169).

After touring a bunch of hands-off museums, squirming kids will enjoy the hands-on activities at the **Leonardo Museum,** where all that human energy can be used to power modern recreations of da Vinci's machines (see page 47).

Climbing the dome of the cathedral is almost like climbing an urban mountain—you'll spiral up in a strange dome-within-a-dome space, see some musty old tools used in the construction, get a bird's-eye peek into the nave from way up, and then pop out with the best city view in town. Arrive by 8:30 to beat the crowds; otherwise it may not be worth the long, slow-moving line (closed Sun; see page 37).

Every kid will want to see Michelangelo's *David* (closed Mon; see Renaissance Walk, page 56). But the most interesting collection of statues—with many bizarre poses—is in the **Bargello** (see Bargello Tour, page 95).

Museo dei Ragazzi (Kids' Museum), in Palazzo Vecchio, offers activities for children (age 4 to teens) on a reservation-only basis. The kids can take a guided English tour with a historically costumed character, or make their own fresco on a souvenir tile (€6 plus €1–2/activity, family rates, no reservation fee, call center to reserve, daily 9:00–18:00, tel. 055-276-8224 or 055-276-8558).

The **Museum of Precious Stones** shows 500 different semi-precious stones and then demonstrates the fascinating techniques of inlay and mosaic work (closed Sun, around corner from *David;* see page 33).

The **Uffizi courtyard** is ringed by statues of all the famous Florentines (Amerigo Vespucci, Machiavelli, Leonardo, and so on)—great for putting a face on a sweep through history (see page 71 of Renaissance Walk).

Florence's various **open-air markets** are fun for kids (see Shopping chapter). Remember to haggle.

The **Boboli and Bardini Gardens** are landscaped wonderlands. While designed to give adults a break from the city, they are kid-friendly compared to streets and museums (closed first and last Mon of month; see page 49). To get to Florence's sprawling public park, **Parco delle Cascine,** head west of the old center along the north side of the river (10-min walk, lots of grass, playground, and swimming pool open June–Sept).

Situated closer to town, the peaceful and breezy **Piazza d'Azeglio** park—complete with playground—can be a welcome refuge from touring madness (daily dawn to dusk, 15-min walk east from Duomo or take bus #12 or #13 from train station or from Via Cavour bus stop just north of Duomo).

Older kids may enjoy or hiking up to **Piazzale Michelangelo**

for the view or taking a **bike tour** through the countryside. Florence by Bike rents bikes of all sizes and city bikes with rear child seats (Via San Zanobi 120 red, tel. 055-488-992, www .florencebybike.it).

For kids running on their gelato buzz well into the evening hours, the vibrant **Piazza della Repubblica** has plenty of goofy street performers and lively musicians. A sparkling **carousel** adds a magical touch, but makes the rounds of different city piazzas throughout the year, so check at the TI.

Of all the side trips, a jaunt to see the leaning tower in **Pisa** is probably the most interesting for kids (see Pisa chapter, page 276).

EATING

For fast and kid-friendly meals in the old center, there are plenty of hamburger and pizza joints. For a good cafeteria, try Self-Service Ristorante Leonardo (a block from the Duomo; see page 207 of Eating). *Gelaterie* such as Festival del Gelato (Via del Corso 75 red) and Perchè No! (Via dei Tavolini 19 red) are brash and neon and provide some of the best high-calorie memories in town.

SHOPPING

Florence is a great shopping town—known for its sense of style since the Medici days. Many people spend entire days shopping. Stores are open 9:00–13:00 and 15:30–19:30, usually closed on Sunday, often closed on Monday, and sometimes closed for a couple of weeks around August 15. Many stores have promotional stalls in the market squares.

For shopping ideas, ads, and a list of markets, see the *Florence Concierge Information* magazine (free from TI and many hotels).

Markets

Busy street scenes and markets abound. Prices are soft in the markets—go ahead and bargain. Perhaps the biggest market fills the streets around the Church of San Lorenzo with countless stalls selling lower-end leather, clothing, T-shirts, handbags, and souvenirs. Beware of fakes (daily 9:00–19:00, closed Mon in winter, between the Duomo and train station). The shops behind the street stalls (and along nearby  Via Faenza) are great for a peek into workaday Florentine life. The neighboring Central Market is a giant covered food market (Mon–Sat 7:00–14:00, closed Sun, a block north of the Church of San Lorenzo).

Other popular shopping centers are the Santa Croce area (known for leather; check out the "leather school," which is actually inside the Santa Croce Church—enter to the right of the altar); Ponte Vecchio (traditional spot for gold and silver); and the old, covered Mercato Nuovo (three blocks north of Ponte Vecchio,

Getting a VAT Refund

Wrapped into the purchase price of your Florentine souvenirs is a Value Added Tax (VAT) that's generally about 20 percent. If you purchase more than €155 worth of goods at a store that participates in the VAT refund scheme, you're entitled to get most of that tax back. Personally, I've never felt that VAT refunds are worth the hassle, but if you do, here's the scoop.

If you're lucky, the merchant will subtract the tax when you make your purchase (this is more likely if the store ships the goods to your home) and you won't have to deal with any paperwork. Paying in cash boosts your chances here. Otherwise, you'll need to:

Get the paperwork. Have the merchant completely fill out the necessary refund document, called a "cheque." You'll have to present your passport.

Get your stamp at the border or airport. Process your cheque(s) at your last stop in the European Union with the customs agent who deals with VAT refunds. It's best to keep your purchases in your carry-on for viewing, but if they're too large or dangerous (such as knives) to carry on, then track down the proper customs agent to inspect them before you check your bag. You're not supposed to use your purchased goods before you leave. If you show up at customs at the airport wearing your new shoes, officials might look the other way—or deny you a refund.

Collect your refund. You must return your stamped document to the retailer or its representative. Many merchants work with services such as Global Refund or Premier Tax Free, which have offices at major airports, ports, or border crossings. These services, which extract a 4 percent fee, can refund your money immediately in your currency of choice or credit your card (within two billing cycles). If you have to deal directly with the retailer, mail the store your stamped documents and then wait. It could take months.

described on page 44).

For antiques, wander the Oltrarno (south side of river), specifically along Borgo San Jacopo and Via Maggio.

A **flea market** litters Piazza dei Ciompi with antiques and odds and ends daily but is really big only on the first Sunday of each month (9:00–20:00, near Piazza Santa Croce).

Boutiques and High Fashion

The entire area between the river and the cathedral is busy with inviting boutiques showing off ritzy Italian fashions. The street Via de' Tornabuoni is best for boutique browsing. The main **Ferragamo** store fills a classy 800-year-old building with a fine selection of shoes and boots and an interesting **shoe museum** upstairs (store: Mon–Sat 10:00–19:30, closed Sun; museum: Mon–Fri 9:00–18:00, closed Sat–Sun; near the S. Trinita bridge at Via de' Tornabuoni 2, tel. 055-292-123). For more boutiques, meander the streets Via della Vigna Nuova (runs west from Via de' Tornabuoni) and Via Strozzi (runs east from Via de' Tornabuoni to Piazza della Repubblica).

Department Stores

Typical chain department stores are **Coin,** the local "Macy's" (Mon–Sat 10:00–20:00, Sun 10:30–20:00, on Via dei Calzaiuoli, near Orsanmichele Church); the similar, upscale **La Rinascente** (Mon–Sat 9:00–21:00, Sun 10:30–20:00, on Piazza della Repubblica, expensive café and view terrace on fourth floor); and **Oviesse,** the local "Penney's," a discount clothing chain (Mon–Sat 9:00–20:00, Sun 10:00-19:30, near train station at intersection of Via Panzani and Via del Giglio).

Souvenir Ideas

Shoppers in Florence can easily buy art reproductions (posters, calendars, books, prints, and so on—a breeze to find in and near the Uffizi and Accademia museums); reproductions of old documents, maps, and manuscripts; traditional stationery (Il Papiro chain stores); silk ties and scarves; ceramics; and goofy knickknacks featuring Renaissance masterpieces (such as Botticelli mouse pads, Raphael lipstick-holders, and plaster *David*s). For soaps, skin creams, herbal remedies, and perfumes, sniff out the antique and palatial perfumery, **Farmacia di Santa Maria Novella** (Via della Scala 16, see page 48).

Edible Goodies

The Central Market is a prime spot for stocking up on culinary souvenirs. Classic purchases include olives, Parmigiano-Reggiano cheese, unusually shaped and colored pasta, and jars of pestos and sauces (such as *pesto Genovese* or *tartufi*—truffle). Upstairs, where produce and bulk products are sold, the price of the dried porcini mushrooms is less than a quarter of what you'll find at the airport Duty Free (but expect all your clothes to smell of it!). While I don't fly with bottles of wine, many bring home a special bottle of Chianti Classico or Brunello di Montalcino.

Customs

You can take home $800 in souvenirs per person duty-free. The next $1,000 is taxed at a flat 3 percent. After that, you pay the individual item's duty rate. You can also bring in duty-free a liter of alcohol (slightly more than a standard-sized bottle of wine), a carton of cigarettes, and up to 100 cigars. As for food, anything in cans or sealed jars is acceptable, but skip dried meat. Don't bring back fresh fruits or veggies. Cheese is permissible only if it's aged (like Parmigiano-Reggiano) and vacuum-packed. To check customs rules and duty rates, visit www.customs.gov.

NIGHTLIFE

With so many American and international college students in town, Florence by night can have a frat-party atmosphere. Nighttime is for eating a late meal, catching a concert, strolling through the old-town pedestrian zone and piazzas, or hitting one of the many pubs.

The latest on nightlife and concerts is listed in several publications available free at the TI (such as the monthly *Florence Concierge Information* or the biweekly *The Florentine*) or for a small price at newsstands (consider the monthly *Firenze Spettacolo,* which has an English section). Also check www.firenzeturismo.it.

The historic center has a good floodlit ambience, ideal for **strolling.** The entire pedestrian zone along Via dei Calzaiuoli, between the Uffizi and the Duomo, is lively with people. The Piazza della Repubblica, lined with venerable 19th-century cafés, offers good people-watching. In the evening it's a hub of activity with opera singers, violinists, harpists, bizarre street performers, and a cover band that plays cheesy tunes for the seating area of one of the piazza's bars. The Ponte Vecchio is a popular place to enjoy river views (and kiss). Of the great squares, only two feel creepy at night—Piazza Santa Maria Novella and, to a lesser extent, Piazza Santo Spirito (south of the Arno)—because they're known as rendezvous spots for drug pushers and users.

Piazzale Michelangelo, perched on a hilltop across the river (bus #12 or #13 from the train station), is awesome for sunsets and is packed with local Romeos and Juliets on weekend evenings. If you're going after dark, it's quicker to get there and back by bus or taxi (rather than take a 60-min round-trip hike). Consider going to **Fiesole** for the sunset (see page 53).

Live Music

Frequent **live concerts** enhance Florence's beautiful setting. In the summertime, piazzas host a wide-range of performers, from American children's choirs to world music. The lovely sounds of classical music also frequently fill churches for special performances.

Orsanmichele Church regularly holds concerts under its Gothic arches. Tickets are sold on the day of the concert from the door facing Via dei Calzaiuoli.

The **Santa Maria de' Ricci Church** hosts a variety of concert performances, from Baroque to children's choirs to operatic singing, practically every night, usually at 21:15. Part of the €11 ticket price goes toward the restoration of the church (between Duomo and Palazzo Vecchio on Via del Corso, tel. 055-289-367).

Live jazz at the **Golden View Open Bar** with the view of the Arno River couldn't be any more. . .golden (Mon, Wed, and Sun at 21:00, near Ponte Vecchio, see Eating, page 209).

The **Box Office** sells tickets for rock concerts and theatre productions in Italian (Mon–Sat 10:00–20:00, closed Sun, on road that runs along west side of train station, Via Alamanni 39, tel. 055-210-804).

Wine Bars

Wine bars *(enoteca)* are fun for sampling local wines and enjoying regional munchies, especially pre-dinner-time. Consider these *enotecas:* **Frescobaldi**'s tasting menu, limited to wines from their own company, is worth a try if you can snag a candlelit table on the tiny, romantic alleyway (€9.50 Sangiovese tasting, €21.50 Super Tuscans, Mon–Sat 12:15–15:30 & 19:00–24:00, closed Sun, Via de' Magazzini 2–4 red, tel. 055-284-724). **All'Antico Vinaio** is bright, cheap, and welcomes drinking on the street (Tue–Thu 8:00–21:30, Fri–Sat 8:00–1:00 in the morning, closed Sun–Mon, Via dei Neri 65 red, between Piazza della Signoria and Santa Croce, tel. 055-282-738). **Boccadama** has snooty service contrasted by a warm countryside kitchen atmosphere and an ever-changing selection of wines from all over Italy (daily 8:00–23:30, also serves lunch and dinner, Piazza Santa Croce 25–26r, tel. 055-243-640).

For the true wine connoisseur, **Le Volpi e l'Uva** is the real deal, specializing in only small wine producers. Its outdoor seating off a little piazza is basically in a parking lot (€15 taste of five wines with samplings of cheese and *salumi*, Mon–Sat 11:00–21:00, closed Sun, Piazza dei Rossi 1, tel. 055-239-8132, run by wine experts Riccardo and Emilio).

For daytime tasting spots, see also Cantinetta dei Verrazzano, I Fratellini, and Casa del Vino under Eating, page 196.

See and Be Scene

The famous-for-its-coffee bar, **Chiaroscuro,** offers a €7 hearty snack buffet of international food with an *aperitivo,* a pre-dinner drink (daily 8:00–21:30, buffet Tue–Wed and Fri 18:30, Via del Corso 36, tel. 055-214-247). **Moyo,** a slick, goldenly lit lounge, offers a happy hour buffet at 19:00 (Sun–Thu 8:00–24:00, Fri–Sat 8:00–2:00 in the morning, just off Piazza Santa Croce, Via de' Benci 23 red, tel. 055-247-738).

To rub elbows with the locals, head across the river towards the tiny Piazza Demidoff (cross the bridge east of the Ponte Vecchio and turn left). These two places have outdoor seating, chi-chi interiors, and Florentines flaunting their latest shoe purchases: **Negroni** (Mon–Sat 8:00–2:00 in the morning, closed Sun, Via dei Renai 17 red, tel. 055-243-647) and **Zoe** (Tue–Sun 8:00–2:00 in the morning, closed Mon, Via dei Renai 13 red, tel. 055-243-111).

TRANSPORTATION CONNECTIONS

Florence is Tuscany's transportation hub, with connections to virtually anywhere in Italy. The city has a train station, bus station (next to train station), and airport (plus Pisa's airport nearby).

Train Station

Florence's main station is Santa Maria Novella, or Firenze S.M.N. (don't get off at Firenze Rifredi or Firenze Campo di Marte). If you arrive by train, there's no need to linger at the station, which generates dazed and sweaty crowds. User-friendly, gray-and-yellow machines take euros and credit cards, and can display schedules, issue tickets, and even make reservations for railpass-holders. You can also get tickets and train info for your next destination from travel agencies away from the congested station (such as American Express, page 27). The fake "Tourist Information" office in the station (next to McDonald's) is actually a room-booking service funded by the hotels. The real TI is across the square from the station (see page 23).

With your back to the tracks, look left to see a 24-hour pharmacy (*Farmacia Comunale,* near McDonald's), city buses, and the entrance to the underground mall/passage that goes across the square to the Church of Santa Maria Novella. (Note: Pickpockets frequent this tunnel, especially the surface point near the church.) Baggage check is near track 16.

Types of Trains

You'll encounter several types of trains in Italy. Along with the various pokey, milk-run trains, there are the slow IR (Interregional) and *diretto* trains, the medium *espresso,* the fast IC (Intercity), and the space-age ES (Eurostar Italia). All of these trains are fully covered by a railpass (except the ES, which requires

Italy's Public Transportation

KEY: — RAIL   •••• SHIP
      ⊥ PRIVATE RAIL --- BUS

railpass-holders to purchase a €10–15 seat reservation). For point-to-point tickets, you'll pay more the faster you go—but even the fastest trains are still affordable (for example, a second-class ticket on a Florence–Venice express train costs about €35; first class costs about €50). Purchasing seat reservations on the train comes with a nasty penalty. Buying tickets or reservations at the station can be a time-waster unless you use the ticket machines (mentioned above). If you're on a tight schedule, you'll want to reserve a few days ahead for fast trains.

Schedules

Newsstands sell up-to-date regional and all-Italy timetables (€4, ask for the *orario ferroviaro*). On the Web, check http://bahn.hafas .de/bin/query.exe/en (Germany's excellent all-Europe Web site) or www.trenitalia.it/en/index.html.

At the station, the easiest way to check schedules is at the handy grayish-blue-and-yellow machines (mentioned above). Enter the date and time of your departure (to or from any Italian station) and you can view all your options. You can also check the low-tech printed schedules posted at the station—departure posters are always yellow. Note that your final destination may be listed in fine print as an intermediate destination. If you're going from Florence to Chiusi or Cortona, scan the schedule and you'll notice that trains that go to Rome usually stop in Chiusi or Terontola (near Cortona) en route. Travelers who read the fine print end up with a greater choice of trains.

Strikes are common. They generally last a day, and train employees will simply say, *"Sciopero"* (strike). But sporadic trains lumber down the tracks during most strikes.

From Florence by Train to: Pisa (2/hr, 1 hr), **Lucca** (9/day, 1.5 hrs), **Siena** (12/day, 1.75 hrs, more with transfer in Empoli; bus is better), **La Spezia** (for the Cinque Terre, 3/day direct, 2 hrs, or change in Pisa), **Milan** (12/day, 3–5 hrs), **Venice** (7/day, 3 hrs), **Assisi** (4/day, 2 hrs, more frequent with transfers, direction: Foligno), **Orvieto** (8/day, 2 hrs), **Rome** (2/hr, 2 hrs), **Naples** (7/day, 4 hrs), **Brindisi** (3/day, 11 hrs with change in Bologna), **Frankfurt** (3/day, 12 hrs), **Paris** (1/day, 12 hrs overnight, important to reserve ahead), **Vienna** (4/day, 9–10 hrs).

Bus Station

The SITA bus station, a block west of the Florence train station, is traveler-friendly. Schedules for regional trips are posted everywhere, and TV monitors show imminent departures. Bus service drops dramatically on Sunday.

By Bus to: San Gimignano (€6, hrly, 1.25–2 hrs, change in Poggibonsi), **Siena** (€6.50, hrly, 75-min *corse rapide* buses are faster

Greater Florence

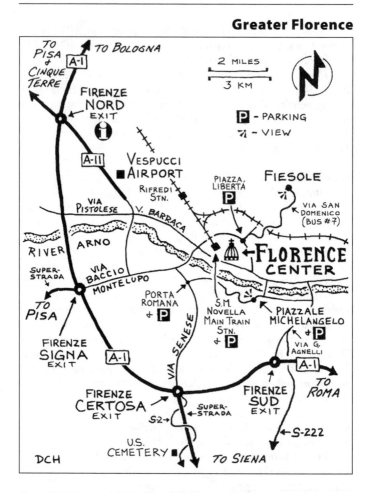

than the train, avoid the 2-hr *diretta* scenic but slow buses), and the **airport** (€4, buy ticket on bus, 2/hr, 20 min). Bus info: tel. 800-373-760 (Mon–Fri 8:30–18:30, Sat–Sun 8:30–12:30); some schedules are in the *Florence Concierge Information* magazine. Several buses cover San Gimignano and Siena in one big day-trip.

Taxis

If you don't want to mess with buses or trains, consider hiring a taxi to take you to nearby towns. For small groups or people with more money than time, this can be a good value. For example, for around €120, you can arrange a ride directly from your Florence hotel to your Siena hotel. Ask your hotel to call a taxi or go to a taxi stand (you'll find them around town and at high-traffic areas such as the train station, Piazza della Repubblica, and Piazza Santa Croce).

Airports

The **Amerigo Vespucci Airport,** several miles northwest of Florence, has a TI, cash machines, and car-rental agencies (airport info tel. 055-306-1300, flight info tel. 055-306-1700—domestic only, www.aeroporto.firenze.it). Frequent shuttle buses connect the airport with Florence's SITA bus station, a block west of the train station (€4, 2/hr, 30 min, from Florence runs 5:30–23:00, from airport 6:00–23:30). Allow about €20 for a taxi.

International and domestic flights often use Pisa's easily navigable **Galileo Galilei Airport** (flight info tel. 050-849-300, www.pisa-airport.com). The airport has a TI (tel. 050-503-700), cash machine, car-rental agencies, and pricey baggage deposit (€7/day per bag, drop-off hours 10:00–18:00, pick-up hours 8:00–20:00). A self-service cafeteria upstairs serves meals (daily 11:15–14:00 & 18:15–21:50).

Trains depart from Pisa's airport to Florence (€5.10 one-way, 2/hr, 90 min, transfer in Pisa) and downtown Pisa (€1.10, 2–4/hr, 5 min, departing 6:20–22:02 from downtown). If arriving by plane, you'll find the trains to your left, at the end of the terminal. Terravision **buses** also head to Florence's Santa Maria Novella station (€7.50 one-way, €13.50 round-trip, depart somewhat hourly 8:40–23:50, 50-min trip, ticket kiosk is at the far end of the terminal from the tracks; catch bus outside and to the far right of the car rental lot). Buses leave for central Pisa as well (€0.80, 3/hr, 15 min), as do taxis (€6).

Tips for Drivers

If you're taking the autostrada (north or south) to Florence, get off at the Certosa exit and follow signs to *Centro;* at Porta Romana, go to the left of the arch and down Via Francesco Petrarca. After driving around and trying to park in Florence, you'll understand why Leonardo never invented the car. Cars flatten the charm of the city.

Don't drive into the historic core of Florence. A system of cameras photographs every car entering the center. You must register your car with your hotel, whether you just drove in to drop off luggage or if you have parking reserved at your hotel. If you don't, a hefty fine will appear on your rental-car statement. If you go into the city beyond the ring road, even accidentally, you need to report your license-plate number to avoid the fine. Non-residents are not allowed to park on the streets anywhere in or near the old center. Cars are not monitored leaving the city.

Many hotels listed in this book have a few parking spots they can rent to guests in the center—most charge around €20 per day. In addition, the city has plenty of **parking lots.** For a short stay, park underground at the train station (€2–3/hr).

Driving in Italy

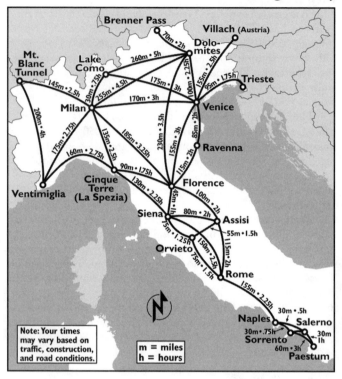

For an overnight stay, consider parking at Piazzale Michelangelo—it's free! Just don't park where the buses drop people off (on the side of the piazza farthest from the view). It's OK to park overnight as long as it's not on a weekly street-cleaning day. Check the signs—a circle with a slash through it and *dispari giovedi, 0,00–06,00* means don't park on Thursdays between midnight and 6 a.m. To get from Piazzale Michelangelo to the center of town, take bus #13 (see Getting Around Florence, page 27).

Other parking options—closer to the center but less economical—include Piazza della Libertà (€15/24 hrs, 4 long blocks east of Fortezza di Basso, on the inner ring road) and Porta Romana (€15/day, exit A1 at Firenze-Certosa, follow signs to *Porta Romana*). For more detailed parking information, ask your hotelier.

TUSCANY
(Toscana)

Tuscany

EMILIA-ROMAGNA

LIG.
LA SPEZIA
APUAN ALPS
CARRARA
CINQUE TERRE
PISTOIA
LUCCA
VESP. AIRPORT
TO BOLOGNA
TO RAVENNA
VIAREGGIO
VINCI
ARNO
FLORENCE
PISA
GALILEO AIRPORT
EMPOLI
US. CEM.
POGG.
CHIANTI
ARNO
TO URBINO
LE MARCHE
SAN SEPOLCRO
LIVORNO
SAN GIMIGNANO
CAST.
SIENA
AREZZO
UMBRIA
VOLTERRA
S-68
S-326
CORTONA
LISCIANO
MONTE-RIGGIONE
ANCAIANO
S-438
S-2
ASCIANO
TER.
ASSISI
MEDI-TERRANEAN SEA
SAN GALGANO
MONTALCINO
S-146
PIENZA
CHIUSI
LAKE TRAS.
MONTE-PULCIANO
PIOMBINO
SANT' ANTIMO
VIA CASSIA
ORVIETO
PORTO-FERRAIO
ELBA
GROSSETTO
MAREMMA
TODI
BAG.
LAKE BOLSENA
A.
MONTE ARGENTARIO
LAZIO
TO ROME

AUTOSTRADA
OTHER ROADS
RAIL
BORDER OF PROVINCE

30 MILES
50 KM

DCH

SIENA

Siena was medieval Florence's archrival. And while Florence ultimately won the battle for political and economic superiority, Siena still competes for the tourists. Sure, Florence has the heavyweight sights. But Siena seems to be every Italy connoisseur's favorite pet town. In my office, whenever Siena is mentioned, someone moans, "Siena? I looove Siena!"

Seven hundred years ago (about 1260–1348), Siena was a major banking and trade center, and a military power in a class with Florence, Venice, and Genoa. With a population of 60,000, it was even bigger than Paris. Situated on the north–south road to Rome (the Via Francigena), Siena traded with all Europe. Then, in 1348, the Black Death (bubonic plague) that swept through Europe hit Siena and cut the population by more than a third. Siena never recovered. In the 1550s, Florence, with the help of Philip II's Spanish army, conquered the flailing city-state, forever rendering Siena a non-threatening backwater. Siena's loss became our sightseeing gain, as its political and economic irrelevance pickled the city in a purely medieval brine. Today, Siena's population is still 60,000, compared to Florence's 420,000.

Siena's thriving historic center, with redbrick lanes cascading every which way, offers Italy's best medieval city experience. Most people do Siena, just 35 miles south of Florence, as a day trip, but it's best experienced at twilight. While Florence has the blockbuster museums, Siena has an easy-to-enjoy soul: Courtyards sport flower-decked wells, alleys dead-end at rooftop views, and the sky is a rich blue dome.

For those who dream of a Fiat-free Italy, pedestrians rule in the old center of Siena. Sit at a café on the main square. Wander narrow streets lined with colorful flags and iron rings to tether horses. Take time to savor the first European city to eliminate automobile traffic from its main square (1966) and then, just to be silly, wonder what would happen if they did it in your home town.

Planning Your Time

On a quick trip, consider spending two nights in Siena (or three nights with a whole-day side trip into Florence). Whatever you do, enjoy a sleepy medieval evening in Siena. The next morning, you can see the city's major sights in half a day.

ORIENTATION

Siena lounges atop a hill, stretching its three legs out from Il Campo. This main square, the historic meeting point of Siena's neighborhoods, is pedestrian-only. And most of those pedestrians are students from the local university.

Everything I mention is within a 15-minute walk of the square. Navigate by three major landmarks (Il Campo, Duomo, and Church of San Domenico), following the excellent system of street-corner signs. The typical visitor sticks to the Il Campo–San Domenico axis. Make a point to stray from the current of this main artery.

Siena itself is one big sight. Its individual sights come in two little clusters: the square (Civic Museum and City Tower) and the cathedral (Baptistery and Duomo Museum with its surprise viewpoint). Check these sights off, and then you're free to wander.

Tourist Information: This TI office is an exasperating place. Employees claim that transit officials and museum officials don't want them to know anything about the town's buses or sights. They do offer a decent free map (daily 9:00–19:00, located on Il Campo at #56, tel. 0577-280-551, www.terresiena.it, incoming@terresiena.it). The helpful booklet *Terre di Siena* lists current hours and prices for sights in Siena and outlying towns. The little TI at San Domenico, while primarily for hotel promotion, sells a €0.50 Siena map and organizes daily walking tours of the old town and San Gimignano (across street from church).

Arrival in Siena

By Train: The small train station, located on the edge of town, has a bar and bus office (no baggage check or lockers). To get from the station to the city center, hike about 20 minutes uphill, or catch a city bus or taxi. The **taxi stand** is to your far right as you exit the station (about €8 to Il Campo, taxi tel. 0577-49-222).

Greater Siena

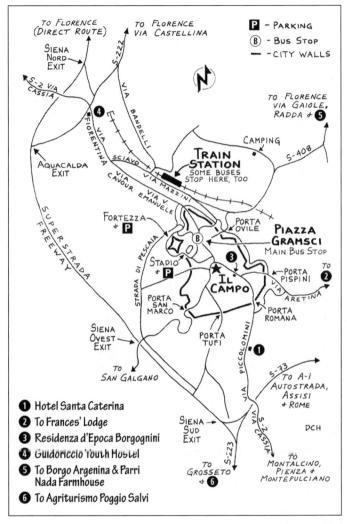

TO FLORENCE (DIRECT ROUTE)

TO FLORENCE VIA CASTELLINA

P - PARKING
B - BUS STOP
— - CITY WALLS

SIENA NORD EXIT

S-222

VIA BANDELLI

S-2 VIA CASSIA

TO FLORENCE VIA GAIOLE, RADDA & ❺

❹

VIA FIORENTINA

E. SCIAVO

CAMPING

S-408

AQUACALDA EXIT

VIA MAZZINI

VIA V. CAVOUR EMANUELE

TRAIN STATION
SOME BUSES STOP HERE, TOO

SUPERSTRADA FREEWAY

FORTEZZA ❖ P

PORTA OVILE

PIAZZA GRAMSCI
MAIN BUS STOP

STRADA DI PESCAIA

B

STADIO ❖ P

★ IL CAMPO

❸

TO ❷

PORTA PISPINI

VIA ARETINA

PORTA SAN MARCO

PORTA ROMANA

SIENA OVEST EXIT

PORTA TUFI

VIA PICCOLOMINI

❶

S-73

TO A-1 AUTOSTRADA, ASSISI & ROME

TO SAN GALGANO

SIENA SUD EXIT

VIA CASSIA S-2

DCH

S-23

TO GROSSETO & ❻

TO MONTALCINO, PIENZA & MONTEPULCIANO

❶ Hotel Santa Caterina
❷ To Frances' Lodge
❸ Residenza d'Epoca Borgognini
❹ Guidoriccio Youth Hostel
❺ To Borgo Argenina & Parri Nada Farmhouse
❻ To Agriturismo Poggio Salvi

To get from the station into town by **city bus,** buy a €1 ticket from the newsstand in the station lobby (daily 6:00–20:00), or from the blue machine in the lobby (touch screen for English and select "urban" for type of ticket). Then walk to the bus stop—a covered shelter 100 yards away—by crossing the parking lot and the wide roundabout in front of the station. Buses only drop off passengers at the station; they pick up travelers at this covered stop. Buses run about every 15 minutes (fewer on Sun and after 21:00).

Every orange bus goes from here to the town center.

(Caution: Blue ones go to other cities.) Confirm by asking *"Centro?,"* punch your ticket in the machine on the bus to validate it, and ride to the last stop, Piazza Gramsci. (Buses also stop at Piazza del Sale and Via della Stufasecca—all within several blocks of each other, so if you don't get dropped off in Piazza Gramsci, just head uphill on the main street to reach it.)

When leaving Siena, just catch the city bus to the train station from any of the three stops just mentioned: Piazza Gramsci, Piazza del Sale, or Via della Stufasecca. Bus stops are marked with a posted schedule and sometimes with yellow lines painted on the pavement, showing a bus-sized rectangle and the word "bus". Confirm with the driver that the bus is going to the *stazione* (stat-zee-OH-nay). Remember to purchase your ticket in advance from a *tabacchi* shop.

By Intercity Bus: Some buses arrive in Siena at the train station (see "By Train," above), others at Piazza Gramsci (a few blocks from city center), and some stop at both. The main bus companies are Sena and the confusingly named Tra-In (TRAH-in). You can store baggage underneath Piazza Gramsci in Sottopassaggio la Lizza (€3.50, daily 7:00–19:45, no overnight).

By Car: Drivers coming from the autostrada take the *Siena Ovest* exit and follow signs for *Centro*, then *Stadio* (stadium, soccer ball). The soccer-ball signs take you to the stadium lot (Parcheggio Stadio, €1.60/hr, pay for number of hours parked when you leave) at the huge, bare-brick Church of San Domenico. The Fortezza lot nearby charges the same amount, or you can park in the lot under the train station. Technically, hotel customers are allowed to drop bags off at their hotel before finding a place to park overnight, but I wouldn't bother. You can park free in the lot west of the Fortezza, in white-striped spots behind Hotel Villa Liberty, behind the Fortezza, and overnight in most city lots from 20:00–8:00. (The signs showing a street cleaner and a day of the week indicate which day the street is cleaned; there's a €100 tow-fee incentive to learn the days of the week in Italian.)

Helpful Hints

Combo-Tickets: A deranged person cobbled together a pile of illogically paired combo-tickets to give some travelers a small savings. Nothing covers everything, and most are conflicting. You can buy a combo-ticket *(biglietto cumulativo)* that gets you into the Duomo, Duomo Museum, Baptistery, and Baptistery crypt (€10, saves €12 if you see all 4 sights, doesn't cover the Duomo when the lovely floors are uncovered mid-Aug–Oct). Another combo-ticket, sold at the City Tower, includes the tower and Civic Museum (€10, saves €3). Yet another is for the Civic Museum and Santa Maria della Scala (€10, saves

€3). There's also a big €13 combo-ticket *(Itinerari d'Arte)* that doesn't include entry to the Duomo or the City Tower but saves you €9 if you visit the Duomo Museum, Santa Maria della Scala, Civic Museum, and the Baptistery (costs €16 Nov–March, so only €6 savings in winter, both versions valid 7 days).

Sightseeing Hours: Note that Siena's museums are often open late on summer Fridays and Saturdays (check with TI for current hours).

Wednesday Morning Market: The weekly market sprawls between the Fortress and Piazza Gramsci along Viale Cesare Maccari and the adjacent Viale XXV Aprile, consisting mainly of clothes, knickknacks, and food.

Internet Access: In this university town, there are lots of places to get plugged in. **Internet Point** is just off Piazza Matteotti, at Via Paradiso 10 (across street and a few steps downhill from McDonald's, Mon–Fri 9:00–13:00 & 15:00–20:00, closed Sat–Sun). **Internet Train** is near Il Campo, at Via di Città 121 (Mon–Sat 10:00–20:00, Sun 12:00–20:00, tel. 0577-226-366). **SkyWeb Internet Center** has fast access and can transfer your digital photos to a backup CD (Mon–Sat 10:00–19:00, closed Sun, Via del Refe Nero 18, just off Via dei Rossi).

Books: **The Book Shop** sells books in English with an emphasis on Italian-related topics (Mon–Sat 10:00–19:30, closed Sun, off Via di Città just before the Pinacoteca at Galleria S. Pietro 19). The **Feltrinelli** bookstore closer to the Campo also sells books and magazines in English (Mon–Sat 9:00–19:30, Sun 11:00–13:30 & 15:30–19:30, Banchi di Sopra 52).

Laundry: Two modern, self-service launderettes are **Lavarapido Wash and Dry** (daily 8:00–22:00, Via di Pantaneto 38, near Logge del Papa) and **Onda Blu** (daily 8:00–22:00, Via del Casato di Sotto 17, 50 yards from Il Campo); last loads are at 21:00 for both.

Travel Agency: Palio Viaggi on Piazza Gramsci sells train and plane tickets but no bus tickets (Mon–Fri 9:00–12:45 & 15:00–18:30, Sat 9:00–13:30, closed Sun, La Lizza 12, tel. 0577-280-828, info@palioviaggi.it).

Local Guides: Roberto Bechi, a hardworking Sienese guide, specializes in off-the-beaten-path tours of the surrounding countryside by minibus (up to six passengers, convenient pick-up at hotel). Married to an American (Patti) and having run restaurants in Siena and the US, Roberto communicates well with Americans. His passions are Sienese culture, Tuscan history, and local cuisine. Ideally, book well in advance, but you might be able to schedule a visit if you call no later than the day before (full-day tours from €70–100

Siena at a Glance

▲▲▲**Il Campo** Best square in Italy. **Hours:** Always open.

▲▲▲**Duomo** Art-packed cathedral with mosaic floors and statues by Michelangelo and Bernini. **Hours:** March–Oct Mon–Sat 9:30–19:00, Sun 13:30–17:30, Nov–Feb Mon–Sat 9:30–17:00, Sun 13:30–16:30.

▲▲**Duomo Museum** Displays cathedral art (including Duccio's *Maestà*) and offers sweeping Tuscan view. **Hours:** Daily March–Oct 9:30–19:00, Nov–Feb 9:30–17:00.

▲**Baptistery** Cave-like building has baptismal font decorated by Ghiberti and Donatello. **Hours:** Daily March–Oct 9:30–19:00, Nov–Feb 9:30–17:00.

▲**Civic Museum** City museum in City Hall with Sienese frescoes of Good and Bad Government. **Hours:** Daily March–Oct 10:00–18:15, Nov–Feb 10:00–16:00. May be open late summer evenings.

▲**City Tower** 330-foot tower climb. **Hours:** Same as Civic Museum.

▲**Pinacoteca** Fine Sienese paintings. **Hours:** Sun–Mon 8:30–13:15, Tue–Sat 8:15–19:15.

▲**Santa Maria della Scala** Museum with vibrant ceiling and wall frescoes depicting day-to-day life in a medieval hospital, much of the original *Fountain of Joy*, and an Etruscan artifact exhibit. **Hours:** Daily mid-March–Oct 10:30–18:30, Nov–mid-March 10:30–16:30.

Church of San Domenico Huge brick church with St. Catherine's head and thumb. **Hours:** Daily March–Oct 7:00–18:30, Nov–Feb 9:00–18:00.

Sanctuary of St. Catherine Home of St. Catherine. **Hours:** Daily 9:00–12:30 & 15:00–19:00.

per person, half-day tours from €25–70 per person, mobile 328-727-3186 or 328-425-5648, www.toursbyroberto.com, tourrob@tin.it). If he's booked, Roberto can recommend other good guides.

Il Casato Viaggi runs half-day bus tours from Siena into the Tuscan countryside. They offer two different itineraries, both including a winery tour and wine-tasting: of the Chianti area (€28, Wed and Fri, includes visits to two medieval villages) and Brunello and the Crete Senesi hills (€35, Sun). Full-day wine-tasting tours in the countryside are also available (€150/person for 2 people, €105/person for 4 people, 10 percent discount with this book; includes 3 tastings, lunch, minivan, and guide; Via Il Casato di Sotto 12 in Siena, tel. 057-746-091, fax 057-727-9863, www.sienaholiday.com).

SIGHTS

Siena's Main Square

Il Campo, a ▲▲▲ sight, is the heart—geographically and meta-phorically—of Siena. Seen from the top of the City Tower, this "heart" appears to pump people through the busy city's veins. The square fans out from the City Hall (Palazzo Pubblico) to create an amphitheater, where the citizens are the stars.

Originally, this area was just a field *(campo)* located outside the former city walls. You can still see some of the old tufa-stone blocks incorporated into today's redbrick Caffè Fonte Gaia (along the right side of the square as you face City Hall).

As the city expanded, Il Campo eventually became the historic junction of Siena's various competing districts, or *contrade,* on the old marketplace. The brick

surface is divided into nine sections, representing the council of nine merchants and city bigwigs who ruled medieval Siena. The square and its buildings are the color of the soil upon which they stand...a color known to artists and Crayola-users as "Burnt Sienna."

City Hall and its 330-foot

Siena

P – PARKING

100 YDS.
100 m

● Sottopassaggio la Lizza (Underground Bus Depot, Bag Storage & Bus Tickets)
❷ Palio al Cinema
❸ Il Casato Viaggi Tours
❹ Palio Viaggi Travel Agency

tower dominate the square. In medieval Siena, this secular building was the center of the city, and the whole focus of the Campo flows down to it.

The City Hall features the various symbols of the city. The sun on the facade remembers St. Bernardino of Siena. Born on the day that St. Catherine of Siena died, he grew up here and went on to travel throughout Italy giving spirited and humorous sermons that preached peace between warring political factions. His sermons often ended with reconciling parties exchanging a *bacio di pace* (kiss of peace). In Siena, he would stand in front of the Palazzo and preach to crowds discreetly segregated by gender with a curtain down the middle. Bernardino personally designed the sun logo to attract crowds, and later he became the patron saint of advertising (and of Siena).

To either side of the sun logo, she-wolf gargoyles lean out and snarl, "Don't mess with Siena, Mister Pope!" Siena, a Ghibelline city, prided itself on its political independence from the papacy; it embraced as a city symbol the pagan she-wolf who suckled Romulus and Remus (Remus' son was Siena's legendary founder). The black-and-white shields over the windows are another city symbol. Near ground level, the metal rings are for tying up your horse, while the fixtures above held flags.

The City Hall's 330-foot-tall **City Tower** (Torre del Mangia), Italy's tallest secular tower, was named after a hedonistic watchman who consumed his earnings like a glutton consumes food— his chewed-up statue is in the courtyard, to the left as you enter. (Tower admission details below.)

The chapel located at the base of the tower was built in 1348 as thanks to God for ending the Black Death (after it killed more than a third of the population). It should also be used to thank God that the tower—just plunked onto the building with no extra foundation—still stands. These days, the chapel is used only to bless the Palio contestants, and the tower's bell only rings for the race.

The ***Fountain of Joy (Fonte Gaia)*** by Jacopo della Quercia marks the square's high point. Find the snake-handler woman,

the two naked guys about to be tossed in, and the pigeons politely waiting their turn to tightrope gingerly down slippery spouts to slurp a drink from wolves' snouts. The relief panel on the left (as you face the fountain) shows God creating Adam by helping him to his feet. It's said that this reclining Adam influenced Michelangelo when he painted his Sistine Ceiling. This fountain is a copy—you can see most of the original fountain in an interesting exhibit at Siena's Santa Maria della Scala, described on page 244.

To say that Siena and Florence have always been competitive is an understatement. In medieval times, a statue of Venus stood on Il Campo. After the plague hit Siena, the monks blamed the pagan statue. The people cut it to pieces and buried it along the walls of Florence.

Siena's Palio

In the Palio, the feisty spirit of Siena's 17 *contrade* (neighborhoods) lives on. These neighborhoods celebrate, worship, and compete together. Each has its own parish church, well, or fountain, and even its own historical museum. *Contrada* pride is evident any time of year in the parades and colorful neighborhood banners, lamps, and wall plaques. (If you hear distant drumming, run to it for some medieval action, often featuring flag-throwers.) But *contrada* passion is most visible twice a year—on July 2 and August 16—when they have their world-famous horse race, the Palio di Siena.

Ten of the 17 neighborhoods compete (chosen by rotation and lot), hurling themselves with medieval abandon into several days of trial races and traditional revelry. Jockeys are considered hired guns...paid mercenaries. But on the big day, the horses are taken into their *contrada*'s church to be blessed. ("Go and return victorious," says the priest.) It's considered a sign of luck if a horse leaves droppings in the church.

On the evening of the big day, Il Campo is stuffed to the brim

The "heart" of Siena beats fastest at Palio time. Picture the Campo when the famous horse races are held (July 2 and Aug

16). Ten snorting horses and their nervous riders (selected from 17 *contrade*, or neighborhoods) line up near the "Antica Siena" shop (right side of square) to await the starting signal. Then they race like crazy three times around the perimeter (the gray pavement), which is covered with dirt. Mattresses pad the sharpest turns. Spectators waving the banners of their neighborhoods cram (for free) into the center of the square or watch from temporary bleachers or, if they have the money, from the balconies. The winner crosses the line, and 1/17th of Siena goes berserk for the next 365 days.

▲**Civic Museum (Museo Civico)**—At the base of the tower is Siena's City Hall, the spot where secular government got its start in early Renaissance Europe. There, you'll find city government with locals and tourists, as the horses charge wildly around the square in this literally no-holds-barred race. A horse can win even if its rider has fallen off. Of course, the winning neighborhood is the scene of grand celebrations afterward. Winners receive a *palio* (banner), typically painted by a local artist and always featuring the Virgin Mary. But the true prize is simply proving your *contrada* is *numero uno*. All over town, sketches and posters depict the Palio. This is not some folkloristic event. It's a real medieval moment. If you're packed onto the square with 15,000 people, all hungry for victory, you won't see much, but you'll feel it. While the actual Palio packs the city, you could side-trip in from Florence to see horse-race trials each of the three days before the main event (usually at 9:00 and around 19:30). For more information, visit www.ilpalio.org.

▲**Palio al Cinema**—This 20-minute film, *Siena, the Palio, and its History,* helps recreate the craziness. See it at the air-conditioned Cinema Moderno in Piazza Tolomei, two blocks from Il Campo (€5.25, with this book pay €4.25/person or €8/two, get the DVD for €10, film shows May–Oct only; May–mid-June and mid-Sept–Oct Mon–Sat 9:30–15:30, from mid-June–mid-Sept Mon–Sat 9:30–17:30, closed Sun; English showings generally hourly at half past the hour—schedule posted on door, tel. 0577-289-201). Call or drop by to confirm when the next English showing is scheduled—there are usually nine a day.

still at work, along with a sampling of local art, including Siena's first fresco (with a groundbreaking down-to-earth depiction of the Madonna). Stroll through the dramatic halls for more frescoes and portraits extolling Siena's greats, saints, and the city-as-utopia.

Take a moment to savor one of those to sigh for rural panoramas out the window of the *Sala della Pace*. The view out the window is essentially the same as that from the top of the big stairs (€7, one €10 combo-ticket includes tower, one €10 combo-ticket includes Santa Maria della Scala, also covered by expensive *Itinerari d'Arte* combo-ticket, daily March–Oct 10:00–18:15, Nov–Feb 10:00–16:00, may be open later on summer evenings, last entry 45 min before closing, ask if audioguides are available, tel. 0577-292-232). See ✪ Civic Museum Tour, page 262.

▲**City Tower (Torre del Mangia)**— Siena gathers around its City Hall, not its church. Medieval Siena was a proud republic, and

this tall tower is the exclamation point of its "declaration of independence." Its 300 steps get pretty skinny at the top, but the reward is one of Italy's best views (€6, €10 combo-ticket with Civic Museum, daily March–Oct 10:00–18:15, Nov–Feb 10:00–16:00, closed in rain, sometimes long lines, avoid midday crowd, limit of 30 tourists at a time, often sold out, mandatory and free bag check).

Near Il Campo

Via Banchi di Sopra and Via Banchi di Sotto—These main drags in town are named "upper row of banks" and "lower row of banks." These were once lined with market tables *(banchi)*, and rents were paid to the city for a table's position along the street. If the owner of a *banco* neglected to pay the rent for his space, thugs came along and literally broke *(rotto)* his table. From this practice—*banco rotto*, or broken table—we get the English word bankrupt.

In medieval times, these two streets were part of the Via Francigena, the main thoroughfare between London and Santiago de Compostela in Spain. The medieval Sienese traded wool with passing travelers, requiring money-changers, which led to banks. As Siena was a secular town, local Christians were allowed to loan money and be bankers. Today, strollers out each evening for their *passegiata* fill via Banchi di Sopra.

▲**Pinacoteca**—It rarely rains in Siena, but when it does, I prefer the Pinacoteca to getting drenched. But others may find this quiet, uncrowded, colorful museum delightful. The museum takes you on a walk through Siena's art chronologically from the 12th through the 16th century, when a revolution in realism was percolating in Tuscany. Here are a few highlights from this large collection:

Room 1 (up two floors and up a little landing to your right) features the art world pre-Duccio. (Duccio is the artist who did the *Maestà* in the Duomo Museum, the Duomo's big stained-glass window, and a fresco in the Civic Museum). Altarpieces emphasize the heavenly and otherworldly, rather than the human realism the Sienese artist helped to pioneer.

Rooms 2–4 contain a number of works by Duccio (and assistants), whose groundbreaking innovations are subtle to the layman's eyes: less gold-leaf background, fewer gold creases in robes, transparent garments, inlaid-marble thrones, and a more human Mary and Jesus.

In **Room 5** are works by Duccio's assistant, Simone Martini, including his *St. Augustine of Siena*. The saint's life is set in pretty realistic Sienese streets, buildings, and landscapes. The saint occasionally pops out at the oddest of angles (difficult to draw) to save the day. (Simone Martini also did the *Maestà* and Guidoriccio frescoes in the Civic Museum.)

In **Room 7** are religious works by the Lorenzetti brothers, best known for the secular masterpiece, *Effects of Good and Bad Government*, in the Civic Museum. The rest of the rooms on this floor are a menagerie of gold-backed saints and Madonnas.

In **Room 12** are two famous, small wooden panels by Sienese painter Ambrogio Lorenzetti: *La Città sul Mare (City by the Sea)* and *Castello in Riva al Lago (Castle on the Lakeshore)*. These works feature the strange, medieval Cubism seen in his contemporary Simone Martini's *Guidoriccio da Folignano* in the Civic Museum. Notice the weird, melancholy light that captures the sense of the Dark Ages. These images are replicated on postcards found throughout the city.

Descend one floor down to **Room 20,** and suddenly the gold is gone—Madonna is set on earth. See works by the painter/biographer Vasari **(Room 22),** a stunning view out the window **(Room 26),** and several colorful rooms **(Rooms 27–30)** dedicated to Domenico Beccafumi (1486–1551). Beccafumi designed many of the Duomo's inlaid pavement panels (including *Slaughter of the Innocents*), and his original cartoons are displayed in **Room 30.** With strong bodies, twisting poses, and dramatic gestures, Beccafumi's works epitomize the Mannerist style.

Room 31 has "Il Sodoma's" sympathetic *Christ on the Column*, and the long **Room 32** displays large-scale works by Il Sodoma, Beccafumi, and others. And finally, Bernardino Mei **(Room 33)** gives a Sienese take on the wrinkled saints and dark shadows of Caravaggio.

To reach the museum from Il Campo, walk out Via di Città and go left on Via San Pietro (€4, Sun–Mon 8:30–13:15, Tue–Sat 8:15–19:15, last entry 30 min before closing, audioguide-€4, free and mandatory bag check, tel. 0577-46-052).

Siena's Cathedral Area

▲▲▲**Duomo**—This 13th-century Gothic cathedral, with its six-story striped bell tower—Siena's ultimate tribute to the Virgin Mary—is heaped with statues, plastered with frescoes, and paved

with art. Soak up the richly ornamented facade before venturing inside, where a passel of popes keeps watch from on high. The interior is a Renaissance riot of striped columns, intricate marble inlays, Michelangelo statues, and Bernini sculptures. The Piccolomini Library features a series of 15th-century frescoes chronicling the adventures of Siena's philanderer-turned-pope, Aeneas Piccolomini.

Cost, Hours, Information: €3 includes cathedral and Piccolomini Library, covered by €10 *biglietto cumulativo* combo-ticket except mid-Aug–Oct when all of the church's intricate inlaid pavements are uncovered and entry costs €6. There's a €3.50 audio-guide for the church and the library; add the Duomo Museum and it's €4.50 (ID required for deposit). The Duomo and Library are both open March–Oct Mon–Sat 9:30–19:00, Sun 13:30–17:30, Nov–Feb Mon–Sat 9:30–17:00, Sun 13:30–16:30, last entry 30 minutes before closing, opening hours can vary—confirm with TI or call 0577-283-048. Modest dress is required to enter, but paper ponchos are provided if needed.

✪ See Siena Duomo Tour on page 248.

▲▲**Duomo Museum (Museo dell'Opera e Panorama)**—On the Il Campo side of the church (look for the yellow signs), Siena's most enjoyable museum was built to house the cathedral's art. Upstairs to the left is Duccio's *Maestà* (*Enthroned Virgin*, 1311), one of the great pieces of medieval art. The flip side of the *Maestà* (displayed on the opposite wall), with 26 panels—the medieval equivalent of pages—shows scenes from the Passion of Christ.

Climb onto the Panorama dal Facciatone. From the first land-ing, take the skinnier second spiral for Siena's surprise view (€6, covered by €10 *biglietto cumulativo* combo-ticket with Baptistery and Duomo except mid-Aug–Oct, also covered by expensive *Itinerari d'Arte* combo-ticket, worthwhile 40-min audioguide-€3, audoguide with Duomo-€4.50, ID required for deposit, daily March–Oct 9:30–19:00, Nov–Feb 9:30–17:00, confirm hours with TI or call tel. 0577-283-048).

✪ See Duomo Museum Tour on page 258.

▲**Baptistery**—Siena is so hilly that there wasn't enough flat ground on which to build a big church. What to do? Build a big church and prop up the overhanging edge with the Baptistery. This dark and quietly tucked-away cave of art is worth a look for its cool tranquility and the bronze panels and angels—by Ghiberti, Donatello, and others—adorning the pedestal of the baptismal font (€3, covered by €10 *biglietto cumulativo* or more expensive *Itinerari d'Arte* combo-ticket, daily March–Oct 9:30–19:00, Nov–Feb 9:30–17:00, confirm with TI).

The "crypt" of the cathedral is important archaeologically, but of little interest to the average tourist (separate €6 entry fee but covered by €10 *biglietto cumulativo* combo-ticket, entrance above the Baptistery). I'd skip it.

▲**Santa Maria della Scala**—This museum (opposite the Duomo entrance) was used as a hospital until the 1980s. Its labyrinthine 12th-century cellars—carved out of tufa and finished with brick—go down several floors, and once stored supplies for the hospital upstairs during medieval times. Today, the hospital and its cellars

St. Catherine of Siena
(1347–1380)

The youngest of 25 children born to a Sienese cloth dyer, Catherine began experiencing heavenly visions as a child. At 16, she became a Dominican nun, locking herself away for three years in a room in her family's house. She lived the life of an ascetic, which culminated in a vision wherein she married Christ. Catherine emerged from solitude to join her Dominican sisters, sharing her experiences, caring for the sick, and gathering both disciples and enemies. At age 23, she lapsed into a spiritual coma, waking with the heavenly command to spread her message to the world. She wrote essays and letters to kings, dukes, bishops, and popes, imploring them to find peace for a war-ravaged Italy. While visiting Pisa during Lent of 1375, she had a vision in which she received the stigmata, the wounds of Christ.

Still in her twenties, Catherine was invited to Avignon, France, where the pope had taken up residence. With her charm, sincerity, and reputation for holiness, she helped convince Pope Gregory XI to return the papacy to the city of Rome. Catherine also went to Rome, where she died young. She was canonized in the next generation (by a Sienese pope) and her relics were distributed to churches around Italy.

are filled with museum exhibits, including these main attractions: the fancy frescoed hall (Pellegrinaio Hall, ground floor), most of the original *Fountain of Joy,* St. Catherine's Oratory chapel (first basement), and the Etruscan collection in the Archaeological Museum (second basement).

Cost and Hours: €6, €10 combo-ticket with Civic Museum, also covered by *Itinerari d'Arte* combo-ticket, daily mid-March–Oct 10:30–18:30, Nov–mid-March 10:30–16:30, last entry 45 minutes before closing. The chapel just inside the door to your left is free (English description inside chapel entrance).

Pellegrinaio Hall: Sumptuously frescoed, this hall shows medieval Siena's innovative health care and social welfare system in action (c. 1442, wonderfully described in English). Starting in the 11th century, the hospital nursed the sick and cared for abandoned children, as is vividly portrayed in these frescoes. The good works paid off, as bequests and donations poured in, creating the wealth that's evident throughout this building.

***Fountain of Joy* Exhibit:** Downstairs you'll find an engaging exhibit on Jacopo della Quercia's early 15th-century *Fountain of Joy (Fonte Gaia)*—and the disassembled pieces of the original fountain itself. In the 19th century, after serious deterioration, the ornate fountain was dismantled and plaster casts were made. (From these casts, they made the replica that graces Il Campo today.) Here you'll see the eroded original panels paired with their restored casts, along with the original statues that used to stand on the edges of the fountain.

On the same floor, pop into the small chapel or oratory where St. Catherine prayed and received visions. A holy nail thought to be from Jesus' cross is on the altar.

Archaeological Museum: Descend into the cavernous second basement under groin vaults to be alone with piles of ancient Etruscan stuff excavated from tombs centuries before Christ (displayed in a labyrinthine exhibit). Remember, the Etruscans dominated this part of Italy before the Roman Empire swept through—even Rome originated as an Etruscan town.

Siena's San Domenico Area

Church of San Domenico—This huge brick church is worth a quick look. The spacious, plain interior (except for the colorful flags of the city's 17 *contrada* or neighborhoods) fits the austere philoso-phy of the Dominicans and invites meditation on the thoughts and deeds of St. Catherine. Walk up the steps in the rear to see paintings from the life of St. Catherine, patron saint of Siena. Halfway up the church on the right, find a metal bust of St. Catherine, a small case containing her thumb (sometimes loaned out to other churches), and a reliquarium on the lowest shelf containing the chain she used to scourge herself. In the chapel (15 feet to the left) surrounded with candles, you'll see Catherine's actual head atop the altar (free, daily March–Oct 7:00–18:30, Nov–Feb 9:00–18:00; WC for €0.50 at far end of parking lot—facing church entrance, it's to your right).

Sanctuary of St. Catherine—Step into Catherine's cool and peaceful home. Siena remembers its favorite hometown gal, a simple, unschooled, but mystically devout soul who, in the mid-1300s, helped convince the pope to return from France to Rome. This schism split the Continent in the 14th century, but because of her intervention, Catherine is honored today as Europe's patron saint. Pilgrims have visited her home since 1464, and architects and artists have greatly embellished what was probably once a humble home (her family worked as wool-dyers). Enter through the courtyard, and walk down the stairs at the far end. The chapel on your right contains the wooden crucifix upon which Catherine was meditating when she received the stigmata. The chapel on your left was originally the kitchen. Go down the stairs to the left of the chapel/kitchen to reach the saint's room. Catherine's bare cell is behind see-through doors. Much of the art throughout the sanctuary depicts scenes from her life (free, daily 9:00–12:30 & 15:00–19:00, Via Tiratoio). It's a few downhill blocks toward the center from San Domenico (follow signs to *Santuario di Santa Caterina*).

SHOPPING AND NIGHTLIFE

Shopping

The main drag, Via Banchi di Sopra, is a can-can of fancy shops. The big local department store is **Upim** (Mon–Sat 8:30–20:00, Sun 9:00–20:00, Piazza Matteotti).

For easy-to-pack souvenirs, get some of the large, colorful scarves/flags that depict the symbols of Siena's 17 different neighborhoods (such as the wolf, the turtle, and the snail). Pick up a few extra to decorate your home (€7 apiece for large size, sold at souvenir stands).

Local Sweets: All over town, **Prodotti Tipici** shops sell Sienese specialties. Siena's claim to caloric fame is its *panforte,* a rich, chewy concoction of nuts, honey, and candied fruits that impresses even fruitcake-haters. There are a few varieties: *margherita,* dusted in powdered sugar, is more fruity; *panpepato* has a spicy, peppery crust. Locals prefer a chewy, white macaroon-and-almond cookie called *ricciarelli.*

Nightlife

Join the evening *passeggiata* (peak strolling time is 19:00) along Via Banchi di Sopra with gelato in hand.

The **Enoteca Italiana** is a good wine bar in a cellar in the Fortezza (sample glasses in three different price ranges: €2, €3, €5.50; Mon 12:00–20:00, Tue–Sat 12:00–24:00, closed Sun; bottles and snacks available; cross bridge and enter fortress, go left down ramp, not to be confused with Enoteca Toscana—same location but not as nice, tel. 0577-288-497).

SIENA DUOMO TOUR

This ornate but surprisingly secular shrine to the Virgin Mary is stacked with colorful art inside and out, from the inlaid-marble floors to the stained-glass windows. Along with sculptures by Bernini and Michelangelo, the church features the Piccolomini Library with a series of captivating frescoes by the Umbrian painter Pinturicchio, telling the story of Aeneas Piccolomini, Siena's consummate Renaissance Man who became Pope Pius II.

ORIENTATION

Cost: €3, covered by €10 *biglietto cumulativo* combo-ticket except mid-Aug–Oct when all of the inlaid floors are uncovered and entry fee is €6 (sold only at the Duomo ticket kiosk inside the entryway).

Dress Code: Modest dress is required, but paper ponchos are provided if needed.

Hours: March–Oct Mon–Sat 9:30–19:00, Sun 13:30–17:30, Nov–Feb Mon–Sat 9:30–17:00, Sun 13:30–16:30, last entry 30 minutes before closing. Opening hours can vary—confirm with TI.

Getting There: Just look up and head for the green- and white-striped tower.

Information: Audioguide for church and library-€3.50; add the Duomo Museum-€4.50 (ID required for deposit). Two headphones are available at a price break. Tel. 0577-283-048.

Photography: No flash permitted.

Length of This Tour: Allow one hour.

THE TOUR BEGINS

Exterior

If the Campo is the heart of Siena, the Duomo is its soul. The white and dark-green church, sitting on an artificial platform atop Siena's highest point, is visible for miles around.

Grab a spot on a stone bench opposite the entry to admire the colorful entrance facade of green, white, pink, and gold. Like a medieval altarpiece, the facade is divided into sections, each frame filled with patriarchs and prophets, studded with roaring gargoyles, and topped with prickly golden pinnacles.

The current structure dates from 1215, with the major decoration done during Siena's heyday from 1250–1350. The lower story, by Giovanni Pisano (worked 1284–1297), features remnants of the fading Romanesque style (round arches over the doors) topped with the pointed arches of the new Gothic style seeping in from France. The upper half, in full-blown Gothic, was done a century later by a different architect.

The six-story bell tower (c. 1315) looks even taller, thanks to an optical illusion: The white marble stripes get narrower toward the top, making the upper part seem farther away.

On a column to the right of the entrance is a statue of the Roman she-wolf suckling Romulus and Remus, the mythical founders of Rome. Legend has it that Remus' son Senio ("Siena") rode north on a black horse to found the city of Siena. Step inside. (With a maximum of 700 allowed in, you may have to wait—current number is indicated on computer screen at turnstile.)

Interior—Nave

The heads of 172 popes peer down from above, looking over the fine inlaid art on the floor. With a forest of striped columns, a coffered dome, a large stained-glass window at the far end, and a museum's worth of early Renaissance art, this is one busy interior. Looking closer at the popes, you see the same four faces repeated over and over.

For almost two centuries (1373–1547), 40 artists paved the marble floor with scenes from the Old Testament, allegories, and intricate patterns. The earliest designs are simple black-and-white with engraved details, but the later ones use inlay technique with many colored marbles. The series starts with historical allegories near the entrance; the larger, more elaborate scenes surrounding the altar are mostly stories from the Old Testament. Many of the floor panels may be protected with sheet flooring.

• *On the floor, find the second pavement panel from the entrance.*

Siena's Duomo

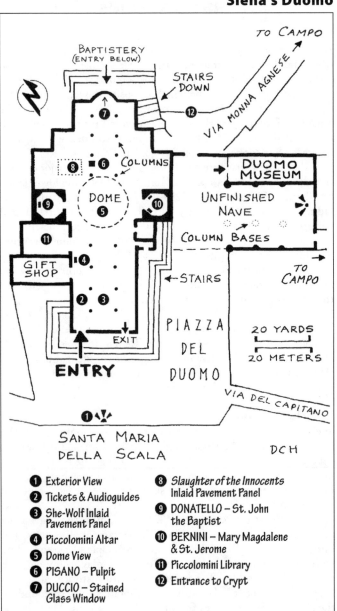

1 Exterior View
2 Tickets & Audioguides
3 She-Wolf Inlaid Pavement Panel
4 Piccolomini Altar
5 Dome View
6 PISANO – Pulpit
7 DUCCIO – Stained Glass Window
8 Slaughter of the Innocents Inlaid Pavement Panel
9 DONATELLO – St. John the Baptist
10 BERNINI – Mary Magdalene & St. Jerome
11 Piccolomini Library
12 Entrance to Crypt

She-Wolf Inlaid Pavement Panel
Depicted as a she-wolf, the proud city of Siena is the center of the Italian universe, orbited by such lesser lights as Roma, Florentia, and Pisa. This is pretty pagan stuff for such prime church real estate. Five yards to the left and right are panels with still more pre-Christian imagery—the ancient Greek prophetesses known as the sibyls.
• *The fourth pavement panel from the entrance is the...*

Fortune Panel
Lady Luck (lower right) parachutes down to earth, where she teeters back and forth (on a ball and a tipsy boat). The lesson? Fortune is an unstable foundation for life. Truth-seekers wind their way up the precarious path to the top, where Socrates accompanies Lady Wisdom. Having attained wisdom, the world's richest man ("Cratis," upper right) realizes that money doesn't buy happiness, and he dumps his jewels out. They fall to earth, and the cycle of Fortune begins again.
• *On the right wall hangs a dim painting (fourth from entrance).*

St. Catherine Painting
Siena's homegrown saint (see page 245) had a vision where she mystically married Christ. Here's the wedding ceremony in heaven. Jesus places the ring on Catherine's finger as her future mother-in-law Mary looks on.
• *On the left wall is a marble altarpiece decorated with statues.*

Piccolomini Altar—in part by Michelangelo
The Piccolomini altar, designed for the tomb of the Sienese-born Pope Pius III, is most interesting for its statues—one by Michelangelo, three by his students.

Michelangelo was originally contracted to do 15 statues, but the marble blocks had been started by another sculptor, and his heart was never in the project. He personally finished only one—St. Paul (lower right, who is clearly more interesting than the bland, bored popes above him).

Paul has the look of Michelangelo's *Moses,* the broken-nosed self-portrait of the sculptor himself, and the dangling hand of his *David.* It was the chance to sculpt *David* in Florence that convinced Michelangelo to abandon the Siena project.

Dome

Grab a seat under the dome. It sits on a 12-sided base but its "coffered" ceiling is actually a painted illusion.

Get oriented to the array of sights by thinking of the church floor as a big 12-hour clock. You're the middle, and the altar is high noon: You'll find the *Slaughter of the Innocents* roped off on the floor at 10:00, Pisano's pulpit between two pillars at 11:00, Duccio's round stained-glass window at high noon, Bernini's chapel at 3:00, the Piccolomini Altar with the Michelangelo statue (next to doorway leading to a shop, snacks, and WC) at 7:00, the Piccolomini Library at 8:00, and a Donatello statue at 9:00.

Attached to columns (at 7:00 and 5:00) are two 65-foot wooden poles—dear to any Sienese heart. These were the **flagpoles** bearing the Florentine flag, captured during the pivotal Battle of Montaperti (1260, fought near Siena), when 20,000 Sienese squared off against 35,000 soldiers from their arch-rival Florence. The two armies battled back and forth all day, until one of the Florentine soldiers—actually, a Sienese spy under cover—attacked the Florentine standard-bearer from behind. Florence's flag fell to the ground, the army lost its bearings and confidence, and Siena seized the moment to counter-attack and win. It was the city's finest hour, ushering in its 80-year Golden Age.

The church was intended to be much larger. Look into the right transept and mentally blow a hole in the wall. You'd be looking down the nave of the massive church, if the original grandiose plan had been completed (see sidebar on next page).

Pisano's Pulpit

The octagonal Carrara marble pulpit (1268) rests on the backs of lions, symbols of Christianity triumphant. Like the lions, the Church eats its catch (devouring paganism) and nurses its cubs. The seven relief panels tell the life of Christ in rich detail. (Buy light from the coin-op machine.) The pulpit is the work of Nicola Pisano (c. 1220–1284), the "Giotto of sculpture," whose revival of classical forms (columns, sarcophagus-like relief panels) signaled the coming Renaissance. His son Giovanni (c. 1250–1314) carved many of the panels, mixing his dad's classicism and realism with the decorative detail and curvy lines of French Gothic—a style that would influence Donatello and the other Florentines.

The Crucifixion panel (facing the nave under the eagle) is proto-Renaissance. Christ's anatomy is realistic. Mary (bottom

---

Siena's Big Plans and Slow Fade

After rival republic Florence began its grand cathedral (1296), proud Siena planned to build one even bigger, the biggest church in all Christendom. Construction began in the 1330s on an extension off the right side of the existing Duomo (today's cathedral would have been used as a transept). The vision was grand, but it underestimated the complexity of constructing such a building without enough land for it to sit upon. That, coupled with the devastating effects of a plague, killed the city's ability and will to finish the project. Many Sienese saw the plague as a sign from God, punishing them for their pride. They canceled their plans and humbly faded into the background of Tuscan history.

---

left) swoons into the arms of the other women, a very human outburst of emotion. And a Roman soldier (to the right, by Giovanni) turns to look back with an easy motion that breaks the stiff, frontal Gothic mold.

If you're visiting Pisa, you'll see two more quite similar Pisano pulpits there. (See pages 287 and 293 for more on the Pisanos and their pulpits).

• *It can be difficult to get a good view of Duccio's stained-glass window. Try viewing it from left of the pulpit.*

Duccio's Stained-Glass Window

Above and behind the altar, the round 20-foot window (1288) is dedicated—like the church and the city itself—to the Virgin Mary. In the window's bottom panel, Mary (in blue) lies stretched across a red coffin (not always visible, sometimes covered by canopy) while a crowd of mourners looks on. Miraculously, Mary was spared the pain of death (the Assumption, central panel), and winged angels carry her up in a holy bubble to heaven (top panel), where Christ sets her on a throne beside him and crowns her.

The work was designed by Siena's most famous artist, Duccio di Buoninsegna (c. 1225–1319). Duccio combined elements from rigid Byzantine icons (Mary's almond-shaped bubble or *mandorla*, and the full-frontal saints that flank her) with a budding sense of 3-D realism (the throne turned at three-quarter angle to simulate depth, with angels behind). Also notice how the angels in the central panel spread their wings out over the border of the window frame.

The Sienese army defeated Florence in the bloody battle of Montaperti, thanks, many believed, to the miraculous help of the Virgin. For the next 80 years of prosperity, Sienese artists cranked out countless Madonnas as a way of saying *grazie*. Bear in mind that the main altar was originally dominated by Duccio's *Maestà*, a huge golden altarpiece of the Virgin in Majesty (now kept in the Duomo Museum—today's altar is less noteworthy), which was bathed in the golden-blue light from this window.

Slaughter of the Innocents Inlaid Pavement Panel

Herod (left), sitting enthroned amid Renaissance arches, orders the massacre of all babies, to prevent the coming of the promised Messiah. It's a chaotic scene of angry soldiers, grieving mothers, and dead babies, reminding locals that a republic ruled by a tyrant will experience misery.

The work was designed by the Sienese Il Beccafumi (1486–1551) and inlaid with a colorful array of marble, including yellow marble, a Sienese specialty quarried nearby.

Donatello—*St. John the Baptist*

The rugged saint in his famous rags stands in a chapel to the right of the library. Donatello, the aging Florentine sculptor, whose style was now considered passé in Florence, came here to build bronze doors for the church (similar to Ghiberti's in Florence). He didn't complete the door project, but he finished this bronze statue (1457).

Bernini Chapel—*Cappella della Madonna del Voto*

To understand why Bernini is considered the greatest Baroque sculptor, step into his sumptuous chapel. This last work in the cathedral, from 1659, is enough to make even a Lutheran light a candle. Move up to the altar and look back at the two Bernini statues: Mary Magdalene in a state of spiritual ecstasy, and St. Jerome playing the crucifix like a violinist lost in beautiful music.

The chapel is classic Baroque, combining colored marble, statues, stained glass, a dome, and golden angels holding an oil painting, creating a multimedia extravaganza that offers a glimpse of heaven.

Over the altar is the *Madonna del Voto,* a Madonna and Child painted by Duccio and adorned with a real crown of gold and jewels. In typical medieval fashion, the scene is set in the golden light of heaven. Mary has the almond eyes, long fingers, and golden folds in her robe that are found in orthodox icons of the time. Still, this Mary tilts her head and looks out sympathetically, ready to listen to the prayers of the faithful. This is the Mary to whom the Palio is dedicated, dear to the hearts of the Sienese.

• *The faithful's prayers to Mary are accompanied by offerings, found outside the chapel, hanging on the wall to the left as you exit.*

Offerings to the *Madonna del Voto*

For untold generations, the Sienese have prayed to the *Madonna del Voto* for her help. In thanks, they give offerings, many of which hang now on the church wall. Silver hearts and medallions express thanks.

Piccolomini Library

If the Piccolomini Library looks crowded, read ahead. Brilliantly frescoed, it captures the exuberant, optimistic spirit of the 1400s, when humanism and the Renaissance were born. The frescoes, never restored, look nearly as vivid today as the day they were finished 550 years ago. (With the bright window light, candles—which would sully the art with soot—were never necessary in this room.) The painter Pinturicchio (c. 1454–1513) was hired to celebrate the life of one of Siena's hometown boys—a man many call "the first humanist," Aeneas Piccolomini (1405–1464). Each of the 10 scenes is framed with an arch, as if Pinturicchio were opening a window onto the spacious 3-D world we inhabit. The line of viewers moves counterclockwise, but start at the window, let your eyes follow the frescos clockwise to trace the following progression:

1. Leaving for Basel: Twenty-seven-year-old Aeneas, riding a white horse and decked out in an outrageous hat, pauses to take one last look back as he leaves Siena to charge off on the first of many adventures in his sometimes sunny, sometimes stormy life. Born poor but noble, he got all A's in his classics classes in Siena. Now, having soaked up all the secular knowledge available, he leaves home to crash a church council in Switzerland, where he would take sides against the pope.

2. Meeting James II of Scotland: Aeneas (with long brown hair) charmed King James and the well-dressed, educated, worldly crowd of Europe's courts. Among his many travels, he visited London (writing home about Westminster Abbey and St. Paul's), barely survived a storm at sea, negotiated peace between England and France, and fathered (at least) two illegitimate children.

3. Crowned poet by Frederick III: Next we find Aeneas in Vienna, working as secretary to the German king. Aeneas kneels to ceremonially receive the laurel crown of a poet. Aeneas wrote love poetry, bawdy stories, and a play, and is best known for his candid autobiography. Everyone was talking about Aeneas—a writer, speaker, diplomat, and lover of the arts and pretty women, who was the very essence of the *uomo universale,* or Renaissance Man.

4. Submitting to Pope Eugene IV: At age 40, after a serious illness, Aeneas changes his life. He journeys to Rome and kisses the pope's foot, apologizing for his heretical opposition. He repents of his wild youth and becomes a priest. (In his autobiography, he says it was time to change anyway, as women no longer aroused him...and he no longer attracted them.)

5. Introducing Frederick III and Eleanora: Quickly named Bishop of Siena, Aeneas (in white, pointed bishop's hat) makes his hometown a romantic getaway for his friend Frederick and his fiancée. Notice the Duomo's bell tower in the distance and the city walls (upper left). Aeneas always seemed to be present at Europe's most important political, religious, and social events.

6. Made Cardinal: Kneeling before the pope, with shaved head and praying hands, Aeneas receives the flat red hat of a cardinal. In many of these panels, the artist Pinturicchio uses all the latest 3-D effects—floor tiles and carpets, distant landscapes, receding lines—to suck you into the scene. He tears down palace walls and lets us peek inside into the day's centers of power.

7. Made Pope: In 1458, at age 53, Aeneas is elected to be Pope Pius II. Carried in triumph, he blesses the crowd. One of his first acts as pope was to declare as heresy the anti-pope doctrines he had championed in his youth. (Pius II fans can visit his birthplace in Pienza—see page 328.)

8. Proclaims a Crusade: He calls on all Europe to liberate the Christian city of Constantinople, which had recently fallen in 1453 to the Ottoman Turks. Europe is reluctant to follow his call, but Aeneas pushes the measure through.

9. Canonizes St. Catherine: From his papal throne, Aeneas looks down on the mortal remains of Catherine (clutching her symbol, the lily) and proclaims his fellow Sienese a saint. The well-dressed candle-holders in the foreground pose proudly.

10. Arrival in Ancona: Old and sick, the pope has to be carried everywhere on a litter because of rheumatic feet. He travels to Ancona, ready to board a ship to go fight the Turks. But only a handful of Venetian galleys arrive at the appointed time, the crusade peters out, and Aeneas, disheartened, dies. He wrote: "I do not deny my past. I have been a great wanderer, wandering away from the right path. But at least I know it, and hope the knowledge has not come too late."

The library also contains intricately decorated, illuminated music scores, and a statue (a Roman copy of a Greek original) of the Three Graces.

• *Exit the Duomo and make a U-turn to the left, walking alongside the church to Piazza Jacopo della Quercia.*

The Unfinished Church

The nave of the Duomo was supposed to be where the piazza is today. Worshippers would have entered the church from the far  end of the piazza through the unfinished wall. Some of the nave's green-and-white-striped columns were built, and are now filled in with a brick wall. Round white stones in the pavement mark where a row of pillars would have been. Look through the unfinished entrance facade, seeing blue sky where the stained-glass windows would have been, and ponder the struggles, triumphs, and failures of the human spirit.

DUOMO MUSEUM TOUR

(Museo dell'Opera e Panorama)

Siena's most enjoyable museum was built to house the cathedral's art. Stand eye-to-eye with the saints and angels who once languished unknown in the church's upper reaches (where copies are found today). The museum's centerpiece—an altarpiece by Duccio—once stood in the center of the church. And the museum's high point is one of the loftiest in town, offering expansive views of the church and the city.

ORIENTATION

Cost: €6, covered by €10 *biglietto cumulativo* combo-ticket except mid-Aug–Oct, when the inlaid floors in the Duomo are uncovered. Also covered by pricey *Itinerari d'Arte* combo-ticket. (See page 234 for more combo-ticket info.)

Hours: Daily March–Oct 9:30–19:00, Nov–Feb 9:30–17:00, confirm hours at TI.

Getting There: It's next to the Duomo, in the skeleton of the unfinished part of the church on the Campo side; look for the yellow signs.

Information: There's a good 40-minute audioguide for €3; add the Duomo audioguide for €4.50 (ID required for deposit). Tel. 0577-283-048.

Length of This Tour: Allow one hour.

Starring: Duccio, the Virgin Mary, and the Tuscan view.

THE TOUR BEGINS

Ground Floor

The ground floor houses the church's original statues, mainly from the facade and exterior. After descending a few steps, turn your back on the hall of statues and wrought-iron gate. You're now face-to-face with **Donatello's** *Madonna and Child,* a round, carved relief. A slender, tender Mary gazes down at her chubby-cheeked baby. The thick folds of her headdress stream down around her smooth face. Her sad eyes say that she knows the eventual fate of her son. Donatello creates the illusion of Mary's three-dimensional "lap" using only a few inches of depth cut into the creamy-rose stone.

Lining the main room are **Giovanni Pisano's statues.** Giovanni spent a decade (c. 1285–1296) carving and orchestrating the decoration of the cathedral—saints, prophets, sibyls, animals, and the original she-wolf with Romulus and Remus. These life-size, robed saints stand in a relaxed *contrapposto,* with open mouths and expressive gestures. Their heads jut out—Giovanni's way of making them more visible from below. Some turn and seem to converse with their neighbors, especially evident with Moses *(Mose)* and the sister who raised him like a mother, Miriam (*Maria di Mose,* on the left side of the room). The copies of these two stand on the right side of the church, where they appear to interact.

Down a few steps in Rooms 11 and 12 are the two lions who once looked down from the church's main entrance, and Giovanni's 12 apostles who once lined the nave. Tastes changed over the centuries, and the apostles were later moved up to the roof, where they eroded. Giovanni's relaxed realism and expressive gestures were a major influence on later Florentine sculptors like Donatello.

• *Upstairs to the left awaits a private audience with Duccio's* Madonna.

Duccio di Buoninsegna—Altarpiece Panels
(*Maestà* and 26 Passion panels, 1311)

The panels in this room were once part of the Duomo's main altarpiece. Grab a seat and study one of the great pieces of medieval art. The former altarpiece was disassembled (and the frame lost) and now most of the pieces are displayed here—the front side (*Maestà,* with Mary and saints) at one end of the room, back side (Passion panels) at the other.

Imagine these separate panels pieced together, set into their original gold, prickly, 15-by-15-foot wood frame and placed on the main altar in the Duomo. For two centuries it gave the congregation something to look at while the priests turned their backs at Communion time. The Christ child stared back.

At the center of the front side sits the Virgin and Child *(Maestà,* or *Enthroned Virgin)* surrounded by angels and saints. Mary's a melancholy queen on an inlaid marble throne. Young angels lean their elbows on the back of the throne and sigh. We see the throne head-on, unnaturally splayed open (a Byzantine style popular at the time in Siena). Mary is massive, twice the size of the saints around her, and she clearly stands out from the golden background. Unlike traditional full-frontal Byzantine icons, she turns slightly sideways to touch her baby, who does not bless us.

The city of Siena is dedicated to this Lady, who backed the Sienese against Florence in the bloody battle of Montaperti in 1260. Here, she's triumphant, visited by Siena's four patron saints (kneeling in front), John the Baptist and other saints (the first choir row), more angels in a row (soprano section), and, chiming in from up in the balcony, James the Great and the 12 apostles.

The painting was revolutionary for the time in its sheer size and opulence, and in Duccio's budding realism that broke standard conventions. Duccio (c. 1225–1319), at the height of his powers, used every innovative arrow in his quiver. He replaced the standard gold-leaf background (symbolizing heaven) with a gold, intricately patterned curtain draped over the throne. Mary's blue robe opens to reveal her body, and the curve of her knee suggests real anatomy beneath the robe. Baby Jesus wears a delicately transparent garment. Their faces are modeled with light—a patchwork of bright flesh and shadowy valleys, as if lit from the left (a technique he likely learned from his contemporary Giotto during a visit to Florence).

Along the base of Mary's throne is an inscription (*"Mater sancta dei..."* or "Holy Mother of God...") asking Mary to bring peace to Siena *(Senis)* and long life to Duccio *(Ducio)*—quite a tribute in a time when painters were usually treated as anonymous craftsmen.

• *Look on the opposite wall.*

The flip side of the altarpiece featured 26 smaller panels—the medieval equivalent of pages—showing colorful **scenes from the Passion of Christ.**

The panels showcase the budding Tuscan style—realism and storytelling. It doesn't take a Bible scholar to "read" these panels, left to right. Christ on a donkey (lower left) makes his triumphal entry into the city gate of Jerusalem (or is it Siena?). Next, he washes his disciples' feet in a realistic, three-dimensional room. But Duccio hasn't fully mastered perspective—in the Last Supper, we see Christ eye-to-eye, but view the table from above. Christ is arrested in Gethsemane, and so on, until the climactic Crucifixion. The Crucifixion is given the standard gold background, but the cross is set on a terraced hillside, amid the crowd. Jesus' followers express human emotion rarely seen in earlier art.

The Passion panels' crowd scenes aren't arranged in neat choir rows, but in more natural-looking groups. Duccio sets figures in motion, with individual faces expressing sorrow, anger, and agitation. Duccio's human realism would be taken to the next level by his Florentine counterpart Giotto, often called the first proto-Renaissance painter.

Duccio and assistants (possibly including Simone Martini) spent three years on this massive altarpiece. It was a triumph, and at its dedication the satisfied Sienese marched it around the Campo and into the church in a public procession.

But by 1506, at the height of the Renaissance, Duccio's medieval altarpiece looked musty and old-fashioned, and was moved to a side altar. In 1771 it was disassembled and stored in the church offices (today's Duomo Museum). Today, scholars debate how to reassemble it accurately, and hail it as a quantum leap in the evolution of art.

• *Continue up the stairs. At the landing just before the top floor, walk past the rooms on the right—a stairwell is through the small doorway. Climb down the steps and then up the claustrophobic spiral staircase to the viewpoint...*

Panorama del Facciatone

Standing on the wall from this high point in the city, you're rewarded with a stunning view of Siena...and an interesting perspective.

Look toward the Duomo and remember this: To outdo Florence, Siena had planned to enlarge this cathedral by turning it into a transept and constructing an enormous nave (see sidebar on page 253). You're standing on top of what would have been the new entrance facade (see map on page 250). The white stones in the pavement mark where columns would have stood. Had the church been completed, you'd be looking straight down the nave toward the altar.

CIVIC MUSEUM TOUR

(Museo Civico)

The City Hall (Palazzo Pubblico), at the base of the City Tower, stands as a symbol of a republic independent of the pope and the Holy Roman Emperor, and of the rising secular society that appeared first in Tuscany before spreading throughout Europe in the Renaissance. Still the seat of city government, the City Hall also has a fine and manageable museum housing a good sample of Sienese art. Stroll through this civic center, featuring day-in-the-life frescoes and an excellent real-life view of the surrounding countryside.

ORIENTATION

Cost: €7, €10 combo-ticket with City Tower, a different €10 combo-ticket with Santa Maria della Scala, or the €16 *Itinerari d'Arte* combo-ticket (also covers Duomo Museum, Santa Maria della Scala, and Baptistery).

Hours: Daily March–Oct 10:00–18:15, Nov–Feb 10:00–16:00, last entry 45 min before closing; may be open late on summer evenings.

Getting There: As the focus of the main square, it's hard to miss.

Information: Audioguides may be available—ask.

Photography: Not allowed.

Length of This Tour: Allow one hour.

THE TOUR BEGINS

Hall of Italian Unification (Sala del Risorgimento)

This hall has dramatic scenes of the 19th-century unification of Italy (surrounded by statues that don't seem to care). See Victor

Siena's Civic Museum

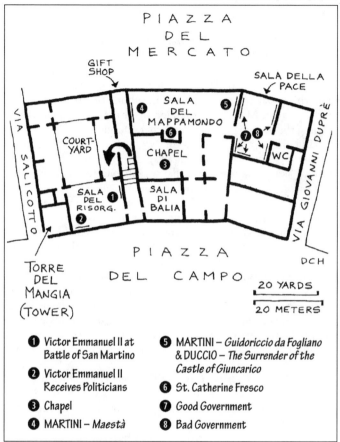

PIAZZA DEL MERCATO

GIFT SHOP

SALA DELLA PACE

SALA DEL MAPPAMONDO

COURT-YARD

CHAPEL

WC

SALA DEL RISORG.

SALA DI BALIA

VIA SALICOTTO

VIA GIOVANNI DUPRÈ

PIAZZA DEL CAMPO

TORRE DEL MANGIA (TOWER)

DCH

20 YARDS

20 METERS

❶ Victor Emmanuel II at Battle of San Martino

❷ Victor Emmanuel II Receives Politicians

❸ Chapel

❹ MARTINI – *Maestà*

❺ MARTINI – *Guidoriccio da Fogliano* & DUCCIO – *The Surrender of the Castle of Giuncarico*

❻ St. Catherine Fresco

❼ Good Government

❽ Bad Government

Emmanuel II (left wall, with beard and pointy moustache), king of a small northern Italian province, on horseback at the Battle of San Martino (1859), leading a united Italian nation against its Austrian oppressors. Beneath the piece, you'll see the coat he's wearing in the painting. Next (long wall), the king's red-shirted troops cheer as he shakes hands with the dashing general Garibaldi. Victorious, Victor receives politicians (next painting) who bow and present the election results that made Italy united and democratic, with Victor as a symbolic head. When Victor Emmanuel died in 1878 (see his funeral on the far wall), Italy was on the road to modern nationhood.

• *Pass through the hallway to the left, and in the second room, turn left to find the chapel where the city's governors and bureaucrats prayed. Continue into the large...*

Sala del Mappamondo

On opposite ends of the room where the Grand Council met, you'll find two large frescoes by Siena's great Simone Martini (c. 1280–1344). His *Maestà* (*Enthroned Virgin*, 1315) was the secular counterpart to Duccio's *Maestà* in the Duomo (now in the Duomo Museum). Mary sits on a throne under a red silk canopy, a model to Siena's city council of what a just ruler should be. Siena's black-and-white coat of arms is woven into both the canopy and the picture frame. Mary is surrounded by saints and angels, clearly echoing the *Maestà* of Simone's teacher, Duccio.

But this is a groundbreaking work. It's Siena's first fresco showing a Madonna not in a faraway, gold-leaf heaven, but under the blue sky of the real world that we inhabit. The canopy creates a 3-D stage, with saints in front of, behind, and under the canopy. Some saints' faces are actually blocked by the support poles. These saints are not a generic conga-line of Byzantine icons, but a milling crowd of 30 individuals with expressive faces. Some look straight out, some are in profile, and some turn at that difficult-to-draw three-quarter angle, grabbing onto the canopy poles. And the Virgin's brooch is painted so well that it almost looks...uh, real.

Facing the *Maestà* is Simone Martini's *Guidoriccio da Fogliano*. It's the year "MCCCXXVIII" (1328), and Siena's renowned mercenary general—one of Martini's compatriots—rides across a barren landscape surveying the two castles his armies have just conquered. Guido and his horse have the same tailor. This is one of Europe's first secular portraits.

The Surrender of the Castle of Giuncarico, by Duccio (1314), shows a man in green about to hand over his sword to the Sienese general (not pictured—the fresco was damaged). In the background is the man's castle and village on a rocky outcrop. Duccio's *Surrender* apparently inspired the 3-D landscape of *Guidoriccio da Folignano*, by Duccio's pupil, Martini.

Also in the room (painted between the arches) are frescoes of two saints with local connections, St. Catherine (see page 245) and St. Bernardino (1380–1444). Bernardino's charismatic sermons in Siena brought together sworn enemies to share a *bacio di pace*—kiss of peace.

Room of Peace
(Sala della Pace, a.k.a. Sala dei Nove)

This is the council room where the Council of Nine met. Looking down on the oligarchy during their meetings were two interesting frescoes showing the *Effects of Good and Bad Government*, by Ambrogio Lorenzetti (1337–1340).

Good Government (on the short wall) is represented by a stately, bearded man on a throne, surrounded by virtuous females, notably the central virtue Peace (Pax), who lounges back on a pile of discarded armor. Justice holds a scale, with angels on either side, to execute her judgments. Wrongdoers (lower right) are rounded up by the authorities. At the foot of the stage, prominent Sienese file by.

On the long wall (with the better-preserved fresco), notice the whistle-while-you-work happiness of the utopian community ruled by the utopian government. Amid Siena's skyline (Duomo at upper left), young people dance to the beat of a tambourine, workers repair roofs, and the conversation flows. The blessings of a good government extend even to the countryside, which feels safe and prosperous. The fields are tilled, the Via Francigena is busy, and angels fly overhead.

But under Bad Government (other long wall, damaged fresco), a horned, fanged, wine-drinking devil sets the vices loose ("Avarice," "Vainglory"). Arsonists torch homes and fields, soldiers rape and pillage, the fields are barren, and frescoes get damaged. Justice slumps at the devil's feet, bound, and too depressed to look up. The message: Without justice, there can be no prosperity.

The rural view out the window is essentially the same view as from the top of the big stairs—enjoy it from here.

SIENA SLEEPING, EATING, AND TRANSPORTATION CONNECTIONS

SLEEPING

Finding a room in Siena is tough during Easter (April 8 in 2007) or the Palio (July 2 and August 16). Call ahead any time of year, as all the guidebooks list Siena's few budget places. While day-tripping tour groups turn the town into a Gothic amusement park in midsummer, Siena is basically yours in the evenings and off-season.

Most of the listed hotels lie between Il Campo and the Church of San Domenico. Part of Siena's charm is its lively, festive char-acter—this means that all hotels can be plagued with noise, even (and sometimes especially) the hotels in the pedestrian-only zone. If tranquility is important for your sanity, ask for a room that's off the street, or consider staying at the recommended places outside the center.

Near Il Campo

Each of these listings is forgettable but inexpensive, and just a horse wreck away from one of Italy's most wonderful civic spaces.

$ Albergo Tre Donzelle is a fine budget value with 28 plain, institutional rooms. Don't hang out here...think of Il Campo, a block away, as your terrace (S-€33, D-€46, Db-€60, T-€65, Tb-€82; with your back to the tower, leave Il Campo to the right at 2:00, Via Donzelle 5; tel. 0577-280-358, fax 0577-223-933, Signora Valentina).

$ Piccolo Hotel Etruria has 20 decent air-conditioned rooms but not much soul. The hotel is a bit overpriced though well-located and sleepable (S-€48, Sb-€53, Db-€86, Tb-€114, Qb-€142, optional breakfast-€5, curfew at 1:00, next to Albergo Tre Donzelle at Via Donzelle 1–3, tel. 0577-288-088, fax 0577-288-461,

---

Sleep Code

(€1 = about $1.20, country code: 39)
S = Single, **D** = Double/Twin, **T** = Triple, **Q** = Quad, **b** = bathroom,
s = shower only.

Breakfast is not included unless noted. If your hotel doesn't provide it, have breakfast on Il Campo or in a nearby bar. Credit cards are generally accepted, but I note if they aren't. (If not, there are ATMs all over town.) Hotel staff generally speak English unless noted otherwise.

To help you sort easily through these listings, I've divided the rooms into three categories based on the price for a standard double room with bath:

  $$$ **Higher Priced**—Most rooms €120 or more.
   $$ **Moderately Priced**—Most rooms between €90–120.
    $ **Lower Priced**—Most rooms €90 or less.

---

www.hoteletruria.com, info@hoteletruria.com, Fattorini family).

$ Locanda Garibaldi is a modest, very Sienese restaurant/ *albergo* (hotel). Gentle Marcello wears two hats, running a busy restaurant downstairs and renting seven pleasant rooms up a funky, artsy staircase (Db-€78, Tb-€100, family deals, cash only, takes reservations only a week in advance, half a block downhill off the square at Via Giovanni Dupre 18, tel. 0577-284-204, Marcello and Sonia speak very little English).

$ Palazzo Bruchi B&B offers nine tranquil rooms situated in a 17th-century palazzo overlooking the Tuscan countryside. Two spacious *luxe* rooms feature Old World, heavy walnut furnishings and period paintings, while seven smaller rooms named for flowers have bright, cheery decor and overlook a quiet interior courtyard. Mariacristina and her daughter Camilla take good care of their guests (Sb-€75, Db-€85, Tb-€120, elevator; take Banchi di Sotto until it turns into Via Pantaneto, located on left, just before the Church of San Giorgio at Via Pantaneto 105; tel. & fax 0577-287-342, www.palazzobruchi.it, masignani@hotmail.com).

$ Hotel Cannon d'Oro, a few blocks up Via Banchi di Sopra, is spacious and comfortable, if a bit noisy and group-friendly (Sb-€71, Db-€90, Tb-€115, Qb-€136, these discounted prices good with this book through 2007, family deals, 30 rooms, includes breakfast, Via Montanini 28, tel. 0577-44-321, fax 0577-280-868, www.cannondoro.com, info@cannondoro.com, Maurizio and Debora). This is just a couple blocks from the bus station.

$ Casa di Antonella B&B, in the heart of town, is neat-as-a-pin, relaxing, and a decent value. Antonella's five rooms have views of the Duomo, San Domenico, or the rooftops of Siena, and

Siena Hotels and Restaurants

1. Piccolo Hotel Etruria
2. Albergo Tre Donzelle
3. Locanda Garibaldi & Rist. Guidoriccio
4. Hotel Cannon d'Oro
5. To Hotel Duomo, Pen. Pal. Ravizza & Ost. Nonna Gina
6. To Hotel Villa Liberty
7. Hotel Chiusarelli
8. Alma Domus
9. Albergo Bernini & Ost. la Chiacchera

10. Casa di Antonella B&B
11. To Hotel Sta. Caterina, Palazzo Bruchi B&B & Res. d'Epoca Borgognini
12. To Hostel
13. Antica Ost. Da Divo
14. To Taverna S. Giuseppe
15. Osteria il Tamburino
16. Le Campane Rest.
17. Nello la Taverna
18. Pizzeria Spadaforte
19. Gelateria la Costarella

20. Ciao Cafeteria, Spizzico Pizza & Key Largo Bar
21. Bar Paninoteca San Paolo
22. Consorzio Agrario Siena Grocery
23. Lavarapido Launderette
24. Onda Blu Launderette

share a communal kitchen and dining room. Four rooms share two baths, and one room has a private bath (D-€65, includes buffet breakfast, no elevator, 3 floors up, located between Piazza Matteotti and Piazza Indipendenza on Via delle Terme 72, tel. & fax 0577-48-436, mobile 330-180-5557, anto.landi@libero.it).

Sleeping Fancy, Southwest of Il Campo

These two classy and well-run places are a 10-minute walk from Il Campo.

$$$ **Hotel Duomo** has 23 spacious rooms and a bizarre floor plan (Sb-€125, Db-€150, Tb-€200, Qb-€250, includes breakfast, air-con, elevator, picnic-friendly roof terrace, free parking; follow Via di Città, which becomes Via Stalloreggi, to Via Stalloreggi 38; tel. 0577-289-088, fax 0577-43-043, www.hotelduomo.it, booking @hotelduomo.it, Alessandra and Stefania). If you arrive by train, take a taxi (€8) or bus #3 to the Due Porte stop just a few steps from the hotel; if you drive, go to Porta San Marco, turn right and follow the signs to the hotel, drop off your bags, and then park in nearby "Il Campo" lot.

$$$ **Pensione Palazzo Ravizza** is elegant and friendly, with an aristocratic feel and a peaceful garden (Sb-€140, small loft Db-€130, standard Db-€172, superior Db-€192—see Web site for room differences, Tb-€220–310, suites available, cheaper mid-Nov–Feb, includes breakfast, back rooms face open country, air-con, elevator, good restaurant, free parking, Via Piano dei Mantellini 34, tel. 0577-280-462, fax 0577-221-597, www.palazzoravizza.it, bureau @palazzoravizza.it).

Near San Domenico Church

These hotels are within a 10-minute walk northeast of Il Campo. Albergo Bernini and Alma Domus, which enjoy views of the old town and cathedral, are about the best values in town.

$$$ **Hotel Chiusarelli** has 49 rooms in a beautiful building with a handy location. Expect traffic noise at night—ask for a quieter room in the back. Readers report the staff is indifferent, except for Barbara, who is super (S-€66, Sb-€85, Db-€125, Tb-€169, suites available, ask for Rick Steves discount when you book, includes buffet breakfast, reasonable dinner menu, air-con, Internet access, pleasant garden terrace, rental bikes-€4/half day, across from San Domenico at Viale Curtatone 15, tel. 0577-280-562, fax 0577-271-177, www.chiusarelli.com, info@chiusarelli.com).

$$ **Hotel Villa Liberty,** a bit farther out, has 18 big, bright, comfortable rooms and lots of street noise (S-€65, Db-€100, can be pricier during high season, includes breakfast, only 2 rooms with twin beds, air-con, elevator, bar, courtyard, free and easy street parking, facing fortress at Viale V. Veneto 11, tel. 0577-44-966, fax

0577-44-770, www.villaliberty.it, info@villaliberty.it).

$ Alma Domus is ideal—unless nuns make you nervous, you need a double bed, or you plan on staying out past the 23:30 curfew (no mercy given). This quasi-hotel (not a convent) is run with firm but angelic smiles by non-English-speaking sisters who offer 43 clean and quiet rooms for a steal and save the best views for foreigners. Bright lamps, quaint balconies, fine views, grand public rooms, top security, and a friendly atmosphere make this a great value. The checkout time is strictly 10:00, but they will store your luggage in their secure courtyard (Db-€60, Tb-€75, Qb-€90, cash only, ask for view room—*con vista*, air-con, elevator; from San Domenico, walk downhill with the church on your right toward the view, turn left down Via Camporegio, make a U-turn at the little chapel down the brick steps to Via Camporegio 37; tel. 0577-44-177, fax 0577-47-601).

$ Albergo Bernini makes you part of a Sienese family in a modest, clean home with nine fine rooms. Friendly Nadia and Mauro and son Alessandro (who speaks English) welcome you to their spectacular view terrace for breakfast and picnic lunches and dinners. Outside of breakfast and checkout time, Mauro, an accomplished accordionist, might play a song for you if you ask (Sb-€78, D-€62, Db-€82, less in winter, breakfast-€7, cash only, non-smoking, midnight curfew, on the main Il Campo-San Domenico drag at Via Sapienza 15, tel. & fax 0577-289-047, www.albergobernini.com, hbernin@tin.it. When full, they recommend their charming, bigger, but more expensive apartments (Db-€100, non-smoking, no curfew, located just a few steps downhill from Albergo).

Southeast of Il Campo, Farther from the Center

The first two places are near each other, in the direction of Porta Romana city gate. The last two are well-served by city buses, but are less convenient. To locate hotels, see map on page 233.

$$$ Hotel Santa Caterina is a three-star, 18th-century place, great for drivers who need air-conditioning. Professionally run with real attention to quality, most of the hotel's 22 comfortable rooms were recently renovated, and there's a delightful garden outside (Sb-€105, small Db-€105, Db-€145, Tb-€195, prices promised through 2007 with this book, includes buffet breakfast, fridge in room, elevator; garden side is quieter, but street side—with multipaned windows—isn't bad; parking-€15/day—request when you reserve, 100 yards outside Porta Romana at Via E.S. Piccolomini 7, tel. 0577-221-105, fax 0577-271-087, www.hscsiena.it, info@hscsiena.it, Lorenza speaks English). A city shuttle bus runs frequently (4/hr) to the town center.

$$$ Frances' Lodge is a small farmhouse B&B a mile out of Siena. Franca and Franco rent four modern rooms and two apartment-suites in a rustic yet elegant old place with a swimming pool, peaceful garden, eight acres of olive trees and vineyards, and great Siena views (Db-€160–190 depending upon room size, Tb-€210–220, Db suite-€220, Tb suite-€250, Qb suite-€280, these prices are promised to our readers through 2007, so let Franca and Franco know when you book, includes great breakfast, easy parking, near shuttle bus "B" into town, Strada di Valdipugna 2, tel. & fax 0577-281-061, www.franceslodge.it, info@franceslodge.it).

$$ Residenza d'Epoca Borgognini is a grand old palazzo with seven cool, solid, and tastefully decorated rooms. You'll find high ceilings, lots of stairs, and a warm welcome from Maria Antonietta (D-normally €80 but €120 in July–Aug, Db-normally €90 but €130 in July–Aug, Tb-€120–150, 10 percent discount with this book in 2007, includes breakfast at nearby bar, Via Pantaneto 160, tel. & fax 0577-44-055, mobile 338-764-0933, www.hotelborgognini.it, hotelborgognini@yahoo.it).

$ Siena's **Guidoriccio Youth Hostel** has 100 cheap beds, but is outside the center. Given the hassle of the bus ride and the charm of downtown Siena at night, I'd skip it (€14 beds in doubles, triples, and dorms with sheets, cash only, cheap breakfast, lockout 9:30–13:30, bus #10 from train station or bus #10 or #15 from Piazza Gramsci—about 20 min, Via Fiorentina 89 in Stellino neighborhood, tel. 0577-52-212, fax 0577-50-277).

Outside of Siena

The following accommodations, best for drivers, are in the lush, peaceful countryside surrounding Siena. To locate these places, see the map on page 233.

$$$ Borgo Argenina is a well-maintained, pricey splurge of a B&B, located a 20-minute drive north of Siena in the Chianti region. It's run by helpful Elena Nappa (Db-€180, beautiful gardens, tel. 0577 747 117, fax 0577-747-228, www.borgoargenina.it, borgoargenina@libero.it).

$ Agriturismo Poggio Salvi, has three inviting, spacious apartments—rentable only by the week—set in a grassy field near the tiny burg of Poggio Salvi, 15 minutes southwest of Siena. Dwellings are separate with modern conveniences (rentals from Sat–Sat, €620/2 people and €940/4 people during high season, e-mail Massimo and ask for Rick Steves discount, Loc. Poggio Salvi 249, 53010 San Rocco a Pilli, tel. & fax 0577-349-443, mobile 333-290-7890, fax 0577-347-686, www.poggiosalvi.net, info@poggiosalvi.net).

$ Parri Nada Farmhouse, a good choice for families, is tucked away in the vineyards in the hills of Chianti 12 miles northeast of Siena. Luca and Elena Masti rent two rooms in their comfortable home (D-€75, T-€90, Q-whole apartment-€110, one-night rentals OK, kitchen, pool, private yard, Località Santa Chiara 4, tel. &

fax 0577-359-072, mobile 333-840-8448 or 338-868-3810, www
.farm-house.it, info@farm-house.it).

EATING

Sienese restaurants are reasonable by Florentine and Venetian
standards. Enjoy ordering high on the menu here without going
broke.

Antica Osteria Da Divo is *the* place for a fine €45 meal.
The kitchen is creative, the ambience is candlelit, and the food
is fresh and top-notch. The lamb goes *baaa* in your mouth. They
offer a basket of fresh, exotic breads and excellent seasonal dishes.
And the chef is understandably proud of his desserts (Wed–Mon
12:00–14:30 & 19:00–22:30, closed Tue, reserve for summer eves;
facing baptistery door, take the far right and walk one long curving block to Via Franciosa 29; tel. 0577-286-054). Readers of this
book enjoy a free welcome drink or can finish their meal with a
complimentary biscotti and *vin santo* or coffee.

Ristorante Guidoriccio, just a few steps below Il Campo,
feels warm, classy, and delightful, with smiling service by Ercole
and Elisabetta and prices good for the locale (pastas-€7, *secondi*-
€13, Mon–Sat 12:30–14:30 & 19:00–22:30, closed Sun, air-con,
Via G. Dupre 2, tel. 0577-44-350).

Taverna San Giuseppe, a local favorite, offers modern Tuscan
cuisine in a dressy grotto atmosphere. Check the posters tacked
around the entry for daily specials. Reserve or arrive early to get
a table (Mon–Sat 12:00–14:30 & 19:00–22:00, closed Sun, 7-min
walk up street to the right of the City Hall, Via Giovanni Dupre
132, tel. 0577-42-286).

Osteria il Tamburino is friendly, popular, and serves up
tasty, inexpensive meals in a narrow dining room (Mon–Sat
12:00–15:00 & 19:00–22:30, closed Sun; from Il Campo, follow
Via di Città—which becomes Stalloreggi—to Via Stalloreggi 11;
tel. 0577-280-306).

Le Campane, two blocks off Il Campo, is more formal than
other Sienese restaurants. It features modern Tuscan fare with an
elegant interior and outdoor tables on a quiet square (pastas-€9,
secondi-€14, Thu–Tue 12:15–14:30 & 19:30–22:00, closed Wed,
reservations smart, indoor/outdoor seating, a few steps off Via di
Città at Via delle Campane 6, tel. 0577-284-035).

Osteria Nonna Gina wins praise from locals for its good
quality and prices (Tue–Sun 12:30–14:30 & 19:30–22:30, closed
Mon, 10-min walk from Il Campo, 2 blocks beyond Hotel Duomo,
Piano dei Mantellini 2, tel. 0577-287-247).

Osteria la Chiacchera is a youthful hole-in-the-brick-wall
playing hip music and serving "peasant food" at peasant prices on

rustic tables and paper place mats (pastas-€4, *secondi*-€5–6, daily 12:00–15:30 & 19:00–24:00, reservations wise, understandably proud of their cakes, skip the *trippa*—tripe, down the street to the left of Pension Bernini at Costa di San Antonio 4, tel. 0577-280-631). Their outside tables cling to a steep lane.

Nello la Taverna, an artsy restaurant with a minimalist dining room, is run by English-speaking Mauro and Simonetta with stylish flair. Their menu features whatever's in season paired with homemade pasta, lots of creative vegetarian options, and well-presented hot desserts (Mon–Sat 12:00–15:00 & 19:00–22:30, closed Sun, a few steps off Il Campo on Via Porrione 28, to the left of City Tower as you're facing it, tel. 0577-289-043).

Locanda Garibaldi offers authentic Sienese dining at a fair price (pastas-€6, *secondi*-€9, €20 *menù*, Sun–Fri 12:00–14:00 & 19:00–21:00, closed Sat, arrive early to get a table, within a block of Il Campo at Via Giovanni Dupre 18, tel. 0187-284-4204). Marcello does a little *piatto misto dolce* (sweet mixed plate) for €4, featuring several local desserts with sweet wine.

Even with higher prices, lousy service, and lower-quality food, consider eating on Il Campo—a classic European experience. Given the real estate, the prices (if you order carefully and are treated fairly) are actually pretty good. Wander across the square, and sit wherever your stomach and heart tell you to. **Pizzeria Spadaforte,** at the edge of Il Campo, has a fine perch, decent food, and slanted tables (€7 pizzas and pastas, daily 12:00–16:00 & 19:30–22:30, to far right of City Tower as you face it, tel. 0577-281-123).

Drinks or Snacks Overlooking Il Campo

Three places have skinny balconies with benches overlooking the main square for their customers. Sipping a coffee or nibbling a pastry here while marveling at the Il Campo scene is one of my favorite things to do in Europe. And it's very cheap. Survey these three places from Il Campo (from the base of the tower, using an imaginary 12-hour clock, they are at 10:00, high noon, and 3:00, respectively).

Gelateria la Costarella has good ice cream, drinks, and light snacks (Mon–Wed & Fri–Sun 8:00–late, closes 22:00 off-season, closed Thu, off Via di Città). **Bar Paninoteca San Paolo,** with a youthful pub ambience, has a row of stools overlooking the square and serves 50 kinds of sandwiches (hot and cold, €3.50 each, €0.50 extra if you sit outside, food served daily 11:30–2:00, on Vicolo di S. Paolo on the stairs leading down to the top of Il Campo). **Key Largo Bar** has two benches in the corner offering a great secret perch (daily 7:00–22:00 or until midnight, closed Sun in winter, on Via Rinaldini). Buy your drink or snack at the bar (no extra charge to sit), climb upstairs, and slide the ancient bar to open the door. Suddenly you're imagining Palio ponies zipping wildly around your corner.

Eating Cheaply in the Center

At the bottom of Il Campo, a **Ciao** cafeteria offers easy self-service meals, no ambience, and no views (daily 12:00–15:00 & 19:00–21:30). The crowded **Spizzico,** a pizza counter in the front half of Ciao, serves huge, inexpensive quarter-pizzas; on sunny days, people take the pizza—trays and all—out on Il Campo for a picnic (daily 11:00–22:00, to left of City Tower as you face it).

Budget eaters look for *pizza al taglio* shops, scattered throughout Siena, selling pizza by the slice. Of all the grocery shops, the biggest is **Consorzio Agrario Siena** (Mon–Sat 8:00–19:30, closed Sun, a block off Piazza Matteotti, toward Il Campo at Via Pianigiani 5).

TRANSPORTATION CONNECTIONS

Siena has sparse train connections, but is a great hub for buses to the hill towns, though frequency drops on Sundays and holidays.

From Siena by Train to: Florence (€5.60, 12/day, 1.75 hrs, more with transfer in Empoli, bus is better), **Pisa** (€6.60, change at Empoli: Pisa–Empoli, hourly, 45 min; Empoli–Siena, hourly, 1 hr), **Rome** (about €17; more if you go on Eurostar via Florence, every 2 hrs, 2.75–4 hrs, transfer in Florence or Chiusi). For more information, visit www.trenitalia.com.

By Bus to: Florence (€6.50, hourly, 75-min *corse rapide* buses are faster than the train, avoid the 2-hr *diretta* slow buses unless you have time to enjoy the beautiful scenery en route, can buy tickets at *tabacchi* shops if bus ticket office is closed), **San Gimignano** (€5.20, 5/day, 75 min, by Tra-In bus, more frequent with transfer in Poggibonsi, tickets also available at *tabacchi* shops), **Assisi** (2/day, 2 hrs, €10, by Sena bus; the morning bus goes direct to Assisi, though the afternoon bus might terminate at Santa Maria degli Angeli—from there catch a local bus to Assisi, 2/hr, 20 min), **Rome** (€17.50, 8/day, 3 hrs, by Sena bus, arrives at Rome's Tiburtina station which is on Metro line B, with easy connections to the Termini train station), **Milan** (€25, 4/day, 4.5 hrs).

Buses depart Siena from Piazza Gramsci, the train station, or both; confirm when you purchase your ticket. You can get tickets for Tra-In buses or Sena buses at the train station: Tra-In buses at the newsstand (Mon–Sat 6:00–20:00, Sun 6:00–16:00), and Sena buses at the window to the left of the train ticket office (Mon–Sat 7:40–12:40 & 14:30–18:30, closed Sun). You can also get tickets under Piazza Gramsci at **Sottopassaggio la Lizza**—look for

stairwells to this underground passageway on sidewalks surrounding Piazza la Lizza (Tra-In bus office: Mon–Sat 5:50–20:00, Sun
6:00–19:30, tel. 0577-204-246, toll-free tel. 800-570-530, www
.trainspa.it; Sena bus office: Mon–Sat 7:45–19:45, closed Sun, if
Sena bus ticket office is closed, buy Sena tickets next door at Tra-
In office, tel. 800-930-960, www.senabus.it).

Sottopassaggio la Lizza, the passageway under Piazza
Gramsci, also has a cash machine (neither bus office accepts credit
cards), luggage storage (€3.50/day, daily 7:00–19:45, no overnight storage), posted bus schedules, TV monitors (listing all the
imminent departures for several bus companies), an elevator, and
expensive WCs (€0.55). Those departing Siena after the bus offices
close can buy the ticket from *tabacchi* shops (only for buses staying within Tuscany). Longer-distance buses all depart before the
bus ticket offices close. On schedules, the fastest buses are marked
corse rapide. I'd stick with these. Note that if a schedule lists your
departure point as either Via Tozzi or Piazza la Lizza, you actually
catch the bus at Piazza Gramsci (Via Tozzi is the street that runs
alongside Piazza Gramsci and Piazza la Lizza is the name of the
bus-hub square). Confusing? Absolutely.

PISA

In A.D. 1200, Pisa's power peaked. For nearly three centuries (1000–1300), Pisa rivaled Venice and Genoa as a sea-trading power, exchanging European goods for luxury items in Muslim lands. As a port near the mouth of the Arno River (six miles from the coast), the city enjoyed easy access to the Mediterranean, plus the protection of sitting a bit upstream. ("Pisa" is an ancient word meaning *delta*.) The Romans had made it a navy base, and by medieval times it was a major player.

Pisa's 150-foot galleys cruised the Mediterranean, gaining control of the islands of Corsica, Sardinia, and Sicily, and trading with Europeans, Muslims, and Byzantine Christians as far south as North Africa and as far east as Syria. European Crusaders hired Pisan boats to carry them and their supplies as they headed off to conquer the Muslim-held Holy Land. The Pisan "Republic" prided itself on its independence from both popes and emperors. The city used its sea-trading wealth to build the grand monuments of the Field of Miracles, including the now-famous Tower.

But the Pisan fleet was routed in battle by Genoa (1284, at Meloria, off Livorno), their overseas outposts were taken away, the port silted up, and Pisa was left high and dry, with only its Field of Miracles and its university keeping it on the map.

Pisa's three important sights—the Duomo, Baptistery, and bell tower—float regally on the best lawn in Italy. The style throughout is Pisa's very own "Pisan Romanesque." Even as the church was being built, the Piazza del Duomo was nicknamed the "Campo dei Miracoli," or Field of Miracles, for the grandness of the undertaking.

The Leaning Tower has reopened after a decade of restoration and topple-prevention. To ascend, you'll have to make a reservation when you buy your €15 ticket (for details, see page 283).

Planning Your Time

Seeing the Tower, visiting the square, and wandering through the church are 90 percent of the Pisan thrill. Pisa is a touristy quickie. By car, it's a headache. By train, it's a joy. Train travelers may need to change trains in Pisa anyway. Hop on the bus and see the Tower (a 15-min ride each way). If you want to climb it, go straight to the ticket booth to snag an appointment—usually for a couple of hours later (or for an extra €2, you can book a time online at www.opapisa.it). Sophisticated sightseers stop more for the Pisano carvings in the Duomo and Baptistery than for a look at the tipsy Tower. There's nothing wrong with Pisa, but I'd stop only to see the Field of Miracles and get out of town. By car, it's a 45-minute detour from the freeway.

If you explore the rest of the city, it stretches southeast of the Field of Miracles, framed by the Arno River on the south and bordered on the east and west by two streets, Borgo Stretto and Via Santa Maria.

ORIENTATION

Tourist Information: One TI is about 200 yards from the train station—exit and walk straight up left side of the street to the big, circular Piazza Vittorio Emanuele II. The TI is on the left, around the corner from #16 (Mon–Fri 9:00–19:00, Sat 9:00–13:30, closed Sun, tel. 050-42-291, www.pisa .turismo.toscana.it). Another, less-enthusiastic TI is behind the Leaning Tower, next to the ticket office (summer daily 8:00–18:00:00, winter Mon–Fri 9:00–18:00, Sat–Sun 10:30–16:30, tel. 050-560-464). There's also a TI at the airport (daily 10:30–16:30 & 18:00–22:00, tel. 050-503-700).

Markets: An open-air produce market attracts picnickers to Piazza della Vettovaglie, one block north of the Arno River near Ponte di Mezzo (Mon–Sat 7:00–18:00, closed Sun). A street market bustles on Wednesday and Saturday mornings between Via del Brennero and Via Paparrelle (just outside of wall, about 6 blocks east of the Tower).

Festivals: The month of June has many events, culminating in a celebration for Pisa's patron saint (June 16–17).

Arrival in Pisa

By Train: If you want to check your baggage upon arrival, look for *deposito bagagli;* if you're facing the tracks, it's to the left at the far end of platform 1, past the police office (€3/bag per 12 hrs, daily 6:00–21:00, they photocopy your passport to check ID, ignore the nonfunctional lockers).

To get to the Field of Miracles from the station, you can **walk**

Pisa

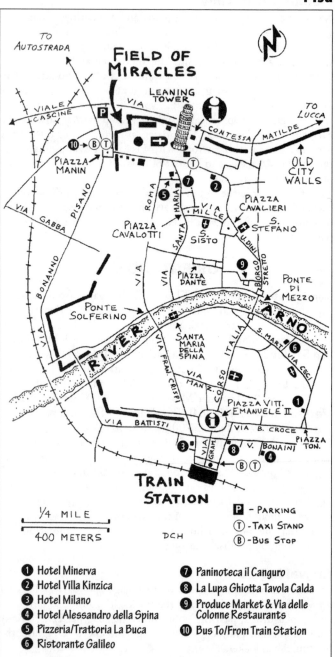

TO AUTOSTRADA

FIELD OF MIRACLES

LEANING TOWER

VIA

TO LUCCA

CONTESSA MATILDE

VIALE CASCINE

P

OLD CITY WALLS

10 B T

PIAZZA MANIN

VIA PISANO

VIA GABBA

7

2

PIAZZA CAVALIERI

S. STEFANO

5

ROMA

SANTA MARIA

VIA MILLE

U. DINI

PIAZZA CAVALOTTI

S. SISTO

BONANNO

VIA

VIA

PIAZZA DANTE

9

BORGO STRETTO

PONTE DI MEZZO

PONTE SOLFERINO

RIVER

ARNO

SANTA MARIA DELLA SPINA

VIA FRAN. CRISPI

VIA MAN.

CORSO ITALIA

S. MART

VIA CECI

6

VIA BATTISTI

PIAZZA VITT. EMANUELE II

1

VIA GRAM.

8 V. BONAINI

4

VIA B. CROCE

PIAZZA TON.

B T

TRAIN STATION

¼ MILE

400 METERS

DCH

P – PARKING

T – TAXI STAND

B – BUS STOP

❶ Hotel Minerva
❷ Hotel Villa Kinzica
❸ Hotel Milano
❹ Hotel Alessandro della Spina
❺ Pizzeria/Trattoria La Buca
❻ Ristorante Galileo

❼ Paninoteca il Canguro
❽ La Lupa Ghiotta Tavola Calda
❾ Produce Market & Via delle Colonne Restaurants
❿ Bus To/From Train Station

(45 min, get free map from TI and they'll mark the best route or follow the walk below), take a **taxi** (€8, at taxi stand at station or tel. 050-541-600; to return, you'll find a taxi stand 30 yards from the Leaning Tower, just in front of the Bar Duomo), or catch a **bus** (15-min ride to the Tower). To go by city bus, take bus #1 (4/hr, after 20:00 3/hr), which stops across the street from the train station, in front of Jolly Hotel Cavaliere. Buy an €0.85 bus ticket from the *tabacchi*/magazine kiosk in the station's main hall or at any *tabacchi* shop (good for 1 hour, round-trip permitted). Before getting on the bus, confirm that your bus is indeed going to "Campo dei Miracoli" (ask driver, a local, or TI) or risk taking a long tour of Pisa's suburbs. The correct buses let you off at Piazza Manin, in front of the gate to the Field of Miracles; drivers make sure that tourists don't miss it. To return to the train station from the Tower, catch the bus across the street from where you got off (again, confirm the destination). You can buy the ticket from the driver for a small extra fee.

By Car: To get to the Leaning Tower, follow signs to the *Duomo* or *Campo dei Miracoli*, located on the north edge of town. If you're coming from the Pisa Nord autostrada exit, you won't have to mess with the city center, but you will likely have to endure some terrible traffic. There's no better option than the €1/hr pay lot just outside the town wall a block from the Tower.

By Plane: From Pisa's airport, take bus #1 (€0.85, 4/hr, after 20:00 3/hr, 15 min) or a taxi (€8) into town.

SELF-GUIDED WALK

Welcome to Pisa:
From the Train Station to the Tower

A leisurely 45-minute stroll from the station to the Tower is a good way to get acquainted with the more subtle virtues of this Renaissance city. It's also a more pleasant alternative to the tourist-mobbed buses. You'll find Pisa to be a student-filled, classy, Old World town with an Arno-scape much like its upstream rival, Florence.

Exit straight out of the station, walking north up Viale Gramsci to the circular Piazza Vittorio Emanuele II (where the TI is). Continue straight north, up the pedestrian-only shopping street Corso Italia, and cross the Arno River over Ponte di Mezzo. This modern bridge, constructed on the same site where the Romans built theirs, is the center of Pisa and the heart of local festivals. Continue north up the elegantly arcaded Borgo Stretto, Pisa's main shopping street.

The first left, Via delle Colonne, is a worthwhile one-block detour, leading to Piazza Vettovaglie, some atmospheric restaurants, and the small but lively open-air produce market just beyond (Mon–Sat 7:00–18:00, closed Sun).

Continue north on Borgo Stretto another 100 yards or so. Take the second left on nondescript Via Ulisse Dini (it's not obvious—turn left immediately after the arcade's end). Continuing on, you pass through Pisa's historic core, including Piazza dei Cavalieri, with its ancient clock, colorfully decorated palace, and statue of Cosimo I de' Medici (the Florentine who ruled Pisa in the 16th century). The frescoes on the exterior of the square's buildings, though damaged by salty sea air and years of neglect, reflect the fading glory of Pisa under the Medicis.

The palace and the compound behind the gates to the right (Scuola Normale) house Pisa's famous university. The university is one of Europe's oldest, with roots in a law school dating as far back as the 11th century. In the mid-16th century, it was a hotbed of controversy, as spacey professors like Galileo Galilei studied the solar system—with results that challenged the church's powerful doctrine. More recently, the blind tenor Andrea Bocelli attended law school in Pisa before embarking on his well-known musical career.

From here, take Via Corsica (to the left of the clock). Take a quick peek into the humble church of San Sisto, ahead on the left (entrance around the corner). With simple bricks, assorted reused columns, heavy walls, and few windows, this is the typical "Romanesque" style compared to the more lavish "Pisan Romanesque" of the Field of Miracles structures.

Follow Via Corsica to Via Santa Maria, where a right turn leads you north, through increasingly touristy claptrap, directly to the Tower.

SIGHTS

▲▲**Field of Miracles (Campo dei Miracoli)**—Scattered across a golf-course-green lawn are four large white buildings that make up Pisa's religious center—the cathedral (or Duomo), its bell tower (the Leaning Tower), Baptistery, and Camposanto Cemetery. The four buildings share similar building materials, comparable decoration, and a tendency toward circular designs—giving the Campo a pleasant visual unity.

The style is dubbed Pisan Romanesque. Where traditional Romanesque has a heavy fortress feel—thick walls, barrel arches, few windows—Pisan Romanesque

Field of Miracles Tickets

Pisa has a scheme to get you into its neglected secondary sights: the Baptistery, the Duomo Museum, Camposanto Cemetery, and the Museum of the Sinopias (fresco pattern museum). Since you may be visiting these lesser sights anyway, I give more sightseeing information on these than they may deserve.

For any one monument, you'll pay €5; for two monuments the cost is €6; for four monuments minus the Duomo it's €8.50; and for the works (including the Duomo) you'll pay €10.50 (cash only). By comparison, the Duomo alone is a bargain (€2).

You can buy any of these tickets at any one of the three ticket offices: behind the Leaning Tower, at the Duomo Museum, or at the Museum of the Sinopias (near the Baptistery, almost suffocated by souvenir stands). All three offices have big, yellow "I" triangle-shaped signs. Keep in mind that the last entrance to all monuments is 30 minutes before closing time.

No matter what ticket you get, you'll still have to pay another €15 to climb the Leaning Tower. Tickets are sold at the three ticket offices (listed above) or online at www.opapisa.it.

is light and elegant. At ground level, most of the structures have a solid Romanesque base of simple pilasters and blind arches (columns and arches in relief). On the upper levels, you'll see a little of everything—tight rows of thin columns borrowed from the Lombards (barbarians); pointed Gothic gables and prickly spires; Byzantine mosaics and horseshoe arches; and geometric designs (such as diamonds) and striped colored marbles inspired by mosques in Muslim lands.

All the Campo's buildings feature bright white marble, a simple ground floor, and rows of delicate columns and arches forming open-air arcades. Architecturally, the Campo is unique and exotic. Theologically, the Campo's buildings mark the main events of every Pisan's life: christened in the Baptistery, married in the Duomo, honored in ceremonies at the Tower, and buried in the Camposanto Cemetery.

Lining this field of artistic pearls is a gauntlet of Europe's tackiest souvenir stands, as well as dozens of amateur mimes "propping up" the Leaning Tower while tourists take photos.

✪ For more information, see Pisa Duomo Tour (page 285) and Field of Miracles Tour (page 291).

▲▲**Leaning Tower**—The Tower is nearly 200 feet tall and 55 feet wide, weighing 14,000 tons and leaning at a 5-degree angle (15 feet

off the vertical axis). It started
to lean almost immediately after
construction began. There are
eight stories—a simple base,
six stories of columns (forming
arcades), and a belfry on top. The
inner structural core is a hollow cylinder built of limestone
bricks, faced with white marble
barged here from San Giuluano,
northeast of the city. The thin

columns of the open-air arcades make the heavy Tower seem light
and graceful.

The Tower was built over two centuries by at least three different architects. You can see how each successive architect tried to
"correct" the problem of leaning—once halfway up (after the 4th
story), once at the belfry on the top.

The first stones were laid in 1173, probably under the direction of the architect Bonanno Pisano (who also designed the
Duomo's bronze back door). Five years later, just as they'd finished
the base and the first arcade, someone said, "Is it just me, or does
that look crooked?" The heavy Tower—resting on a very shallow
13-foot foundation—was obviously sinking on the south side into
the marshy, multilayered, unstable soil. (Actually, all the Campo's
buildings tilt somewhat.) They carried on anyway, until they'd
finished four stories (the base plus three arcade floors). Then,
construction was suddenly halted—no one knows why—and for a
century the Tower sat half-finished and visibly leaning.

Around 1272, the next architect continued, trying to correct
the problem by angling the next three stories backward, in the
opposite direction of the lean. The project then again sat mysteri-
ously idle for nearly another century. Finally, Tommaso Pisano put
the belfry on the top (c. 1350–1372), also kinking it backward.

Man versus Gravity: After the Tower's completion, several
attempts were made to stop its slow-motion fall. The architect/art-
ist/writer Giorgio Vasari reinforced the base (1550), and it actually worked. But in 1838, well-intentioned engineers pumped out
groundwater, destabilizing the Tower, and causing it to lean at a
rate of a millimeter a year.

It got so bad that in 1990 the Tower was closed for repairs,
and 30 million dollars were spent trying to stabilize it. Engineers
dried the soil with steam pipes, anchored the Tower to the ground
with steel cables, and buried 600 tons of lead on the north side as
a counterweight (not visible)—all with little success. The breakthrough came when they drilled 15-foot holes in the ground on the
north side and sucked out sixty tons of soil, allowing the Tower to

sink on the north side. The Tower has actually been straightened by about six inches, turning the clock back 200 years on the still-leaning (and probably still falling) Tower.

As well as gravity, erosion threatens the Tower. Since its construction, 135 of the Tower's 180 marble columns have had to be replaced. Stone decay, deposits of lime and calcium phosphate, accumulations of dirt and moss, cracking from the stress of the lean—all of these are factors in its decline.

Thanks to the Tower's lean, there are special trouble spots. The lower south side (which is protected from cleansing rain and wind) is black from dirty airborne particles, while the stone on the upper areas, though clean, has more decay (from eroding rain and wind).

The Tower, now stabilized, is getting cleaned. Cracks are filled, and accumulations removed, using atomized water sprays and poultices of various solvents.

Climbing the Tower: Every 30 to 40 minutes, 30 people can clamber up the 294 tilting stairs to the top (€15, daily 8:30–20:30, off-season 9:00–17:00, ticket office opens 30 min early).

To make the necessary reservation in person (rather than online), go straight to the ticket office behind the Tower, on the left in the yellow building. You choose a (30–40 min) time slot for your visit at the time of purchase. During the tourist season it will likely be a couple of hours before you're able to go up (you can see the rest of the monuments and grab lunch while waiting), but the wait will probably be much shorter if you arrive at the beginning or end of the day. For an extra €2, you can book a time at www .opapisa.it. Online bookings are accepted no more than 45 days—and no fewer than 14 days—in advance.

You can pick up your tickets at any time, but do so at least an hour before your time slot in case there's a line. You must show up 10 minutes before your appointment at the meeting point outside the ticket office. You can't take any bags up the Tower, but day-bag-sized lockers are available at the ticket office. Even though the ticket-office sign says the visit is guided, that only means you'll be accompanied by a museum guard to make sure you don't stay up past your scheduled appointment time. Not including the climb, you'll have about 15 minutes for vertigo on top.

Caution: There are no railings, the steps are slanted, and rain makes the marble slippery. Anyone with balance issues of any sort should think twice before ascending.

▲▲**Duomo (Cathedral)**—The gargantuan Pisan Romanesque church has a Pisano pulpit, modest dress code, and no baggage check (€2, summer Mon–Sat 10:00–20:00, Sun 13:00–19:45; spring and fall Mon–Sat 10:00–17:30, Sun 13:00–17:30; winter Mon–Sat 10:00–12:30 & 15:00–16:30, Sun 15:00–16:30). ✪ See Pisa Duomo

Tour on page 285.

▲**Baptistery**—The round Baptistery next to the cathedral has superb acoustics and another fine Pisano pulpit (daily, spring–fall 9:00–19:00, winter 10:00–17:00, located in front of the Duomo). ✪ See Field of Miracles Tour on page 291.

Camposanto Cemetery—Lined with faint frescoes, the ancient cemetery is famous for its "Holy Land" dirt, said to reduce a body to a skeleton within a day. Artillery fire during World War II set the lead roof ablaze, greatly damaging the building and its frescoes (same hours as Baptistery, on north side of Field of Miracles). ✪ For more about the cemetery, see page 294.

Museum of the Sinopias (Museo delle Sinopie)—Housed in a 13th-century hospital, the museum displays some of the original sketches (made on walls) that were used to make the frescoes in the Camposanto Cemetery (same hours as Baptistery, entrance nearly obscured by souvenir stands, across from Baptistery). ✪ For additional info, see page 296.

Duomo Museum (Museo dell'Opera del Duomo)—The museum is big on Pisan art, displaying treasures of the cathedral, paintings, silverware, and sculptures (from the 12th–14th centuries, particularly by the Pisano dynasty), as well as ancient Egyptian, Etruscan, and Roman artifacts (same hours as Baptistery, behind Leaning Tower, Piazza Arcivescovado 18). ✪ See page 297.

Panoramic Walk on the Wall—This much-advertised walk, which includes just a small section of the 12th-century wall, isn't worth your time or €2 (Jun–Aug daily 11:00–14:00 & 15:00–18:00, entrance near Baptistery, at Porta Leone).

Museo Nazionale di San Matteo—On the river and in a former convent, this art museum displays 12th- to 15th-century sculptures, illuminated manuscripts, and paintings by Martini, Ghirlandaio, Masaccio, and others (€4, Mon–Sat 8:30–19:00, Sun 8:30–13:00, closed some Mon, near Piazza Mazzini at Lungarno Mediceo, tel. 050-541-865).

PISA
DUOMO
TOUR

The huge Pisan Romanesque cathedral, with its carved pulpit by Giovanni Pisano, is artistically more important than its more famous bell tower.

ORIENTATION

Cost: €2 (see page 281 for combo-ticket info).

Hours: Summer—Mon–Sat 10:00–20:00, Sun 13:00–20:00. Spring and fall—Mon–Sat 10:00–19:00, Sun 13:00–19:00. Winter—Mon–Sat 10:00–13:00 & 15:00–17:00, Sun 15:00–17:00. Last entry 30 min before closing.

Dress Code: Shorts are OK as long as they're not too short, but shoulders should be covered (although it's not really enforced).

Baggage: Big backpacks are not allowed, nor is storage provided; if you're climbing the Tower, you can leave your daybag in its locker room (see page 283). Technically, these small lockers are for Tower climbers, but they could work for clever cathedral visitors.

Length of This Tour: Allow one hour.

THE TOUR BEGINS

Exterior

The Duomo is the centerpiece of the Field of Miracles' complex of religious buildings. Begun in 1063, it was financed by a galley-load of booty ransacked that year from the Muslim-held capital of Palermo, Sicily. The architect Buschetto created the style of Pisan Romanesque that set the tone for the Baptistery and Tower. Five decades later (1118), the architect Rainaldo added the impressive main-entrance facade (which also leans out about a foot).

The lower half of the church is simple Romanesque, with blind arches. The upper half has four rows of columns that form arcades. Stripes of black and white marble, mosaics, stone inlay, and even recycled Roman tombstones complete the decoration.

• *Tourists enter the church at the facade, opposite the Baptistery.*

Bronze Back Doors (Porta San Ranieri)

Designed by Bonnano Pisano (c. 1186)—who was thought by some historians to be the first architect of the tower—the doors have

24 different panels that show Christ's story using the same simple, skinny figures found in Byzantine icons. (The doors are actually copies; the originals are housed in the Duomo Museum.)

It starts in the lower right panel ("Magis"), as the three Wise Men ride up a hill, heading toward...the panel to the left, where tiny baby Jesus lies in a manger while angels and shepherds look down from above. Above the manger scene, King Herod ("Erodi") sits under a canopy (in Pisan Romanesque style) and orders a soldier to raise his sword to kill all potential Messiahs. The terrified mother pulls her hair out. In the panel to the right, John the Baptist stands under a swaying palm and baptizes the adult Jesus. Jesus wears the rippling River Jordan like a blanket.

Cast using the lost-wax technique, this door was an inspiration for Lorenzo Ghiberti's bronze doors in Florence.

Nave

The 320-foot nave was the longest in Christendom when it was built. The model comes from traditional Roman basilicas—68 Corinthian columns of granite that divide the nave into five aisles. But the striped marble and arches-on-columns give it an exotic, almost mosque-like feel. Dim light filters in from the small upper windows of the galleries, where the women worshipped. The gilded coffered ceiling has shields of Florence's Medicis, including the round symbols (pills). This powerful family—who began as medics, later became cloth merchants, and finally bankers—took over Pisa after its glory days.

• *In the apse (behind the altar) is the...*

Apse Mosaic

The mosaic (c. 1300, partly done by Cimabue) shows Christ as the Ruler of All (Pantocrator) between Mary and John the Evangelist. The Pantocrator image of Christ is a bit foreign to Protestants, Catholics, and secularists, but is standard fare among Eastern Orthodox Christians—that is, the "Byzantine" people who were Pisa's partners in trade.

As King of the Universe, Christ sits on a throne, facing directly out with penetrating eyes. He wears a halo divided with a cross, worn only by Christ. In his left hand is a Bible open to the verse, "Ego Lux Sum Mundi"—"I am the light of the world." Christ blesses with his right hand, with the fingers forming the Greek letters chi and rho, the first two letters of "Christos." The thumb (almost) touches the fingers, symbolizing how Christ unites both his divinity and his humanity.

Dome

Looking up into the dome, the heavens open, and rings of saints and angels spiral up to a hazy God. Beneath the dome is an inlaid-marble, Cosmati-style mosaic floor.

• *Near the center of the church you'll find...*

Giovanni's Pulpit (1301–1311)

The 15-foot-tall, octagonal pulpit by Giovanni Pisano (c. 1250–1319) is the last, biggest, and most complex of the four pulpits by

the Pisano father-and-son team. Giovanni's father, Nicola, started the family tradition four decades earlier, carving the pulpit in the Baptistery. Giovanni grew up working side-by-side with dad on numerous projects. Now on his own, he crams everything he's learned into his crowning achievement.

Giovanni left no stone uncarved in his pursuit of beauty. Four hundred intricately sculpted figures smother the pulpit, blurring the architectural outlines. In addition, the relief panels are actually curved, making it look less like an octagon than a circle. The creamy-white Carrara marble has the look and feel of carved French ivories, which the Pisanos loved. Originally, this and the other pulpits were frosted with paint, gilding, and colored pastes.

At the base, lions roar and crouch over their prey, symbolizing how Christ (the lion) triumphs over Satan (the horse, as in the

Four Horsemen of the Apocalypse).

Four of the pulpit's support "columns" are statues. The central "column" features three graceful ladies representing Faith, Hope, and Charity, the three pillars of Christianity. They in turn stand on the sturdy base of knowledge, represented by the liberal arts taught at the U. of Pisa. Another "column" is Hercules, standing *contrapposto,* nude, holding his club and lion skin. Nearby, Lady Church suckles the babies of the Old and New Testaments, while at her feet are the Four Virtues, including Justice (with her scales), Moderation (modestly covering her nakedness), Courage (holding a lion), and Wisdom (with a horn of plenty).

Around the top of the pulpit, Christ's life unfolds in a series of panels saturated with carvings. The panels tilt out from the top, so the viewer below has a better look, and they're bordered on top with a heavy cornice as a backdrop. Since the panels are curved and unframed, you "read" Christ's life less like a nine-frame comic strip and more like a continuous scroll.

The story unfolds from left to right, beginning at the back near the stairs.

1. Story of Elizabeth and Zechariah: John the Baptist's parents.

2. Nativity: Mary lounges across a bed, unfazed by labor and delivery. Her pose is clearly inspired by carved Roman sarcophagi (which you can see in the Camposanto Cemetery), showing the dearly departed relaxing for eternity atop their coffins. Mary and the babe are surrounded by angels (above) and shepherds (right).

3. Adoration of the Magi: The wise men ride in with horses and camels.

4. Presentation in the Temple (left side): Joseph and Mary hold baby Jesus between them. On the right side of the panel, Giovanni adds the next scene in the story, when the nuclear family gets on a donkey and escapes into Egypt.

5. Massacre of the Innocents: Herod (at the top) turns and gestures dramatically, ordering the slaughter of all babies. A mother (bottom left corner) grabs her head in despair. Giovanni uses thick lips and big noses to let the faces speak the full range of human emotions. The soldiers in the tangled chaos are almost freestanding.

6. Kiss of Judas: Jesus is betrayed by a kiss (left side).

7. Crucifixion: An emaciated Christ is mourned by his followers who turn every which way. A Roman horseman (bottom right corner) rides directly away from us—an example of Renaissance "foreshortening" a century before its time.

8. and 9. Last Judgment: Christ sits in the center, the dead rise from their graves, and he sends the good to heaven (left) and hell (right).

Giovanni was a better pure sculptor than his father. Armed with more sophisticated chisels, he could cut even deeper into the marble, freeing heads from the marble backdrop, creating almost-freestanding, 3-D figures. Where Nicola shows figures either facing forward or in profile, Giovanni mastered the difficult three-quarters angle.

If the pulpit seems a bit cluttered and asymmetrical, blame Mussolini. Originally, Giovanni built the pulpit standing on the right side of the altar (the traditional location). But after a massive fire in 1595 (when the roof burned), the pulpit was disassembled and stored away for three centuries. In 1926, they pulled it out of storage, reassembled it on this spot...and ended up with pieces left over (now in other museums), leading scholars to debate the current look.

• *Hanging from the ceiling of the north transept (to the left of the altar) is...*

Galileo's Lamp

The bronze incense burner is said to be the one (actually, this is a replacement for the original) that caught teenage Galileo's attention one day in church. Someone left a church door open, and a gust of wind set the lamp swinging. Galileo timed the swings, and realized that the burner swung back and forth in the same amount of time regardless of how wide the arc. (This pendulum motion was a constant that allowed Galileo to measure this ever-changing universe.)

Galileo Galilei (1564–1642) was born in Pisa, grew up here on Via Giuseppe Giusti (where the family home still stands, adorned with a humble plaque), and taught math at the university (1584–1591). Legend says he threw things off the Tower to time their falls, fascinated by gravity.

• *Find the following two sights in the right (south) transept, near the tourists' entrance*

Emperor Henry VII's Tomb

In the corner of the south transept, pause at the tomb of Holy Roman Emperor Henry VII, whose untimely death plunged Pisa into its centuries-long decline. Henry lies sleeping, arms folded, his head turned to the side, resting on a soft pillow.

This German king (c. 1275–1313) invaded Italy and was welcomed by Pisans as a nonpartisan leader who could bring peace to Italy's warring Guelphs and Ghibellines. In 1312, he was crowned Emperor by the pope in Rome. He returned to his base in Pisa and was preparing to polish off the last opposition when he caught a fever (or was poisoned by a priest) and died. Ghibelline Pisa was suddenly at the mercy of Guelph rivals such as rising Florence, and Pisa never recovered.

St. Ranieri's Body

In a glass-lined casket on the altar, Pisa's patron saint lies mummified, encased in silver at his head and feet, with his hair shirt covering his body.

Ranieri Scuggeri (1117–1161) was born into the city of Pisa at its peak, when the Field of Miracles was a construction zone. (Ranieri was a year old when this Duomo was consecrated in thanks for Pisa's lucrative victory over the Muslims.) The son of a rich sea-trader, Ranieri chose the life of a hard-partying, popular, touring musician. Backstage one night, he met a mysterious stranger who changed his life. Ranieri was inspired to take his musical instrument and set it on fire, while opening his arms to the heavens (à la Jimi Hendrix). He returned to his father's shipping business and amassed a fortune. Then, one day, he smelled something funky—his own money. He gave it all away, joined a monastery, and put on a hair shirt.

The former wandering troubadour, traveling salesman, and pilgrimaging monk finally settled down in his hometown of Pisa. He devoured the Bible, then used his showmanship to wow audiences here—in the Duomo—when he took stage atop the pulpit to deliver spirited sermons.

Ranieri, honored in grand style on June 16 and 17, is cause for Pisa's biggest local event—the "Luminara"—celebrated along the Arno with tens of thousands of candles lining the buildings and floating on the river. The next day, rowing teams play a game of capture-the-flag, racing to a boat in the Arno and shinnying up a long rope to claim the prize.

FIELD OF MIRACLES TOUR

The Leaning Tower nearly steals the show from the massive cathedral, which muscles out the other sights. But if you have extra time to wander and ponder in Pisa, consider exploring the rest of the Field of Miracles: the Baptistery, Camposanto Cemetery, Museum of the Sinopias (sketches), and the Duomo Museum.

ORIENTATION

Cost: €8.50 for the four sights, €10.50 includes the Duomo (cash only, see "Field of Miracles Tickets" on page 281).

Hours: The sights are open daily from spring through fall (9:00–19:00) and in winter (10:00–17:00). The only exception is the Duomo itself, which has shorter hours, especially during the winter (summer Mon–Sat 10:00–20:00, Sun 13:00–19:45; spring and fall Mon–Sat 10:00–17:30, Sun 13:00–17:30; winter Mon–Sat 10:00–12:30 & 15:00–16:30, Sun 15:00–16:30).

Location: The Baptistery is located in front of the Duomo's facade. The Camposanto Cemetery is on the north side of the Field of Miracles. The Museum of the Sinopias is hidden behind souvenir stands, across the street from the Baptistery entrance. The Duomo Museum is housed behind the Tower (Piazza Arcivescovado 18).

Length of This Tour: Allow one hour.

THE TOUR BEGINS

Baptistery
Pisa's Baptistery is Italy's biggest. It's interesting for its pulpit and interior ambience, and especially great for its acoustics.

Pisa's Field of Miracles

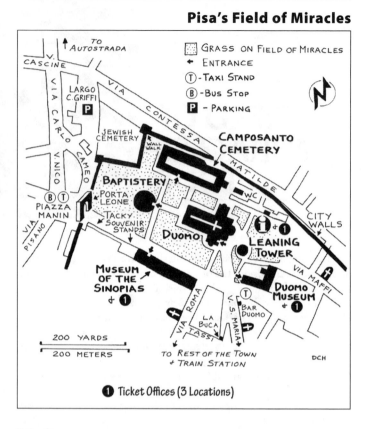

LEGEND:
- Grass on Field of Miracles
- ← Entrance
- (T) - Taxi Stand
- (B) - Bus Stop
- (P) - Parking

TO AUTOSTRADA
V. CASCINE
VIA CARLO CAMEO
LARGO C. GRIFFI
V. NICO
VIA CONTESSA MATILDE
JEWISH CEMETERY
WALL WALK
CAMPOSANTO CEMETERY
(B) (T) PIAZZA MANIN
PORTA LEONE
BAPTISTERY
TACKY SOUVENIR STANDS
Duomo
WC
LEANING TOWER
CITY WALLS
VIA PISANO
MUSEUM OF THE SINOPIAS
VIA ROMA
LA BUCA
TASSI
V. S. MARIA
BAR DUOMO
(T)
DUOMO MUSEUM
VIA MAFFI

200 YARDS
200 METERS

TO REST OF THE TOWN & TRAIN STATION

DCH

❶ Ticket Offices (3 Locations)

Exterior

The building is 180 feet tall—John the Baptist on top looks eye-to-eye with the tourists atop the nearly 200-foot Leaning Tower. Notice that the Baptistery leans nearly six feet to the north (the Tower leans 15 feet to the south). The building (begun 1153) is modeled on the circular domed Church of the Holy Sepulchre in Jerusalem, seen by Pisan Crusaders who occupied Jerusalem in 1099.

From the outside, you see three distinct sections reflecting changing tastes that span the 150-year construction: simple Romanesque blind arches at the base (1153), ornate Gothic spires and pointed arches in the middle (1250), and a Renaissance dome (15th-century). The roofing looks unfinished but was intentionally designed with red tiles on the seaward side and the more-prestigious lead tiles (which would corrode) on the sheltered side. The statues of the mid-section are by Nicola Pisano, who sculpted the pulpit inside.

Interior

Inside, it's simple, spacious, and baptized with light. Tall arches atop thin columns once again echo the Campo's architectural theme of arches above blank spaces. The columns encircle just a few pieces of religious furniture.

In the center sits the **octagonal font** (1246). A statue of the first baptist, John the Baptist, stretches his hands and says, "Welcome to my Baptistery." The font contains plenty of space for baptizing adults by immersion (the medieval custom), plus four wells for dunking babies.

Baptismal fonts—where sinners symbolically die and are reborn—are traditionally octagons. The shape suggests a cross (symbolizing Christ's death), and the eight sides represent the eighth day of Christ's ordeal, when he was resurrected. The font's sides, carved with inlaid multicolored marble, feature circle-in-a-square patterns, indicating the interlocking of heaven and earth. The circles are studded with interesting faces, both human and animal. Behind the font, the altar features similar inlaid-marble work.

Nicola Pisano's Pulpit

Is this the world's first Renaissance sculpture? It's the first authenticated (signed) work by the "Giotto of sculpture," working in what came to be called the "Renaissance" style. It's a freestanding sculpture with classical columns, realistic people and animals, and 3-D effects in the carved panels.

The 15-foot-tall, hexagonal pulpit is by Nicola Pisano (c. 1220–1278, Giovanni's father), the earliest (1260) and simplest of the four pulpits by the Pisano father-and-son team. Nicola, born in southern Italy, settled in Pisa, where he found steady work. Ten-year-old Giovanni learned the art of pulpit-making here at the feet of his father.

The speaker's platform stands on columns that rest on the backs of animals, representing Christianity's triumph over paganism. The white Carrara-marble panels are framed by dark rose-colored marble, making a pleasant contrast. Originally, this and the other pulpits were touched up with paint, gilding, and colored pastes.

The relief panels, with scenes from the life of Christ, are more readable than the Duomo pulpit. It shows bigger, simpler figures in dark-marble "frames." Read left to right, starting from the back.

1. Nativity: Mary reclines across a bed like a Roman matron, a pose inspired by Roman sarcophagi, which had been found around Pisa in Nicola's day (also on display in the Camposanto).

2. Adoration of the Magi: The three kings kneel before baby Jesus in simple profile; but notice the strong 3-D of the horses' heads coming straight out of the panel.

3. Presentation in the Temple: It lacks the star of the scene, baby Jesus, who got broken off, but on the panel's right side, a powerful, bearded man in a voluminous robe epitomizes Nicola's solemn classical style.

4. Crucifixion: Everyone faces either straight out or in profile; the Roman in front has to actually look back over his shoulder to razz Christ.

5. Last Judgment: Christ reigns over crowded, barely controlled chaos. The pulpit's lectern is an eagle clutching its prey, echoing the theme of the base.

Acoustics
Make a sound in here and it echoes for a good 10 seconds (a 10-second decay). A priest standing at the baptismal font (or a security guard today) can sing three tones within the 10 seconds—"Ave Maria"—and make a chord, singing haunting harmonies with himself. This medieval form of digital delay is due to the 250-foot-wide dome. Recent computer analysis suggests that the 15th-century architects who built the dome intended this building to be not just a Baptistery but also a musical instrument. A security guard sings every half-hour starting at 10:00.

Climb to the Galleries
Climb 75 steps to the interior gallery (midway up) for an impressive view back down on the baptismal font. Ascend 75 more steps to the upper gallery with views outside—through grills or dirty windows—looking over the town and across to the Leaning Tower.

Camposanto Cemetery
The long white building (1278–1465) with a nondescript entrance borders the Field of Miracles on the north. This site has been a cemetery since ancient times. Highlights are the building's cloistered interior courtyard, some ancient sarcophagi, and the large 14th-century fresco, *The Triumph of Death* (same hours as Baptistery).

Inside is a delightful open-air **courtyard,** surrounded by an arcade with intricately carved tracery in the arches. The courtyard's grass grows on special dirt (said to turn a body into a skeleton in a day) originally shipped by returning Crusaders from Mount Calvary, where Christ was crucified.

The arcade floor is paved with the **coats-of-arms** of some 600 dearly departed Pisans. Displayed in the arcade are dozens of ancient Roman sarcophagi. These coffins once held dead Romans (not currently buried here). Just to the right of the entrance door, you'll find the third-century A.D. rectangular **Roman sarcophagus** carved with mythological scenes. Along the side we see a couple—the deceased—shown relaxing atop their coffin. Carved reliefs like this inspired Nicola and Giovanni Pisano.

Circle the courtyard clockwise, noticing **traces of fresco** on the bare-brick walls. (We'll see some reconstructed frescoes later.) The huge **chains** on the west wall once stretched across the mouth of Pisa's harbor as a defense. Then Genoa attacked, broke the chains, carried them off as a war trophy, and gave them to Pisa's arch-rival Florence. Finally, they were returned here as a token of friendship.

Straight ahead is the cemetery's oldest object, an ochre-colored Greek tombstone—the fourth-century B.C. **stele,** dating from the time of Alexander the Great. It shows a woman (seated) who's just given birth. A maid (standing) shows the baby while the mother gazes adoringly. In the floor 10 yards away by the corner of the courtyard is one of the newest memorials, a **pavement slab** dedicated to an American artist, Deane Keller. After serving in Italy in World War II, he helped rebuild the Camposanto Cemetery and restore its frescoes.

At the back of the courtyard (opposite where you entered), step through the door to see **photos** of the Camposanto bombed during World War II (yikes!). By the summer of 1944, Allied troops had pushed Nazi forces to the north bank of the Arno, and German Field Marshal Kesselring dug in at Pisa, surrounded by the United States' 91st Infantry. Germans and Americans lobbed artillery shells at each other. (The Americans even considered blowing up the Leaning Tower—the "Tiltin' Hilton" was suspected to be the German lookout point.) Most of the Field of Miracles was miraculously unscathed, but the Camposanto took a direct hit with a Yankee incendiary grenade. It melted the lead-covered arcade roof and peeled historic frescoes from the walls. The Americans liberated the city on September 2 and rebuilt the Camposanto. Some restored (but still much-damaged) frescoes are now displayed in the adjoining room.

The 1,000-square-foot *Triumph of Death* (on the left wall, c. 1350, artist unknown, perhaps Francesco Traini or Bonamico

Buffalmacco) captures Pisa's mood in the wake of the bubonic plague (1348), which killed one in three Pisans. Well-dressed ladies and gents (left half of the painting) are riding gaily through the countryside when they come across three coffins with corpses (bottom left). Confronted with death, they each react differently—a woman puts her hand thoughtfully to her chin, a man holds his nose against the stench, while a horse leans in for a better whiff. Above them, a monk scours the Bible for the meaning of death. Mr. Death, a winged demon with a scythe, stands to the right of center and eyes his future victims.

In the right half of the painting, young people gather in a garden (bottom right) to play music (symbolizing earthly pleasure), oblivious to the death around them. Winged demons swoop down from above to pluck souls from a pile of corpses, while winged angels fight them for the souls. The action continues in the next fresco (the room's far wall), where Christ and Mary judge the dead at the Last Judgment. The wicked are led away to hell (the right wall of the room) to be tortured by a horned Satan. Grim stuff, but appropriate for the Camposanto's permanent residents.

Museum of the Sinopias

Housed in a 13th-century hospital, this museum (Museo delle Sinopie) features the preparatory sketches (sinopias) for the Camposanto's frescoes. If you loved *The Triumph of Death* and others in the Camposanto, or if you're interested in fresco technique, this museum is worthwhile. If not, you'll wonder why you're here.

Climb the stairs to the first floor to find (along the right wall) the red-tinted sinopias for *The Triumph of Death*, the *Last Judgment*, and (at the far end) the multi-ringed, earth-centric, Ptolomaic universe of the *Theological Cosmography*.

Sinopias are sketches in red paint painted directly on the wall just before the final colored version. The master always did the sinopia himself. It was a way for him (and for those who paid for the work) to see exactly how the scene would look in its designated spot. If it wasn't quite right, the master changed a detail here and there. Assistants then copied or traced the sinopia onto paper to make a cartoon. Then the wall was covered with plaster (completely covering up the sinopia), and the assistants redrew the outlines—either by tracing a cut-out of the cartoon or by perforating the drawing on the cartoon and coloring it with a powdered bag of charcoal to make dotted lines to follow on the plaster. While the plaster was still wet, the master quickly filled in the color and details, producing the final frescoes (now on display at the Camposanto). The sinopias—never meant to be seen—were uncovered by the bombing and restoration of the Camposanto and brought here.

Duomo Museum

Near the Tower is the entrance to the Duomo Museum (Museo dell'Opera del Duomo), which houses many of the original statues that once adorned the Campo's buildings (where copies stand today), notably the statues by Nicola and Giovanni Pisano. You can stand face-to-face with the Pisanos' very human busts that ring the outside of the Baptistery. Giovanni Pisano's stone *Madonna del Colloquio* solemnly exchanges gazes with baby Jesus in her arms. The most charming piece is Giovanni's carved ivory *Madonna and Child*. Mary leans back gracefully to admire baby Jesus, her pose matching what she's carved from—an elephant's tusk.

You'll see a mythical sculpted hippogriff (a medieval jackalope) and other oddities brought back from the Holy Land by Pisan Crusaders. The museum also has several large-scale wooden models of the Duomo and Baptistery. The church treasury is here, with vestments, chalices, and bishops' staves. There are some Etruscan funerary urns upstairs with reclining people—the inspiration for the Roman sarcophagi that inspired the Pisanos.

Beyond the Etruscan collection are beautiful small-scale copies of the Camposanto frescoes, painted in the 1830s. There's also a scene showing what the building looked like inside before it was bombed.

The museum's interior courtyard has a two-story, tourist-free view of the Tower, Duomo, and Baptistery.

PISA SLEEPING, EATING, AND TRANSPORTATION CONNECTIONS

SLEEPING

To locate the hotels, see the map on page 278.

$$$ Hotel Alessandro della Spina, in a nondescript neighborhood near the train station, has 16 elegant and colorful rooms, each named after a flower (Sb-€105, Db-€125, discount off-season, air-con, free parking; head straight out of train station, turn right onto Viale F. Bonaini, take third right onto Via Alessandro della Spina and follow signs to Via Alessandro della Spina 2/7/9; tel. 050-502-777, fax 050-20-583, www.hoteldellaspina.it, info @hoteldellaspina.it).

$$ Hotel Minerva, a seven-minute walk from the train station, is a classy, peaceful place with all the comforts (Sb-€95, Db-€120, Tb-€135, air-con, garden terrace, Piazza Toniolo 20; head straight out of station to Piazza Vittorio Emanuele, turn right onto Viale B. Croce, at next square—Piazza Toniolo—turn left; tel. 050-501-081, fax 050-501-559, www.hotelminerva.pisa.it, info @hotelminerva.pisa.it).

$$ Hotel Villa Kinzica, with 33 decent rooms, is just steps away from the Field of Miracles—ask for a room with a view of the Tower (Sb-€78, Db-€108, Tb-€124, Qb-€135, elevator, air-con, attached restaurant, Piazza Arcivescovado 2, tel. 050-560-419, fax 050-551-204, www.hotelvillakinzica.it, info@hotelvillakinzica.it).

$ Hotel Milano, near the station, offers 10 spacious, tidy rooms handy for train travelers (D-€55, Db-€75, breakfast-€3, air-con, Via Mascagni 14, tel. 050-23-162, fax 050-44-237, www .hotelmilano.pisa.it, info@hotelmilano.pisa.it).

Sleep Code

(€1 = about $1.20, country code: 39)
S = Single, **D** = Double/Twin, **T** = Triple, **Q** = Quad, **b** = bathroom,
s = shower only.
Unless otherwise noted, credit cards are accepted and breakfast is included, and English is generally spoken.

To help you sort easily through these listings, I've divided the rooms into three categories based on the price for a standard double room with bath:

$$$ **Higher Priced**—Most rooms €120 or more.
 $$ **Moderately Priced**—Most rooms between €80–120.
  $ **Lower Priced**—Most rooms €80 or less.

EATING

For a quick lunch or dinner, the pizzeria/trattoria **La Buca,** just a block from the Tower, is adequate and convenient (Sat–Thu 12:00–15:30 & 19:00–22:30, closed Fri, at Via Santa Maria 171 and Via A. G. Tassi, tel. 050-560-660).

Ristorante Galileo, south of the Arno, has excellent pizza and pasta (€4.50–8, Wed–Mon 12:00–15:00 & 19:30–22:00, closed Tue, Via Silvestri 12, tel. 050-28-287).

At **Paninoteca il Canguro,** friendly Fabio makes warm, hearty sandwiches to order. Try their popular primavera sandwich (Mon–Fri 10:00–24:00, Sat 10:30–17:00, closed Sat night and Sun, Via Santa Maria 151, tel. 050-561-942).

For a cheap, fast, and tasty meal a few steps from the train station, drop by cheery **La Lupa Ghiotta Tavola Calda.** It's got everything you'd want from a *ristorante* at half the price with faster service (build your own salad—5 ingredients for €4.50; Mon and Wed–Sat 12:15–15:00 & 19:15–24:00, Tue 12:15–15:00 only, closed Sun, Viale F. Bonaini 113, tel. 050-21-018).

The street that houses the daily market, **Via delle Colonne** (a block north of the Arno, west of Borgo Stretto), has a few atmospheric, mid-priced restaurants and several fun, greasy take-out options.

TRANSPORTATION CONNECTIONS

From Pisa by Train to: Florence (2/hr, 1 hr, €5), **Rome** (about hourly, 4 hrs), **La Spezia,** gateway to Cinque Terre (hourly, 1 hr), **Siena** (change at Empoli: Pisa–Empoli, hourly, 45 min; Empoli–Siena, hourly, 1 hr), **Lucca** (hourly, 2/day Sun, 30 min). Even the fastest trains stop in Pisa, so you might be changing trains here whether you plan to stop or not.

By Car: The drive between Pisa and Florence is that rare case where the non-autostrada highway (free, more direct, and at least as fast) is a better deal than the autostrada.

Pisa's Airport: For information on Pisa's Galileo Galilei Airport, see page 227.

LUCCA

Surrounded by well-preserved ramparts, layered with history, alternately quaint and urbane, Lucca charms its visitors. Romanesque churches seem to be around every corner, as do fun-loving and shady piazzas filled with soccer-playing children. Despite Lucca's appeal, few tourists seem to put it on their maps, and it remains a city for the Lucchesi (loo-KAY-zee).

ORIENTATION

Tourist Information

The main TI is just inside the Porta Santa Maria gate, on Piazza Santa Maria (daily April–Oct 9:00–20:00, Nov–March 9:00–13:00

& 15:00–18:00, Internet access, Piazza Santa Maria 35, tel. 0583-919-931, fax 0583-469-964, www.luccatourist.it, info@luccaturismo.it).

Another TI, on Piazzale Verdi, offers information, a room-booking service, Internet access, and baggage check (daily 9:00–19:00, off-season 9:00–17:30, bike rental, 80-min city-walk audioguide-€9, €6 more for each additional audioguide; bag storage-€2/hr per bag or €5 for up to 5 hours, they need to photocopy your passport; futuristic WC, tel. 0583-583-150).

Arrival in Lucca

To reach the city center from the train station, walk toward the walls and head left, to the entry at Porta San Pietro. Taxis are sparse at midday, but try calling 0583-333-434 or 0583-955-200. There is no baggage check at the train station, but you can leave bags at the TI on Piazzale Verdi (see "Tourist Information," above).

Helpful Hints

Combo-Tickets: A €6 combo-ticket includes visits to the Ilaria del Carretto tomb in San Martino Cathedral (€2), the Cathedral Museum (€4), and San Giovanni Church (€2.50). A different €6 ticket combines the Guinigi Tower (€4) and the Clock Tower (€3.50). Yet another combo-ticket covers Palazzo Mansi and Villa Guinigi for €6.50 (€4 each if purchased separately).

Shops and Museums Alert: Shops close most of Sunday and Monday mornings. Many museums are closed on Monday as well.

Markets: Lucca's atmospheric markets are worth visiting. Every third Saturday and Sunday of the month, one of the largest **antiques markets** in Italy unfurls in the blocks around Piazza Antelminelli (8:00–15:00). The last weekend of the month, local artisans sell **arts and crafts** throughout the town (also 8:00–15:00). At the **general market,** held Wednesdays and Saturdays, you'll find produce and household goods (8:00–13:00, outside of the walls, a few blocks north of Porta Elisa around the stadium).

Concerts: San Giovanni Church hosts several musical concerts each week throughout the year, featuring highlights from hometown composer Giacomo Puccini (get schedule at church or TI, or check www.puccinielasualucca.com).

Festival: On September 13 and 14, the city celebrates Volto Santo ("Holy Face"), with a procession of the treasured local crucifix and a fair in Piazza Antelminelli.

Internet Access: You can get online at either TI (see "Tourist Information," above). **Mondo Chiocciola** has several terminals (Mon–Fri 15:30–20:00, Sat 9:30–13:00 & 15:30–20:00, closed Sun, Via del Gonfalone 12, near launderette recommended below, tel. 0583-440-510).

Laundry: Lavanderia Self-Service Niagara is just off Piazza Santa Maria at Via Rosi 26 (daily 8:00–22:00).

Bike Rental: Several places with identical prices cluster around Piazza Santa Maria (€2.50/hr, €12.50/day, tandem bikes available, open daily, last rental around 19:00). These easygoing shops rent good bikes: **Antonio Poli** (Piazza Santa Maria 42, tel. & fax 0583-493-787, enthusiastic Cristiana) and **Cicli Bizzarri** (Piazza Santa Maria 32, tel. 0583-496-031). A one-hour rental gives you two leisurely loops around the ramparts.

The History of Lucca

Lucca began as a Roman settlement. In fact, the grid layout of the streets (and the shadow of an amphitheater) survives from Roman times. Trace the rectangular Roman wall—indicated by today's streets—on the map. As in typical Roman towns, two main roads quartered the fortified town, crossing at what was the forum (main market and religious/political center)—today's Piazza San Michele.

Christianity came here early; it's said that the first bishop of Lucca was a disciple of St. Peter. While churches were built here as early as the fourth century, the majority of Lucca's elegant Romanesque churches date from around the 12th century.

Feisty Lucca, though never a real power, enjoyed a long period of independence (maintained by clever diplomacy). Aside from 30 years of being ruled from Pisa in the 14th century, Lucca was basically an independent city-state (until Napoleon came to town).

In the Middle Ages, wealthy Lucca's economy was built on the silk industry, dominated by the Guinigi (gwee-NEE-gee) family. Without silk, Lucca would have been just another sleepy Italian town. In 1500, the town had 3,000 silk looms employing 25,000 workers. Banking was also big. Many pilgrims stopped here on their way to the Holy Land, deposited their money for safety...and never returned to pick it up.

In its heyday, Lucca packed 160 towers—one on nearly every corner—and 70 churches within its walls. Each tower was the home of a wealthy merchant family. Towers were many stories tall, with single rooms stacked atop each other: ground-floor shop, upstairs living room, and top-floor fire-safe kitchen, all connected by exterior wooden staircases. The rooftop was generally a vegetable garden with trees providing shade. Later, the wealthy city folk moved into the countryside, trading away life in their city palazzos to establish farm estates complete with fancy villas. (You can visit some of these villas today—the TI has a brochure—but they're convenient only for drivers and are generally not worth the cost of admission.)

In 1799, Napoleon stormed into Italy and took a liking to Lucca. He liked it so much that he gave it to his sister as a gift. It was later passed on to Napoleon's widow, Marie Louise. With a feminine sensitivity, Marie Louise was partially responsible for turning the city's imposing (but no longer particularly useful) fortified wall into a fine city park that is much enjoyed today.

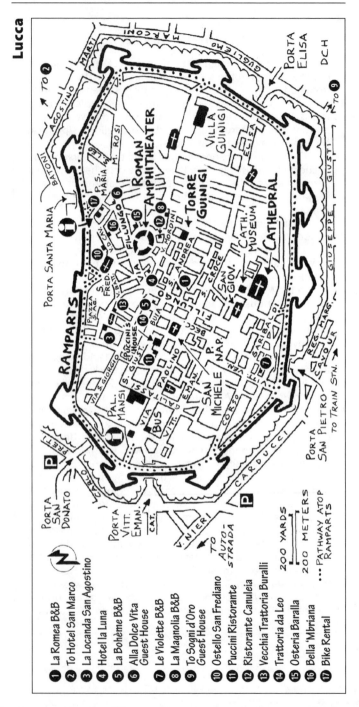

Lucca

SIGHTS AND ACTIVITIES

▲▲**Bike the Ramparts**—Lucca's most remarkable feature, its Renaissance wall, is also its most enjoyable attraction—especially when circled on a rental bike. Stretching for 2.5 miles, this is an

ideal place to come for an overview of the city by foot or bike.

Lucca has had a protective wall for 2,000 years. You can read three walls into today's map: the first rectangular Roman wall, the later medieval wall (nearly the size of today's), and the 16th-century Renaissance wall.

With the advent of cannons, thin medieval walls were suddenly vulnerable. A new design—the same one that stands today—was state-of-the-art when it was built (1550–1650). Much of the old medieval wall (look for the old stones) was incorporated into the Renaissance wall (with uniform bricks). The new wall was squat: a 100-foot-wide mound of dirt faced with bricks, engineered to absorb a cannonball pummeling. The townspeople cleared a wide no-man's-land around the town, exposing any attackers from a distance. Ten heart-shaped bastions (inviting picnic areas today) were designed to minimize exposure to cannonballs and to maximize defense capabilities. The ramparts were armed with 130 cannons.

The town invested a third of its income for over a century to construct the wall, and—since it kept away the Florentines and nasty Pisans—it was considered a fine investment. In fact, nobody ever bothered to try to attack the wall. Locals say that the only time it actually defended the city was during an 1812 flood, when the gates were sandbagged and its ramparts kept the high water out.

Today the ramparts seem made-to-order for a leisurely bike ride (20-min pedal, wonderfully smooth). You can rent bikes cheaply and easily from one of several bike-rental places in town (see "Helpful Hints," above).

Roman Amphitheater—Just off the main shopping street, the architectural ghost of a Roman amphitheater can be felt in the delightful Piazza Anfiteatro. With the fall of Rome, the theater (which seated 10,000) was gradually cannibalized for its stones and inhabited by a mishmash of huts. The huts were cleared away at the end of the 19th century to better appreciate the town's illustrious past. Today the square is a circle of touristy shops and mediocre restaurants that becomes a lively bar-and-café scene after dark. Today's street level is nine feet above the original arena floor. The only bits of surviving Roman stonework are a few arches on the northwest exterior (Via Fillungo 42).

Via Fillungo—This main pedestrian drag, *the* street to stroll, takes you from the amphitheater almost all the way to the cathedral. Along the way you'll get a taste of Lucca's rich past, including several elegant, century-old storefronts. Many of the original storefront paintings, reliefs, and mosaics survive—even if today's occupant of that shop sells something entirely different.

At #97 is a classic old **jewelry store** with a rare storefront that has kept its T-shaped arrangement (when closed, you see a wooden T, and during open hours it unfolds with a fine old-time display). This design dates from a time when the merchant sold his goods in front, did his work in the back, and lived upstairs.

Di Simo Caffè at #58 has long been the hangout of Lucca's artistic and intellectual elite. Composer and hometown boy Giacomo Puccini tapped his foot while sipping coffee here. Pop in to check out the 1880s ambience.

A surviving five-story **tower house** is at #67. Remember, there was a time when each corner sported its own tower. The stubby stones that still stick out once supported wooden staircases (there were no

interior connections up or down). So many towers cast shadows over this part of town that the next street is called Via Buia ("Dark Street").

At #45 and #43, you'll see two more good examples of tower houses. Across the street, the **Clock Tower** (Torre delle Ore) has a hand-wound Swiss clock that has clanged four times an hour since 1754 (€3.50 to climb up and see the mechanism flip into action on the quarter hour, covered by €6 combo-ticket with Guinigi Tower, daily 10:00–19:00).

The intersection of Via Fillungo and Via Roma/Via Santa Croce marks the center of town (where the two original Roman roads crossed). As you go down Via Santa Croce, you'll pass a Leonardo exhibit (€5 to see a room full of "don't touch" modern models of his sketches...not worth the money, open daily 9:30–19:30) before reaching **Piazza San Michele** (once the Roman

Forum). Towering above the church's fancy Pisan Romanesque facade, the archangel Michael stands ready to flap his wings—which he actually did on special occasions. (See the stairs behind the facade, which church officials would climb to pull some strings and wow their gullible flock.) Piazza San Michele is as fun a people center today as it has been since Roman times.

▲**San Martino Cathedral**—This church, begun in the 11th century, is an entertaining mix of architectural and artistic styles. Its elaborate Pisan-Romanesque **facade**—featuring Bible scenes, animals, and candy-cane-striped columns—dominates the piazza. The central figure of the facade is St. Martin, a Roman military officer from Hungary who, by offering his cloak to a beggar, more fully understood the beauty of Christian compassion. (The impressive original, a fine example of Romanesque sculpture, is just inside, hiding from the pollution.) Each of the columns on the facade is unique. Notice how the facade is asymmetrical: The clock tower was already in place when the cathedral was built, so the builders cheated on the right side to make it fit the space. On the lower right, the architect Guideo from Como holds a document declaring he finished the facade in 1204. On the right (at eye level), a labyrinth set into the wall relates the struggle and challenge our souls face in finding salvation. The Latin plaque just left of the main door is where moneychangers and spice traders met to seal deals (on the doorstep of the church—to underscore the reliability of their promises). Notice the date: An Dni MCXI (A.D. 1111).

The **interior** features Gothic arches, Renaissance paintings, and stained glass from the 19th century. On the left side of the nave, a small, elaborate temple displays the wooden crucifix called Volto Santo. It's said to have been sculpted by Nicodemus in Jerusalem and set afloat in an unmanned boat that landed on the coast of Tuscany, from where wild oxen miraculously carried it to Lucca in 782. The sculpture (which is actually 12th-century Byzantine-style) has quite a jewelry collection, which you can see in the Cathedral Museum (see below).

On the right side of the nave, the sacristy houses the enchantingly beautiful **memorial tomb of Ilaria del Carretto** by Jacopo della Quercia (1407). This young bride of silk baron Paolo Guinigi is decked out in the latest, most expensive fashions, with the requisite little dog curled up at her feet in eternal sleep. She's so realistic that the statue was nicknamed "sleeping beauty." Her nose is partially worn off because of a long-standing tradition of lonely young ladies rubbing it for luck in finding a boyfriend (cathedral entry is free, Ilaria tomb-€2, included in €6 combo-ticket with Cathedral Museum and San Giovanni Church, Mon–Fri 9:30–17:45, Sat 9:30–18:45; Sun open sporadically between Masses: 9:00–9:50 & 13:00–17:45; Piazza San Martino).

Cathedral Museum (Museo della Cattedrale) —This beauti-fully presented museum houses original paintings, sculptures, and vestments from the cathedral and other Lucca churches. The first room displays jewelry made to dress up the Volto Santo crucifix, including gigantic gold shoes. Upstairs, notice the fine red bro-caded silk—a reminder that this precious fabric is what brought riches and power to the city. The exhibits in this museum take on meaning only with the €1 audioguide—if you're not in the mood to listen to this, I'd skip the place altogether (€4; included in €6 combo-ticket with Ilaria tomb and San Giovanni Church; peak season daily 10:00–18:00; off-season Mon–Fri 10:00–14:00, Sat–Sun 10:00–17:00; next to cathedral on Piazza Antelminelli).

San Giovanni Church—This first cathedral of Lucca is interest-ing only for its archaeological finds. The entire floor of the 12th-century church has been excavated (1969–1992), revealing layers of Roman houses, early churches, and ancient hot tubs dating back to the time of Christ. Eager students can request an English transla-tion of the floor plans from the ticket office to know what's what. As you climb under the church's present-day floor and wander the lanes of Roman Lucca, remember that the entire city sits on similar ruins (€2.50, included in €6 combo-ticket with Ilaria tomb and Cathedral Museum; peak season daily 10:00–18:00; off-season Sat–Sun 10:00–17:00, closed Mon–Fri; kitty-corner from cathedral at Piazza San Giovanni).

Puccini's House—Opera enthusiasts (but nobody else) will want to visit the home where Giacomo Puccini (1858–1924) grew up. The museum has the great composer's piano and a small collection of his personal belongings (€3; June–Sept daily 10:00–18:00; Oct–May Tue–Sun 10:00–13:00 & 15:00–18:00, closed Mon; Corte San Lorenzo 9, tel. 0583-584-028).

Guinigi Tower (Torre Guinigi)—Many Tuscan towns have tow-ers, but none quite like the Guinigi family's. Up 227 steps is a small garden with fragrant trees surrounded by fan-tastic views (€4, daily mid-June–mid-Sept 9:00–24:00, mid-Sept–late Oct 9:30–18:00, late Oct–March 9:30–16:30, April–mid-June 9:00–20:00, Via S. Andrea, tel. 336-203-221). Tower-climbers can also purchase a combo-ticket (€6) that covers both the Guinigi Tower and the medieval **Clock Tower** (Torre delle Ore—described on page 306; €3.50 for Clock Tower alone, daily 10:00–19:00, on corner of Via Fillungo and Via del'Arancio).

Palazzo Mansi—Minor paintings by Tintoretto, Pontormo, Veronese, and others vie for attention, but the palazzo itself, a furnished and decorated 17th-century confection, steals the show. This is your chance to appreciate the wealth of Lucca's silk merchants (€4, €6.50 combo-ticket includes Villa Guinigi, Tue–Sat 8:30–19:30, Sun 8:30–13:30, closed Mon, last entry 30 min before closing, no photos, no English descriptions—politely suggest they make some for future visitors; Via Galli Tassi 43, tel. 0583-55-570). All visitors must be accompanied by a museum custodian, so there may be a bit of a wait during high season.

Villa Guinigi—Built by Paolo Guinigi in 1418, the family villa is now a stark museum displaying artifacts, sculptures, and paintings. Monumental paintings by multitalented Giorgio Vasari are the best reason to visit (€4, €6.50 combo-ticket includes Palazzo Mansi, Mon–Sat 8:30–19:30, Sun 8:30–13:30, last entry 30 min before closing, may have to wait in high season for a museum custodian to accompany you, Via della Quarquonia, tel. 0583-496-033).

SLEEPING

$$$ La Romea B&B, in an air-conditioned, restored 14th-century palazzo near Guinigi Tower, feels like a royal splurge. Its four posh rooms and one suite are lavishly decorated in handsome colors, with stately parquet floors (Db-€130–140, Qb suite-€160, 3 percent cheaper with cash; from Via Fillungo, take Via Sant'Andrea to the Church of Sant'Andrea and turn right on Vicolo delle Ventaglie to #2; tel. 0583-464-175, fax 0583-471-280, www.laromea.com, info@laromea.com, Giulio and his wife Gaia).

$$$ Hotel San Marco, a seven-minute walk outside the Porta Santa Maria, is a postmodern place decorated à la Stanley Kubrick. Its 42 rooms are sleek, with all the comforts (Sb-€87, Db-€126, includes nice breakfast spread, air-con, elevator, pool, free parking,

---

Sleep Code

(€1 = about $1.20, country code: 39)
S = Single, **D** = Double/Twin, **T** = Triple, **Q** = Quad, **b** = bathroom. Unless otherwise noted, credit cards are accepted, English is spoken, and breakfast is included (but usually optional).

To help you sort easily through these listings, I've divided the rooms into three categories based on the price for a standard double room with bath:

$$$ Higher Priced—Most rooms €120 or more.
$$ Moderately Priced—Most rooms between €80–120.
$ Lower Priced—Most rooms €80 or less.

taxi from station-€6, Via San Marco 368, tel. 0583-495-010, fax 0583-490-513, www.hotelsanmarcolucca.it, info@hotelsanmarcolucca.com).

$$$ La Locanda San Agostino, run by gracious Sarah, has three tastefully decorated, romantic, spacious rooms. The vine-draped terrace and quaint views invite you to relax (Db-€150, extra bed-€25, 5 percent discount with cash and this book in 2007, one room has air-con, free Internet access, from Via Fillungo take Via San Giorgio to Piazza San Agostino 3, best to reserve by e-mail, tel. & fax 0583-467-884, www.locandasantagostino.it, info@locandasantagostino.it).

$$ Hotel la Luna has 29 classy, spotless rooms in the heart of the city. Updated rooms are split between two adjacent buildings right off of the main shopping street. Frescoed top-floor suites are a palatial, romantic splurge (Sb-€82–96, Db-€96–110, suite-€175, overpriced breakfast-€11, air-con, elevator, parking-€11/day, Via Fillungo Corte Compagni 12, tel. 0583-493-634, fax 0583-490-021, www.hotellaluna.com, info@hotellaluna.com, Barbieri family).

$$ La Bohème B&B has a cozy yet elegant ambience, offering five spacious, charming, chandeliered rooms, each painted with a different rich color scheme (Db-€110, less off-season, 5 percent discount with cash and this book in 2007, air-con, Via del Moro 2, tel. & fax 0583-462-404, www.boheme.it, info@boheme.it, run by gracious Ranieri).

$ Alla Dolce Vita Guest House is a good value, with four clean, comfortable, and spacious rooms in a handy location right next to the medieval gate at the end of Via Fillungo (Db-€67, Tb-€77, communal kitchen; follow Via Fillungo to the medieval gate, turn left and head to the small piazza on the right to #232—right of the bar; Via Fillungo 232, tel. 0583-467-768, mobile 329-582-5062, fax 0583-957-612, www.luccabed.com, info@luccabed.com, run by helpful Davide).

$ At Le Violette B&B, kindly Anna (still learning English, her granddaughter Sara speaks English) will settle you into one of her six homey, tidy, quiet rooms just a couple of blocks away from the train station inside Porta San Pietro (D-€55, Db-€65, extra bed-€15, communal kitchen, €5 to use washer and dryer—but only if you're staying several days; once inside Porta San Pietro, head inward on Via G. Saladini and turn left onto Via F. Carrara, then right onto Via Girolamo, then left onto Via della Polveriera to #6; tel. 0583-493-594, mobile 349-823-4645, fax 0583-980-064, www.leviolette.it, leviolette@virgilio.it).

$ La Magnolia offers five clean, quiet rooms with an intimate atmosphere and relaxing garden in a central location (Sb-€50–65 Db-€70–85, includes breakfast at a nearby bar, 5 percent discount with cash and this book in 2007, 1 block behind the Roman amphitheater at Via Mordini 63, tel. 0583-467-111, www.lamagnolia.com, info @lamagnolia.com, Andrea and Laura).

$ Sogni d'Oro Guest House ("Sleep like Gold"), run by Davide from Alla Dolce Vita (listed above), is a handy budget option for drivers, with five basic rooms, dingy halls, and a communal kitchen (grocery store next door). It's a 10-minute walk from the train station, and a five-minute walk from the city walls (D-€50, Db-€65; from the station, head straight out to main boulevard Viale Regina Margherita and turn right, following the street as it turns into Viale della Curtatone, then taking a right onto Via A. Cantore to #169, tel. 0583-467-768, mobile 333-498-3045, fax 0583-957-612, www.bbsognidoro.com, info@bbsognidoro.com).

$ Ostello San Frediano, in a central palazzo with a peaceful garden, is a cut above the average hostel. The rooms are bright and modern, and some have fun lofts (Db-€47, Qb-€95, €19 beds in 6- to 8-person dorms, €3 extra for non-members, cash only, lockout 11:00–15:00, no curfew, Internet access, cheap restaurant, free parking, Via della Cavallerizza 12, tel. 0583-469-957, fax 0583-461-007, www.ostellolucca.it, info@ostellolucca.it).

EATING

Puccini Ristorante is the place to splurge for a fancy €50 dinner. Fish and meat are featured here, as well as homemade bread, pasta, and desserts, with gourmet preparations and elegant presentation. Skip the basic sidewalk seats for the classy, modern art–strewn dining room (€40–45 tasting *menùs*, Wed 19:30–22:30, Thu-Mon 12:30–14:30 & 19:30–22:30, closed Tue, reserve on weekends, across the street from Puccini's House, Corte San Lorenzo 1, tel. 0583-316-116).

Ristorante Canuleia makes everything fresh in their small kitchen. While the portions aren't huge, the food is tasty. You can eat in their tiny dining room or garden courtyard. Reserve ahead for dinner (daily 12:30–14:00 & 19:30–21:30, Via Canuleia 14, tel. 0583-467-470).

Vecchia Trattoria Buralli, on quiet Piazza San Agostino, is a good bet for traditional cooking, with fine indoor and piazza seating, though the service can be uneven (€20–40 dinner, Thu–Tue 12:00–14:45 & 19:15–22:30, closed Wed, Piazza San Agostino 10, tel. 0583-950-611).

Trattoria da Leo, a cousin of Vecchia Trattoria Buralli above, packs in chatty locals for typical, low-priced home-cooking. Arrive early or reserve a spot (daily 12:00–14:30 & 19:30–22:30, cash only, exit Piazza San Salvatore on Via Asili and take the first left, Via Tegrimi 1, tel. 0583-492-236).

Osteria Baralla, a few steps from the Roman Amphitheater, is popular with locals for its quality meals. They have a breezy, spacious dining room under medieval vaults or a few quiet tables on the pedestrian street (Mon–Sat 12:30–14:30 & 19:30–22:30, closed Sun, reservations smart for dinner, Via Anfiteatro 7/9, tel. 0583-440-240).

Bella 'Mbriana focuses on doing one thing very well: turning out piping hot, wood-fired pizzas to happy locals in a cheery wood-paneled dining room. Order at the counter, and they bring your pizza to you on a cutting board. Prices range from €3.50 for your basic *Napolitano* to €12 for their specialty, with buffalo mozzarella and other gourmet ingredients (Wed–Mon 12:30–14:30 & 18:30–23:30, closed Tue, to the right as you face San Frediano Church, Via della Cavalerizza 29, tel. 0583-495-565).

TRANSPORTATION CONNECTIONS

From Lucca by Train to: Florence (9/day, 90 min), **Pisa** (hourly, 2/day Sun, 30 min), **Milan** (nearly hourly except Sun, 4–5 hrs, transfer in Florence or Prato), **Rome** (hourly except Sun, 3 hrs, change in Florence or Pisa).

Drivers: Lucca has a serious lack of public parking places. Try parking lots at Porta Santa Maria and Porta Sant'Anna, or consider parking outside of the gates near the train station or on the boulevard surrounding the city.

TUSCAN
HILL TOWNS

Tuscany is rich in history, and proud locals will remind you that their ancestors, the Etruscans, were thriving long before anyone had heard of Julius Caesar. The region offers a delightful mix of scenic beauty and rich history...and a taste of the rustic Italian good life.

Many of the hill towns—so emblematic of Tuscany—trace their roots to Etruscan times (well before ancient Rome). Others date from the fall of Rome, when barbarian invasions chased lowland townsfolk to the hills, where they built fortified communities. The Middle Ages were formative times for many cities, when warring factions divided towns between those loyal to the Pope (Guelphs) and the Holy Roman Emperor (Ghibellines). Cities developed monumental defensive walls and built great towers. Then, the Black Death swept through Tuscany in 1348 and devastated the region. The plague, plus the increasing dominance of Florence, turned many bustling cities into docile backwaters. Ironically, what was bad news in the 14th century is good news today: The hill towns enjoy a tourist-fueled affluence and retain a unique, medieval charm.

Tuscan towns are best enjoyed by adapting to the pace of the countryside. So...slow...down...and savor the delights that Tuscany offers. Spend the night if you can, as many hill towns are mobbed by day-trippers from Florence and Siena.

But how in Dante's name does a traveler choose from the literally hundreds of Tuscan hill towns? I've listed some of my favorites in this chapter. The ones you visit will depend on your interests, time, and mode of transportation. Multi-towered San Gimignano is a classic, but peak-season crowds can overwhelm the town. Wine aficionados head for Montalcino and Montepulciano—each a happy gauntlet of wine shops and art galleries (the latter being my

Tuscan Hill Towns

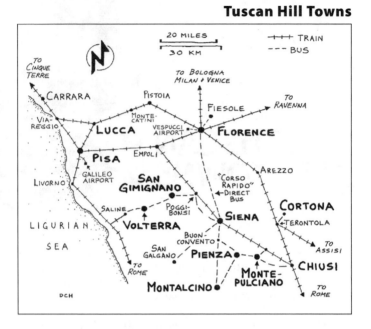

favorite). Art-lovers and those enamored by Frances Mayes' novel *(Under the Tuscan Sun)* make the pilgrimage to Cortona. Fans of architecture and urban design appreciate Pienza's well-planned streets and squares. And, for rustic vitality not trampled by tourist crowds, Volterra is the clear winner.

One of the greatest Tuscan treats—the food—varies wildly depending on where you are. The areas around Florence and Siena are famed for serving hearty "farmer food," but as you move west, dishes become lighter, based more on seafood and grains. While Siena is the town that excels at sweets, you can find good local desserts anywhere (watch for the phrase "*fatta in casa,*" or homemade). Wine is good throughout Tuscany, with pleasing selections for both amateurs and connoisseurs (see page 316 for a description of Tuscan wines).

Getting Around Tuscany

You'll find manageable public transportation in most places, but to really explore the countryside with flexibility and at your own pace, you need a car.

By Bus or Train: Traveling by public transportation is cheap and connects you with the locals. While trains link some of the towns, hill towns—being on hills—don't quite fit the railroad plan. Stations are likely to be in the valley a couple of miles from the town center, usually connected by a local bus.

Buses are often the best, if not the only, choice to get between destinations. Siena is a hub of bus lines and, therefore, a practical home base. Find schedules at local TIs and buy tickets at newsstands or *tabacchi* shops (with the big *T* signs). Confirm the departure point *(Dov'è la fermata?)*—some piazzas have more than one bus stop, so double-check that the posted schedule lists your destination and departure time. In general, orange buses are local city buses, and blue buses are for long distances.

Once the bus arrives, confirm the destination with the driver. You are expected to stow big backpacks underneath the bus (open the luggage compartment yourself if it's closed).

Sundays and holidays are problematic; even from large cities like Siena, schedules are sparse, departing buses are jam-packed, and ticket offices are often closed. Plan ahead and buy your ticket in advance. Most agencies book bus and train tickets with little or no commission.

By Car: Exploring small-town Tuscany by car is a great experience. But since a car is an expensive, worthless headache in big cities (such as Florence and Siena), wait to pick up your car until the last big city you visit. Then use it for lacing together the hill towns and exploring the countryside. Buy a big, detailed Tuscany road map (at a newsstand or gas station). Although roads are numbered on maps, actual road signs don't list any route numbers. Instead, roads are indicated by blue signs with a city name on them (e.g., if you want to take the road heading west out of Montepulciano— marked route #146 on your map—you'd follow signs to Pienza, the next town along this route). The signs are inconsistent—they may direct you to the nearest big city or simply the next town along the route. For scenic drives in this area, see page 341.

If you are staying overnight, ask your hotelier for parking suggestions. Keep valuables out of sight and locked in the trunk of the car.

By Tour: Il Casato Viaggi runs bus tours from Siena to the Tuscan countryside, with plenty of wine-tasting opportunities (see "Helpful Hints," page 237; Via Il Casato di Sotto 12 in Siena, tel. 057-746-091, fax 057-727-9863, www.sienaholiday.com).

SLEEPING

Hotels, Rooms, and Apartments

In small towns, there are often few hotels to choose from. Prices are lower than in Florence, but a nice double will still run around €80,

Wines in Tuscany

The region of Tuscany produces some of the most famous and tastiest wines in Italy. The characteristics of the soil, temperature, and exposure make each wine unique to its area. Even if you don't often drink wine, try some in Tuscany.

Choosing a wine can be intimidating, but the Italian government tries to help you choose something decent, even if you're clueless. In general, wines are designated to one of four categories:

Vino da Tavola (table wine) is the lowest grade—drink this one with pizza. While inexpensive *vino della casa*, or "house wines," fall into this category, they can be decent. Many restaurants, even modest ones, take pride in their house wine, bottling their own or working with local wineries.

Denominazione di Origine Controllata (DOC), a cut above table wine, is usually cheap, but can be surprisingly good. Over 700 wines have earned the DOC designation. You'll see plenty of DOC wines in Tuscany, since many come from the Chianti region, located between Florence and Siena.

Denominazione di Origine Controllata e Guarantita (DOCG) is the highest grade, and can be identified by the pink or

including breakfast. Many towns have an abundance of *affita camere*, or rental rooms. This can be anything from a set of keys and a basic bed to a cozy B&B with your own Tuscan grandmother. TIs book rooms and apartments and have lists of each. Private rooms are generally a good budget option, but since they vary in quality, shop around to find the best value. Apartments usually offer a couple of bedrooms, a sitting area, and a teensy *cucinetta*, typically stocked with dishes and flatware—a great value for families traveling together who'd rather cook than eat out all the time.

Agriturismo

Agriturismo (agricultural tourism), or rural B&Bs, began in the 1980s as a way for small farmers to survive in a modern economy where, like in the US, so many are run out of business by giant agricultural corporations. By renting rooms to travelers, farmers can remain on their land and continue to produce food. A peaceful home base for exploring the region, these rural Italian B&Bs are ideal for those traveling by car—especially families.

green label on the neck and the scary price tag on the shelf. Only 21 wines in Italy can be called DOCG. They're generally a good bet if you want a quality wine, but don't know anything else about the winemaker.

A recently created category called **Indicazione Geographica Tipica** (IGT) is a broad group of wines that range from basic to some of Italy's best. It includes the "Super Tuscans"—wines that don't follow the strict "recipe" required for DOC or DOCG status, but that give local vintners more opportunity to be creative. Super Tuscans are made from a mix of international grapes (such as Cabernet) grown in Tuscany and aged in small oak barrels for only two years. The result is a lively full-bodied wine that dances all over your head...and is worth the steep price.

Visit a Tuscan *enoteca* (wine bar) and sample some of these wines side-by-side to figure out what you like—and what suits your pocketbook.

Words to Live By, or... How to Describe Wine in Italian

dry	*secco*	SAY-koh
sweet	*dolce*	DOHL-chay
earthy	*terre*	TAY-ray
fruity	*fruttoso*	froo-TOH-zoh
full-bodied	*corposo*	kor-POH-zoh

It's wise to book several months in advance for high season (May–Sept). Weeklong stays are preferred in July and August, but shorter stays are possible off-season. In the winter you might be charged extra for heat, so confirm the price ahead of time. Payment policies vary, but generally a 25 percent deposit is required (lost if you cancel), and the balance is due one month before arrival.

As the name implies, *agriturismi* are in the countryside,

although some are located within a mile of town. Most are family-run and vary wildly in quality. Some properties are rustic, while others are downright luxurious, offering amenities such as swimming pools and riding stables. The rooms are usually clean and comfortable. Breakfast is often included, and *mezza pensione* (half-pension, which in this case, means a home-cooked dinner) might be built into the price whether

Tips for Enjoying an *Agriturismo* or Farmhouse Stay

- To sleep cheap, avoid peak season. Rental prices follow the old rule of supply and demand. For instance, a Tuscan farmhouse that rents for as much as $2,000 a week at peak times can go for as little as $700 in late September or October.
- Make sure your trip fits their requirements. Many properties rent on a traditional Saturday-to-Saturday time period. You might be unable to rent for a different or shorter time, especially during peak season.
- If you want amenities, be willing to pay more. A private pool can add substantially to the cost, but at the height of summer, could be worth every extra euro.
- Consider renting a rural apartment rather than an entire villa or farmhouse. Often the owners have renovated an original rambling farmhouse or medieval estate into a series of well-constructed apartments with private kitchens, bathrooms, living areas, and outdoor terraces. They usually share a common pool.
- You will need private transportation, such as a rental car, to fully enjoy—or even reach—your accommodations.
- To make the most of your time, ask an expert—the owner—for suggestions on local restaurants, sights, and activities. Make sure you know how to operate the appliances.
- Slow down. One of the joys of staying for at least a week in one location is you can develop a true *dolce far niente* (sweetness of doing nothing) attitude. If it rains, grab a book from the in-house library and curl up on the sofa.
- While your time in the countryside may not be action-packed, staying put in one spot leaves you open to the unexpected pleasures that come when you just let the days unwind without a plan.

you want it or not. Most places serve tasty homegrown food; some are vegetarian or organic, others are gourmet. Kitchenettes are often available to cook up your own feast.

To qualify officially as an *agriturismo*, the farm must still generate more money from its farm activities, thereby insuring that the land is worked and preserved.

Some farmhouse B&Bs are simply that, and are not really working farms, though are still fine places to stay. But if you want the real thing, make sure the owners call their place an *agriturismo*.

In this chapter, I've listed some *agriturismi* and farmhouses under the towns that they're nearest, but there are many, many more. Local TIs can give you a list of farms in their area, and many *agriturismi* now have their own Web sites. For a sampling, visit www.agriturismoitaly.it or do a Web search for *agriturismo*. For a booking agency, consider Farm Holidays in Tuscany (closed Sat–Sun, tel. 0564-417-418, www.byfarmholidays.com, info @byfarmholidays.com).

South Tuscany

Montalcino

On a hill overlooking vineyards and valleys, Montalcino—famous for its delicious and pricey Brunello di Montalcino red wines—is a must-sip for wine lovers.

In the Middle Ages, Montalcino (mohn-tahl-CHEE-noh) was considered Siena's biggest ally. Originally allied with Florence, the town switched sides after the Sienese beat up Florence in the battle of Montaperti in 1260. The Sienese persuaded the Montalcini to join their side by forcing them to sleep one night in the bloody Florentine-strewn battlefield.

Montalcino prospered under Siena, but like its ally, it waned after the Medici family took control of the region. The village regained fame when, in the late 19th century, the Biondi Santi family created a fine, dark red wine, calling it "the brunette."

Non–wine-lovers may find Montalcino a bit too focused on *vino*, but one sip of Brunello makes even wine skeptics believe that Bacchus was on to something. Note that Rosso di Montalcino (a younger version of Brunello) is also very good, at half the price. Those with sweet tooths will enjoy munching Ossi di Morta ("bones of the dead"), a crunchy cookie with almonds.

Sitting atop a hill amidst a sea of vineyards, Montalcino is surrounded by walls and dominated by the Fortezza (a.k.a. "La Rocca"). From here, roads lead down into the two main squares: Piazza Garibaldi and Piazza del Popolo.

Day-trippers be warned: Montalcino has no baggage-check service. In a jam, try the TI.

Tourist Information: The TI, just off Piazza Garibaldi in the City Hall, can find you a room (Db-€50–60) for no fee (daily 10:00–13:00 & 14:00–17:50, closed Mon in winter, tel. & fax 0577-849-331, www.prolocomontalcino.it). **Market day** is Friday (7:00–13:00) on Viale della Libertà.

Montalcino

P –Parking

100 YARDS
100 METERS

TO
VIA CASSIA,
SIENA, PIENZA &
MONTEPULCIANO

DCH

1 Palazzina Cesira B&B
2 Hotel il Giglio
3 Ristorante il Moro Rooms
4 Affittacamere Mariuccia
5 To La Crociona Agriturismo

6 Taverna il Grappolo Blu
7 Trattoria l'Angolo
8 Osteria al Giardino
9 Café Fiaschetteria Italiana
10 Co-op Supermarket

SIGHTS

Fortezza—This 14th-century fort, built under the rule of Siena, is now little more than an empty shell. People visit for its *enoteca*, or wine bar (see below). Climb the ramparts to enjoy a panoramic view of the Asso and Orcia valleys, or enjoy a picnic in the park surrounding the fort (€3.50 for rampart walk, €6 combo-ticket includes Civic Museum, daily 9:00–20:00, closed Mon off-season).

Civic Museum (Museo Civico)—Gothic art is the star of this museum, with works from Montalcino's heyday, the 13th to 16th centuries. Wooden sculptures and religious objects round out the collection. A new archaeological section will debut in 2007 (€4.50, €6 combo-ticket includes Fortezza, Tue–Sun 10:00–13:00 & 14:00–17:50, closed Mon, Via Ricasoli, tel. 0577-846-014).

Wineries—While there are plenty of *enoteche*, there are no real wineries inside the city. The nearby countryside, however, is littered with them, and most wineries will give tastings. While some require an appointment, many also are happy to serve a potential buyer a glass and show them around. Banfi, the most touristy, produces well-respected wines (daily 10:00–17:00, tours Mon–Fri at 16:00, reserve in advance, 10-minute drive south of Montalcino in Sant'Angelo Scalo, tel. 0577-840-111, www.castellobanfi.com, reservations@banfi.it).

The Montalcino TI can give you the list of more than 150 regional wineries. Or check with the vintners' consortium (tel. 0577-848-246, www.consorziobrunellodimontalcino.it, info @consorziobrunellodimontalcino.it).

SLEEPING

$$ Palazzina Cesira, right in the heart of the old town, rents five spacious and tastefully decorated rooms in a fine 13th-century residence with a palatial lounge. You'll enjoy a refined and tranquil ambience and the chance to get to know Lucilla and her American husband Roberto (Db-€85, suites-€100–110, cash only, 2-night minimum, Via Soccorso Saloni 2, tel. & fax 0577-846-055, www .montalcinoitaly.com, cesira@mail.montalcinoitaly.com).

$$ Hotel il Giglio, although lacking in warmth, has 12 comfortable rooms, some with vaulted ceilings. Ask for a room with a view (Sb-€58, Db-€90–100, Tb-€110, 10 percent discount with this book and cash in 2007, breakfast-€6.50, Via Soccorso Saloni 5, tel. 0577-846-577, tel. & fax 0577-848-167, www.gigliohotel.com, info@gigliohotel.com).

$ Ristorante il Moro rents four pleasant, modern rooms around the corner from their restaurant. The two upper rooms

Sleep Code

(€1 = about $1.20, country code: 39)
S = Single, **D** = Double/Twin, **T** = Triple, **Q** = Quad, **b** = bathroom,
s = shower only. Unless otherwise noted, credit cards are accepted and breakfast is included (but usually optional). English is generally spoken, but I've noted exceptions.

To help you sort easily through these listings, I've divided the rooms into three categories based on the price for a standard double room with bath:

$$$ Higher Priced—Most rooms €100 or more.
$$ Moderately Priced—Most rooms between €70–100.
$ Lower Priced—Most rooms €70 or less.

have views, the lower rooms have terraces, and they all share a cozy common room with a kitchen (Db-€50, no breakfast, 100 yards from bus station at Via Mazzini 44, tel. 0577-849-384, Alessandro and Julia).

$ Affittacamere Mariuccia has three basic, drab rooms, but it's central and cheap (Db-€46, no breakfast, check-in at Enoteca Pierangioli, Piazza del Popolo 16, rooms across the street at #28, tel. & fax 0577-849-113, www.enotecapierangioli.com, enotecapierangioli@hotmail.com, Stefania doesn't speak English).

Near Montalcino: **$$ La Crociona,** an *agriturismo* farm and working vineyard, rents seven fully equipped apartments. Fiorella Vannoni and Roberto and Barbara Nannetti offer cooking classes and tastes of the Brunello wine grown and bottled on the premises (Db-€95 but €65 in Oct–mid-May, Qb-€130 but €95 in Oct–mid-May, lower weekly rates, laundry load-€8, pool, La Croce 15, tel. 0577-847-133, tel. & fax 0577-848-007, www.lacrociona.com, crociona@tin.it). The farm is two miles south of Montalcino on the road to the Sant'Antimo Monastery (look for big yellow *Piombaia La Crociona* sign on left, then follow directions to Tenuta Crocedimezzo e Crociona). A good restaurant is next door.

EATING

Taverna il Grappolo Blu is unpretentious and friendly, serving local specialties and vegetarian options to an enthusiastic crowd (€6-pastas, €11-*secondi*, daily 12:00–15:00 & 19:00–22:00, near the main square, a few steps off Via Mazzini at Scale di Via Moglio 1, tel. 0577-847-150).

Trattoria l'Angolo, a family-run hole-in-the-wall, has nine small tables and homemade desserts (pastas-€7, meat-€8, Wed–

Mon 12:00–14:30 & 19:00–21:30, closed Tue, Via Ricasoli 9, tel. 0577-848-017).

Osteria al Giardino serves near-gourmet local cuisine at the bus station end of town. Owner and chef Giovanni Luca makes everything fresh, from the bread to the desserts (pastas-€7, *secondi*-€12, Thu–Tue 12:30–15:00 & 19:30–22:00, closed Wed, Piazza Cavour 1, tel. 0577-849-076).

Gather ingredients for a picnic at the **Co-op supermarket** on Via Sant'Agostino, just off Via Ricasoli in front of the Sant'Agostino Church, then enjoy your feast in front of the Fortezza.

Wine Tasting

While wine snobs turn up their noses, the medieval setting inside Montalcino's fort at **Enoteca la Fortezza** is a hit for most visitors. Spoil yourself with Brunello in the cozy *enoteca* or at outdoor tables (3 tastes for €12, snacks for 2 people-€9, daily 9:00–20:00, closes at 18:00 in off-season, inside the Fortezza, tel. 0577-849-211, www.enotecalafortezza.it).

Café Fiaschetteria Italiana was founded by Ferruccio Biondi-Santi, who created the famous Brunello wine. The wine library in the back of the café boasts many local wine choices, including a prized bottle from 1955, a vintage year. A meeting place since 1888, this grand café also serves light lunches and espresso to tourists and locals alike (€15 for a glass of Brunello and plate of snacks, daily 7:30–23:00, Piazza del Popolo 6, tel. 0577-849-043).

TRANSPORTATION CONNECTIONS

From Montalcino by Bus to: Siena (€3, 6/day, 90 min), **Montepulciano/Pienza** (10/day, change to line #114 in Torrenieri, one hour plus changing time). Anyone going to Rome or Florence changes in Siena. The town bus station is on Piazza Cavour. Bus tickets are sold at *tabacchi* shops or the bar on Piazza Cavour—not on board. Check schedules at the TI or the bus station.

Drivers coming in for a short visit should drive right through the old gate under the fortress (it looks almost forbidden) and grab a spot in the pay lot at the fortress. Otherwise, there is free parking a short walk away.

Montepulciano

Curving its way along a ridge, Montepulciano (mohn-tay-pull-chee-AH-noh) delights visitors with *vino* and views. Alternately under Sienese and Florentine rule, the city still retains its medieval *contrade* districts, each with a mascot and flag. The neighborhoods compete the last Sunday of August in the Bravio delle Botti, where teams of men push large wine casks uphill from Piazza Marzocco to Piazza Grande, all hoping to win a banner and bragging rights.

The city is a collage of architectural styles, but the elegant San Biagio Church, at the base of the hill, is its most impressive Renaissance building. Most ignore the architecture and focus more on the city's other creative accomplishment, the tasty Vino Nobile di Montepulciano red wine.

The action in Montepulciano centers on two streets, the steep Via di Gracciano nel Corso (nicknamed Corso) and Via Ricci, but

the quiet back streets are well worth a visit. Most visits to Montepulciano begin at the fortified Porta al Prato gate, near the bus station. From the gate, it's a 15-minute walk uphill along the Corso, the bustling main drag (note the Etruscan reliefs on the foundation of Palazzo Bucelli—see photo) to the main square, Piazza Grande. If you arrive at the bus station, ask about a shuttle bus that will bring you closer to the Piazza Grande; it's a good strategy to take the bus up and walk back down.

Tourist Information: The TI is on Piazza Don Minzoni (Mon–Sat 9:30–12:30 & 15:00–18:00, Sun 9:30–12:30, tel. 0578-757-341, www.comune.montepulciano.si.it, prolocomp@bccmp.com).

Helpful Hints: Market day is Thursday. Public WCs are located next to Palazzo Communale and the Church of St. Augustine.

SIGHTS

Piazza Grande—This pleasant, lively piazza is surrounded by a grab bag of architectural sights. The medieval Palazzo Comunale

may remind you of Palazzo Vecchio in Florence—that's because Florence dominated this town in the 15th and 16th centuries. The crenellations along the roof were never intended to hide soldiers—they're there just to symbolize power. Climbing the **clock tower** rewards you with a windy, but beautiful view

Montepulciano

1 Mueble il Riccio Rooms
2 Camere Bellavista Rooms
3 Ai Quattro Venti
4 Osteria dell'Aquacheta

TO SIENA & A-1 AUTOSTRADA FREEWAY

SANT' AGNESE

VIA E. BERNABEI

PIAZZA MARZOCCO

PIAZZA DON MINZONI

POGGIO-FANTI GARDENS

V. CAL.

VIA DELLE LETTERE

WC

SANG

PORTA AL PRATO

VIALE I MAGGIO

VIA DELLE

PALAZZO BUCELLI

ST. AUGUSTINE

WC

NEL CORSO

BUS STATION

S. LUCIA

Post

PIANA

ARCHI

SAN FRAN.

POGGIOLO

VIA GRACCIANO

VIA DI ORIOLO

★ PIAZZA GRANDE

P —PARKING

TO SAN BIAGIO

VIA DI SAN BIAGIO

VIA RICCI

CIVIC MUSEUM

V. TALOSA

V. VOLTI

GESÙ

VIA SAN PIETRO

CIRCONVALLAZIONE

PALAZZO COMUNALE

WC

★

1 CONTUCCI CANTINA

DUOMO

FIOR. VECCHIA

V. DEL OPIO CORTO

P

VIA COLLAZZI

VIA DONATO

V. TEATRO

PORTA DI FARINE

FORTEZZA

BUS STOP

VIA DI

VIA FILOSOFI

100 YARDS

100 METERS

V. POLIZIANO

S. MARIA

TO PIENZA

from the terrace below the clock. Go into the Palazzo Comunale and head up the stairs (€1.60, daily 10:00–18:00). The Palazzo de' Nobili-Tarugi is a Renaissance arcaded confection; meanwhile, the unfinished Duomo looks glumly on, wishing the city hadn't run out of money for its facade. Many such churches were built until they had a functional interior, and then, for various practical reasons, the facades were left unfinished. You can see the rough stonework just waiting for the final marble veneer. Step inside the Duomo, and you are rewarded with a beautiful della Robbia *Altar of the Lilies* behind the baptismal font (on the left as your enter) and a luminous, early-Renaissance Assumption triptych by Taddeo di Bartolo, an artist from Siena. The Contucci Palace (left of the church) is lucky enough to have a 16th-century Renaissance facade. The Contucci family still lives in their palace, producing and selling their own wine. The town is fortunate to be graced with so many bold and noble palazzos—Florentine nobility favored Montepulciano as a breezy and relaxed place for a summer or secondary residence.

▲▲ **Contucci Cantina**—Montepulciano's most popular attraction isn't made of stone...it's the famous wine, Vino Nobile. This robust red can be tasted in any of the cantinas lining Via Ricci and Via di Gracciano nel Corso, but the cantina in the basement of the Contucci Palace is the most fun. While the palace has a formal wine-tasting showroom facing the square, head down the lane on the right to the actual cellars, where you'll meet lively Adamo, who has been making wine since 1953 and welcomes tourists into his cellar. Adamo usually has a dozen bottles open (tasting is free, no food, daily 8:30–12:30 & 14:30–18:30, Piazza Grande 7, tel. 0578-757-006). Groups are welcome with a reservation.

After sipping a little wine with Adamo, explore the 13th-century vaults of the palace basement, now filled with huge bar-rels of wine. Countless barrels of Croatian, Italian, and French oak (1,000 to 2,500 liters each) cradle the wine through a two-year in-the-barrel aging process, while the wine picks up the personality of the wood. After about 35 years, an exhausted barrel has nothing left to offer its wine, and it's retired. Adam explains that the French oak gives the wine "pure elegance,"  the Croatian is more masculine, and the Italian oak is a marriage of the two. Each barrel is labeled with the size in liters, the year the wine was barreled, and the percentage of alcohol (determined by how much sun shone in that year). "Nobile"-grade wine needs a minimum of 13 percent alcohol.

The information office for the "Strada del Vino" (Wine Road) organizes **wine tours** in the city and minibus winery tours farther afield (Piazza Grande, tel. 0578-717-484, www.stradavinonobile.it, info@stradavinonobile.it).

Civic Museum (Museo Civico)—Small and eclectic, the highlight of this well-presented museum is its colorful della Robbia ceramic altarpieces and Etruscan artifacts (€4.10, Tue–Sun 10:00–13:00 & 15:00–18:00, Sun 10:00–18:00, closed Mon, Via Ricci 10, tel. 0578-717-300).

San Biagio Church—Down a picturesque driveway lined with cypress, this church—designed by Antonio da Sangallo—is Renaissance perfection. The proportions of the Greek cross plan give the building a pleasing rhythmic quality. The lone tower was supposed to have a twin, but it was never built. The soaring interior, with a high dome and lantern, creates a fine Renaissance space (daily 9:00–13:00 & 15:00–19:00). The street Via di San Biagio, leading from the church up into town, makes for an enjoyable, if challenging, walk.

SLEEPING

(€1 = about $1.20, country code: 39)

$$ Mueble il Riccio ("hedgehog" in Italian) is medieval-elegant, with six modern rooms, an awesome roof terrace, and friendly owners (Sb-€75, Db-€85, Tb-€101, breakfast-€8, air-con, a block below the main square at Via Talosa 21, tel. & fax 0578-757-713, www.ilriccio.net, info@ilriccio.net, Gio and Ivana speak English). Gio (or his son) gives country tours (€25/hr) in one of their classic Italian cars; for tour details, see their Web site.

$ Camere Bellavista has 10 simple rooms, some with better views than others. Room 6 has a view terrace worth reserving (Db €55, nicer Db-€65, breakfast-€2.50, cash only, no elevator, Via Ricci 25, mobile 347-823-2314, bellavista@bccmp.com, little English spoken).

EATING

Ai Quattro Venti is fresh, flavorful, fun, and right on Piazza Grande, offering good indoor and outdoor seating (pastas-€7, Fri–Wed 12:30–14:00 & 19:30–22:30, closed Thu, next to City Hall on Piazza Grande, tel. 0578-717-231).

Osteria dell'Aquacheta serves pastas and salads at reasonable prices, with a mix of locals and tourists (€5 pastas and salads, Wed–Mon 12:30–15:00 & 19:30–22:30, closed Tue, Via del Teatro 22, tel. 0578-717-086).

TRANSPORTATION CONNECTIONS

From Montepulciano by Bus to: Siena (4/day, 75 min, none on Sun), **Pienza** (8/day, 30 min). All buses leave from Piazza Pietro Nenni. There are hourly bus connections to Chiusi, a town on the main Florence–Rome rail line; Chiusi is a much better bet than the distant Montepulciano station (5 miles away), which is served only by milk-run trains.

Drivers: Route #146 to Montalcino is particularly scenic (see "Crete Senese Drives," page 341). It isn't wise to tackle the tiny roads inside the city, so park outside the walls, either at the bus station or the numerous lots on the edge of town.

Pienza

Set on a crest, surrounded by green, rolling hills, the small town of Pienza packs a lot of Renaissance punch. In the 1400s, locally born

Pope Pius II of the Piccolomini family decided to remodel his birthplace in the style that was all the rage—Renaissance. Propelled by papal clout, the town of Corsignano was transformed—in only five years' time—into a jewel of Renaissance architecture. It was renamed Pienza, after Pope Pius. The plan was to remodel the entire town, but work ended in 1564 when both the pope and his architect, Bernardo Rossellino, died. The architectural focal point is the square Piazza Pio II, surrounded by the Duomo and the pope's family residence, Palazzo Piccolomini. While the Piazza Pio II is Pienza's pride and joy, the entire town—a mix of old stone-work, potted plants, and grand views—is fun to explore, especially with a camera or sketchpad in hand. You can walk each lane in the tiny town in a few minutes. Nearly every shop sells the town's specialty—Pecorino cheese—a pungent sheep's cheese available fresh *(fresco)* or aged *(secco)*. **Market day** is Friday.

Tourist Information: The TI is 10 yards up the street from Piazza Pio II (Mon–Sat 10:00–13:00 & 15:00–19:00, closed Sun, tel. & fax 0578-749-905). The TI will let you leave your bags there.

SIGHTS

▲**Piazza Pio II**—One of Italy's classic piazzas, this square is famous for its elegance and artistic unity. The square and the surrounding buildings were all designed by Rossellino to form an "outdoor room." Spinning around, you'll see the City Hall (13th-century bell tower with a Renaissance facade and a fine loggia), the Bishop's Palace (now an art museum), the Piccolomini family palace (well worth touring—see below), and the Duomo. Just to the left of the church, a lane leads to the best viewpoint in town.

Duomo—Its classic, symmetrical Renaissance facade—with the Piccolomini family coat of arms (modestly) front and center—dominates Piazza Pio II. The interior is charming, with several Gothic altarpieces and painted arches. Windows feature the crest of Pius II, with five half-moons advertising the number of crusades that his family funded.

▲▲Palazzo Piccolomini—The home of Pius II (see page 328) and the Piccolomini family (until 1962) can be visited with a guided tour. While the 30-minute tour (in English and Italian) visits only six rooms and the loggia, it offers a fascinating slice of 15th-century aristocratic life and is the sightseeing highlight of the town. In fact, it's the most impressive small-town palace experience I've found in Tuscany. Don't miss this one. Check out the well-preserved painted courtyard for free. In Renaissance times, most buildings were covered with elaborate paintings like these (€3.50, Tue–Sun 10:00–12:30 & 15:00–18:00, closed Mon and in winter, tel. 0578-749-071).

Diocesan Museum (Museo Diocesano)—This collection of religious paintings from local churches fills the cardinal's Renaissance palace. The art is provincial Sienese, displayed in chronological order from 12th through 17th centuries, conveniently all on one floor (€4.10, Wed–Mon 10:00–13:00 & 15:00–19:00, closed Tue, in winter open Sat–Sun only, Corso il Rossellino 30).

View Terrace—Facing the church, a lane leads left to the panoramic promenade. Views from the terrace include the Tuscan countryside and Monte Amiata, the largest mountain in southern Tuscany, in the distance.

SLEEPING

(€1 = about $1.20, country code: 39)
$$ Agriturismo Terrapille sits just below Pienza, on a little grassy bluff surrounded by 360 degrees of dreamy Tuscan scenery. It's private and rustic yet cozy and romantic. Four country rooms and two apartments come with modern comforts (Db-€95, Qb-€160, breakfast-€7.50, dinner available on request for €25, pool, about a mile out of town, take road #18 in direction of Monticchiello, tel. & fax 0578-749-146 at farm, www.terrapille.it, terrapille@bccmp.com). Lucia, who runs the place, lives in Pienza (home tel. 0578-748-434, mobile 338-920-4470).

$ Oliviera Camere, which has six simple rooms in the town center, is run by soft-spoken Nello, who doesn't speak English (Db-€50, breakfast in room, cash only, Via Condotti 4, tel. 0578-748-205, mobile 338-952-0459).

$ Il Giardino Segreto Camere rents six humble rooms with a lush, peaceful garden (Db-€62, apartment Db-€67, Via Condotti 13, tel. 0578-748-539, mobile 338-899-5879, www.ilgiardinosegreto .toscana.nu, muccirossi@bcc.tin.it).

EATING

Latte di Luna, lively with great indoor and outdoor seating, is a good, quality choice (Wed–Mon 12:30–14:30 & 19:30–21:30, closed Tue, at Porta al Giglio, Via San Carlo 2, tel. 0578-748-606).

La Taverna di Re Artu serves bruschetta and a variety of wines (daily 10:30–20:30, Via della Rosa 4).

Ristorante dal Falco, a modern place just outside the town wall, is out of the tourist zone and therefore forced to offer a fine value to survive. Its comfortable indoor and outdoor seating and lack of tourists make it a favorite with tour guides (pastas-€6, *secondi*-€11, Sat–Thu 12:00–15:00 & 19:00–22:00, closed Fri, Piazza Dante Alighieri 3, tel. 0578-749-856).

Assemble a picnic at any of the numerous cheese and wine shops, and dine with a fantastic view along the walls of the view terrace.

TRANSPORTATION CONNECTIONS

Bus tickets are sold at the bar just inside Pienza's town gate.

From Pienza by Bus to: Siena (6/day, 90 min), **Montepulciano** (8/day, 30 min).

Cortona

Cortona blankets a 1,700-foot hill surrounded by dramatic Tuscan and Umbrian views. Frances Mayes' books, such as *Under the Tuscan Sun,* have placed this town in the touristic limelight, just as Peter Mayle's books popularized the Luberon region in France. But long before Mayes ever published a book, Cortona was popular with Romantics and considered one of the classic Tuscan hill towns. Unlike San Gimignano, Cortona maintains a rustic and gritty personality—even with its long history of foreigners who, enamored with its Tuscan charm, made this their adopted home.

The city began as one of the largest Etruscan settlements, the remains of which can be seen at the base of the city walls, as well as

in the nearby tombs. It grew to its present size in the 13th to 16th centuries, when it was a colorful and crowded city, eventually allied with Florence. The farmland that fills almost every view from the city was marshy and uninhabitable until about 200 years ago, when it was drained and turned into some of Tuscany's most fertile land.

Art-lovers know Cortona as the home of Renaissance painter Luca Signorelli, Baroque master Pietro da Cortona (Berretini), and the 20th-century Futurist artist Gino Severini. The city's museums and churches reveal many of the works of these native sons.

ORIENTATION

Most of the main sights, shops, and restaurants cluster around the level streets on the Piazza Garibaldi–Piazza del Duomo axis, but Cortona will have you huffing and puffing up some steep hills.

Tourist Information: The helpful TI is on the main drag at Via Nazionale 42 (daily March–Oct 9:00–13:00 & 15:00–19:00, shorter hours off-season, sells train and bus tickets, tel. 0575-630-352, www.apt.arezzo.it, www.cortona-musei.it for museums, infocortona@apt.arezzo.it). **Market day** is Saturday on Piazza Signorelli (early–14:00).

Private Guide: Giovanni Adreani exudes energy and a love of his city and Tuscan high culture. He is great at bringing the fine points of the city to life and can take visitors around in his car for no extra price. As this region is speckled with underappreciated charms, having Giovanni for a day as your driver/guide promises to be a fascinating experience (€110/half-day, €180/day, tel. 0575-630-665, mobile 347-176-2830, www.adreanigiovanni .com, adreanigiovanni@libero.it).

Arrival in Cortona: Buses stop at Piazza Garibaldi. From here, it's a level five-minute walk down bustling, shop-lined Via Nazionale (stop by the TI) to Piazza della Repubblica, the heart of the town, dominated by City Hall (Palazzo della Comune). From this square, it's a two-minute stroll past the interesting Etruscan Museum and theater to Piazza del Duomo, where you'll find the recommended Diocesan Museum. Steep streets, many of them stepped, lead from Piazza della Repubblica up to the San Niccolo and Santa Margherita churches and the Medici Fortress (a 30-minute climb from Piazza della Repubblica).

Cortona

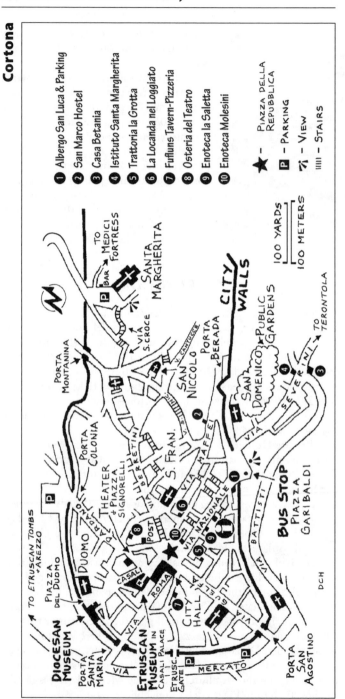

1 Albergo San Luca & Parking
2 San Marco Hostel
3 Casa Betania
4 Istituto Santa Margherita
5 Trattoria la Grotta
6 La Locanda nel Loggiato
7 Fufluns Tavern-Pizzeria
8 Osteria del Teatro
9 Enoteca la Saletta
10 Enoteca Molesini

★ – PIAZZA DELLA REPUBBLICA
P – PARKING
↟ – VIEW
‖‖‖ – STAIRS

100 YARDS
100 METERS

SELF-GUIDED WALK

Welcome to Cortona

This introductory walking tour will take you from the Piazza Garibaldi, up the main strip, to the town center, its piazzas, and the Duomo.

• *Start at the bus stop in...*

Piazza Garibaldi: Many visits start and finish in this square, thanks to its bus stop. While the piazza, bulging like a big turret out from the town fortifications, looks like part of an old rampart, it's really a souvenir of those early French and English Romantics—the ones who first created the notion of a dreamy, idyllic Tuscany. During the Napoleonic age, the French built this balcony (and the scenic little park behind the adjacent San Domenico Church) simply to enjoy a commanding view of the Tuscan countryside.

With Umbria about a mile away, Cortona marks the end of Tuscany. This is a major cultural divide, as Cortona was the last town in Charlemagne's empire and the last under Medici rule. Umbria, just to the south, was papal territory for centuries. These deep-seated cultural disparities were a great challenge for the visionaries who unified the fractured region to create the modern nation of Italy during the 1860s. A statue in the center of this square honors one of the heroes of the struggle for Italian unification—the brilliant revolutionary general, Giuseppe Garibaldi.

Enjoy the commanding view from here. Assisi is just over the ridge on the left. Lake Trasimeno peeks from behind the hill, looking quite normal today. But, according to legend, it was blood-red after Hannibal defeated the Romans here in 217 B.C. and 15,000 died in the battle. The only sizable town you can see, on the right, is Montepulciano. Cortona is still defined by its Etruscan walls—remnants of these walls, with stones laid 2,500 years ago, stretch from here in both directions.

Frances Mayes put Cortona on the map for many Americans with her book and the movie, *Under the Tuscan Sun.* Her book describes her real-life experience buying, fixing up, and living in a rundown villa in Cortona with her husband Ed. The movie romanticized the story, turning Frances into a single, recently divorced writer who restores the villa and her peace of mind. Frances' villa isn't "under the Tuscan sun" very often; it's named Bramasole—literally, "craving sun." On the wrong side of the hill, it's in the shade after 15:00. She and her husband still live there part of each year and are respected members of their adopted community (outside the walls, behind the hill on the left).

• *From this square, head into town along...*

Via Nazionale: The only level road in town, locals have nicknamed Via Nazionale the *ruga piana* (flat wrinkle). This is the main commercial street in this town of 2,500, and it's been that way for a long time. Every shop seems to have a medieval cellar or an Etruscan well. Notice the crumbling sandstone door frames. The entire town is constructed out of this grainy, eroding rock.

• *Via Nazionale leads to...*

Piazza della Repubblica: The City Hall faces Cortona's main square, where three flags fly: Europe, Italy, and peace (Tuscany is famously left-wing and likes peace). Note how the City Hall is a clever hodgepodge of twin medieval towers, with a bell tower added to connect them, and a grand staircase to lend some gravitas. Notice also the fine wood balconies on the left. In the Middle Ages, wooden extensions such as balconies were common features on the region's stone buildings. These balconies (not original, but rebuilt in the 19th century) would have fit right in the medieval cityscape. These days, you usually see only the holes that once supported the long-gone wooden beams.

This square has been the town center since Etruscan times. Four centuries before Christ, an important street led from here up to the hill-capping temple. Later, the square became the Roman forum. Opposite the City Hall is a handy grocery store for good, cheap sandwiches (see "Eating," page 338). Above that is the loggia—once a fish market, now a recommended restaurant.

• *The second half of the square, to the right of the City Hall, is...*

Piazza Signorelli: Dominated by Casali Palace, this square was the headquarters of the Florentine captains who used to control the city. Every six months, Florence would send a new captain to Cortona, who would help establish his rule by inserting his family coat of arms into the palace's wall. These date from the 15th to the 17th century, and were once painted with bright colors. Cortona's fine Etruscan Museum (listed in "Sights," below) is in the Casali Palace courtyard, which is lined with many more of these family coats of arms. The inviting Café del Teatro fills the loggia of the theater that is named for the town's most famous artist, Luca Signorelli.

• *Head down the street just to the right of the museum to the...*

Piazza del Duomo: Here you'll find the Diocesan Museum (see "Sights," below), cathedral, and a statue of Sta. Margherita. If the cathedral seems a little underwhelming and tucked away, that's because it is. Cortona loves its patron saint, Margherita, and put the energy it would normally invest in its cathedral into Santa Margherita Basilica at the top of the hill. Margherita was a 13th-century rich girl who took good care of the poor and was an early follower of St. Francis and Sta. Clare. Many locals believe that Margherita protected Cortona from WWII bombs. (Many also thank her for the best public toilets in town—clean and free, just under her statue.)

The Piazza del Duomo terrace comes with a commanding view of the Tuscan countryside. Find the town cemetery in the distance. If you were standing here before the time of Napoleon, you'd be surrounded by tombstones. But Cortona's graveyards—like urban graveyards throughout Napoleon's realm—were cleaned out in the early 1800s to reclaim land and improve hygiene.

• *Next, enter the...*

Duomo: The Cortona cathedral is not—strictly speaking—a cathedral, because it no longer has a bishop. The white-and-gray Florentine Renaissance–style interior is mucked up with lots of Baroque chapels filling once spacious side niches. In the rear (on the right) is an altar cluttered with relics. Technically any Catholic altar, in order to be consecrated, needs a relic embedded in it. Go ahead—gently lift up the tablecloth. The priest here doesn't mind. You'll see a little marble patch that holds a bit of a saint.

• *From here, you can visit the nearby Diocesan Museum or head back to the Piazza della Repubblica to visit the Etruscan Museum (see "Sights," below, for both), or to get a bite to eat (see "Eating" on page 338).*

SIGHTS

▲**Etruscan Museum (Museo dell'Accademia Etrusca)**— Established in 1727, this was one of the first galleries dedicated to artifacts from the Etruscan civilization. Along with lots of gold and jewelry, you'll find a seventh-century B.C. grater (for some really old Parmesan cheese) and a magnificent fourth-century B.C. bronze oil lamp with 16 spouts, set in a small, four-pillared temple. Don't miss the library of the Etruscan Academy upstairs. The academy was founded in 1727 to promote an understanding of the city through the study of archaeology. This eclectic museum, recently expanded in 2006, also has an Egyptian section, fine Roman mosaics, and a room dedicated to modern works by Severini (€7, April–Oct Tue–Sun 10:00–19:00, Nov–March Tue–Sun 10:00–17:00, closed Mon, Casali Palace on Piazza Signorelli, tel. 0575-637-235).

▲**Diocesan Museum (Museo Diocesano)**—This collection of art from the town's many churches has works by Fra Angelico and Pietro Lorenzetti, and masterpieces by hometown hero and Renaissance master Luca Signorelli.

Don't miss Fra Angelico's sumptuous *Annunciation*. In this scene, Mary says, "Yes," consenting to bear God's son. Notice how the house sits on a pillow of flowers...the new Eden. The old Eden, featuring the expulsion of Adam and Eve from Paradise, is in the upper left. The painting comes with comic-like narration: The angel's lines are top and bottom, Mary's answer is upside down (logically, since it's directed to God, who would be reading from heaven).

Another highlight is Luca Signorelli's *Mourning of the Dead Christ (Compianto sul Cristo Morto)*. Signorelli was a generation ahead of Michelangelo and, with his passion for painting ideas, was an inspiration for the young artist. Everything in his painting has a meaning: The skull of Adam sits under the sacrifice of Jesus; the hammer represents the Passion (the Crucifixion leading to the Resurrection); the lake is blood; and so on. I don't understand all of the medieval symbolism, but it's intense (€5, helpful audio-guide-€3, daily April–Oct 10:00–19:00; Nov–March Tue–Sun 10:00–17:00, closed Mon; Piazza del Duomo 1, tel. 0575-62-830). For more on Signorelli, see page 342.

Church of St. Francis—Established by St. Francis' best friend, Brother Elias, this church dates from the 13th century. Francis fans visit for its precious Franciscan relics. In the sacristy you'll find his tunic, the little Gospel that he always carried, and his pillow. If the church is closed, you can ring the bell from the cloister of the adjacent Franciscan Monastery and ask to be let in.

San Niccolo Church—Signorelli enthusiasts will want to make the pilgrimage up to this tiny church. Ring the bell, and the caretaker might give you a short tour in Italian (€1 donation, daily in summer 9:00–12:00 & 15:00–19:00, daily off-season 9:00–12:00 & 15:00–17:00). The highlight of this humble church is an altarpiece painted on both sides by Signorelli. The caretaker activates a tricky arm mechanism that moves the picture away from the wall to reveal the painting behind it.

Santa Margherita Basilica—From San Niccolo Church, a steep path leads uphill 10 minutes to this basilica, which houses the remains of the town's favorite saint. Sta. Margherita, an unwed mother from Montepulciano, found her calling with the Franciscans in Cortona, tending to the sick and poor. Her son eventually became a Franciscan monk.

Still need more altitude? Head uphill five more minutes, to the Medici Fortezza (usually open daily 9:00–12:00 & 15:00–19:00). The views are stunning, stretching all the way to distant Lake Trasimeno.

Etruscan Tombs near Cortona—Guided tours to nearby "Il Sodo" tombs (called *melone* for their melon-like shape) are complicated to arrange. But the excavation site and bits of the ruins are easy to visit and can be seen from outside the fence in the morning. It's just a couple miles out of Cortona on the Arezzo road (#71), at the edge of Camucia at the foot of the Cortona hill; ask anyone for "Il Sodo."

SLEEPING

(€1 = about $1.20, country code: 39)

$$$ Albergo San Luca, perched on a cliff side, has 57 modern, business-class, impersonal rooms, half with stunning views of Lago Trasimeno. It's friendly, well-run, and conveniently located right at the bus stop (Sb-€75, Db-€110, request a view room when you reserve, popular with Americans and groups, Piazza Garibaldi 1, tel. 0575-630-460, fax 0575-630-105, www.sanlucacortona.com, info@sanlucacortona.com). If driving, there's a small public parking lot at the hotel where you might find a spot (cheap and easy meters).

$ Casa Betania, a big wistful convent with a large, inviting view terrace, rents 35 fine rooms (only twin beds) for the best price in town. While it's primarily for "thoughtful travelers," anyone looking for a peaceful place to call home will feel welcome in this pilgrims' resort (S-€26, Sb-€31, D-€37, Db-€42, breakfast-€3, about a third of a mile out of town, a few minutes' walk below Piazza Garibaldi at Via Gino Severini 50, tel. 0575-62-829, fax 0575-604-299, casabetaniacortona@interfree.it).

$ Istituto Santa Margherita, run by the Suore Serve di Maria Riparatrici sisters, rents 25 cheap and simple beds in a smaller and more institutional-feeling convent across the street (Sb-€32, Db-€46, breakfast-€3, Viale Cesare Battisti 15, tel. 0575-630-336, fax 0575-630-549, comunitacortona@smr.it).

$ San Marco Hostel, at the top of town, housed in a remodeled 13th-century palace, is one of Italy's best hostels (€12.50/bed in dorms with 2, 4, or 8 beds, includes breakfast, Via Maffei 57, tel. 0575-601-392).

Near Cortona

$$$ Casa San Martino, 12 miles east of Cortona near the isolated village of Lisciano Niccone, is a 250-year-old countryside farmhouse run as a B&B by American Italophile Lois Martin. While Lois reserves the summer (June–Aug) for one-week stays, she'll take guests staying a minimum of three nights for the rest of the year (Db-€140, 10 percent discount for my readers in 2007—mention this book when you reserve, pool, washer/dryer, house rental available, off-season cooking and painting classes, Casa San Martino 19, Lisciano Niccone, tel. 075-844-288, fax 075-844-422, csm@tuscanyvacation.com). Lois' neighbors, Ernestine and Gisbert Schwanke, run the tidy **La Villetta di San Martino B&B** (Db-€100, 2-night minimum, cash only, common kitchen and sitting room, San Martino 36, tel. & fax 075-844-309, www.tuscanyvacation.com, erni@netemedia.net).

$$ Castello di Montegualandro is a well-preserved castle on a hill opposite Cortona, overlooking the lake and countryside. The Marti family rent four charming medieval apartments, formerly peasants' quarters, inside the peaceful castle walls. Each one is unique and named for its former use—the Fornacci's sunken living room used to be a kiln. The castle's chapel is a popular spot for weddings (3- or 4-person apartment starts at €133, 3-night minimum, mention this book for a 7 percent discount in 2007, discounts for longer stays, cash only, 10 min southeast of Cortona, Tuoro sul Trasimeno, tel. & fax 075-823-0267, www.montegualandro.com, info@montegualandro.com).

EATING

Trattoria la Grotta, just off Piazza della Repubblica, is a traditional, cave-like place with daily specials and an enthusiastic following (pastas-€7, meat-€8, Wed–Mon 12:00–14:30 & 19:00–22:00, closed Tue, Piazza Baldelli 3, tel. 0575-630-271).

La Locanda nel Loggiato serves up big portions of Tuscan cuisine on the loggia overlooking Piazza Repubblica. While they have fine indoor seating, I'd eat here only for the chance to gaze at the square over a meal (pastas-€7, meat-€7–15, Thu–Tue 12:15–15:00 & 19:15–23:00, closed Wed, Piazza Pescheria 3, tel. 0575-630-575).

Fufluns Tavern Pizzeria (that's the Etruscan name for Dionysus) is easy-going, friendly, and remarkably unpretentious for its location in the town center. It's popular with locals for its good, inexpensive Tuscan cooking and friendly staff (cheap, lots of pizzas but plenty more, good house wine, Wed–Mon 12:15–14:30 & 19:15–22:30, closed Tue, a block below Piazza della Repubblica at Via Ghibellina 3, tel. 057-560-4140, run by Alessio and Simona).

Osteria del Teatro tries very hard to create an Old World atmosphere and does it well. It serves nicely presented and tasty Tuscan standards amid feminine, nostalgic elegance (closed Wed, 2 blocks uphill from the main square at Via Maffei 2, tel. 0575-630-556).

Enoteca la Saletta, dark and classy, is good for some fine wine and a light meal. You can sit inside surrounded by wine bottles or outside to people-watch on the town's main drag (Thu–Tue 7:30–24:00, closed Wed, Via Nazionale 26, tel. 057-560-3366).

For a Picnic: On the main square, the chic little grocery store, **Enoteca Molesini,** makes tasty sandwiches (see list on counter and order by number) and sells whatever you might want for a picnic (daily including Sun morning, Piazza della Repubblica 23). Munch your picnic across the square on the steps of City Hall, or just past Piazza Garibaldi in the public gardens behind San Domenico Church.

TRANSPORTATION CONNECTIONS

Cortona connects with the rest of Italy by train. To get from Cortona down to the town's train station, at the foot of the hill, take a taxi or bus (€1, 2/hr between Piazza Garibaldi and station, buy tickets at newsstand or *tabacchi* shop).

From Cortona by Train to: Rome (10/day, 2.25 hrs), **Florence** (hourly, 90 min), **Assisi** (6/day, 60 min), **Montepulciano** (10/day, 75 min, change in Chiusi). Most trains stop at Cortona's Camucia train station (tel. 0575-603-018), but fast trains from Rome and Florence stop at Terontola, 10 miles away (tel. 0575-670-034).

Drivers: Some free parking is available inside the town walls, if you can find it (best bets: Piazzale del Mercato and Piazzale di Santa Margherita). But I'd just grab a spot in one of several free lots right outside the walls. Piazza Garibaldi is perfectly central (where the buses stop, 2 minutes' walk from Piazza della Repubblica) and has a handful of pay spots (blue lines, plug the meter, cheap, free from 20:00–8:00). The small town is actually very long, and it can be smart to drive to the top for sightseeing there (parking at Santa Margherita Basilica).

San Galgano Monastery

Of southern Tuscany's several evocative monasteries, San Galgano is the best. Set in a forested area called the Montagnolo ("medium-

sized mountains"), the isolated abbey and chapel are postcard-perfect.

San Galgano was a 12th-century saint who renounced his past as a knight to become a hermit. Lacking a cross to display, he created his own by miraculously burying his sword up to its hilt into a stone, à la King Arthur, but in reverse. After his death, a large Cistercian monastery complex grew. Today, all you'll see is the roofless, ruined abbey and, on a nearby hill, the Chapel of San Galgano with its fascinating dome and sword in the stone.

Getting There: Although a bus reportedly comes here from Siena, this sight is realistically accessible only for drivers. It's just outside of Monticiano (not Montalcino), about an hour south of Siena.

The Abbey: This picturesque, Cistercian abbey was once a powerful institution in Tuscany. Known for their skill as builders, the Cistercians oversaw the construction of Siena's cathedral. But the abbey, after losing most of its population in the plague of 1348, never really recovered and was eventually deconsecrated.

The Cistercian order was centered in France, and the architecture of the abbey shows a heavy French influence. Notice the large, high windows and the pointy, delicate arches. This is pure French Gothic, a style that never fully caught on in Italy (compare it with the chunky, elaborately decorated cathedral in Siena, built about the same time).

As you enter the church, notice the small section of the cloister wall to the left. This used to surround the garden, and was the only place that the monks were allowed to talk, for one hour each day. From inside the church, the empty windows frame the view of the chapel up on the hill.

The Chapel: A path from the abbey leads up the hill to the Chapel of San Galgano. The unique, beehive-like interior houses San Galgano's sword and stone, recently confirmed to date back to the 12th century. Don't try and pull the sword from the stone. The small chapel to the left displays the severed arms of the last guy who tried. The chapel also contains some deteriorated frescoes and more interesting sinopie, or fresco sketches. The adjacent gift shop sells a little bit of everything, from wine to postcards to herbs, some of it monk-made (free, daily 8:00–sunset). For a quick snack, a small, touristy bar at the end of the driveway is your only option.

Other more accessible Tuscan monasteries worth visiting include Sant'Antimo (6 miles south of Montalcino) and Monte Oliveto Maggiore (15 miles south of Siena, mentioned in "Crete Senese Drives" on next page).

MORE SOUTH TUSCAN SIGHTS

▲**Chiusi**—This small hill town (rated ▲▲ for Etruscan fans), once one of the most important Etruscan cities, is now a key train junction on the Florence–Rome line. The region's trains (to Siena, Orvieto, and Assisi) go through or change at this hub.

Highlights include the Archaeological Museum and the Etruscan tombs located just outside of town near Lago di Chiusi (€4, daily 9:00–20:00, Via Porsenna 93, tel. 0578-20-177). One of the tombs is multichambered, with several sarcophagi. Another, the Tomba della Scimmia (Tomb of the Monkey), has some well-preserved frescoes. Visiting the tombs requires a guide, arranged through the TI or the Archaeological Museum (5 people allowed to view at a time).

Troglodyte alert! The Cathedral Museum on the main square has a dark, underground labyrinth of Etruscan tunnels (bring a flashlight). The mandatory guided tour of the tunnels ends in a large Roman cistern from which you can climb the church bell tower for an expansive view of the countryside (museum–€2, labyrinth–€3, combo-ticket–€4, daily 9:30–12:45 & 16:00–19:00, tunnel tours at 11:00 and 16:00, Piazza Duomo 1, tel. 0578-226-490).

The TI is on the main square (Mon–Fri 10:00–13:00, maybe afternoons in summer, closed Sat–Sun, tel. 0578-227-667, prolocochiusi@bcc.tin.it). Trains connect Chiusi with Rome, Florence, Siena, and more. Buses link the train station with the town center two miles away.

▲**US Cemetery**—The compelling sight of endless rows of white marble crosses and Stars of David recalls the heroism of the young

Americans who fought so valiantly to free Italy (and ultimately Europe) from the grips of fascism. This particular cemetery is the final resting place of more than 4,000 Americans who died in the liberation of Italy during World War II. Climb the hill past the perfectly manicured lawn, lined with grave markers, to the memorial, where maps and a history of the Italian campaign detail the Allied advance (daily mid-April–Sept 9:00–18:00, Oct–mid-April 9:00–17:00, 7 miles south of Florence, off Via Cassia that parallels the *superstrada* between Florence and Siena, 2 miles south of Florence Certosa exit on A-1 autostrada). Buses from Florence stop just outside the cemetery.

▲▲**Crete Senese Drives**—South of Siena, the hilly area known as the "Sienese Crests" is full of colorful fields and curvy, scenic roads. You'll see an endless parade of classic Tuscan scenes, rolling hills topped with medieval towns, olive groves, rustic stone farmhouses, and a skyline punctuated with cypress trees. You won't find many wineries here, since the clay soil is better for wheat and sunflowers, but you will find the pristine, panoramic Tuscan countryside that you find on calendars and postcards.

During the spring, the fields are painted in yellow and green with fava beans and broom, dotted by red poppies on the fringes. Sunflowers decorate the area during July and August, and expanses of wind-blown grass fill the landscape almost all year.

Most roads to the southeast of Siena will give you a taste, but one of the most scenic stretches is the Laurentina road (Siena–Asciano–San Giovanni d'Asso, #438 on road maps, can easily continue to Montalcino). There are plenty of turnouts on this road for panoramic photo opportunities, and a few roadside picnic areas.

For a break from the winding road, about 15 miles from Siena, you'll find the quaint and non-touristy village of **Asciano.** With a medieval town center and several interesting churches and museums, this is a great place for lunch (TI at Corso Matteotti 18, tel. 0577-719-510). If you're in town on Saturday, gather a picnic at the outdoor market (Via Amendola, 8:00–14:00).

Five miles south of Asciano, the **Abbey of Monte Oliveto Maggiore** houses a famous fresco cycle of the life of St. Benedict, painted by Renaissance masters Il Sodoma and Luca Signorelli (free, daily April–Oct 9:15–12:00 & 15:15–18:00, Nov–March closes at 17:00, Gregorian chanting Sun at 11:00 and Mon–Fri at 18:15, call to confirm, tel. 0577-707-611). Once you reach the town of **San Giovanni d'Asso,** it's only another 12 miles southwest to Montalcino.

Another scenic drive is the lovely stretch between Montalcino and Montepulciano (#146 on road maps). This route alternates between the grassy hills of the Crete Senese and sun-bathed vineyards of the Orcia River valley. Stop by Pienza en route.

Sleeping in the Crete Senese: **Agriturismo il Molinello** rents four apartments, two built over a medieval mill. Hardworking Alessandro and Elisa share their organic produce and sometimes offer wine-tastings. With children, friendly dogs, toys, and a swimming pool, this is ideal for families (Qb-€70–100, apartment for up to 8-€130, 1-week stay required in summer, discounts and 2-night minimum off-season, mountain-bike rentals, near Asciano, 30 min southeast of Siena, tel. 0577-704-791, mobile 335-692-5720, fax 0577-705-605, www.molinello.com, info@molinello.com).

North Tuscany

San Gimignano

The epitome of a Tuscan hill town, with 14 medieval towers still standing (out of an original 60 or so), San Gimignano is a perfectly preserved tourist trap. The locals seem corrupted by the easy money of tourism, and most of the rustic is faux. But San Gimignano is so easy to visit and visually so beautiful that it remains a good stop.

In the 13th century, back in the days of Romeo and Juliet, feuding noble families ran the towns. They'd periodi-

cally battle things out from the protection of their respective family towers. Pointy skylines, like San Gimignano's, were the norm

San Gimignano

To Ponte a Nappo Rooms

1. To Ponte a Nappo Rooms
2. Hotel la Cisterna
3. Arco di Goro Rooms
4. Santa Fina Rooms
5. Tortoli Rooms
6. Palazzo al Torrione
7. Trattoria Chiribiri
8. La Grotta Ghiotta
9. Locanda il Pino & Rist. il Pino
10. La Mangiatoia
11. Locanda di Sant'Agostino
12. Co-op Supermarket

in medieval Tuscany.

While the basic three-star sight here is the town of San Gimignano itself, there are a few worthwhile stops. From the town gate, head straight up the traffic-free town's cobbled main drag to Piazza della Cisterna (with its 13th-century well). The town sights cluster around the adjoining Piazza del Duomo.

Tourist Information: The helpful TI is in the old center on Piazza del Duomo (daily March–Oct 9:00–13:00 & 15:00–19:00, Nov–Feb 9:00–13:00 & 14:00–18:00, free maps, sells bus tickets, books rooms, tel. 0577-940-008, www.sangimignano.com, prolocsg@tin.it). You can drop your bag at the TI. The TI rents **audioguides** (€5 for 2-hr tour, exteriors only).

The town offers a two-hour **guided walk** in English and Italian at 15:00 daily except Sunday, March–Oct (€15, pay and meet at small TI—actually a hotel booking office—at Porta San Giovanni).

Helpful Hints: Thursday is **market day** on Piazza del Duomo, but for local merchants, every day is a sales frenzy. A public **WC** is just off Piazza della Cisterna (€0.50). A little electric **shuttle bus** does its laps all day from Porta San Giovanni to Piazza della Cisterna to Porta San Matteo (€0.50, 2/hr, buy ticket from TI or *tabacchi* shop).

SELF-GUIDED WALK

Welcome to San Gimignano

This quick walking tour will take you from the bus stop at Porta San Giovanni through the town's main squares to the Duomo and Sant'Agostino Church.

• *Start, as most tourists do, at the Porta San Giovanni gate at the bottom end of town.*

Porta San Giovanni: San Gimignano lies about 25 miles from both Siena and Florence, a good stop for pilgrims en route to those cities, and on a naturally fortified hilltop that encouraged settlement. The town's walls were built in the 13th century, with gates that helped regulate who came and went. Today, modern posts keep out all but service and emergency vehicles. The small square just outside the gate features a memorial to the town's WWII dead. Follow the pilgrims' route (and flood of modern tourists) through the gate and up the main drag.

About 100 yards up, on the right, is a pilgrims' shelter (12th-century, Pisan Romanesque). The Maltese cross indicates that this was built by the Knights of Malta. It was one of 11 such shelters in town. Today, only this shelter's wall remains.

• *Carry on, up to the town's central Piazza della Cisterna. Sit on the steps of the well.*

Piazza della Cisterna is named for the cistern that is served by the old well standing in the center of this square. A clever system of pipes drained rainwater from the nearby rooftops into the underground cistern. This square has been the center of the town since the ninth century. Each Thursday, it fills with a weekly market—as it has for over a thousand years.

• *Notice San Gimignano's famous towers.*

The Towers: Of the original 60 or so towers, only 14 survive. Before effective walls were developed, rich people fortified their own homes with these towers: They provided a handy refuge when ruffians and rival city-states were sacking the town. These towers became a standard part of medieval skylines. Even after town walls were built, the towers continued to rise—now to fortify noble families feuding within a town (Montague and Capulet style).

In the 14th century, San Gimignano's good times turned very bad. In the year 1300, about 13,000 lived within the walls. Then in 1348, a six-month plague decimated the population, leaving the once-mighty town with barely 4,000 alive. Once fiercely independent, now crushed and demoralized, San Gimignano came under Florence's control, and was forced to tear down its towers. (The Banca Toscana building is the remains of one such toppled tower.) And, to add injury to injury, Florence redirected the vital trade route away from San Gimignano. The town never recovered, and poverty left it in a 14th-century architectural time warp. That well-preserved cityscape, ironically, explains the town's prosperity today.

• *From the well, walk 30 yards uphill to the adjoining square with the cathedral.*

Piazza del Duomo faces the former cathedral. The twin towers to the right are 10th-century, among the first in town. The stubby tower opposite the church is typical of a merchant's tower: main door on ground floor, warehouse upstairs, holes to hold beams that once supported wooden balconies and exterior staircases, heavy stone on the first floor, cheaper and lighter brick for upper stories.

On the piazza are the Civic Museum and Torre Grossa, worth checking out (see "Sights," below). You'll also see the...

Duomo (or Collegiata): Walk inside San Gimignano's Romanesque cathedral. Sienese Gothic art (14th-century) lines the nave with parallel themes, Old Testament on the left and New Testament on the right. (For example: the suffering of Job opposite the suffering of Jesus; Creation facing the Annunciation; and the birth of Adam facing the Nativity.) This is a classic use of art to teach. Study the fine Creation series (top left). Many scenes are portrayed with a local 14th-century "slice of life" setting, to help lay townspeople relate to Jesus—in the same way that many white

Christians are more comfortable thinking of Jesus as white (€3.50, €5.50 combo-ticket includes mediocre Religious Art Museum, Mon–Fri 9:30–19:30, Sat 9:30–17:00, Sun 12:30–17:30).

From the church, hike uphill (passing the church on your left) following signs to *Rocca e Parco di Montestaffoli*. You'll enter a peaceful hilltop park and olive grove within the shell of a 14th-century fortress. A few steps take you to the top of a little tower (free) for the best views of San Gimignano's skyline; the far end of town and the Sant'Agostino Church (where this walk ends); and a commanding 360-degree view of the Tuscan countryside. San Gimignano is surrounded by olives, grapes, cypress trees and—in the Middle Ages—lots of wild dangers. Back then, farmers lived inside the walls and were thankful for the protection.

• *Return to the bottom of Piazza del Duomo, turn left, and continue your walk across town, cutting under the double arch (from the town's first wall) and into the new section where a line of fine noble palaces—now a happy can-can of wine shops and galleries—cheers you down Via San Matteo to...*

Sant'Agostino Church: This tranquil church, at the opposite end of town, has fewer crowds and more soul. Behind the altar, a lovely fresco cycle by Benozzo Gozzoli (who painted the exquisite Chapel of the Magi in the Medici-Riccardi Palace in Florence—see page 149) tells of the life of St. Augustine, a North African monk who preached simplicity. The kind, English-speaking friars (from England and the US) are happy to tell you about their church and way of life, and also have Mass in English on Sundays at 11:00. Pace the tranquil cloister before heading back into the tourist mobs (free, but €0.50 lights the frescoes, daily 7:00–12:00 & 15:00–19:00).

SIGHTS

Civic Museum (Museo Civico)—This small, fun museum is inside City Hall (Palazzo Comunale). Enter the room called Sala di Consiglio (a.k.a. Danti Hall). It's *molto* medieval and covered in festive frescoes, including the *Maestà* by Lippo Memmi. This virtual copy of Simone Martini's *Maestà* in Siena proves that Memmi doesn't have quite the same talent as his famous brother-in-law. Upstairs, the Pinacoteca displays a classy little painting collection, with a 1422 altarpiece by Taddeo di Bartolo honoring St. Gimignano. You can see the saint, with the town in his hands, surrounded by events from his life. As you exit, be sure to stop by the Camera del Podesta to check out the medieval dating scene (€5, includes Torre Grossa, audioguide-€2, daily March–Oct 9:30–19:00, Nov–Feb 10:00–17:00, Piazza del Duomo).

Torre Grossa—The city's tallest tower, at 200 feet, can be climbed

(€5, includes Civic Museum, same hours as museum, Piazza del Duomo).

SLEEPING

(€1 = about $1.20, country code: 39)
Although a zoo during the daytime, when evening comes, locals outnumber tourists, and San Gimignano becomes peaceful and enjoyable.

$$ Hotel la Cisterna, right on Piazza della Cisterna, offers 49 overpriced, predictable rooms, some with panoramic view terraces (Sb-€70, Db-€98, Db with terrace-€122, Db with view-€130, buffet breakfast, elevator, good restaurant with great view, discounts off-season, closed Jan–Feb, Piazza della Cisterna 23, tel. 0577-940-328, fax 0577-942-080, www.hotelcisterna.it, info@hotelcisterna.it, Alessio).

$$ Ponte a Nappo, run by enterprising Carla Rossi (who doesn't speak English) and her son Francisco (who does), has comfortable rooms and apartments in a farm just outside San Gimignano (Db-€70, apartments for 2–6 people €90–180 with this book in 2007, breakfast-€8, air-con, parking, 15-min walk or 5-min drive from Porta San Giovanni, tel. 0577-955-041, mobile 349-882-1565, fax 0577-941-268, www.accommodation-sangimignano.it, info@rossicarla.it). A picnic dinner—lounging on their comfy garden furniture as the sun sets—is good Tuscan living. About 100 yards below the monument square at Porta San Giovanni, find Via Vecchia (not left or right, but down a tiny road toward several listed accommodations).

$$ Palazzo al Torrione, just inside Porta San Giovanni, is quiet and handy. They have 10 modern rooms, generally better than hotels at two-thirds the price, but they don't have a full-time reception (Db-€70-110, breakfast-€5-10, family suites, cheap parking, inside and left of gate at Via Berignano 76; run from *tabacchi* shop which is 2 blocks away, just inside the gate on the main drag at Via San Giovanni 59; tel. 0577-940-480, mobile 338-938-1656, fax 0577-955-605, www.palazzoaltorrione.com, palazzoaltorrione@palazzoaltorrione.com, Francesco).

$ In-Town Rossi Apartments, owned by the same family, are in the town center (rooms are named Arco di Goro, Santa Fina, and Tortoli, Db-€55 with this book in 2007, fancy Db overlooking square-€85, same contact info as Ponte a Nappo farm, above). See their Web site for details on their confusing array of rooms for rent.

$ Locanda il Pino is tiny (5 rooms), super-clean, and quiet, run by a family above their elegant restaurant just inside Porta San Matteo (Db-€55, no breakfast, easy parking just outside the gate,

Via Cellolese 4, tel. 0577-940-415, laurabeconcini@supereva.it). While far from the bus stop, this is a great value for those with a car.

EATING

Trattoria Chiribiri, just inside Porta San Giovanni, serves home-made pastas and desserts at a remarkably fair price (daily 11:00–23:00, Piazza della Madonna 1, tel. 0577-941-948).

La Mangiatoia is a good local splurge, especially if you like wild game and candlelight (pastas-€10, *secondi*-€16, Wed–Mon 12:30–14:30 & 19:30–22:00, closed Tue, good outdoor seating, near Porta San Matteo at Via Mainardi 5, tel. 0577-941528).

Ristorante il Pino, run by the same family since 1929, is subdued, pricey, and dressy. It's *the* place for "dainty game" on pink tablecloths under medieval arches (Fri–Wed 12:30–14:00 & 19:30–22:00, closed Thu, seafood as well as game, Via Cellolese 8, tel. 0577-940-415).

La Grotta Ghiotta makes good soup and sandwiches that can be packed up *portare via*—to go (daily 12:00–20:00, Via Santo Stefano 10, tel. 0577-942-074).

Locanda di Sant'Agostino spills out onto the peaceful square, facing Sant'Agostino Church. It's cheap and cheery, serving lunch and dinner daily. Dripping with onions and atmosphere on the inside, there's shady on-the-square seating outside (closed Jan, tel. 0577-943-141).

Picnics: The big, modern **Co-Op supermarket** sells all you need for a nice spread (Mon–Sat 8:30–20:00, closed Sun, at parking lot below Porta San Giovanni). Or browse the little shops guarded by wild boar heads within the town walls; they sell boar meat (*cinghiale;* cheeng-gee-AH-lay). Pick up 100 grams (about a quarter pound) of boar, cheese, bread, and wine and enjoy a picnic in the garden at the Rocca or the park outside Porta San Giovanni.

TRANSPORTATION CONNECTIONS

From San Gimignano by Bus to: Florence (hourly, 1.25–2 hrs min, change in Poggibonsi), **Siena** (5/day, 75 min, more with change in Poggibonsi), **Volterra** (4/day, 2 hrs, change in Colle di Val d'Elsa). Sunday buses are few, far between, and crowded. Bus tickets are sold at the bar just inside the town gate or at the TI. While the town has no formal baggage-check service, the TI will let you park your bags there for free.

Drivers: You can't drive within the walled town of San Gimignano, but a parking lot waits just a few steps outside the town. San Gimignano is an easy 45-minute drive from Florence (exit Florence via Porta Romana, follow blue signs to Siena, Route SS2; exit the freeway at Poggibonsi). San Gimignano has three pay lots a short walk outside the walls, and free places farther away. The handiest lot (Parcheggio Montemaggio, just outside Porta San Giovanni) fills up early, but those arriving from the north can wait for a spot—as one car leaves, the gate allows another to enter (€2/hr).

Volterra

Encircled by impressive walls and topped with a grand fortress, Volterra sits high above the rich farmland. More than 2,000 years ago, Volterra was one of the most important Etruscan cities, a city much larger than the one we see today. Greek-trained Etruscan artists worked here, leaving a significant stash of art, particularly funerary urns. Eventually absorbed into the Roman Empire, the city bitterly fought against the Florentines in the Middle Ages, but like many Tuscan towns, it lost in the end and was given a fortress atop the city to "protect" its citizens.

Compact and walkable, the city stretches out from the pleasant Piazza dei Priori to the old city gates. Unlike other famous towns in Tuscany, Volterra feels not cutesy or touristy...but real, vibrant, and almost oblivious to the allure of the tourist dollar. A refreshing break from its more commercial neighbors, it's my favorite small town in Tuscany.

Tourist Information: The helpful TI is on the main square, at Piazza dei Priori 20 (daily 10:00–13:00 & 14:00–18:00, €5 audio-guides discounted 20 percent with this book, tel. 0588-87257). **Market day** is on Saturday.

Local Guide: American Annie Adair married into the local community, organizes American marriages in Tuscany, and is an excellent private guide (€100/half-day, €200/day, mobile 347-143-5004, tel. & fax 0588-87774, www.tuscantour.com, info @tuscantour.com).

SIGHTS

▲**Porta all'Arco**—Volterra's most famous sight is its Etruscan Gate, built of massive, volcanic tufa stones in the fourth century B.C. Volterra's original wall was four miles around—twice the size of the wall that encircles it today. With 25,000 people, Volterra was a key Etruscan trade center—one of 12 leading towns that made up the Etruscan Dodecapolis (a league of Etruscan cities). The three seriously eroded heads, dating from the first century

Volterra

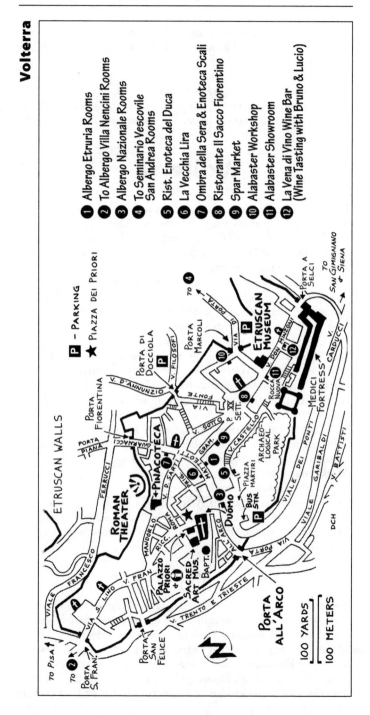

1. Albergo Etruria Rooms
2. To Albergo Villa Nencini Rooms
3. Albergo Nazionale Rooms
4. To Seminario Vescovile San Andrea Rooms
5. Rist. Enoteca del Duca
6. La Vecchia Lira
7. Ombra della Sera & Enoteca Scali
8. Ristorante Il Sacco Fiorentino
9. Spar Market
10. Alabaster Workshop
11. Alabaster Showroom
12. La Vena di Vino Wine Bar (Wine Tasting with Bruno & Lucio)

P – PARKING

★ PIAZZA DEI PRIORI

B.C., show what happens when you leave something outside for 2,000 years. The newer stones are part of the 13th-century city wall, which incorporated parts of the much older Etruscan wall.

A plaque just outside remembers June 30, 1944. Near that time, Nazi forces were planning to blow up the arch to slow the Allied advance. To save their treasured landmark, Volterrans ripped up the stones that pave Via Porta all'Arco and plugged the gate, managing to convince the Nazi commander that there was no need to blow up the arch. Today, all the stones are back in their places, and, like silent heroes, they welcome you through the oldest-standing Etruscan gate into Volterra.

Pass through the arch. Wander up Via Porta all'Arco 50 yards, then climb left up Via Laberinti to a viewpoint. (On a clear day you can see the Mediterranean and the mountains of Corsica.) Continue uphill, pondering the town's nickname, "The City of Wind and Rock," until Vicolo degli Abbandonati deposits you on Piazza San Giovanni, where you face the cathedral.

Duomo—A common arrangement in the Middle Ages was for the church to face the baptistery (you couldn't enter the church until you were baptized)...and for the hospital to face the cemetery. All of these overlooked the same square. That's how it is in Pisa, as it is here.

This 12th-century church is not as elaborate as its cousin in Pisa, but the simple facade and central nave flanked by monolithic stone columns are beautiful examples of the Pisan Romanesque style. The chapel to the left of the entry has unusual, large dioramas with painted terra-cotta figures. The interior was decorated mostly in the late 16th century, during Florentine rule under the Medici family (and much restored in the 19th century). You'll see a lot of the Medici coat of arms (with the six pills, representing the family's first trade—as doctors or *medici*). The 12th-century pulpit is beautifully carved. All of the apostles are together except Judas, who's under the table with the evil dragon (his name is the only one not carved onto the relief). The dreamy painted-and-gilded-wood Deposition (Jesus being taken down from the cross, 13th-century) is restored true to its original form, showing emotion and motion way ahead of its time. Recorded Gregorian chants add to the church's wonderful ambience (free, daily 8:00–12:30 & 15:00–17:00).

Sacred Art Museum—This humble three-room museum collects sacred art from deconsecrated churches and small, unguarded

Under the Etruscan Sun
(c. 900 B.C.–A.D. 1)

Around 550 B.C.—just before the Golden Age of Greece—the Etruscan people of central Italy had their own Golden Age. Though their origins are mysterious, their mix of Greek-style art with Roman-style customs helped lay a civilized foundation for the rise of Rome. As you travel through Tuscany (from "Etruscan") you'll find traces of this long-lost people.

Etruscan tombs and artifacts are still being discovered, often by farmers in the countryside. Museums in Volterra and Cortona house fine collections of urns, pottery, and devotional figures. You can visit several domed tombs outside of Cortona.

The Etruscans first appeared in the ninth century B.C., when a number of cities sprouted up in sparsely populated Tuscany and Umbria, including today's hill towns of Cortona, Chiusi, and Volterra. Perhaps they were immigrants from Turkey, but more likely they were local farmers who moved to the city, became traders and craftsmen, and welcomed new ideas from Greece.

More technologically advanced than their neighbors, the Etruscans mined metal, exporting it around the Mediterranean, both as crude ingots and as some of the finest-crafted jewelry in the known world. They drained and irrigated large tracts of land, creating the fertile farmland of central Italy's breadbasket. With their disciplined army, warships, merchant vessels, and (from the Greek perspective) pirate galleys, they ruled central Italy and the major ports along the Tyrrhenian Sea. For nearly two centuries (c. 700–500 B.C.), much of Italy lived a golden age of peace and prosperity under the Etruscan sun.

Judging from the many luxury items that have survived, the Etruscans enjoyed the good life. Frescoes show men and women looking remarkably like how the Greeks and Romans described them: healthy, vibrant, and well-dressed, playing flutes, dancing with birds, or playing party games. Etruscan artists celebrated individual people, showing their wrinkles, crooked noses, silly smiles, and funny haircuts.

Thousands upon thousands of surviving ceramic plates, cups, and vases attest to the importance of food. Men and women ate together, propped on their elbows on dining couches, surrounded by colorful frescoes and terra-cotta tiles. According to contemporary accounts, the Etruscans were Europe's best-dressed people, even their slaves. The banqueters were entertained with music and dancing and served by elegant and well-treated slaves.

Scholars today have deciphered the Etruscans' Greek-style alphabet and some individual words, but they've yet to fully master the grammar or crack the code.

Much of what we know of the Etruscans comes from their

The Etruscan Empire

tombs, often clustered in a necropolis. The tomb was a home in the hereafter, fully furnished for the afterlife, complete with all the deceased's belongings. The sarcophagus might have a statue on the lid of the deceased at a banquet—lying across a dining couch, spooning with his wife, smiles on their faces, living the good life for all eternity.

Seven decades of wars with the Greeks (545–474 B.C.) disrupted the trade routes and drained the League, just as a new Mediterranean power was emerging...Rome. In 509 B.C., the Romans overthrew their Etruscan king, and Rome expanded, capturing Etruscan cities one by one (the last in 264 B.C.). Etruscan resisters were killed, the survivors intermarried with Romans, their kids grew up speaking Latin, and the culture became Romanized. By Julius Caesar's time, the only remnants of Etruscan culture were Etruscan priests, who became Rome's professional soothsayers, or fortune-tellers. Interestingly, the Etruscan prophets had foreseen their own demise, having predicted that Etruscan civilization would last 10 centuries.

But Etruscan culture lived on in Roman religion (pantheon of gods, household gods, and divination rituals), art (realism), lifestyle (the banquet), and in a taste for Greek styles—the mix that became our "Western civilization."

churches from nearby villages (€8 combo-ticket includes Etruscan Museum and Pinacoteca, daily 9:00–13:00 & 15:00–18:00, morning only in winter, well-explained in English, next to the Duomo at Via Roma 1).

▲**Etruscan Museum (Museo Etrusco Guarnacci)**—Filled top to bottom with rare Etruscan artifacts, this museum—even with few English explanations—makes it easy to appreciate how advanced this pre-Roman culture was. The exhibit, while pretty dusty and old school, is considered the third-best Etruscan museum anywhere, after the Vatican and the British Museum. It starts with the pre-Etruscan Villanovian artifacts (c. 1500 B.C.). The seemingly endless collection of funerary urns (designed to contain the ashes of cremated loved ones) all show the subject lounging, as if kicking back with the gods at some heavenly banquet, popping grapes and just enjoying the moment. They indicate that the Etruscans believed you'd have fun in the afterlife. Artifacts such as mirrors, coins, and jewelry offer a peek into this fascinating culture. Giacometti fans will be amazed at how the tall, skinny figure called *The Shadow of Night (L'Ombra della Sera)* looks just like the modern Swiss sculptor's work—only 2,500 years older (€8, includes—like it or not—the Pinacoteca and Sacred Art Museum, daily 9:00–19:00, Nov–March closes at 13:45, mildly interesting English pamphlet available, audioguide-€3, Via Don Minzoni 15, tel. 0588-86-347). An alabaster workshop and a recommended wine bar are across the street; see listings below.

Pinacoteca—This museum fills a 14th-century palace with fine paintings that feel more Florentine than Sienese—a reminder of whose domain this town was in. Its highlights are Luca Signorelli's beautifully lit *Annunciation*, an example of classic High Renaissance (from the town cathedral), and (to the right) *Deposition from the Cross*, the ground-breaking Mannerist work by Rosso Fiorentino (note the elongated bodies and harsh emotional lighting and colors). Notice also Ghirlandaio's *Christ in Glory*. The two devout-looking, kneeling women are actually pagan, pre-Christian Etruscan demi-goddesses, Attinea and Greciniana, but the church identified them as obscure saints to make the painting acceptable (€8 combo-ticket includes Etruscan and Sacred Art museums, daily April–Oct 9:00–19:00, Nov–March closes at 13:45, Via dei Sarti 1, tel. 0588-87-580).

Roman Theater—Built around 10 B.C., this well-preserved theater is considered to have some of the best acoustics of its kind. Because of the fine aerial view you get from the city wall promenade, you may find it unnecessary to pay admission to enter. Belly up to the 13th-century wall and look down. The wall you're standing on divided the theater from the town center...so, naturally, the theater became the town dump. Over time, the theater was forgotten—

covered in the garbage of Volterra. Luckily, it was rediscovered in the 1950s.

The stage wall was standard Roman design—with three levels from which actors would appear: one for humans, one for heroes, and the top one for gods. Parts of two levels still stand. Gods leaped out onto the third level for the last time in the fourth century A.D., when the town decided to abandon the theater and to use its stones to build fancy baths instead. You can see the remains of the baths behind the theater, including the round sauna with brick supports to raise the heated floor (€2, but you can view the theater free from Via Lungo le Mure, April–Oct daily 10:30–17:30, Nov–March Sat–Sun only 10:00–16:00).

From the vantage point on the city wall promenade, you can trace Volterra's vast Etruscan wall. Find the church in the distance, on the left, and notice the stones just below. They are from the Etruscan wall that followed the ridge into the valley and defined Volterra five centuries before Christ.

Palazzo dei Priori—Volterra's City Hall (c. 1209) claims to be the oldest of any Tuscan city-state. It clearly inspired the more famous Palazzo Vecchio in Florence. Town halls like this were emblematic of an era when city-states were powerful. They were architectural exclamation points declaring that, around here, no pope or emperor called the shots. Towns such as Volterra were truly city-states—proudly independent and relatively democratic. They had their own armies, taxes, and even weights and measures. Notice the horizontal "cane" cut into the City Hall wall. For a thousand years, this square hosted a market and the "cane" was the local yardstick. When not in use for meetings, the city council chambers—lavishly painted and lit with fun dragon lamps—are open to visitors (daily April–Oct 10:30–17:30, Nov–March Sat–Sun only 10:00–17:00).

▲Via Matteotti—The town's main drag, named after the popular socialist leader killed by the Fascists in 1924, provides a good cultural scavenger hunt and guided walk. Start your walk just 30 yards from the Palazzo dei Priori (City Hall) at the start of Via Matteotti. At #1 there's a typical Italian bank security door. (Step in and say, "Beam me up, Scotty.") Look up and all around. Find the medieval griffin torch holder—symbol of Volterra—and imagine the town torch lit. The pharmacy sports the symbol of its medieval guild. As you head down Via Matteotti, notice how the doors show centuries of refitting work—be careful. There's a wild boar, which is a local delicacy, at #10.

At #12, notice how the typical palace, once the home of a single rich family, is now occupied by many middle-class families (judging from the line of doorbells). After the social revolution in the 18th century and the rise of the middle class, former palaces were condominium-ized. Even so (like in *Dr. Zhivago*), the original family still lives here. Apartment #1 is the home of Count Guidi.

At #19, La Vecchia Lira is a lively cafeteria (see page 358). The Bar L'Incontro is a favorite for homemade gelato and pastries. Until recently, #20 was the headquarters of the local Communist party. Americans get all Khrushchev-nervous when confronted with euro-communism, but in Western Europe it's actually a mild form of socialism that remains pretty strong today. Bologna is famously red, as is Tuscany in general. In the 1970s, 60 percent of Tuscany voted communist. The strength of the local Communist party has its roots in WWII anti-fascism.

Across the street, up Vicolo delle Prigioni, is a fun bakery. They're happy to sell small quantities if you want to try the local *cantuccini* (almond biscotti) or munch a cannoli.

At #27, look up and imagine heavy beams cantilevered out, supporting extra wooden rooms, and balconies crowding out over the street. Throughout Tuscany, today's stark and stony old building fronts once supported a tangle of wooden extensions. Doors that once led to these extra rooms are now half-bricked up to make windows. Imagine the density in the 14th century, before the plague thinned out the population.

At #30, pop into an alabaster showroom. Alabaster, quarried nearby, has long been a big industry here. Volterra alabaster—softer and more porous than marble—was sliced thin to serve as windows for Italy's medieval churches. At #51, a bit of Etruscan wall is artfully used to display more alabaster art. And #56 is the surreal alabaster art gallery of Paolo Sabatini.

Locals gather early each evening at #57 for the best cocktails in town—served with free munchies. The cinema is across the street. Movies in Italy are rarely in *versione originale*. Italians are used to getting their movies dubbed into Italian.

At #66, the end of the street is marked by another Tuscan tower. This noble house has a ground floor with no interior access to the safe upper floors. Rope ladders were used to get upstairs. The tiny door was wide enough to let in your skinny friends...but definitely no one wearing armor and carrying big weapons.

Alabaster Workshop—Alab'Arte offers a fun peek into the art of alabaster. Their showroom is across from the Etruscan Museum. A block downhill is their powdery workshop, where you can watch Roberto Chiti and Giorgio Finazzo at work. Lighting shows off the translucent quality of the stone and the expertise of these artists (Mon–Sat 9:00–13:00 & 15:00–19:00, closed Sun, showroom at Via Don Minzoni 18, workshop at Via Orti Sant'Agostino 28, tel. 0588-85-506). If you want to see more artisans in action, ask the TI for their list of the town's many workshops open to the public.

Wine Tasting with Bruno and Lucio—La Vena di Vino, also just across from the Etruscan Museum, is a fun *enoteca* where two guys have devoted themselves to the wonders of wine and share it with a fun-loving passion. Each day Bruno and Lucio open six or eight bottles, serve your choice by the glass, pair it with characteristic munchies, and offer fine music (guitars available for patrons) and an unusual decor (the place is strewn with bras). Here is your chance to try the latest phenom in the wine world, the Super Tuscan—a creative mix of international grapes grown in Tuscany. According to Bruno, "While the Brunello (€6 a glass) is just right for wild boar, the Super Tuscan (€5) is just right for meditation" (Wed–Mon 12:00–24:00, closed Tue, Via Don Minzoni 30, tel. 0588-81-491).

Medici Fortress and Archaeological Park—The Parco Archeologico marks what was the acropolis of Volterra from 1500 B.C. until A.D. 1472, when Florence conquered the pesky city and burned its political and historic center, turning it into a grassy commons (today's park) and building the adjacent Medici Fortezza. The old fortress—a symbol of Florentine dominance—now keeps people in rather than out. It's a maximum-security prison housing only 60-or-so special prisoners. (Note that when you're driving from San Gimignano to Volterra, you pass another big, modern prison—almost surreal in the midst of all the Tuscan wonder.) Authorities prefer to keep organized crime figures locked up far away from their family ties in Sicily.

SLEEPING

(€1 = about $1.20, country code: 39)
$$ Albergo Etruria, on Volterra's main drag, rents 21 fresh, modern, and spacious rooms within an ancient stone structure. They have a welcoming TV lounge and a great roof garden (Sb-€70, Db-€90, Tb-€110, 10 percent discount with cash and this book in 2007, Via Matteotti 32, tel. 0588-87377, fax 0588-92784, www.albergoetruria.it, info@albergoetruria.it). Lisa and Giuseppina take very good care of their guests.

$$ Albergo Villa Nencini, just outside of town, is big, modern, and professional, with 36 fine rooms, a large pool, and free parking (Sb-€62, Db-€83, Tb-€112, 10 percent discount with cash and this book in 2007, Borgo San Stefano 55, a 10-minute walk to main square, tel. 0588-86386, fax 0588-80601, www.villanencini.it, info@villanencini.it, run by Nencini family).

$$ Albergo Nazionale, with 38 big rooms, is clean, simple, and steps from the bus stop (Sb-€56, Db-€81, Tb-€112, less off-season, Via dei Marchesi 11, tel. 0588-86284, fax 0588-84097, www.hotelnazionale-volterra.com, info@hotelnazionale-volterra.com).

$ Seminario Vescovile San Andrea has been training priests for 500 years. Today, the remaining eight priests still train students, and their 30 rooms—separated by vast and holy halls—are rented very cheap to travelers (S-€14, Sb-€18, D-€28, Db-€36, T-€42, Tb-€54, breakfast-€3, closed at 24:00, groups welcome, Viale Vittorio Veneto 2, tel. 0588-86028, semvescovile@diocesivolterra.it).

EATING

Ristorante Enoteca del Duca, with a locally respected chef, serves refined Tuscan cuisine. You can dine under a medieval arch, with walls lined with wine bottles, or on a nice little patio out back (food-sampler menù-€40, pastas-€8, *secondi*-€15, a good place for truffles, fine wine list, closed Tue, near City Hall at Via di Castello 2, tel. 0588-81510).

La Vecchia Lira is a classy self-serve eatery that's a hit with locals as a quick and cheap lunch spot by day, and a fancier fish restaurant at night (Fri–Wed 12:00–15:00 & 19:30–22:30, closed Thu, Via Matteotti 19, tel. 0588-86180).

Ombra della Sera serves the best pizza in town and more (Tue–Sun 12:00–15:00 & 19:00–22:00, closed Mon, Via Guarnacci 16, tel. 0588-85274).

Ristorante Il Sacco Fiorentino is a local favorite for traditional cuisine (Thu–Tue 12:00–14:45 & 19:00–21:45, closed Wed, Piazza XX Settembre 18, tel. 0588-88537).

For fresh sandwiches and wine, try friendly **Enoteca Scali** (daily 9:00–22:00, Via Guarnacci 3, tel. 0588-81170).

Picnics: You can assemble a picnic at the few *alimentari* around town (try Spar Market at Via Gramsci 12) and eat in the breezy Archaeological Park.

TRANSPORTATION CONNECTIONS

From Volterra by Bus to: Florence (4/day, 2 hrs, change in Colle Val d'Elsa), **Siena** (4/day, 2 hrs, change in Colle di Val d'Elsa), **San Gimignano** (4/day, 2 hrs, change in Colle di Val d'Elsa), **Pisa** (9/day, 2 hrs, change in Pontedera). Buses come and go from Volterra's Piazzi Martiri della Libertà (buy tickets at any *tabacchi* shop). For Siena, Florence, and San Gimignano, Tra-In bus tickets only get you as far as Colle di Val d'Elsa; you must then buy another ticket (from another bus company) at the newsstand near the bus stop. There is virtually no bus service in or out of Volterra on Sundays or holidays.

Drivers: The town is ringed with easy and free parking lots. The most central (and only underground) lot is a pay lot at Piazza Martiri della Libertà (La Dobana, €1.40/hr or €10/24 hrs).

MORE NORTH TUSCAN SIGHTS

Chianti Sculpture Park—This unique, outdoor, contemporary sculpture park lies within a peaceful 35-acre forest, and features large works by renowned artists from five continents. Most pieces were designed for a specific site within the park and are gracefully integrated with their natural surroundings (€7.50, April–Oct daily 10:00–sunset, Nov–March by reservation only, gift shop sells sculptures, located roughly between Florence and Siena, La Fornace 48/49, tel. 0577-357-151, fax 0577-357-149, www.chiantisculpturepark.it).

FLORENTINE HISTORY

EIGHT CENTURIES IN 10 PAGES

59 B.C.–A.D. 1200:
Roman, Early Christian, Medieval

It's the usual Rome story—military outpost, thriving provincial cap-
ital, conversion to Christianity, overrun by barbarians—except Florence really didn't fall. Proud medieval Florentines traced their roots back to civilized Rome, and the city remained a Tuscan commercial center during the Dark Ages.

Sights
- Piazza della Repubblica (the old Forum)
- Find the ancient Roman military camp on today's street map. You can still see the rectangular grid plan—lined up with compass points, rather than the river.
- Baptistery (built c. 1050), likely on site of Roman temple
- Roman and Etruscan fragments (Duomo Museum)

1200s: Urban Growth

Woolen cloth manufacture, trade, and banking made urban mer-
chants—organized into guilds—more powerful than rural, feudal nobles. Florence, now a largely independent city-state, allied with nearby cities.

Sights
- Bargello (it was built as the City Hall)
- Santa Croce and Santa Maria Novella churches
- Baptistery interior mosaics

1300s: Prosperity, Plague, Recovery

As part of a budding democracy with civic pride, Florence's guilds and merchants financed major construction projects (some begun in late 1200s). But the population of 90,000 was suddenly cut nearly in half by the Black Death (bubonic plague) of 1348. Recovery was slowed by more plagues, bank failures, and political rivalries.

Sights
- Duomo and Campanile (original decorations in Duomo Museum)
- Palazzo Vecchio
- Orsanmichele Church
- Santa Croce, Santa Maria Novella, and Giotto's bell-tower design and his paintings in Uffizi

1400s: Renaissance and Medicis

While 1500 marks Europe's Renaissance, in Florence—where the whole revival of classical culture got its start—the Renaissance

began and ended in the 1400s (the Quattrocento). The Medicis (MED-ee-chee), a rich textile-and-banking family whose wealth gave them political leverage around Europe, ruled the most prosperous city in Italy, appeasing the masses with philanthropy and public art.

Sights
- Brunelleschi's Duomo dome and Pazzi Chapel
- Donatello's statues in Bargello, Duomo Museum, and on Orsanmichele exterior
- Ghiberti's two bronze doors on Baptistery (originals in Duomo Museum)
- Botticelli's paintings in Uffizi
- The Uffizi, tracing painting from medieval to Michelangelo
- The Bargello, tracing sculpture

- Masaccio's frescoes in Santa Maria Novella and Brancacci Chapel
- Fra Angelico paintings (and Savonarola history) in San Marco Museum

1500–1800:
Decline, Medici Dukes, Renaissance Goes South

Bankrupt, the anti-democratic Medicis were exiled to Rome, where they married into royalty and returned—backed by foreign powers—as even less democratic nobles. The
"Renaissance spirit" moved elsewhere, taking Michelangelo, Leonardo, and Raphael with it. In succeeding centuries, the Medici dukes ruled an economically and politically declining city, but still financed art.

Sights
- Michelangelo's Florentine works—*David*, Medici Chapels, and Laurentian Library
- Pitti Palace and Boboli Gardens (the later Medici palace)
- Later paintings (Uffizi) and statues (Bargello)
- Destruction of the original Duomo facade (Duomo Museum)
- Medici Chapels—pompous tombs of (mostly) later Medicis
- Ponte Vecchio cleaned up for jewelry shops
- Baroque interiors of many older churches
- Galileo's finger, telescopes, and experiments in Science Museum

1800s: Italian Unification

After years of rule by Austrian nobles, Florence peacefully booted

the *ausländers* and joined the Italian unification movement. It even briefly served as modern Italy's capital (1865–1870). Artistic revival of both medieval (neo-Gothic) and Renaissance (Neoclassical) styles.

Sights
- Duomo's current neo-Gothic facade
- Piazza della Repubblica, commemorating unification, fine 19th-century cafés

1900s:
Uncontrolled Urbanization, Urban Renewal

Population growth, rapid industrialization, WWII destruction,

and the 20-foot-high flood of 1966 made Florence a chaotic, noisy, dirty, traffic-choked city. In the last 30 years, however, the tourist zone has been cleaned and cleared, museums revamped, hours extended, and the people have adapted to welcoming foreign visitors. Now if they could just do something about those Vespas....

FLORENCE TIMELINE

500 B.C.–A.D.1000:
Etruscans, Romans, and "Barbarians"

c. 550 B.C. Etruscans settle in Fiesole, near Florence.

59 B.C. Julius Caesar establishes the Roman town of Florentia (meaning flowering or flourishing) at a convenient crossing point of the Arno River.

c. A.D. 200 Thriving Roman city, pop. 10,000.

c. 350 In the wake of Constantine's legalization of Christianity, Bishop (and Saint) Zenobius builds a church where the Duomo stands today.

450 Rome falls. Ostrogoths from the east, Byzantines from modern-day Turkey, and Germanic barbarians sweep through in waves. But Florence survives as a small trading town.

800 Charlemagne's Franks sweep through; he becomes the first Holy Roman Emperor. Florence is part of the Empire for the next 300 years, and is the regional capital (rather than Fiesole).

1000–1400:
Medieval Rise and Political Squabbles

c. 1050 Baptistery built, likely on site of ancient Roman temple.

1100 Matilda, Countess of Tuscany, allies with the pope and rises against the German-based Holy Roman Empire, gaining independence for Florence.

1200 Florence is the leading city in Tuscany, thriving on wool manufacture, trade, banking, and moneylending.

Guelphs vs. Ghibellines

Pope	Emperor
Middle-class merchants and craftsmen	Aristocrats of feudal order
Urban (new economy)	Rural (traditional economy)
Independence of city-states under local Italian leaders	Unification of small states under traditional dukes and kings

But really, the fight was about power, not ideology. (It wasn't what you believed, but with whom you were allied.) The names always mean something different depending on the particular place and time.

1215 Political assassination of Buondelmonte epitomizes power struggles among nobles (Ghibellines), rich merchants and craftsmen (Guelphs), and laborers. The different factions seek support from outsiders—Guelphs ally with pope, Ghibellines with emperor. In general, Ghibellines dominate in first half of 1200s.

1222–1235 Florentine armies defeat Pisa, Siena, and Pistoia. Florence is the dominant city-state in Tuscany, heading a rich, commercial marketplace.

1252 Gold florin minted, one of Europe's strongest currencies.

1266 Merchants and craftsmen (Guelphs), organized into guilds, oust nobles and establish the *primo popolo*, the first "rule by the people."

1293 Guelphs solidify rule by the rich middle class, establishing a constitution that forbids nobles and laborers from holding office. The Ghibellines are gone, but bitter political infighting continues, with Florence divided between Black and White Guelphs.

1296 Construction begins on the Duomo. Santa Croce and Santa Maria Novella are also being built.

1302 The poet Dante, a prominent White Guelph, is exiled. Traveling around Europe and Italy, he writes his epic poem *The Divine Comedy*.

1347 Florence's population is 90,000, making it one of Europe's biggest cities.

1348 Population nearly halved after the horrific bubonic plague. In addition, recent bank failures and ongoing political squabbles make recovery more difficult.

1378 The Ciompi revolt, led by wool-factory workers, is suppressed by rich merchant families. The guilds (workers' unions) lose power as a few wealthy families rise—the Strozzi, Ricci, Alberti, and...Medici.

1400s, The "Quattrocento": A Prosperous Renaissance City Under Medici Princes

1401 Baptistery door competition energizes an already civic-minded city.

1406 Florence, by conquering Pisa, gains a port and becomes a sea-trading power.

1421 Giovanni de' Medici, a shrewd businessman, expands the Medici family business from wool manufacture into banking.

1434 Cosimo the Elder (Giovanni's son) returns triumphant from exile to rule Florence. Outwardly, he honors the Florentine constitution, but, in fact, he uses his great wealth to rule as a tyrant, buying popularity with lavish patronage of public art.

1436 Dedication of the Duomo, topped by Brunelleschi's dome.

1440 Battle of Anghiari—Florence defeats Milan.

c. 1440 Donatello's *David*.

1458 Cosimo the Elder creates a rubber-stamp Council of the Hundred.

1464 Cosimo's son, Piero the Gouty, rules stiffly but ably.

1469 Lorenzo the Magnificent, Cosimo's grandson, rules over the most powerful city in Italy. He is a popular politician but a so-so businessman.

1492 Lorenzo dies. Many Medici banks go bankrupt. Lorenzo's son, Piero the Unfortunate, facing an invasion force from France, appears to side with the foreigners.

1494 The Medici family, reviled as bankrupt morally, financially, and politically, is exiled. In the political vacuum, the monk Girolamo Savonarola appears as a voice of moral authority. He re-establishes the Florentine constitution.

1498 Savonarola is hanged and burned on Piazza della Signoria by political enemies and a citizenry tired of his morally strict rule. The constitution-driven republic continues.

1500–1800:
The "Later" Medicis Oversee Florence's Decline

1501 Michelangelo begins sculpting *David*.

1512 The Medici family, having established a power base in Rome, returns to take political power as tyrants, backed by the pope and the Spanish army of Holy Roman Emperor Charles V.

1513 Lorenzo the Magnificent's son, Giovanni, becomes Pope Leo X.

1523 Lorenzo's nephew becomes Pope Clement VII.

1527 Renegade, unpaid mercenary troops loot Rome. In the political chaos that follows, Florentines drive the Medicis from Florence, reestablishing a republic.

1530 After a year-long siege, Pope Clement VII and Charles V retake Florence, abolishing the republic and reinstalling Medici rulers.

1533 The Medicis marry off Catherine de' Medici to the future King Henry II of France.

1537 Cosimo the Younger, a Medici descended from Cosimo the Elder's brother, is made Duke of Florence. He and his wife, Eleanor of Toledo, rule as tyrannical nobles but beautify the city with the Uffizi, a renovated Palazzo Vecchio, and a rebuilt Pitti Palace.

1574 Francesco I becomes duke, soon to be followed by various Ferdinandos and Cosimos. Florence is now a minor player in world affairs, a small dukedom with a stagnant economy.

1587 The medieval facade of the Duomo is torn down. It remains bare brick for the next 200 years while different proposals are debated.

1600 Maria de' Medici marries Henry IV to become Queen of France.

1610–1633 Galileo, backed by the Medici family, works in Florence.

1737 Gian Gastone, the last of the Medici line, dies. Florence is ruled by Austrian Hapsburg nobles.

1800–Present:
Florence Enters the Modern World

1799 Napoleon "liberates" the city, briefly establishing a pseudo-democracy with his sister as duchess.

1814 Napoleon falls, and the city returns to Austrian rule, under a distant descendant of the Medici family.

1848 Florentine citizens join an uprising all over Italy against foreign rule. The Risorgimento is on.

1860 Florence joins the kingdom of Victor Emmanuel, forming the nucleus of united, democratic, modern Italy.

1865 Florence is made Italy's capital (until the liberation of Rome in 1870).

1944 Under Nazi occupation as the Allies close in, all of the Arno bridges except the Ponte Vecchio are blown up.

1966 A disastrous flood, up to nearly 20 feet high, covers the city's buildings and art treasures in mud. The city is a cultural, economic, and touristic mess. An international effort of volunteer "mud angels" slowly brings these treasures back into view.

1993 The Mafia tries to strike terror with a bomb that destroys a section of the Uffizi, but the museum and the city recover. With a thriving university, scads of Internet cafés, and sparkling clean museums, Florence is a model cultural destination.

2007 You visit Florence, the art capital of Europe.

RENAISSANCE FLORENCE: CRADLE OF THE MODERN WORLD

There was something dynamic about the Florentines. Pope Boniface VIII said there were five elements: earth, air, fire, water... and Florentines. For 200 years, starting in the early 1300s, their city was a cultural hub.

Florence's contributions to Western culture are immense: the whole revival of the arts, humanism, and science; the seeds of democracy; the modern Italian language (which grew out of the popular Florentine dialect); the art of Botticelli, Leonardo, and Michelangelo; the writings of Machiavelli, Boccaccio, and Dante; and the explorations of Amerigo Vespucci, who gave his name to a newly discovered continent. Florentines considered themselves descendants of the highly cultured people of the Roman Empire. But Florence, even in its Golden Age, was always a mixture of lustiness and refinement. The streets were filled with tough-talking, hardened, illiterate merchants who strode about singing verses from Dante's *Divine Comedy*.

Florentine culture came from money, and that money came from the wool trade, silk factories, and banking. The city had a large middle class and strong guilds (labor unions for skilled craftsmen). Success was a matter of civic pride, and Florentines showed that pride in the mountains of money they spent to rebuild and beautify the city.

Technically, Florence was a republic, ruled by elected citizens rather than nobility. While there was some opportunity for upward mobility among the middle class, most power was in the hands of a few wealthy banking families. The most powerful was the Medici family. The Medici bank had branches in 10 cities in Europe, including London, Geneva, Bruges (Belgium), and Lyon (France). The pope kept his checking account in the Rome branch. The Florentine florin was the monetary standard of the Continent.

Florence dominated Italy economically and culturally, but not militarily. The independent Italian city-states squabbled and remained scattered until the nationalist movement four centuries later. (When someone suggested to the Renaissance Florentine Niccolò Machiavelli that the Italian city-states might unite against their common enemy, France, he wrote back, "Don't make me laugh.")

Lorenzo de' Medici (1449–1492), inheritor of the family's wealth and power and his grandfather Cosimo's love of art, was a central figure of the Golden Age. He was young (20 when he took power), athletic, and intelligent, in addition to being a poet, horseman, musician, and leader. He wrote love songs and humorous dirty songs to be sung loudly and badly at carnival time. His marathon drinking bouts and illicit love affairs were legendary. He learned Greek and Latin and read the classics, yet his great passion was hunting. He was the Renaissance Man—a man of knowledge and action, a patron of the arts, and a scholar and man of the world. He was Lorenzo the Magnificent.

Lorenzo epitomized the Florentine spirit of optimism. Born on New Year's Day and raised in the lap of luxury (Donatello's *David* stood in the family courtyard) by loving parents, he grew up feeling that there was nothing he couldn't do. Florentines saw themselves as part of a "new age," a great undertaking of discovery and progress in man's history. They boasted that within the city walls, there were more "nobly gifted souls than the world has seen in the entire thousand years before." These people invented the term "Dark Ages" for the era that preceded theirs.

Lorenzo surrounded himself with Florence's best and brightest. They formed an informal "Platonic Academy," based on that of ancient Greece, to meet over a glass of wine under the stars at the Medici villa and discuss literature, art, music, and politics—witty conversation was considered an art in itself.

Their "neo-Platonic" philosophy stressed the goodness of man and the created world; they believed in a common truth behind all religion. The Academy was more than just an excuse to go out with the guys: The members were convinced that their discussions were changing the world and improving their souls.

Botticelli was a member of the Platonic Academy. He painted scenes from the classical myths that the group read, weaving contemporary figures and events into the ancient subjects. He gloried in the nude body, which he considered God's greatest creation.

Artists such as Botticelli thrived on the patronage of wealthy individuals, government, the Church, and guilds. Botticelli commanded as much as 100 florins for one work, enough to live for a year in high style, which he did for many years. In Botticelli's art we see the lightness, gaiety, and optimism of Lorenzo's court.

Another of Lorenzo's protégés was the young **Michelangelo.** Impressed with his work, Lorenzo took the poor, unlearned 13-year-old boy into the Medici household and treated him like a son.

Michelangelo's playmates were the Medici children, later to become Popes Leo X and Clement VII, who would give him important commissions. For all the encouragement, education, and contacts Michelangelo received, his most important gift from Lorenzo was simply a place at the dinner table, where Michelangelo could absorb the words of the great men of the time and their love of art for art's sake.

Even with all the art and philosophy of the Renaissance, violence, disease, and warfare were present in medieval proportions. For the lower classes, life was as harsh as it had always been. Many artists and scholars wore swords and daggers as part of everyday dress. This was the time of the ruthless tactics of the Borgias (known for murdering their political enemies) and of other families battling for power. Lorenzo himself barely escaped assassination in the cathedral during Easter Mass; his brother died in the attack.

The center of the Renaissance gradually shifted to Rome, but its artists were mostly Florentine. In the 15th century, the Holy City of Rome was a dirty, decaying, crime-infested place. Then a series of popes, including Lorenzo's son and nephew, launched a building and beautification campaign. They used fat commissions (and outright orders) to lure Michelangelo, Raphael, and others to Rome. The Florentine Renaissance headed south.

APPENDIX

Let's Talk Telephones

Here's a primer on making phone calls. For information specific to Italy, see "Telephones" in the Introduction.

Making Calls Within a European Country: About half of all European countries use area codes; the other half use a direct-dial system without area codes.

To make calls within a country that uses a direct-dial telephone system (Italy, Belgium, the Czech Republic, Denmark, France, Portugal, Norway, Spain, and Switzerland), you dial the same number whether you're calling across the country or across the street.

In countries that use area codes (such as Austria, Britain, Finland, Germany, Ireland, the Netherlands, and Sweden), you dial only the local number when calling within a city, and you add the area code if calling long distance within the country.

Making International Calls: You always start with the international access code (011 if you're calling from the US or Canada, or 00 from Europe), then dial the country code of the country you're calling (see chart below).

What you dial next depends on the phone system of the country you're calling. If the country uses area codes, drop the initial zero of the area code, then dial the rest of the number.

Countries that use direct-dial systems (no area codes) vary in how they're accessed internationally by phone. For instance, if you're making an international call to Italy, the Czech Republic, Denmark, Norway, Portugal, or Spain, simply dial the international access code, country code, and phone number. But if you're calling Belgium, France, or Switzerland, drop the initial zero of the phone number.

European Calling Chart

Just smile and dial, using this key:
AC = Area Code, LN = Local Number

European Country	Calling long distance within ...	Calling from the US or Canada to ...	Calling from a European country to ...
Austria	AC + LN	011 + 43 + AC (without the initial zero) + LN	00 + 43 + AC (without the initial zero) + LN
Belgium	LN	011 + 32 + LN (without initial zero)	00 + 32 + LN (without initial zero)
Britain	AC + LN	011 + 44 + AC (without initial zero) + LN	00 + 44 + AC (without initial zero) + LN
Croatia	AC + LN	011 + 385 + AC (without initial zero) + LN	00 + 385 + AC (without initial zero) + LN
Czech Republic	LN	011 + 420 + LN	00 + 420 + LN
Denmark	LN	011 + 45 + LN	00 + 45 + LN
Finland	AC + LN	011 + 358 + AC (without initial zero) + LN	00 + 358 + AC (without initial zero) + LN
France	LN	011 + 33 + LN (without initial zero)	00 + 33 + LN (without initial zero)
Germany	AC + LN	011 + 49 + AC (without initial zero) + LN	00 + 49 + AC (without initial zero) + LN
Greece	LN	011 + 30 + LN	00 + 30 + LN
Hungary	06 + AC + LN	011 + 36 + AC + LN	00 + 36 + AC + LN
Ireland	AC + LN	011 + 353 + AC (without initial zero) + LN	00 + 353 + AC (without initial zero) + LN
Italy	LN	011 + 39 + LN	00 + 39 + LN

European Country	Calling long distance within ...	Calling from the US or Canada to ...	Calling from a European country to ...
Netherlands	AC + LN	011 + 31 + AC (without initial zero) + LN	00 + 31 + AC (without initial zero) + LN
Norway	LN	011 + 47 + LN	00 + 47 + LN
Poland	AC + LN	011 + 48 + AC (without initial zero) + LN	00 + 48 + AC (without initial zero) + LN
Portugal	LN	011 + 351 + LN	00 + 351 + LN
Slovakia	AC + LN	011 + 421 + AC (without initial zero) + LN	00 + 421 + AC (without initial zero) + LN
Slovenia	AC + LN	011 + 386 + AC (without initial zero) + LN	00 + 386 + AC (without initial zero) + LN
Spain	LN	011 + 34 + LN	00 + 34 + LN
Sweden	AC + LN	011 + 46 + AC (without initial zero) + LN	00 + 46 + AC (without initial zero) + LN
Switzerland	LN	011 + 41 + LN (without initial zero)	00 + 41 + LN (without initial zero)
Turkey	AC (if no initial zero is included, add one) + LN	011 + 90 + AC (without initial zero) + LN	00 + 90 + AC (without initial zero) + LN

- The instructions above apply whether you're calling a fixed phone or mobile phone.
- The international access codes (the first numbers you dial when making an international call) are 011 if you're calling from the US or Canada, or 00 if you're calling from anywhere in Europe.
- To call the US or Canada from Europe, dial 00, then 1 (the country code for the US and Canada), then the area code and number. In short, 00 + 1 + AC + LN = Hi, Mom!

Country Codes
After you've dialed the international access code (00 if you're calling from Europe, 011 if you're calling from the US or Canada), dial the code of the country you're calling.

Austria—43
Belgium—32
Britain—44
Canada—1
Croatia—385
Czech Rep.—420
Denmark—45
Estonia—372
Finland—358
France—33
Germany—49
Gibraltar—350
Greece—30
Ireland—353

Italy—39
Morocco—212
Netherlands—31
Norway—47
Poland—48
Portugal—351
Slovakia—421
Slovenia—386
Spain—34
Sweden—46
Switzerland—41
Turkey—90
US—1

Useful Italian Phone Numbers
Emergency (English-speaking police help): 113
Emergency (military police): 112
Ambulance: 118
Road Service: 116
Directory Assistance (for €0.50, an Italian-speaking robot gives the number twice, very clearly): 12
Telephone Help (in English; free directory assistance): 170

Festivals in Florence and National Holidays in 2007
This list includes Florence's major festivals, plus national holidays observed throughout Italy. Many sights close down on national holidays. Note that this isn't a complete list; holidays strike without warning.

For specifics and a more comprehensive listing of festivals, contact the Italian tourist information office in the US (www.italiantourism.com, see page 6) and visit www.discoveritalia.com, www.whatsonwhen.com, and www.hostetler.net.

Jan 1:	New Year's Day
Jan 6:	Epiphany
Mid-Feb:	Carnival Celebrations/Mardi Gras in Florence (costumed parades, street water fights, jousting competitions).
April 8:	Easter Sunday (2007). Explosion of the

2007

JANUARY
S	M	T	W	T	F	S
	1	2	3	4	5	6
7	8	9	10	11	12	13
14	15	16	17	18	19	20
21	22	23	24	25	26	27
28	29	30	31			

FEBRUARY
S	M	T	W	T	F	S
				1	2	3
4	5	6	7	8	9	10
11	12	13	14	15	16	17
18	19	20	21	22	23	24
25	26	27	28			

MARCH
S	M	T	W	T	F	S
				1	2	3
4	5	6	7	8	9	10
11	12	13	14	15	16	17
18	19	20	21	22	23	24
25	26	27	28	29	30	31

APRIL
S	M	T	W	T	F	S
1	2	3	4	5	6	7
8	9	10	11	12	13	14
15	16	17	18	19	20	21
22	23	24	25	26	27	28
29	30					

MAY
S	M	T	W	T	F	S
		1	2	3	4	5
6	7	8	9	10	11	12
13	14	15	16	17	18	19
20	21	22	23	24	25	26
27	28	29	30	31		

JUNE
S	M	T	W	T	F	S
					1	2
3	4	5	6	7	8	9
10	11	12	13	14	15	16
17	18	19	20	21	22	23
24	25	26	27	28	29	30

JULY
S	M	T	W	T	F	S
1	2	3	4	5	6	7
8	9	10	11	12	13	14
15	16	17	18	19	20	21
22	23	24	25	26	27	28
29	30	31				

AUGUST
S	M	T	W	T	F	S
			1	2	3	4
5	6	7	8	9	10	11
12	13	14	15	16	17	18
19	20	21	22	23	24	25
26	27	28	29	30	31	

SEPTEMBER
S	M	T	W	T	F	S
						1
2	3	4	5	6	7	8
9	10	11	12	13	14	15
16	17	18	19	20	21	22
23/30	24	25	26	27	28	29

OCTOBER
S	M	T	W	T	F	S
	1	2	3	4	5	6
7	8	9	10	11	12	13
14	15	16	17	18	19	20
21	22	23	24	25	26	27
28	29	30	31			

NOVEMBER
S	M	T	W	T	F	S
				1	2	3
4	5	6	7	8	9	10
11	12	13	14	15	16	17
18	19	20	21	22	23	24
25	26	27	28	29	30	

DECEMBER
S	M	T	W	T	F	S
						1
2	3	4	5	6	7	8
9	10	11	12	13	14	15
16	17	18	19	20	21	22
23/30	24/31	25	26	27	28	29

Cart *(Scoppio del Carro)* in Florence (fireworks, bonfire in wooden cart).

April 9:	Easter Monday (2007)
April 25:	Liberation Day
May 1:	Labor Day
May 17:	Ascension Day (2007). Annual Cricket Festival in Florence (music, entertainment, food, crickets sold in cages).
June 1–30:	Annual Flower Display in Florence (carpet of flowers on the main square, Piazza della Signoria)
June 2:	Anniversary of the Republic
June 24:	Festival of St. John in Florence (parades, dances, boat races). Also Calcio Fiorentino (costumed soccer game on Florence's Piazza Santa Croce)

Late June–Early Sept:	Florence's annual outdoor cinema season (contemporary films)
July–August:	Annual Florence Dance Festival
July 2:	Palio horse race in Siena
Aug 15:	Assumption of Mary
Aug 16:	Palio horse race in Siena
Sept, first week:	Festa della Rificolona in Florence (children's procession with lanterns, street performances, parade)
Oct:	Musica dei Popoli Festival in Florence (ethnic and folk music and dances)
Nov 1:	All Saints' Day
Dec 8:	Feast of the Immaculate Conception
Dec 25:	Christmas
Dec 26:	St. Stephen's Day

Numbers and Stumblers

- Europeans write a few of their numbers differently than we do: 1 = 1 , 4 = 4 , 7 = 7 . Learn the difference or miss your train.
- In Europe, dates appear as day/month/year, so Christmas is 25/12/07.
- Commas are decimal points and decimal points commas. A dollar and a half is $1,50 and there are 5.280 feet in a mile.
- When pointing, use your whole hand, palm down.
- When counting with fingers, start with your thumb. If you hold up your first finger to request one item, you'll probably get two.
- What Americans call the second floor of a building is the first floor in Europe.
- European pedestrians keep the left "lane" open for passing on escalators and moving sidewalks. Keep to the right.

Metric Conversion (approximate)

1 inch = 25 millimeters	32 degrees F = 0 degrees C
1 foot = 0.3 meter	82 degrees F = about 28 degrees C
1 yard = 0.9 meter	1 ounce = 28 grams
1 mile = 1.6 kilometers	1 kilogram = 2.2 pounds
1 centimeter = 0.4 inch	1 quart = 0.95 liter
1 meter = 39.4 inches	1 square yard = 0.8 square meter
1 kilometer = 0.62 mile	1 acre = 0.4 hectare

Florence's Climate Chart

First line, average daily low; second line, average daily high; third line, days of no rain.

J	F	M	A	M	J	J	A	S	O	N	D
32°	35°	43°	49°	57°	63°	67°	66°	61°	52°	43°	35°
40°	46°	56°	65°	74°	80°	84°	82°	75°	63°	51°	43°
25	21	24	22	23	21	25	24	25	23	20	24

Converting Temperatures: Fahrenheit and Celsius

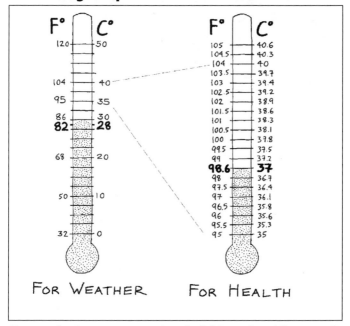

FOR WEATHER   FOR HEALTH

Europe takes its temperature using the Celsius scale, while we opt for Fahrenheit. For weather, remember that 28°C is 82°F—perfect. For health, 37°C is just right.

Roman Numerals

In the US, you'll see Roman numerals—which originated in ancient Rome—used for copyright dates, clocks, and the Super Bowl. In Italy, you're likely to observe these numbers chiseled on statues and buildings. If you want to do some numeric detective work, here's how. In Roman numerals, as in ours, the highest numbers (thousands, hundreds) come first, followed by smaller numbers. Many numbers are made by combining numerals into sets: V = 5, so VIII = 8 (5 plus 3). Roman numerals follow a subtraction principle for multiples of fours (4, 40, 400, etc.) and nines (9, 90, 900, etc.); the number four, for example, is written as IV

(1 subtracted from 5), rather than IIII. The number nine is IX (1 subtracted from 10).

The title of the book you're holding—with the year written in Roman numerals—would be *Rick Steves' Florence & Tuscany MMVII*. Big numbers such as dates can look daunting at first. The easiest way to handle them is to read the numbers in discrete chunks. For example, Michelangelo was born in MCDLXXV. Break it down: M (1,000) + CD (100 subtracted from 500, or 400) + LXX (50 + 10 + 10, or 70) + V (5) = 1475. It was a very good year.

M = 1000	XL = 40
CM = 900	X = 10
D = 500	IX = 9
CD = 400	V = 5
C = 100	IV = 4
XC = 90	I = duh
L = 50	

Italian Survival Phrases

English	Italian	Pronunciation
Good day.	Buon giorno.	bwohn JOR-noh
Do you speak English?	Parla inglese?	PAR-lah een-GLAY-zay
Yes. / No.	Sì. / No.	see / noh
I (don't) understand.	(Non) capisco.	(nohn) kah-PEES-koh
Please.	Per favore.	pehr fah-VOH-ray
Thank you.	Grazie.	GRAHT-seeay
I'm sorry.	Mi dispiace.	mee dee-speeAH-chay
Excuse me.	Mi scusi.	mee SKOO-zee
(No) problem.	(Non) c'è un problema.	(nohn) cheh oon proh-BLAY-mah
Good.	Va bene.	vah BEHN-ay
Goodbye.	Arrivederci.	ah-ree-vay-DEHR-chee
one / two	uno / due	OO-noh / DOO-ay
three / four	tre / quattro	tray / KWAH-troh
five / six	cinque / sei	CHEENG-kway / SEHee
seven / eight	sette / otto	SEHT-tay / OT-toh
nine / ten	nove / dieci	NOV-ay / deeAY-chee
How much is it?	Quanto costa?	KWAHN-toh KOS-tah
Write it?	Me lo scrive?	may loh SKREE-vay
Is it free?	È gratis?	eh GRAH-tees
Is it included?	È incluso?	eh een-KLOO-zoh
Where can I buy / find...?	Dove posso comprare / trovare...?	DOH-vay POS-soh kohm-PRAH-ray / troh-VAH-ray
I'd like / We'd like...	Vorrei / Vorremmo...	vor-REHee / vor-RAY-moh
...a room.	...una camera.	OO-nah KAH-meh-rah
...a ticket to ___.	...un biglietto per ___.	oon beel-YEHT-toh pehr
Is it possible?	È possibile?	eh poh-SEE-bee-lay
Where is...?	Dov'è...?	DOH-veh
...the train station	...la stazione	lah staht-seeOH-nay
...the bus station	...la stazione degli autobus	lah staht-seeOH-nay DAYL-yee OW-toh-boos
...tourist information	...informazioni per turisti	een-for-maht-seeOH-nee pehr too-REE-stee
...the toilet	...la toilette	lah twah-LEHT-tay
men	uomini, signori	WOH-mee-nee, seen-YOH-ree
women	donne, signore	DON-nay, seen-YOH-ray
left / right	sinistra / destra	see-NEE-strah / DEHS-trah
straight	sempre diritto	SEHM-pray dee-REE-toh
When do you open / close?	A che ora aprite / chiudete?	ah kay OH-rah ah-PREE-tay / keeoo-DAY-tay
At what time?	A che ora?	ah kay OH-rah
Just a moment.	Un momento.	oon moh-MAYN-toh
now / soon / later	adesso / presto / tardi	ah-DEHS-soh / PREHS-toh / TAR-dee
today / tomorrow	oggi / domani	OH-jee / doh-MAH-nee

In the Restaurant

I'd like...	**Vorrei...**	vor-REHee
We'd like...	**Vorremmo...**	vor-RAY-moh
...to reserve...	**...prenotare...**	pray-noh-TAH-ray
...a table for one / two.	**...un tavolo per uno / due.**	oon TAH-voh-loh pehr OO-noh / DOO-ay
Non-smoking.	**Non fumare.**	nohn foo-MAH-ray
Is this seat free?	**È libero questo posto?**	eh LEE-bay-roh KWEHS-toh POH-stoh
The menu (in English), please.	**Il menù (in inglese), per favore.**	eel may-NOO (een een-GLAY-zay) pehr fah-VOH-ray
service (not) included	**servizio (non) incluso**	sehr-VEET-seeoh (nohn) een-KLOO-zoh
cover charge	**pane e coperto**	PAH-nay ay koh-PEHR-toh
to go	**da portar via**	dah POR-tar VEE-ah
with / without	**con / senza**	kohn / SEHN-sah
and / or	**e / o**	ay / oh
menu (of the day)	**menù (del giorno)**	may-NOO (dayl JOR-noh)
specialty of the house	**specialità della casa**	spay-chah-lee-TAH DEHL-lah KAH-zah
first course (pasta, soup)	**primo piatto**	PREE-moh peeAH-toh
main course (meat, fish)	**secondo piatto**	say-KOHN-doh peeAH-toh
side dishes	**contorni**	kohn-TOR-nee
bread	**pane**	PAH-nay
cheese	**formaggio**	for-MAH-joh
sandwich	**panino**	pah-NEE-noh
soup	**minestra, zuppa**	mee-NEHS-trah, TSOO-pah
salad	**insalata**	een-sah-LAH-tah
meat	**carne**	KAR-nay
chicken	**pollo**	POH-loh
fish	**pesce**	PEH-shay
seafood	**frutti di mare**	FROO-tee dee MAH-ray
fruit / vegetables	**frutta / legumi**	FROO-tah / lay-GOO-mee
dessert	**dolci**	DOHL-chee
tap water	**acqua del rubinetto**	AH-kwah dayl roo-bee-NAY-toh
mineral water	**acqua minerale**	AH-kwah mee-nay-RAH-lay
milk	**latte**	LAH-tay
(orange) juice	**succo (d'arancia)**	SOO-koh (dah-RAHN-chah)
coffee / tea	**caffè / tè**	kah-FEH / teh
wine	**vino**	VEE-noh
red / white	**rosso / bianco**	ROH-soh / beeAHN-koh
glass / bottle	**bicchiere / bottiglia**	bee-keeAY-ray / boh-TEEL-yah
beer	**birra**	BEE-rah
Cheers!	**Cin cin!**	cheen cheen
More. / Another.	**Ancora un po.' / Un altro.**	ahn-KOH-rah oon poh / oon AHL-troh
The same.	**Lo stesso.**	loh STEHS-soh
The bill, please.	**Il conto, per favore.**	eel KOHN-toh pehr fah-VOH-ray
tip	**mancia**	MAHN-chah
Delicious!	**Delizioso!**	day-leet-seeOH-zoh

For hundreds more pages of survival phrases for your trip to Italy, check out *Rick Steves' Italian Phrase Book & Dictionary* or *Rick Steves' French, Italian, and German Phrase Book*.

Making Your Hotel Reservation

Most hotel managers know basic "hotel English." Faxing or e-mailing are the preferred methods for reserving a room. They're more accurate than telephoning and much faster than writing a letter. Use this handy form for your fax or find it online at www.ricksteves.com/reservation. Photocopy and fax away.

One-Page Fax

To: _____ @ _____
      hotel   **fax**

From: _____@ _____
        name   **fax**

Today's date: _____ / _____ / _____
                day   **month**   **year**

Dear Hotel _____ ,
Please make this reservation for me:

Name: _____

Total # of people:_____ # of rooms:_____ # of nights: _____

Arriving: _____ /_____ /_____   My time of arrival (24-hr clock): _____
          day **month** **year**   (I will telephone if I will be late)

Departing:____ /_____/_____
          day **month** **year**

Room(s): Single _____Double ____Twin _____Triple ____ Quad_____

With: Toilet _____ Shower_____Bath _____ Sink only _____

Special needs: View___ Quiet ____ Cheapest ____ Ground Floor ____

Please fax, mail, or e-mail confirmation of my reservation, along with the type of room reserved and the price. Please also inform me of your cancellation policy. After I hear from you, I will quickly send my credit-card information as a deposit to hold the room. Thank you.

_____
Signature

_____
Name

_____
Address

_____
City   *State*   *Zip Code*   *Country*

_____
E-mail Address

INDEX

Travel smart…carry on!

The latest generation of Rick Steves' carry-on travel bags is easily the best—benefiting from two decades of on-the-road attention to what really matters: maximum quality and strength; practical, flexible features; and no unnecessary frills. You won't find a better value anywhere!

Rick Steves' Convertible Carry-On

This is the classic "back door bag" that Rick Steves lives out of for three months every summer. It's made of rugged, water-resistant 1000-denier nylon. Best of all, it converts easily from a smart-looking suitcase to a handy backpack with comfortably-curved shoulder straps and a padded waistbelt.

This roomy, versatile 9" x 21" x 14" bag has a large 2500 cubic-inch main compartment, plus three outside pockets (small, medium and huge) that are perfect for often-used items. And the cinch-tight compression straps will keep your load compact and close to your back—not sagging like a sack of potatoes.

Wishing you had even more room to bring home souvenirs? Pull open the full-perimeter expando-zipper and its capacity jumps from 2500 to 3000 cubic inches. When you want to use it as a suitcase or check it as luggage (required when "expanded"), the straps and belt hide away in a zippered compartment in the back. Choose from five great traveling colors: black, navy, blue spruce, evergreen or merlot.

Rick Steves' 21" Roll-Aboard

At 9" x 21" x 14" our sturdy 21" Roll-Aboard is rucksack-soft in front, but the rest is lined with a hard ABS-lexan shell to give maximum protection to your belongings. We've spared no expense on moving parts, splurging on an extra-long button-release handle and big, tough inline skate wheels for easy rolling on rough surfaces.

Wishing you had even more room to bring home souvenirs? Pull open the full-perimeter expando-zipper and its capacity jumps from 2500 to 3000 cubic inches.

Rick Steves' 21" Roll-Aboard features exactly the same three-outside-pocket configuration and rugged 1000-denier nylon fabric as our Convertible Carry-On, plus a full lining and a handy "add-a-bag" strap.

Choose from five great traveling colors: black, navy, blue spruce, evergreen or merlot.

For great deals on a wide selection of travel goodies, begin your next trip at the Rick Steves Travel Store!

Visit the Rick Steves Travel Store at
www.ricksteves.com

FREE-SPIRITED TOURS FROM
Rick Steves

Small Groups
Great Guides
No Grumps

**Best of Europe ■ Family Europe
Italy ■ Village Italy ■ South Italy
France ■ Eastern Europe ■ Prague
Scotland ■ Britain ■ Ireland
Scandinavia ■ Spain-Portugal
Germany-Austria-Switzerland ■ Turkey ■ Greece ■ London-Paris
Paris ■ Venice-Florence-Rome...and much more!**

Looking for a one, two, or three-week tour that's run in the Rick Steves style?
Check out Rick Steves' educational, experiential tours of Europe.

Rick's tours are an excellent value compared to "mainstream" tours. Here's a taste
of what you'll get...

- **Small groups:** With just 24-28 travelers, you'll go where typical groups of
  40-50 can only dream.

- **Big buses:** You'll travel in a full-size 40-50 seat bus, with plenty of empty
  seats for you to spread out and be comfortable.

- **Great guides:** Our guides are hand-picked by Rick Steves for their wealth of
  knowledge and giddy enthusiasm for Europe.

- **No tips or kickbacks:** To keep your guide and driver 100% focused on giving
  you the best travel experience, we pay them well—and prohibit them from
  accepting tips and merchant kickbacks.

- **All sightseeing:** Your tour price includes all group sightseeing, with no
  hidden extra charges.

- **Central hotels:** You'll stay in Rick's favorite small, characteristic, locally-run
  hotels in the center of each city, within walking distance of the sights you
  came to see.

- **Visit www.ricksteves.com:** You'll find all our latest itineraries, dates and
  prices, be able to reserve online, and request a free copy of our "Rick Steves
  Tour Experience" DVD!

Rick Steves' Europe Through the Back Door, Inc.
130 Fourth Avenue North, PO Box 2009, Edmonds, WA 98020 USA
Phone: (425) 771-8303 ■ Fax: (425) 771-0833 ■ www.ricksteves.com

Start your trip at
www.ricksteves.com

Rick Steves' Web site is packed with over 3,000 pages of timely travel information. It's also your gateway to getting FREE monthly travel news from Rick— and more!

Free Monthly European Travel News
Fresh articles on Europe's most interesting destinations and happenings. Rick will even send you an e-mail every month (often direct from Europe) with his latest discoveries!

Timely Travel Tips
Rick Steves' best money-and-stress-saving tips on trip planning, packing, transportation, hotels, health, safety, finances, hurdling the language barrier...and more.

Travelers' Graffiti Wall
Candid advice and opinions from thousands of travelers on everything listed above, plus whatever topics are hot at the moment (discount flights, packing tips, scams...you name it).

Rick's Annual Guide to European Railpasses
The clearest, most comprehensive guide to the confusing array of railpass options out there, and how to choo-choose the railpass that best fits your itinerary and budget. Then you can order your railpass (and get a bunch of great freebies) online from us!

Great Gear at the Rick Steves Travel Store
Enjoy bargains on Rick's guidebooks, planning maps and TV series DVDs, and on his custom-designed carry-on bags, roll-aboard bags, day packs and light-packing accessories.

Rick Steves Tours
This year more than 10,000 lucky travelers will explore Europe on a Rick Steves tour. Learn more about our 25 different one-to-three-week itineraries, read uncensored feedback from our tour alums, and sign up for your dream trip online!

Rick on Radio and TV
Download free podcasts of our weekly *Travel with Rick Steves* public radio show; read the scripts and see video clips from public television's *Rick Steves' Europe*.

Respect for Your Privacy
Ordering online from us is secure. When you buy something from us, join a tour, or subscribe to Rick's free monthly travel news e-mails, we promise to never share your name, information, or e-mail address with anyone else. You won't be spammed!

Have fun raising your Travel I.Q. at
www.ricksteves.com

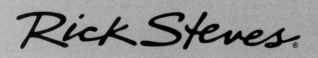

More *Savvy.* More *Surprising.* More *Fun.*

COUNTRY GUIDES 2007

Croatia & Slovenia
England
France
Germany & Austria
Great Britain
Ireland
Italy
Portugal
Scandinavia
Spain
Switzerland

CITY GUIDES 2007

Amsterdam, Bruges & Brussels
Florence & Tuscany
Istanbul
London
Paris
Prague & The Czech Republic
Provence & The French Riviera
Rome
Venice

BEST OF GUIDES

Best of Eastern Europe
Best of Europe

As the #1 authority on European travel, Rick gives you inside information on what to visit, where to stay, and how to get there—economically and hassle-free.

PHRASE BOOKS & DICTIONARIES

French
French, Italian & German
German
Italian
Portuguese
Spanish

MORE EUROPE FROM RICK STEVES

Easy Access Europe
Europe 101
Europe Through the Back Door
Postcards from Europe

RICK STEVES' EUROPE DVDs

All 43 Shows 2000-2005
Britain
Eastern Europe
France & Benelux
Germany, The Swiss Alps & Travel Skills
Ireland
Italy
Spain & Portugal

PLANNING MAPS

Britain & Ireland
Europe
France
Germany, Austria & Switzerland
Italy
Spain & Portugal

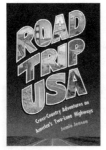

CREDITS

Researchers

To update this book, Rick relied on the help of these *fantastica* researchers:

Amanda Scotese

Amanda Scotese freelances as a journalist and editor in San Francisco. Her travels in Italy include a stint selling leather jackets in Florence's San Lorenzo Market, basking in the Sicilian sun, and of course, helping out with Rick Steves' guidebooks and tours.

Karin Kibby

Karin Kibby has been living in Italy for the past six years. When she is not researching guidebooks or guiding tours, you can find her in the countryside picking grapes and olives, and generally enjoying *la dolce vita*.

Rick Steves' Guidebook Series

Country Guides
Rick Steves' Best of Europe
Rick Steves' Best of Eastern Europe
Rick Steves' Croatia & Slovenia (new in 2007)
Rick Steves' England
Rick Steves' France
Rick Steves' Germany & Austria
Rick Steves' Great Britain
Rick Steves' Ireland
Rick Steves' Italy
Rick Steves' Portugal
Rick Steves' Scandinavia
Rick Steves' Spain
Rick Steves' Switzerland

City and Regional Guides
Rick Steves' Amsterdam, Bruges & Brussels
Rick Steves' Florence & Tuscany
Rick Steves' Istanbul (new in 2007)
Rick Steves' London
Rick Steves' Paris
Rick Steves' Prague & the Czech Republic
Rick Steves' Provence & the French Riviera
Rick Steves' Rome
Rick Steves' Venice

Rick Steves' Phrase Books
French
German
Italian
Spanish
Portuguese
French/Italian/German

Other Books
Rick Steves' Europe Through the Back Door
Rick Steves' Europe 101: History and Art for the Traveler
Rick Steves' Easy Access Europe
Rick Steves' Postcards from Europe
Rick Steves' European Christmas

(Avalon Travel Publishing)

.vel Publishing
.n Street, Suite 250
ville, CA 94608

.alon Travel Publishing
An Imprint of Avalon Publishing Group

Printed in the United States of America by Worzalla

Portions of this book were originally published in *Rick Steves' Mona Winks* © 2001, 1998,
1996, 1993, 1988 by Rick Steves and Gene Openshaw, and in *Rick Steves' Italy* © 2006,
2005, 2004, 2003, 2002, 2001 by Rick Steves.
ISBN (10): 1-56691-810-3 ISBN (13): 978-1-56691-810-7 ISSN: 1538-1609

For the latest on Rick's lectures, guidebooks, tours, public radio show, and public television
series, contact Europe Through the Back Door, Box 2009, Edmonds, WA 98020, tel.
425/771-8303, fax 425/771-0833, www.ricksteves.com, rick@ricksteves.com.

Europe Through the Back Door Managing Editor: Risa Laib
ETBD Senior Editor: Jennifer Hauseman
ETBD Editors: Jennifer Madison Davis, Cathy McDonald, Gretchen Strauch
Avalon Travel Publishing Editor and Series Manager: Madhu Prasher
Avalon Travel Publishing Project Editor: Patrick Collins
Research Assistance: Amanda Scotese, Karin Kibby
Copy Editor: Ellie Behrstock
Proofreader: Janet Walden
Indexer: Laura Welcome
Production & Typesetting: Holly McGuire, Patrick David Barber
Interior Design: Amber Pirker, Jane Musser, Laura Mazer
Cover Design: Kari Gim, Laura Mazer
Maps & Graphics: David C. Hoerlein, Laura VanDeventer, Lauren Mills, Rhonda Pelikan,
    Barb Geisler, Mike Morgenfeld
Front Cover Photos: Front image, Ponte Vecchio © Ben Cameron; Back image, View
    from tower, San Gimignano, north Tuscany © Mike Potter
Front matter color photo: p. i, Michelangelo's Tomb of Giuliano © Europe Through the
    Back Door; p. iii, Siena Duomo © Mike Potter
Interior photography: Rick Steves, Gene Openshaw, David C. Hoerlein, Jennifer
    Hauseman